MAKING POLICY IN TURBULENT TIMES

CHALLENGES AND PROSPECTS FOR HIGHER EDUCATION

EDITED BY

**Paul Axelrod, Roopa Desai Trilokekar,
Theresa Shanahan, Richard Wellen**

Queen's Policy Studies Series
School of Policy Studies, Queen's University
McGill-Queen's University Press
Montreal & Kingston • London • Ithaca

© 2013 School of Policy Studies, Queen's University at Kingston, Canada

SCHOOL OF
Policy Studies

Publications Unit
Robert Sutherland Hall
138 Union Street
Kingston, ON, Canada
K7L 3N6
www.queensu.ca/sps/

The preferred citation for this book is:
Axelrod, P., R.D. Trilokekar, T. Shanahan, and R. Wellen, eds. 2013. *Making Policy in
Turbulent Times: Challenges and Prospects for Higher Education.* Montreal and Kingston:
Queen's Policy Studies Series, McGill-Queen's University Press.

Library and Archives Canada Cataloguing in Publication

Making policy in turbulent times : challenges and prospects for higher
education / edited by Paul Axelrod, Roopa Desai Trilokekar, Theresa Shanahan,
Richard Wellen.

(Queen's policy studies series)
Papers based on the conference Policy Formation in Post-secondary Education: Issues
and Prospects in Turbulent Times, sponsored by the Faculty of Education at York
University, Toronto, 2012.
Issued in print and electronic formats.
Includes bibliographical references and index.
ISBN 978-1-55339-332-0 (pbk.) — ISBN 978-1-55339-336-8 (ebook) —
ISBN 978-1-55339-341-2 (pdf)

1. Higher education and state—Congresses. I. Axelrod, Paul Douglas, author,
writer of introduction, editor of compilation II. Wellen, Richard, 1958-, author, editor of
compilation III. Shanahan, Theresa, 1963-, author, editor of compilation IV. Trilokekar,
Roopa Desai, author, editor of compilation V. Queen's University (Kingston, Ont.).
School of Policy Studies, issuing body VI. York University (Toronto, Ont.). Faculty
of Education, sponsoring body VII. Policy Formation in Post-secondary Education:
Issues and Prospects in Turbulent Times (Conference) (2012 : Toronto, Ont.) VIII. Series:
Queen's policy studies series

LC165.M34 2013   378.1   C2013-903518-4
                                                           C2013-906327-7

TABLE OF CONTENTS

ACKNOWLEDGEMENTS

The chapters in this volume were presented in earlier versions at a workshop held at York University, Toronto, Canada, in March 2012, entitled "Policy Formation in Post-secondary Education: Issues and Prospects in Turbulent Times." Each session was facilitated by individuals who contributed in substantial ways to the discussion and assessment of the papers. Our thanks go to George Fallis, Ross Finnie, Ruth Hayhoe, Lorna Marsden, Ken Norrie, and Richard Wellen. Funds in support of the workshop and/or the publication of this book were provided by York University's Office of the Vice-President, Research and Innovation; the Faculty of Education; the Faculty of Liberal Arts and Professional Studies; and the Social Sciences and Humanities Research Council of Canada. We thank Zainab Kizilbash, Yvette Munroe, and Margo Novak for their assistance at the workshop; Laura Crane for her technical assistance on the book; and Trish Skrzypczyk, who helped prepare the manuscript for publication. Finally, we thank Keith Banting of the School of Policy Studies; Mark Howes and Valerie Jarus in the Publications Unit, who undertook the production and copy editing of the manuscript for McGill-Queen's University Press; and Stephanie Stone, who performed the copy editing.

INTRODUCTION

Paul Axelrod

The recent dramatic reduction of teaching and research budgets in the universities of several European countries highlights the impact of economic strain and the paradoxes of policy-making in contemporary higher education. Universities have scarcely been insulated from the economic turmoil rippling across the globe since 2008. And while they are still perceived as engines of the emerging "knowledge economy," post-secondary educational institutions throughout the world appear to lack the resources they require to adequately fulfill their economic, social, and educational objectives. They face growing accessibility demands and shifting paradigms in government policy, and they endure increasing government oversight notwithstanding the erosion of public sector funding.

International experiences are hardly identical – and the differences matter immensely – but turbulent times do appear to be altering the landscape of higher education. How is policy being forged in this context? Are current policy decisions transformative or temporary in their impact? Do we require new tools to interpret and understand policy-making in higher education (and other fields), or are prevailing conceptual approaches still viable and relevant?

These and other questions were the subject of an international workshop sponsored by the Faculty of Education at York University in Toronto in March 2012. Leading thinkers from around the globe explored policy formation in turbulent times and reflected on the past, present, and future of post-secondary education. This anthology contributes significantly to new research, and we hope that it will engage the attention of scholars and practitioners alike.

Making Policy in Turbulent Times: Challenges and Prospects for Higher Education, ed. P. Axelrod, R.D. Trilokekar, T. Shanahan, and R. Wellen. Kingston: School of Policy Studies, Queen's University.

Research on the development of policy in post-secondary education in Canada and abroad is limited, although, in some important respects, promising. There are numerous studies on policy outcomes (e.g., state-university relations, funding decisions, student assistance plans, etc.) but relatively little literature on the ways in which policy is conceived, formed, and implemented. Scholars in the field of policy development and public administration have contributed conceptually, though rarely empirically, in the case of post-secondary education, to researchers' understanding of policy-making, and our anthology seeks to help fill this gap. Among other matters, contributors to this volume explore the importance of research in policy development, the impact of globalization on decision-makers' choices, the adoption of institutional alliances in higher education, the changing role of university presidents, and the ways in which emerging industrial powers, such as China, are forging higher educational policy pathways. A particular strength of this volume is its situating of Canada in a comparative international context, something rarely done in the post-secondary educational literature.

The anthology's contributors address a number of important questions on policy development. How *is* policy made? For the advocate, being well informed, assembling solid research, even being right are not sufficient. Numerous elements affect the development and implementation of policy: ideology, party platforms, constituencies, lobbying networks, election priorities, pragmatism, politicians' individual idiosyncrasies, and overriding economic concerns.

In a wide-reaching historical analysis (1945–2011), Michael Shattock traces the complex ways in which social pressures, economic drivers, and distinctive political structures have influenced higher education policy in the United Kingdom. He explains how Britain's centralized approach to university governance was mediated, to some degree, by a variety of agencies and constituencies with discrete agendas. Shattock writes, "This balance between a distributed unitary centre, heavily influenced by government-wide financial considerations, and institutional independence, … with occasional shifts in the weightings, has created a uniquely British policy context." Roopa Desai Trilokekar et al. propose a conceptual framework that provides context to policy-making, identifies key policy determinants and their interactions since the 1990s, and offers insights into federal-provincial tensions and other distinctive Canadian features of the policy-making process. While the chapter's analysis of the fluid way that policy determinants interact is based on a Canadian case study, the analysis has implications for practices elsewhere.

With reference to national contexts, it is important to ask whether higher education policy has converged internationally. The anthology addresses this question in a vigorous manner. Nelly P. Stromquist argues that political economy has shaped university developments around the world, pointing to the role of neo-liberal ideology and global economic power in the diffusion of educational policies. Analyzing data from developments in American research universities, she sees convergence in resource competition, management and governance, professional identity, and internationalization. Further, she suggests that managerialism, quality assurance, accountability instruments, the prioritizing of science and technology over the humanities and social sciences, and the homogenizing impact of agencies such as the World Bank are identifiable trends across the globe.

But in their respective chapters, Bjørn Stensaker as well as Chuo-Chun Hsieh with Jeroen Huisman question the convergence thesis, refuting the contention that globalization has led to growing uniformity in organizational forms and functions. They argue that in Europe, while there are undeniable pressures to standardize funding and accreditation practices through initiatives related to the Bologna Process and the European University Association, individual nations and institutions have found ways to negotiate these pressures and reflect unique cultural and national goals. Institutions are focusing on their distinctive traits in order to compete successfully in the academic marketplace. The very economic pressures that have led to convergence may also provide incentives for universities to distinguish themselves. Taken together, these chapters identify both international trends in policy development and the particularities of institutional practice in different jurisdictions.

The anthology's contributors also consider the effectiveness of national and pan-national post-secondary education policies, particularly in the recent era of economic turmoil. Harry de Boer and Frans van Vught contend that the reforms introduced by the European Union (through the Lisbon Strategy 2000–10) to promote economic growth and educational innovation have largely failed. Too little research is underway, and higher educational attainment and participation levels remain stubbornly low. While the authors are cautiously optimistic about the prospects for change, new initiatives (such as the Europe 2020 Strategy) designed to infuse dynamism into European higher education will continue to be challenged by Europe's ongoing economic crises.

By contrast, Chinese higher education, according to Qiang Zha and Fengqiao Yan, has experienced tremendous growth, arising from the government's ambition to cultivate "world-leading innovative talents" and "world-class universities." On closer examination, the simultaneous pursuit of efficiency, quality, and equity strains the system overall. Furthermore, there is an inherent tension between China's ambitions for innovation and an academic culture that remains politically constrained and academically narrow; this tension could result in thwarting the country's ambitions. To meet its goals, say the authors, China's intellectual culture requires more openness, and its institutions require more autonomy.

Research is a core function of higher education, and several authors examine the way research has been used to shape the direction of post-secondary education. Drawing from American case studies, David D. Dill questions the reliability and durability of "the new institutional economics," which he believes may be "undermining the traditional contributions that universities have made to the public good." He raises concerns about the effectiveness of measures such as quality assurance mechanisms and performance-based funding to regulate universities in their pursuit of efficiency and the provision of equitable social benefits.

Creso M. Sá, Merli Tamtik, and Andrew Kretz examine the performance of research funding agencies based on their qualitative study of key informants from representative Canadian funding agencies. This chapter explains how Canadian national research agencies use (or choose not to use) evidence to design and implement their own programs, and it discusses policy trends affecting funding research agencies across Canada, the United States, and Europe, noting the increased role of government in setting and adjudicating research policy.

Ian Clark and Ken Norrie challenge Canadian universities to make it possible for a stronger research culture to thrive. Their chapter explores two paradoxes in universities: the institutions value research but have little by way of scholarly effort to improve research performance; and they value evidence but are reluctant to act when evidence calls for change in core practices. Clark and Norrie urge academia to use the evidence at hand, which shows that universities cannot afford uniformly to provide high quality in both research and teaching. In this respect, institutional differentiation is, for the authors, the most rational and promising route to follow.

Access to higher education, a theme that recurs internationally, has implications both for economic growth and for social equity. Ideally, universities would contribute to both of these missions, but as a number of authors show, there are tensions between them. Claire Callender describes the 2012–13 higher education reforms in the UK and considers the ideological, political, and economic forces that have shaped British policy over the past two decades. She contends that educational reforms represent a fundamental change in the role of the state, which, in providing higher education, favours growth (through increased privatization) over equity, thus deepening social inequalities.

Lesley Vidovich tracks a similar process in Australia using a case study of the quality and equity policies that the government has introduced to drive national competitiveness in the global marketplace. She notes the ways in which discourses on quality, influenced by international trends, are trumping discourses on equity, which remain "marginal" in post-secondary education-policy formation. She also notes that the Australian academic community has altered the course of some contested government initiatives, particularly with respect to research rankings and quality measurements. "[L]obbying by universities and academics has been able to achieve reversals of some quality policy details, suggesting

at least a limited degree of localized agency in Australian higher education policy processes."

The phenomenon of globalization has led many institutions to collaborate with partners abroad in generating educational and investment
opportunities. Sheila Embleton analyzes Canada-India alliances – how
they came to be and what they have sought to achieve – and the effect on
these relationships of a shared colonial history, a large and active Indian
diaspora in Canada, and the cultivation of binational professional and
institutional associations. Maria Slowey presents the case of Ireland to
demonstrate the development of academic alliances, regional clusters,
and strategic networks at the European level. In discussing these various modes of collaboration, she explores the ways in which the state has
steered higher education to meet its social and economic objectives, both
regionally and nationally.

What do we know about policy actors in higher education? This anthology includes contributions from several Canadian administrators who
have been at the centre of policy discussions and who have had responsibility for implementing policy agendas. Former university presidents
Judith Woodsworth and Harvey P. Weingarten describe both successful
strategies for securing government resources and failed attempts, arising
from external and internal resistance, to reform academic institutions.
Weingarten offers specific advice to universities on how to improve their
relations with government and thus their potential to influence its policy.
Woodsworth explores the challenges and attributes of successful leadership in higher education and highlights the gendered nature of these
experiences. She examines the role of strategic planning, the influence
of external factors, and the range of internal controversies that affect the
policy-making and implementation processes.

In her former role as vice-president academic, Embleton explains how
creative individual initiatives and good timing can effect policy change.
Glen A. Jones augments this discussion with an analysis of the increasingly important role of Ontario networks and lobbyists in helping frame
university and college policy initiatives. He suggests that the "whining
and begging" approach of higher education leaders has been replaced
by more sophisticated advocacy strategies, at both the institutional and
the sectoral levels.

In a poignant afterword, Jane Gaskell revisits key themes in this anthology, reminding readers of the recurring and serendipitous character of
policy development. She pays special attention to the place of research
in policy formation, noting its limits and potential, and to international
policy patterns, which are propelling post-secondary institutions in
similar but not identical directions.

In sum, this book identifies challenges facing universities everywhere
in troubling economic times; it compares policy developments in numerous jurisdictions; it demonstrates the ways in which networks and

lobbyists achieve results; and it provides historically informed and nu-anced analyses of policy dynamics. It is a substantial contribution to our understanding of contemporary higher education.

I

POLICY-MAKING:
THE NATURE OF
THE PROCESS

CHAPTER 1

POLITICS, MONEY, ECONOMIC ADVANTAGE, AND LAST, BUT PERHAPS NOT LEAST, UNIVERSITY AUTONOMY: ASSESSING THE POLICY DRIVERS IN BRITISH HIGHER EDUCATION

Michael Shattock

THE POLICY BACKGROUND

This chapter examines the development of policy in British higher education over the post–World War II period from 1945 to 2011. The period begins with the emergence of the universities from the war years and ends with the publication of the white paper *Higher Education: Students at the Heart of the System* (BIS 2011). It thus covers a growth in the national age participation rate from 3 percent to 43 percent and a change from a fully state-funded higher education system – a new development in 1945 – to a largely privatized model, except in Scotland, prescribed in the white paper. The chapter shows how the prime locus of policy changed in the period but also how the structures of policy-making contributed to British exceptionalism and created a distinctive British model. It also demonstrates how in a highly centralized state, with a well-developed parastatal and institutional infrastructure, higher education tends to cherish institutional autonomy while at the same time remaining highly integrated with the decision-making apparatus of the state. To do this, the chapter focuses on key sets of decision-making.

Making Policy in Turbulent Times: Challenges and Prospects for Higher Education, ed. P. Axelrod, R.D. Trilokekar, T. Shanahan, and R. Wellen. Kingston: School of Policy Studies, Queen's University.

The two main policy drivers in British higher education throughout the period were the pressure of the demand for places and the decisions required to enable the expansion of student numbers and of higher education institutions to be paid for. In the 1980s, a new driver appeared with the recognition that the growth of the modern knowledge economy' demanded investment in university-based research so that questions of research concentration, on both scientific and fiscal grounds, came to introduce a powerful new structural agent into the development of the higher education system. Decision-making fitted Lindblom's definition of "disjointed incrementalism" (Lindblom 1980), but policies emerged, not fully formed, but as a result of "a bargaining process" (Minogue 1983) or from what Lindblom called "partisan mutual adjustment" (Lindblom 1965).

Viewed from the perspective of policy process theory, British higher education represents a somewhat aberrant field of study. Policy was not consistently made top down or bottom up (Sabatier 1986). In the first place, the "top" is hard to define because it comprised not only the responsible government minister but also the Treasury, the intermediary bodies – the University Grants Committee (UGC), the National Advisory Body for Public Sector Higher Education (NAB), the Universities Funding Council (UFC) and the Higher Education Funding Councils, and, between 2001 and 2004, the Prime Minister's Office.

For its part, the "bottom" was made up of the institutions themselves and their powerful representative bodies: the Committee of Vice-Chancellors and Principals (CVCP), the Committee of Polytechnic Directors (CDP), and, after these two bodies merged, Universities UK (UUK) and the Russell Group (an elite group of research-intensive universities) together with, on significant occasions, the National Union of Students (NUS). All of these organizations had their own close links at various points with ministers, officials, and the intermediary bodies. In addition, there were the research councils, the Royal Society, and many other academic bodies.

The "top" might appear to be represented by a draconian letter from a secretary of state to a funding council, but policy almost never sprang fully developed from a secretary of state: it may have been virtually dictated by the Treasury or prepared by officials who, in higher education, were almost certainly, from the 1990s on, more influential in policy matters than ministers. Officials would themselves have tested out issues with UUK, and the draft would have been shown to the intermediary body for comment and, occasionally, modification.

Major policy decisions rarely went higher than the secretary of state: Tony Crosland, secretary of state in the Labour Government of 1964–70, did not take the most far-reaching decision to the Cabinet – to reject a main plank of the report of the Robbins Committee (Committee on Higher Education 1963), create the polytechnics, and impose the binary line (that is, the rigid separation of the new polytechnic sector from the university sector of higher education) – so there was no discussion of the proposals outside the Department of Education and Science itself. When a secretary of state in a Conservative Government, Kenneth Clark, was persuaded by his officials in 1991 to abolish the binary line and redesignate the polytechnics as universities, he put it to a Cabinet committee, which nodded it through without discussion. (He was so concerned that they might have missed the item altogether that he asked an official to contact all of the members to check that they had understood the implications [Personal interview].)[1]

Political parties bickered in the House of Commons about individual higher education policies, but most of the major decisions – such as the creation of the polytechnics in 1965, the creation of the NAB in 1981 to create a parallel body to the UGC for higher education controlled at the local authority level, the removal of the polytechnics from local authority control in 1988, the ending of the binary line in 1992, and the creation of the Dearing Committee (National Committee of Inquiry into Higher Education) in 1996 – were essentially bipartisan. And even though the Conservative Party in opposition voted against the Labour Government's proposals to introduce "top-up" fees in 2004, it did so only on tactical grounds and went on in the coalition government to raise fees to new high levels in the 2011 white paper.

The policy dialogue was mostly about technical issues and was conducted by civil servants in the Treasury, the Department of Education and Skills (DES), and the intermediary bodies; it was also conducted among the higher representative bodies (the CVCP, CDP, and UUK), all three of which were engaged in an interlocking policy network largely driven by questions of resource constraint. Higher education did not for the most part produce high policy issues. The reception of the Robbins Report with its forecast of student numbers up to 1980 was one exception, and the parliamentary decision to impose top-up fees, to come into effect in 2006, was another, but key decisions were usually taken below the political radar and, for the most part, behind closed doors.

FROM PRIVATE TO PUBLIC CONTROL OF HIGHER EDUCATION

It could be said that the universities have "had a good War." In the 1920s and 1930s, two-thirds of their income came from non-state sources – student fees, endowments, local authority and other grants – and the UGC's recurrent support was given on a deficiency basis, that is, by providing a subsidy to non-state sources. Universities were legally independent and historically autonomous. Their scientists played an outstanding role in winning World War II (although the contribution at Bletchley was not made public until the 1990s), and the importance of their intellectual

independence, compared to the collapse of the German universities under
Nazism, was referred to constantly, from Truscott's *Red Brick University* in
1943 to Moberly's *The Crisis in the University* in 1949. (In 1944, for example,
a senior university educationalist argued that the merger of teacher training colleges with universities would protect the colleges if totalitarianism
were to raise its head in Britain [Browne 1979, 71].)

The need for investment in universities was a theme of the later war
years, and when the demand for places began to grow as a result of
demobilization, the Labour Government readily agreed to take over
university funding. Before the war, state finance came directly from
the Treasury through the UGC because the Board (later the Ministry) of
Education was regarded as too school-oriented to be entrusted with the
universities. The Treasury continued to be the responsible ministry under
the new funding regime, and the UGC was primarily an academic body
responsible for the disbursement of funding to individual institutions.
Because the Treasury made no pretence to be able to formulate university
policy, the UGC took on the role of being a "collective Minister" (Carswell
1985, 12), a role it was to continue to play until 1981.

The UGC was founded in 1919 specifically to be a vehicle for the
distribution of state funding to universities and to protect universities'
independence from the state. Its membership comprised part-time senior
academics, who swore impartiality toward their own institutions, and
a full-time chairman, normally a senior academic figure. The secretariat was provided by civil servants seconded mostly from the Treasury.
It was described as a "buffer" body between the government and the
universities.

> From the Government's point of view it is the accepted source of expert
> advice on university affairs including the allocation of resources which
> the Government makes available; from the universities' it is the accepted
> medium for representing their opinions and needs to the Government
> and for ensuring the allocation is equitable. (Public Accounts Committee,
> 1966–67, para. 10, Question 24)

At the same time, the UGC was part of the Treasury for the purposes of
financial control and was described by a senior Treasury official as "in our
minds part of the Treasury. Their job is to do our job ... we regard them
as our agents and trustworthy agents" (Select Committee on Estimates
1951–52). It had very close contacts with the CVCP as the representative
body of all heads of university institutions. These were personal as well
as official: Keith (later Lord) Murray, chairman between 1953 and 1963,
used to dine in the Athenaeum Club the evening before each monthly
CVCP meeting so that vice-chancellors could have a word with him
before their meeting (Sir James Mountford, interview by J.J. Walsh); he
dined every month with the permanent secretary of the Treasury (Lord

Murray, interview by J.J. Walsh). In 1962, the Financial Secretary of the Treasury, a ministerial appointment, opened a meeting with the vice-chancellors to discuss the grant to universities by saying that one of the vice-chancellors present had been his tutor and another had played on the same Oxford college hockey team (CVCP Archive 1962). The Treasury, the UGC, and the CVCP were part of a common culture that owed a great deal to shared experience in wartime.

Throughout the period 1945 to 1961, demand increased and student numbers expanded. In the universities, numbers grew from about 60,000 to 110,000; in teacher training, from about 15,000 to 50,000; and in advanced further education, conducted in local colleges, from about 7,000 to 40,000. The age participation rate had risen from 3 percent to 8 percent. In 1961, the government accepted the recommendation that students in higher education should receive a maintenance grant for living costs and fees, to be paid for by the government through their local authority. In spite of the extreme austerity of the immediate post-war years, the government matched the demand for places in the universities with financial support.

The universities, on their side, met targets recommended for recruiting science and technology students, and 13 of them had been rewarded with significant new capital investment in applied science and technology. (The universities also won a significant battle to preserve their monopoly of degree-awarding powers, condemning local authority colleges to awarding diplomas through a national awards agency; the UGC, with the support of the Chancellor of the Exchequer, thus outgunned the Ministry of Education [UGC 1950–55].)

In 1953, the UGC began the task of tracking the growth in demand. Growth was coming from two sources: one was "the trend" for more students to stay on in school after age 16 and go on to higher education, while the other was "the bulge," the demographic rise in 18-year-olds deriving from demobilization, which was due to peak in the early 1960s (Sir Edward Hale, personal correspondence with J.J. Walsh). To anticipate this, the UGC had already created seven new universities (Sussex, East Anglia, York, Essex, Kent, Warwick, and Lancaster) but was forecasting a need for 170,000 to 175,000 more places by the early 1970s.

Such a level of expansion raised all kinds of problems: student numbers were anticipated to rise much faster than gross domestic product (GDP), and if capital costs, recurrent funding, and student support costs rose *pro rata*, this expansion would compete with other national priorities: infrastructure (roads, etc.) and the rising costs of the Welfare State. In addition, the universities' location under the Treasury would become increasingly anomalous, bearing in mind the Treasury's explicit role in controlling public expenditure across all government departments. Parallel levels of unplanned expansion were also taking place in local authority colleges and in teacher training colleges, although expansion in the latter was supposed to be controlled by the Ministry of Education against teaching manpower needs. A policy was needed to determine the long-term pattern of higher education.

The answers to these questions were referred to the Robbins Committee on Higher Education, which reported in 1963. The committee was well funded and had a substantial research team. Membership fairly accurately reflected the ascendancy of the universities since 1945: Lord Robbins, its chairman, was a distinguished economist at the London School of Economics who had worked closely with Keynes in the war years, and over half of its membership was drawn from the universities; Keith Murray, the chairman of the UGC and the architect of university development in the 1950s, was an "assessor" and attended all of its meetings; only one member had a local authority background. The committee – whose report is regarded in Britain as one of the great liberal documents of the post-war years, comparable in its way to the 1943 Beveridge Report, which had laid the groundwork for the Welfare State – forecast a growth in the qualified demand for places from 216,000 in 1962–63 to 558,000 in 1980–81 (Committee on Higher Education 1963, 69, Table 30). It recommended that the bulk of the expansion should be university-based, that the teacher training colleges should be brought academically and administratively under the universities, and that up to ten local authority colleges might be expected to have advanced to a point where they could be upgraded to universities by 1980.

The precedent here was a group of nine Colleges of Advanced Technology (CATs) that had been separated out from other local authority colleges for advanced status in 1956. They had been transferred from local authority to Ministry of Education control in 1961, and the committee now recommended them for immediate upgrading to university status. The committee went on to recommend that the universities be transferred from Treasury control to a new minister of arts and science and not to the minister of education, thus accepting the arguments, presented in university evidence to the committee, against a transfer to the ministry. The report contained a Note of Reservation by the one local authority member, who argued that education was "one and indivisible," that universities should be transferred to the Ministry of Education, and that teacher training colleges should not be separated from their local authorities and put wholly under the universities (Committee on Higher Education 1963, 293–296).

The Conservative Government immediately accepted both the growth numbers forecast by the committee, thus committing itself to funding for the next decade, and the upgrading of the CATs to university status; but it deferred decisions on structural issues. It was replaced in 1964 by a Labour Government that, in opposition, had supported a unitary university-based system but, once in office, was persuaded by Ministry of Education officials led by Toby (later Sir Toby) Weaver and local authority figures like Sir William (later Lord) Alexander, general secretary of the Association of Education Committees, a powerful local authority body, to reverse its position and support the principles of the Note of Reservation.

Weaver and later Tony Crosland, Secretary of State for Education and Science in a new Department of Education and Science (essentially the former Ministry of Education with responsibility for the research councils transferred to it), rejected the idea that the majority of higher education should be located in an "autonomous sector," believing that it should be developed in the more socially relevant environment of the local authorities. This position had been strongly argued by the local authorities themselves as well as the relevant trade union, the Association of Teachers in Technical Institutions, whose general secretary wrote the key policy paper "The Future of Higher Education within the Further Education System" (Sharp 1987), and by a group of non-university–based Labour Party educationalists, notably Eric Robinson and Tyrrell Burgess, who were based in local authority colleges and had strong trade union links; Robinson's book, *The New Polytechnics* (1968), provided the intellectual substructure of the polytechnic idea.

Crosland's Woolwich speech in 1965 announcing the rejection of the Robbins Committee's recommendations on structure, the creation of 30 polytechnics, and the reinforcement of the binary line between the university and what became known as the public sector of higher education represented a resounding defeat for the universities and asserted an alternative vision of a more vocational, less disciplinarily focused, community-based higher education that gave more emphasis to part-time programs and home-based students. This development did not, however, immediately translate into a reduction in the role of the UGC or the extent to which policy toward the universities was largely a function of the close links between the CVCP and the UGC. Weaver, indeed, argued that the creation of the public sector of higher education represented a protection for the autonomy of the university sector (Weaver 1973).

The university sector survived, with difficulty, the shocks of the oil crisis in 1973–74 and the impact of rapid inflation and further financial crises in the later 1970s; being transferred to the DES did not, in practice, increase government intervention. The university sector remained controlled by the UGC, the public sector institutions, polytechnics, and colleges and remained subject to the bureaucracy of local government; however, thanks to a pooling system for financing further and advanced further education run by the local authorities themselves, it was free to develop on the basis of student demand.

The turning point came with the arrival of the Thatcher Government in 1979 and the imposition of significant cuts in public expenditure. These were not directed specifically toward higher education but rather at government expenditure as a whole. The UGC, which over the period 1980 to 1984 faced a budget cut of 15 percent (which included the decision to cease subsidizing international student fees), was also concerned to reflect the impact of a 10 percent cut in the unit of resource (that is, the resource per student provided by the government) over the 1970s, and it responded by cutting student numbers in universities by 3 percent to restore the unit of resource and by imposing cuts differentially on universities against quality criteria and subject mix (Shattock 1994).

This produced a public outcry within Parliament as well as in higher education itself. The UGC had acted autonomously and had not consulted the DES, which would have been opposed to cutting numbers and would probably have preferred a policy of equal misery across the sector. A new secretary of state, Sir Keith Joseph (his predecessor had been sacked as one of the Cabinet "wets" who tacitly opposed Thatcher's economic policies), found himself defending the cuts in the House of Commons without having authorized the policy. Almost immediately, he announced to the UGC that henceforward, he intended to take responsibility for major policy decisions in the university sector (Shattock 1994, 133–134).

Although the UGC itself continued in being until 1989, when it was replaced by the UFC, which continued to exercise UGC-type functions until 1992, this marked a decisive shift from private, in other words university-centred, to public control over the universities. The UGC's 1981 cuts represented the last hurrah of a set of what were traditional university values – maintaining relatively low student/staff ratios, rewarding institutional excellence, making policy for the sector through academically dominated bodies, and respecting autonomy.

In the public sector, the imposition of the spending cuts in the early 1980s led to the capping of the pool and the creation of the NAB, a mixed local authority and DES body chaired by a minister and designed to coordinate allocations to institutions and act as a "public sector" equivalent of the UGC. This represented, however, only a stage in the process of removing polytechnics and colleges of higher education altogether from local authority control in 1988 and bringing them under a Polytechnics and Colleges Funding Council, which paralleled the UFC. It was only a short step to bring the two sectors together in 1992 with the re-designation of the polytechnics as universities under a common set of Higher Education Funding Councils.

On one reading, the abolition of the binary line can be seen as a return to Robbins principles. (The growth of student numbers between 1963 and 1992 would certainly have justified the redesignation of 30 local authority institutions.) But on another, it can be viewed as a massive centralization, albeit one that was somewhat mitigated by the establishment of separate Scottish and Welsh funding councils. This reflected both a technical and a political issue: one reason why the UGC had been put under the Treasury in 1919 was that the Scottish Education Department (SED) was sensitive to Scottish universities being placed under an English Board of

Education; in 1992, bringing all higher education under a single funding council would have involved stripping the SED of its central institutions (i.e., polytechnics) and its teacher training colleges. Apart from the Scottish decision not to charge tuition fees, the policies of the Scottish and Welsh funding councils have broadly shadowed the policies of the Higher Education Funding Council for England (HEFCE); the breakdown of higher education institutions is England, 131; Scotland, 19; Wales, 11; and Northern Ireland, 4.

The merger of the two sectors in 1992 had been proposed by officials in the DES and approved by ministers. It offered them some important advantages: first, it created a better platform for central policy-making, and second, by averaging the unit costs of teaching across the two sectors, it produced substantial economies because polytechnic unit costs, which did not include any element of resource for research, were significantly lower than those of universities.

The new funding councils were lay rather than academically dominated bodies and were deliberately defined as funding rather than planning institutions. Theoretically, this gave the funding councils increased independence, but in practice, since their relations with the institutions were governed by a contract, the funding councils held all the cards. Very rapid expansion occurred in the period 1989–1994, and in 1994, the Treasury stepped in (in England) to freeze numbers, with HEFCE threatening to fine institutions that overshot prescribed targets. This system was later extended to withdrawing funds if institutions undershot. Policies were delivered by means of letters of guidance from the secretary of state to the funding council, and they were translated into incentives through competitions to fund new policy departures.

To meet the requirements of public accountability, governing bodies and vice-chancellors were required to sign a Financial Memorandum, which year by year became more prescriptive. In 1991, the then chief executive of the UFC (previously chairman of the UGC) stated publicly that "the UFC has suffered far more nit-picking interference from DES civil servants in the last two years [since the UFC had been given statutory status] than the UGC did in the previous five. Moreover the Financial Memorandum which relates relations between the DES and the UFC manifests in every line that the DES is not prepared to rely on the UFC's competence and good sense" (Swinnerton Dyer 1991).

New public management (NPM) approaches, begun under the 18-year period of Conservative Government and pursued with enthusiasm in the ten years of Blair – creating markets, stimulating competition, introducing quality measures such as key performance indicators and student satisfaction surveys – combined to impose new levels of bureaucracy on the university system. These, translated down to the institutions, created what organizational theorists call the neo-institutional/archetype phenomenon, whereby institutional isomorphism dictates that dominant cultural values and policy priorities and structures generate irresistible cultural pressures to conform to external organizational forms (Deem, Hillyard, and Reed 2007).

Universities themselves became more managerial, spent a high proportion of their income on bureaucracy, and devoted more time to meeting targets that they had not designed themselves but that were dictated to them by external bodies or the various league tables presented in the media (Hazelkorn 2011). The change from private to public control reflected the centralization of modern government in Britain; the scale of mass; moving toward universal, higher education; and the increasing integration of the higher education system into the aspirations and policy demands of the knowledge economy.

THE ECONOMY, THE TREASURY, AND THE FINANCING OF BRITISH HIGHER EDUCATION

The fundamental problem for British higher education since 1945 has been that the demand for higher education has exceeded by many times the growth of GDP. In 1945, the state committed itself to an expensive model for funding universities, and in 1961, it compounded the problem by adopting a generous financial support system for students. It found these models increasingly hard to sustain in the face of the demands placed on it by other parts of the public sector of the economy: health, social security, and national infrastructure. The compromises and conflicts that derived from this dilemma represented key drivers of policy throughout the period, especially in a situation where the national economy was unstable and overstretched.

One consequence of this was that the need to control public expenditure and the particular processes adopted to do so gave the Treasury an important policy-making role. Between 1945 and 1962, the Treasury treated the UGC's claims for resources to meet increased demand with considerable understanding. Universities were funded on a five-year basis: they submitted their plans for development to the UGC, the UGC assessed and coordinated them through an elaborate range of subject-based committees, and the UGC then presented a bill to the Treasury. This encouraged a sense of entitlement.

When the CVCP complained that the settlement for 1957–62 was an improvement of only 8.3 percent, the chairman of the UGC, Keith Murray, was forced to respond that in 1958–59, other areas of government expenditure were being cut back and that universities should consider themselves as being in "a privileged position" (CVCP Archive 1957). Up to this point, universities had been funded out of the back pocket, as it were, of the Treasury, but in 1962, the Treasury official in charge of public expenditure told the UGC, "The scale of university finance was now such that decisions could no longer be taken by the Treasury Ministers on their own but had become the responsibility of the Government as a whole" (UGC 1962).

The introduction of new machinery to control public expenditure, the Public Expenditure Survey Committee (PESC), meant that for the first time, the universities' case had to be examined in direct competition with other departmental bids for increases in public expenditure. Although minor variations were introduced over the years, the PESC (later changed to the Public Expenditure Survey, or PES, because the committee itself no longer met) made the post of Chief Secretary to the Treasury, a political appointment with Cabinet membership, the arbiter, in the first instance, of public expenditure bids.

Under the new system, the Cabinet established a target for the whole of public expenditure; this provided an envelope within which departmental bids had to fit. Departments submitted their bids through their principal finance officer, and discussions took place first at officer level and later at chief secretary/ministerial level. Ministers had the right to appeal to the full Cabinet or, in a very tight year, if agreement could not be reached, to a Star Chamber of ministers appointed by the prime minister (Personal interview). The process put the Treasury at the heart of decision-making on priorities. The universities' budget was particularly sensitive because of the resource implications of the increase in student demand. Public sector higher education was, however, not directly exposed to the PES until the creation of the NAB in 1981 because polytechnic and college numbers were grouped as one element in the much larger local authorities' budgets, notionally controlled by the Department of the Environment.

The first year in which the PESC operated, 1962, provided a foretaste of the policy issues that the new machinery was to raise for higher education. The Treasury position was that with GDP not rising above 2.5 percent, public expenditure had to be constrained to something between 40 percent and 45 percent of total national expenditure (UGC 1962). The chief secretary had to admit to Parliament that he had been unable to accept the UGC's student number targets for the early 1970s or even the capital bid up to 1966–67. The CVCP immediately issued a statement that the government had taken the unprecedented step of rejecting the UGC's advice, and there was an uproar in Parliament, not just from the Labour opposition but also from the government's own backbenches (Berdahl 1962). The following year, the government quietly reversed its decision, and the chief secretary was replaced, but the strength of the reaction both in Parliament and in the media was why, when the Robbins forecasts for the demand for places up to 1980–81 were published the following year, the government accepted them (including a target of 217,000 by 1973–74) within 24 hours.

In doing so, the government seems knowingly to have misled itself. The Treasury, in its evidence to Robbins, expressly forecast a 2.5 percent per annum rate of economic growth and canvassed the economies that might have to be made in the higher education budget if it was to accommodate the growth in demand. Robbins, however, took an alternative forecast of 4 percent provided by the National Economic Development Corporation, and the chief secretary to the Treasury adopted it in the paper that he drafted to the Cabinet recommending acceptance of the Robbins forecasts (Boyd-Carpenter 1963, 173). Thus, the commitment to expansion was embarked upon on a false financial prospectus.

The original Treasury forecast turned out to be correct. Had the Robbins Committee accepted the lower figure as its planning baseline, its discussion of loans and fee levels might have hardened, and funding policies might have been very different. The committee would almost certainly have had to point out that fully funding both the education and the living costs of an expansion of student numbers necessary to meet demand was likely to be unaffordable and that some contribution from the students themselves and a student loan scheme was inevitable.

The introduction of the PES machinery meant that higher education (and in the 1970s this remained primarily university) policy was subject to scrutiny behind closed doors in dialogues between the DES and Treasury officials and occasionally between the secretary of state and the chief secretary. This was (and still is) a bargaining process, with the Treasury, which had its own views on policy, fighting to keep a departmental bid down against compelling bids from other departments pursuing politically popular programs in order to contain expenditure within the Cabinet-approved expenditure envelope (Personal interview).

Bargaining could also take place within a department's budget so that the universities' case had to be balanced, within the DES, by primary and secondary schools' issues such as the costs of raising the school-leaving age. Crosland, for example, conceded a discriminatory rise in fees for international students over home students in 1967 in order to protect schools from charging for school meals. This decision excited student protest all round the country, and the CVCP carried on a concerted campaign to reverse it right up to 1979–80 (Lee 1998). In 1977, just as a solution was about to be reached by lowering both home and overseas fees, home tuition fees (which were paid by the state through local authority budgets) were increased specifically to meet local authority education deficits (Personal interview).

In 1979, within three days of the Thatcher Government taking office, the Treasury told the new secretary of state that funding for universities could be preserved by removing the subsidy from international student fees altogether. This launched a major change in policy, one that saw Margaret Thatcher come under severe attack at the Commonwealth Prime Ministers' Conference later in the year. Within 12 months, the secretary of state had to announce further reductions of 8.5 percent, which precipitated the UGC cuts of 1981. Booth provides an account of the year-by-year impact of Treasury interventions into student number targets, tuition fee levels, and capital expenditure planning over one decade and gives an insider's assessment of the extent of the Treasury's influence on higher education policy (Booth 1983).

Up to the mid-1980s, a central element in the DES's arguments with the Treasury on behalf of the UGC and the NAB had been preserving expansion at given levels of unit cost. With a demographic-led decline in the number of 18-year-olds, the Treasury had endorsed a policy of "tunnelling through the hump" and had calculated its forecast expenditure accordingly. As a result, the DES published an extremely pessimistic and much criticized green paper (DES 1985). A new secretary of state, Kenneth (now Lord) Baker, anxious to change the climate and persuaded by industry that a return to expansion was called for on industrial manpower grounds, made a virtue of abandoning the unit-of-resource argument, which he described in his autobiography as "an ingenious system" developed by the UGC that "became sacrosanct" and gave the Treasury control of the rate of expansion (Baker 1993, 283). Fortunately, we have an alternative account provided by John Major, the future prime minister, from his time as chief secretary to the Treasury conducting the PES round. Baker, he wrote,

> would bound in full of enthusiasm and with lots of ideas all of which, he assured me, would be hugely popular with the electorate and would guarantee another election victory.... When detailed questioning on cost [was] put to Ken he was often poorly briefed. His spending plans were grossly inflated and it never took long to reduce the padding. At the end of our negotiations, Ken bounded out as cheerfully as he had come in, but with much less money than he had sought. (Major 1999, 103)

Baker became the apostle of expansion, arguing in 1989 that he wished to see the participation rate rise to one in three by 2000. But a consequence of this was a decrease in the unit of resource of some 45 percent between 1980 and 1997, so that while expansion continued, it did so at worsening student/staff ratios. This decrease was to have a determining influence on the development of higher education and, in particular, the future of the two sectors: whereas the universities resisted various market-led incentives to expand at the lower cost offered by the UFC, the polytechnics, newly freed from the local authorities but short of cash, seized the opportunity to expand at marginal cost. This was to have a profound impact on their position after 1992 in a hierarchy determined by research.

The account provided by Booth of the Treasury's influence in the 1970s can be taken as offering an accurate picture for the 1980s and beyond. It is safe to say that the DES never embarked on a significant policy change without consulting the Treasury and, at significant points, such as the rationalization of costs after the merger of the two sectors in 1992 and the negation of the Dearing proposals on funding in 2000, its voice was decisive. The 2010 Comprehensive Spending Review and the substitution of tuition fees for recurrent grant may be regarded as the final evidence of the impact of the Treasury and the PES process on the development of policy in British higher education.

RESEARCH AND THE RESTRUCTURING OF BRITISH HIGHER EDUCATION

Evaluating research performance and using the results as a policy tool came relatively late in the development of higher education. From 1945, universities benefited from dual funding: UGC funding within the recurrent grant to provide a research "floor" and funding from the research councils, awarded competitively, providing funding for individual research projects. The Robbins Committee took what was the traditional view: "There is no borderline between teaching and research; they are complementary and overlapping activities" (Committee on Higher Education 1963, 182, para. 557). And in 1982, the chairman of the UGC could tell the Public Accounts Committee of the House of Commons, "We give block grants to universities ... so it is for the university itself to decide on a disposition of resource between departments' teaching and research.... That is what is meant by university autonomy" (Public Accounts Committee 1982, 175).

However, new pressures emerged in the 1980s. The first came from an interdepartmental review of government-sponsored research and development, which demonstrated that there were clear overlaps among research programs initiated within government but that the universities could claim to be doing about half the nation's fundamental research. The second was that the Treasury wanted to see a disaggregation of research funding from teaching funding in the UGC's recurrent grant, claiming that there was a "black hole" in the research element because the allocation methodology took insufficient account of the differentiation of research capability between institutions. The third pressure came from the research councils, which argued for more selectivity and concentration in research funding; they coupled this with the claim that research funding could be more efficiently delivered if the element for research in the UGC's resources was transferred to them.

In the wake of the 1981 cuts, the secretary of state sought public advice from the UGC and the NAB on a strategy for higher education. To guide its response, the UGC invited universities to answer 28 questions, one of which suggested greater selectivity in funding of research; only two universities responded positively to this idea, and the CVCP in opposing it said that the UGC "should not be involved directly in making assessments" between institutions (CVCP Archive 1984).

But the UGC pressed ahead, introducing the first Research Assessment Exercise (RAE) in 1985–86. This was a discipline-by-discipline, not an institutional, assessment, and it was translated into a methodology whereby 25 percent of the block grant was distributed according to research performance criteria. The RAE was repeated in 1989, 1992, 1995, 2001, and 2008 and is due to operate again in 2014 as the Research Evaluation Framework. It was not embarked upon in 1985–96 as a long-term restructuring process but as a short-term measure to achieve greater concentration in research. However, with the increasing tweaks to the methodology to reward the most successful departments at the expense of the rest, it has become so: four universities receive 25 percent of the funding, and 25 universities receive 75 percent, a position that has been confirmed in three successive RAEs.

The dual-funding system did not apply in the public sector of higher education, although staff members in polytechnics and colleges were eligible to apply for grants from the research councils. In 1987, the Advisory Board for the Research Councils (ABRC) issued a report, *A Strategy for the Science Base* (ABRC 1987), which argued that the future pattern of higher education provision, appropriate to the needs of research, required a structuring of the system into R (research) institutions, T (teaching) institutions, and X (mixed research and teaching) institutions. The report was never acknowledged to be government policy, but the ABRC's heavyweight membership, which included the chairman of the UGC, gave support to the view that it represented official thinking. When the two sectors were merged in 1992 and the former polytechnics entered the RAE, the R, T, and X forecast appeared to be confirmed.

The arrival of a Labour Government in 1997 led to a reinforcement of the policy: on the one hand, a white paper argued that research and innovation was central to growth in a knowledge economy (DTI, HM Treasury, and DES 2002), and, on the other, the Prime Minister concluded "that the future of developed nations such as ours ... depends on having a vibrant, dynamic and world class higher education system," which he strongly associated with research excellence (Blair 2010, 482). A white paper issued by the Department for Education and Skills (DfES), *The Future of Higher Education*, confirmed that the Government would invest "in our very best research institutions, enabling them to compete effectively with the world's best universities" (DfES 2003, 23). The policy of concentration in disciplines had morphed into an institutional league table philosophy.

Research performance has, therefore, become a powerful restructuring agent. However, the results are not as clear cut as the R, T, and X policy might have anticipated. The methodology of the 2008 RAE deliberately highlighted the existence of excellent research performance wherever it might be identified rather than on the basis of a whole department. It showed that 49 universities had some research in the top grade and 118 institutions were represented in the two highest grades ("world leading" and "internationally excellent in originality, significance and rigour").

The position becomes even more variegated if one looks at research grant and contract income because although income is concentrated in the top four universities (Oxford, Cambridge, Imperial College London, and University College London (with Manchester, after the merger with the University of Manchester Institute of Science and Technology, close behind), there are at least 35, not 25, universities that could justify the claim of being research-intensive. But excellent research is spread much more widely than this, including in nearly all of the universities that might be thought to fall into the T category. What the data seem to be pointing to is that the government's ambition to concentrate research in fewer universities has been frustrated by the universities' own ambition to succeed in the RAE and by the reluctance of staff members to allow themselves to be constrained by the institutional model of being a teaching-only university. The RAE has restructured upward, not down.

INSTITUTIONAL AUTONOMY AND THE POLICY-MAKING RESILIENCE OF THE HIGHER EDUCATION SYSTEM

In 2011, the European University Association (EUA) published a report entitled *University Autonomy in Europe: The Scorecard* (Estermann, Nokkala, and Steinel 2011), which rated European universities' autonomy in the categories of organizational autonomy, financial autonomy, staffing autonomy, and academic autonomy. The scorecard clearly demonstrated that the British university system was the most autonomous in Europe. This partly reflects the comparative lack of autonomy implicit, even after reforms, in the Humboldtian and Napoleonic forms of state governance that still persist in continental Europe, but it also underlines the historic legal and academic independence of the British university model. When the civic universities, which had been established by local citizens, not by the state, were granted royal charters in the late 19th and early 20th centuries, it was to give them the same rights and privileges as Oxbridge or the University of London. When the UGC founded the 1960s new universities, although it was in response to local bids, these institutions inherited the same legal status. Academic freedom and university autonomy were hard wired into the nation's cultural constitution.

In 1945, this autonomy could have been threatened when the state assumed responsibility for the funding of universities, and many senior university figures were concerned about it, but the reform of the UGC and the formal confirmation of its buffer, as well as its planning, role had the effect of reinforcing universities' sense of independence even though, financially, they were nearly 80 percent dependent on UGC recurrent grant. The Robbins Report argued that "the maximum [degree] of independence compatible with the necessary degree of public control is good in itself, as reflecting the ultimate values of a free society" (Committee on Higher Education 1963, 230, para. 709), and although Parliament decided in 1966 against the universities' continued immunity from scrutiny by the Comptroller and Auditor General, it established safeguards to reassert the importance of preserving institutional autonomy.

The public sector had no such protection. Indeed, an important rationale for the creation of the polytechnics was that they should not be autonomous but be subject to "social control." Local authority control, however, demonstrably failed, and the 1988 decision to remove them emphasized the government's wish to provide them with a governance structure that ensured autonomy. Nevertheless, when the decision was taken four years later to abolish the binary line, one of the implicit aims in establishing the funding council system was to create a vehicle that, by applying funding formulas and incentives, would render the higher education system more responsive to government policies.

But government found itself in a dilemma. Both Conservatives and later Labour were intellectually wedded to NPM approaches as a way of reducing the increasing cost of public services and making them more efficient. Introducing the idea of a market and creating autonomous structures that would compete in a marketplace were central to these ideas (e.g., creating Foundation Trust hospitals and a patient-led market in the National Health Service). Higher education might have seemed a natural test bed for such policies. However, when Keith Joseph, in the mid-1980s, had proposed substituting loans for student maintenance grants and using the savings to invest in science, he had been shouted down at a Conservative Party 1922 Committee by his own backbenchers, anxious not to upset their middle class constituents (Denham and Garnett 2001). Six years later, in 1991, John Major told the CVCP over a dinner that he would fight any proposal for top-up fees (CVCP 1991) on the (unstated) grounds that it would be electorally unpopular.

In 1994, the Treasury was forced to extinguish Kenneth Baker's market in student places at marginal cost because it had had to provide substantial supplementary grants to the DES in 1992 and 1993 to cover unbudgeted student support costs. Controls increased: successive letters of guidance from secretaries of state to HEFCE grew more directive (the Labour secretary of state's guidance letter after the 2003 white paper contained 41 instructions [Blunkett 2003]), and the funding councils' guidance to the institutions became much more frequent. (The UGC might have written no more than four or five circulars a year to universities, but the chairman would have had considerable individual correspondence with vice-chancellors; between 2006 and 2010, HEFCE sent out an average of 42 circulars a year.) The Financial Memorandum that set out accountability issues between institutions and the funding councils rose from four to 49 pages between 1989 and 2009. And the proportion of managerial staff in universities rose from around 10 percent to 20 percent between the late 1990s and 2010 (Whitchurch 2012). Institutional autonomy, which was a fundamental precept of the NPM market approach, turned out to demand an increasing amount of state steering. The more universities were urged to generate funds from non-state sources, the greater the tendency of the state seemed to be to micromanage the system.

While bureaucracy increased, particularly in the area of quality assurance, the principle of institutional autonomy remained a key element of policy at both government and funding council levels. Universities were not just legally independent, but it was accepted by the state that their academic freedom was bound up with their autonomy in decision-making. Legislation to create the higher education funding councils in 1992 sought to reinforce such autonomy by denying the funding councils a formal planning role such as had been exercised by the UGC.

But as the unit of resource continued to fall, institutional representative bodies became more aggressive in seeking solutions. The DES might have thought that a merged pre- and post-1992 CVCP would be more quiescent in the face of funding shortfalls, but in February 1996, faced with further budget reductions, the committee decided to recommend that universities charge a top-up fee (that is, a fee over and above the tuition fee paid by the local authorities on behalf of the government) from 1997–98 unless the government committed itself to some improvement in its funding policies. With a General Election in the offing, and with neither main political party wanting higher education funding to form part of the election campaign, the Government agreed with the Opposition to set up the National Committee of Inquiry into Higher Education under the chairmanship of Lord Dearing.

The Treasury nullified the Dearing Committee's eventual proposals on tuition fees, which were in any case quite modest, but the Blair Private Office remained interested in the fees question. At a dinner with a subset of vice-chancellors in late 2001, Blair writes, "Once the university chiefs laid out the problem I knew we had to act" (Blair 2010, 483). His justification was the Shanghai Jiao Tong University league table, the threat of investment in universities in China and India, and the example of the United States: "They were more entrepreneurial; they went after their alumni and built up big endowments; their bursary system allowed them to attract poorer students; and their financial flexibility meant they could attract the best academics. Those who paid the top dollar got the best. Simple as that" (Blair 2010, 482). The narrow parliamentary vote in 2004 in favour of introducing tuition fees represented a triumph for bottom-up policy-making – that is, policy-making driven from a higher education interest group. It was the only occasion since the mid-19th century when a prime minister played a decisive role in the development of British higher education.

It would be easy to assume that the growing power of the modern state would stifle the entrepreneurial spirit of individual institutions. While it is clear that institutional autonomy could be said to be exercised on a narrower front, in one area – the development of global reach – it might be said to far outreach the golden age of the UGC. No one, neither the Treasury nor the universities, believed that in 1980, the decision to charge full-cost fees to international students was anything but a severe blow to the higher education system. Yet 30 years later, the Department for Business, Innovation and Skills (BIS) was reporting higher education as a triumph for the export industry, generating £4 billion (CAN$46.2 billion) in direct tuition fees and nearly £8 billion (CAN$12.4 billion) more in off-campus expenditure. Reducing unit costs forced universities to look elsewhere for funding – a world of international agents, officers, and academic partners and campuses was the result. If, on the one hand, we regret the encroachment of state policy on higher education and its intrusiveness, we should remember the extraordinary exercise of institutional autonomy in the international higher education market.

POLICY FORMULATION: THE BRITISH CHARACTERISTICS

The value of examining policy formulation over such a long period is that it enables us to determine whether policy grows out of an intrinsic higher education dynamic (Clark 1983) or whether it should more properly be regarded as one thread in a country's intellectual, cultural, and political history. National systems may vary in this respect. In Britain, however, it has been a characteristic that autonomous universities have always been very much part of the state and that higher education policy has evolved as much, if not more, because of changes external to higher education than because they were driven by some higher education logic. Even in what some might regard as the golden age of independence, before 1960, universities were closely enmeshed with the state. Policies did not spring fully developed from think tanks, policy reviews, or ambitious ministers (though the Weaver/Crosland duo might be cited as a partial exception) but rather from a network of interlocking policy decision-making centres in government, in the intermediary bodies, in the research councils, and in the representative bodies of the institutions themselves and, occasionally, the NUS.

The evidence above suggests that this process shaped British higher education in distinctive ways. The pre-1992 universities have lost the privileged, private status that they once had, where policy was created entirely within the sector, and are now subject to a much more directive relationship with the state. The post-1992 institutions, however, have acquired new freedoms by the abolition of the binary line. Overall, the merger of the two sectors and the creation of the funding council system have enhanced the ability of the state to steer – or, it might be argued, drive – higher education to fit with short-term political, economic, or social objectives.

The process by which this was achieved has been dominated by financial considerations: how to contain the growth of higher education within an overstretched government budget. The PES process has given the Treasury a policy role that has ensured that the development of higher education policies has been reactive and episodic. The one consistent policy since the mid-1980s (which has been to restructure the system according to a research achievement model) has been only partly successful and has been vitiated by institutions' (and their staff members') own ambition to conform to a traditional university model. The historical concept of university autonomy, which might philosophically have resonated with NPM approaches, has proved to be a corrective to policies initiated in Whitehall rather than a supplement to them; the most extreme shift in policy, the introduction of top-up fees in 2006, was sparked by the institutions themselves.

Because policy was largely driven by the relentless growth in student demand and the question of how it could be paid for, policy was neither coherent nor consistent. Two comments from leading participants might convey the picture, both drawn from the 1980s. The first is from Richard Bird, the senior civil servant in the DES during that period.

> [M]ost of the significant developments of the decade happened in a piecemeal and pragmatic fashion. There were certainly overall trends in policy, though these could by no means be assembled into any kind of grand strategy. Indeed in my judgement, the creation of an embracing strategy was always beyond reach because of the Government's refusal to appoint royal commissions … and the usual insistence that actions could "brook no delay." (Bird 1994)

The second is from a very senior policy-maker who was brought in from academic life.

> My experience of government was shocking for me. I had expected that the nearer one got to the commanding heights the more rational it would all be. The more calmness, the more rationality, the more careful looking at evidence. I discovered the opposite. Ministers were in a constant state of mild panic rushing from one thing to the next, never having time to grasp any issue, needing to make a decision in extraordinary short periods of time and often trying to make decisions without having grasped the issues. Then officials tried to rush around to clear up the mess. (Interview by Kogan 1995 for Kogan and Hannay 2000)

Policy formulation in British higher education was distinctive in a number of ways. First, unlike Canada, the US, Germany, and Spain, higher education policy was centrally controlled by a unitary state; regional governance did not exist, and local governance was widely seen as having failed. Whereas in Ontario, California, Baden-Württemberg, or Valencia, regional governments could shape their higher education systems, in Britain such power was reserved for central government. (Although after 1992, separate funding councils were established under devolved governments in Wales and Scotland, there was close alignment with HEFCE, and the RAE, for example, was undertaken by HEFCE on behalf of all of the funding councils. Scotland's decision to resist top-up fees was a political decision taken outside the confines of Scottish higher education.)

Compared with European countries with highly centralized systems such as Austria, France, and Italy, historically characterized by micromanagement by state bureaucracies, the British system of central government established intermediary bodies to protect institutional autonomy and institutional self-management from state interference. Although HEFCE describes itself now as "a broker" rather than a buffer (HEFCE 2010, 2), the continued existence of an intermediary body represents a second distinctive feature. The dispersal of policy-making influence in the centre was increased by the range of representative bodies, research councils, and learned societies that contributed to the policy dialogue. This meant that the context of British decision-making was quite unlike any other of the states where higher education was subject to unitary governance.

But a third important feature is the role played by the Treasury through the PES process. The Treasury has never been, since Gladstone, merely a ministry of finance, but has always exercised a wider role. With the creation of the PES process, a system was devised that made it the arbiter of all public spending, with the ability to weigh up priorities across the whole of government. In the 50 years since it was introduced, only one education secretary of state, Gillian Shephard, has challenged the PES's decision on the education budget and exercised her right to take it to the full Cabinet; and she lost the Cabinet vote.

The PES process represents not simply a year-by-year "shootout" but a continuous dialogue as spending departments try out new plans on officials on the public expenditure side of the Treasury. Whereas some countries may "top slice" the education budget, in Britain it competes on a three-year cycle with budgets for health, social services, crime prevention, and infrastructure. This has inevitably tipped the balance more toward higher education's contribution to wealth creation, an indication of which was its transfer from the former DES to the new BIS. This close involvement of the Treasury has had the effect of making higher education policy-making more dependent than in many countries on the ebb and flow of government policies. It may also have protected it from what might have been more ideological approaches to policy formation if policy had resided solely in the jurisdiction of a single government department or was subject to major influence by one or other major political party.

Finally, British higher education is distinctive in its continued respect for institutional autonomy. While some aspects of institutional strategic autonomy may have been narrowed as we have moved from mass to near universal higher education, the extent to which operational autonomy is protected both de jure and de facto, as exemplified in the EUA report, mentioned above, and in institutions' international activities, represents a critical element in the formulation of policy. Whether it can be sustained in equal measure across all institutions in the face of the pressures imposed by the modern state remains an important policy issue for the future.

This balance between a distributed unitary centre, heavily influenced by government-wide financial considerations, and institutional independence, a situation that has broadly prevailed for nearly a century, with occasional shifts in the weightings, has created a uniquely British policy context. What this emphasizes, however, is how difficult it is in Britain to discuss higher education policy without relating it to its political and economic setting. And the existence of institutional autonomy has done much to obscure the extent to which the policy drivers in higher education are integrally embedded in the shifting evolution of government policies as a whole.

NOTE

1.   The author conducted a number of confidential interviews, mostly with former senior officials, on the basis of anonymity for this chapter. The names of the interviewees are therefore withheld.

REFERENCES

ABRC. 1987. *A Strategy for the Science Base*. London: HMSO.

Baker, K. 1993. *The Turbulent Years in My Life in Politics*. London: Faber and Faber.

Berdahl, R. 1962. "University-State Relations Re-examined." *Keele Sociological Review*, 15–29.

Bird, R. 1994. "Reflections on the British Government and Higher Education in the 1980s." *Higher Education Quarterly* 48 (2):73–85.

BIS. 2011. *Higher Education: Students at the Heart of the System*. Cm. 8122. London: HMSO.

Blair, T. 2010. *The Journey*. London: Harper Collins.

Blunkett, D. 2003. "Higher Education Funding and Delivery to 2005–06." Letter to the Chairman of HEFCE. January.

Booth, C. 1983. "DES and Treasury." In *Resources in Higher Education*, ed. A. Morris and J. Sizer. Guildford: Society for Research into Higher Education.

Boyd-Carpenter, J.A. 1963. "The Robbins Report: Memorandum by the Chief Secretary to the Treasury and Paymaster General." C(63). 1 October.

Browne, J.D. 1979. *Teachers of Teachers*. London: Hodder and Stoughton.

Carswell, J. 1985. *Government and the Universities 1960–1980*. Cambridge: Cambridge University Press.

Clark, B.R. 1983. *The Higher Education System*. Berkeley: University of California Press.

Committee on Higher Education (Robbins Committee). 1963. *Higher Education*. Cmnd. 2154. London: HMSO.

CVCP Archive. 1957. Minutes of CVCP meeting with UGC, 22 November. MSS.399. University of Warwick Modern Records Centre, Coventry.

—. 1962. Minutes of deputation to Chief Secretary of the Treasury. 26 January. University of Warwick Modern Records Centre, Coventry.

—. 1984. Minutes of meeting on 17 February. University of Warwick Modern Records Centre, Coventry.

Deem, R., S. Hillyard, and M. Reed. 2007. *Knowledge, Higher Education and the New Managerialism*. Oxford: Oxford University Press.

Denham, A., and M. Garnett. 2001. *Keith Joseph*. Chesham: Acumen.

DES. 1985. *The Development of Higher Education into the 1990s*. Cmnd. 9254. London: HMSO.

DfES. 2003. *The Future of Higher Education*. Cm. 5735. London: Stationery Office.

DTI (Department of Trade and Industry), HM Treasury, and DES. 2002. *Investing in Innovation: A Strategy for Science, Engineering and Technology*. London: Stationery Office.

Estermann, T., T. Nokkala, and M. Steinel. 2011. *University Autonomy in Europe: The Scorecard*. Brussels: European University Association.

Hazelkorn, E. 2011. *Rankings and the Re-shaping of Higher Education*. London: Palgrave Macmillan.

HEFCE. 2010. *Model Financial Memorandum between HEFCE and Institutions*. July 2010/19.

Kogan, M., and S. Hannay. 2000. *Reforming Higher Education*. London: Jessica Kingsley.

Lee, J.M. 1998. "Overseas Students in Britain: How their Presence was Politicised in 1966–76." *Minerva* XXXVI (4):305–321.

Lindblom, C.E. 1965. *The Intelligence of Democracy: Decision Making through Mutual Adjustment*. New York: Free Press.

—. 1980. *The Policy-Making Process*, 2nd ed. Englewood Cliffs, NJ: Prentice Hall.

Major, J. 1999. *The Autobiography*. London: Harper Collins.

Minogue, M. 1983. "Theory and Practice in Public Policy and Administration." *Policy and Politics* 11:63–85.

Moberly, W. 1949. *The Crisis in the University*. London: SCM Press.

Public Accounts Committee. 1967. *Parliament and Control of University Expenditure: Special Report 1966–67*. HC 179. London: HMSO.

—. 1982. *Eleventh Report 1981–82: Minutes of Evidence*. HC 175. London: HMSO.

Robinson, E. 1968. *The New Polytechnics*. London: Cornmarket.

Sabatier, P.A. 1986. "Top-down and Bottom-up Approaches to Implementation Research: A Critical Analysis and Suggested Synthesis." *Journal of Public Policy* 6:21–45.

Select Committee on Estimates. 1951–52. *Fifth Report: Minutes of Evidence*. HC 163. London: HMSO.

Sharp, P.R. 1987. *The Creation of the Local Authority Sector of Higher Education*. London: Falmer Press.

Shattock, M.L. 1994. *The UGC and the Management of British Universities*. Buckingham: Open University Press.

Swinnerton Dyer, Sir P. 1991. "Policy on Higher Education and Research." *Higher Education Quarterly* 45 (3):204–218.

Truscott, B. 1951. *Red Brick University*. Harmondsworth: Penguin.

UGC. 1950–55. Minutes and papers. Files 1/3, 1/4. The National Archive, Kew.

—. 1962. 16 January. The National Archive, Kew.

Walsh, J.J. Correspondence with Sir Edward Hale. Papers. MS 1774. Leeds University Library, Leeds.

—. Interview with Sir James Mountford. Papers. MS 1774. Box 1. Leeds University Library, Leeds.

—. Interview with Lord Murray. Papers. MS 1774. Leeds University Library, Leeds.

Weaver, T. 1973. "Higher Education and the Polytechnics." Joseph Payne Memorial Lecture 1973–74 of the College of Preceptors, Bloomsbury House, London, 25 October.

Whitchurch, C. 2012. *Reconstructing Identities in Higher Education: The Rise of "Third Space" Professionals*. London: Routledge.

CHAPTER 2

MAKING POST-SECONDARY EDUCATION POLICY: TOWARD A CONCEPTUAL FRAMEWORK

ROOPA DESAI TRILOKEKAR, THERESA SHANAHAN,
PAUL AXELROD, AND RICHARD WELLEN

INTRODUCTION

In this chapter, we offer a conceptual framework for how public policy is made in Canadian post-secondary education (PSE). The chapter's central objectives are to provide a context for explaining post-secondary policy-making in Canada, to identify key policy influences and how they interact within our framework, and to offer insight into the distinctive features of Canadian policy-making in PSE. This chapter draws on data from our current project, funded by the Social Sciences and Humanities Research Council of Canada (SSHRC).[1] It relies on extensive interviews with federal and provincial (Ontario) government and education officials involved directly in policy-making, employed at all levels of government and in various locations in PSE. We also draw from a number of policy documents and government reports.

THE CONTEXT OF CANADIAN POST-SECONDARY EDUCATION

In Canada, constitutional responsibility for higher education rests with the provinces.[2] Provincial governments have exclusive law-making authority over education and have responsibility for regulation,

Making Policy in Turbulent Times: Challenges and Prospects for Higher Education, ed. P. Axelrod, R.D. Trilokekar, T. Shanahan, and R. Wellen. Kingston: School of Policy Studies, Queen's University.

organization, and funding of the public education system. Nevertheless, the federal government's role in education is significant; it consists of a number of direct and indirect policy instruments that derive from its legitimate constitutional powers over other areas of jurisdiction. For example, the federal government pursues its role in national development, and especially in promoting economic and social growth and equality of opportunity, in part through its financial support to post-secondary institutions and students. Universities and colleges also prepare young people for the labour force; enable interprovincial labour market mobility; deliver adult training and retraining as well as vocational training; and support bilingualism, technological development, international relations, and research.

The federal government also has responsibility for funding higher educational opportunities for Aboriginal peoples under the *Indian Act*. Despite the federal government's embedded role in educational policy and support, Canada has no federal department of higher education. Interprovincial relations are addressed through the Council of Ministers of Education, Canada, and federal-provincial government relations, especially around jurisdictional issues, are at times discordant.

Each provincial system of education has developed independently, making each provincial PSE system distinct. In Ontario, the Ministry of Training, Colleges and Universities (MTCU) has responsibility for the PSE system, which is the largest in the country. This means that the provincial government is responsible for the legislation, regulation, coordination, and, in the case of publicly funded PSE institutions, the funding of the PSE system. Funding comes in the form of provincial operating grants to each institution and is drawn from the province's general revenue coffers. Provincial general revenue includes federal government transfer payments to the province; therefore, fluctuations in federal transfer payments to Ontario invariably affect provincial support for PSE.

Historically, the system in Ontario has been divided along degree-granting (universities) and non-degree-granting (colleges) lines in a classic binary fashion, without the feeder function for colleges that exists in other provinces and countries. Ontario's PSE system is made up of 20 publicly funded universities and 24 colleges of applied arts and technology (CAATs). In addition, there are 20 private institutions with limited degree-granting authority[3] and over 600 private career colleges, or PCCs (in the "shadow" or "phantom" sector). The publicly funded sectors dominate PSE policy since the number of students in private institutions is significantly smaller than in the public education sector. Unlike in other provinces, governments in Ontario engage with universities individually (as they are legally independent, not-for-profit corporations with distinct governance structures); governments may also deal with universities through their collective association, the Council of Ontario Universities (COU), whereas the CAATs are governed as a sector under legislation.

CONCEPTUAL FRAMEWORK

Our research data are drawn from our SSHRC project on PSE policy-making. For this project, we conducted interviews[4] with policy-makers and stakeholders that focus on four domains of higher education: funding, research and development (R&D), accessibility and student assistance, and internationalization at both the provincial and the federal levels. We are primarily concerned with the decision-making aspects of the policy-making process – for example, variables such as the context of policy-making, the structures of decision-making, how policy issues or agendas are identified, and who determines policy paths and options.

Our framework suggests that there is a constellation of factors that *determine* policy-making in ways that are idiosyncratic, complex, and dynamic. We suggest that this process is neither linear nor cyclical, but that different variables have different levels of influence on policy, and we differentiate these policy determinants between core, *direct* influencers and circuitous forces and factors that influence policy *indirectly*. We propose that policy determinants that have a direct influence can be issues, persons, conditions, or factors that act as the impetus or catalyst for the creation of policy and course of action taken by government, whereas those that influence policy more indirectly can be forces, conditions, structures or ideologies, or networks or communities that provide a "container," thus affecting the course, shape, and development of policy. While we distinguish between the direct and indirect influence of individuals, ideologies, policy-development structures, networks, lobbying, and external social and economic pressures, our perspective allows us to analyze the interrelationships among these variables that contribute to policy-making (see Figure 1).

POLICY DETERMINANTS – DIRECT

People, power, and position

Our research suggests that understanding individuals and their positions with respect to power is necessary to understanding PSE policy-making. Specific individuals or groups of individuals can be important drivers of policy by virtue of the particular positions they occupy in the government and/or the access they have to those in power. Particularly important are "policy entrepreneurs" (Kingdon 1995) and "policy brokers" (Sabatier 1988), who work with government but also through larger networks to advance new ideas and initiatives. Since the PSE policy community is narrow and because Canada's parliamentary system is strongly leader-focused (Savoie 1999), these policy entrepreneurs and brokers can and must often work closely and directly with political leaders and their political staff.

FIGURE 1
Conceptual framework for post-secondary policy-making

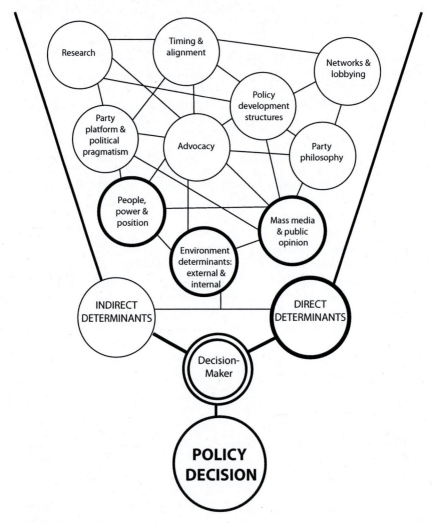

Source: Authors' compilation.

The prime minister and the premier

Our study demonstrates that at both the federal and the provincial levels, the key individuals in policy-making are the prime minister and the premier. Unquestionably, there is a political agenda behind policy-making, as well as a variety of socio-economic and institutional influences, but personal motivations may often be decisive. Leaders frequently seek to make a major imprint or leave a cherished legacy on the policy landscape.

At the federal level, the creation of the Canada Millennium Scholarship Foundation (CMSF), inaugurated in 2000, illustrates the role of leadership and personal motivations in the emergence of high priority initiatives. Viewed by Prime Minister Jean Chrétien (1993–2003) as a "momentous millennium project," the CMSF originated with Chrétien's policy adviser, Eddie Goldenberg, who proposed to the prime minister the creation of a $2.5 to $3 billion dollar national scholarship program. Chrétien liked the idea and told Goldenberg to consult with the Department of Finance which was favourably disposed to the plan (Goldenberg 2006, 346–351). In order to preserve the initiative as it was first conceived and to keep control of the federal surplus funds that were being used to finance it, Chrétien's office decided to bypass the formal decision-making process and not consult the Cabinet and other ministers (Savoie 1999, 155, 317). In other words, the PM circumvented the "normal" decision-making process to achieve his policy objective. (Axelrod et al. 2011)

Savoie describes this as "policy-making by announcement," where, for example, the prime minister delivers a major speech and simply proclaims a new policy initiative, one that has not been discussed by the Cabinet or vetted by any of the ministers or their departments (2010, 139). Similarly, he suggests that all prime ministers take office with a few "pet projects" (139, 140) and that there is "no stopping them" (140). One official concluded, "In the end, the strategy of the Prime Minister's Office [PMO] has a call on everything" (Interview, 10 August 2009); another civil servant observed, "This couldn't have happened if it wasn't supported by the PMO" (Interview, 9 September 2009).

Similarly, at the provincial level, the premier's policy direction prevails. For example, Ontario Premier Dalton McGuinty (2003–2013) fashioned himself at the outset of his term as the Education Premier, setting the stage for his initiation of major policy changes in education. A former deputy minister stated,

> From time to time, there's direction from the premier's office to do something and it gets done and implemented.... So if you've got a premier like Premier McGuinty or Premier Campbell [British Columbia] previously, who is intensely interested in public post-secondary with lots of ideas, you often spend a lot of time working with them and the premier's office. (Interview, 25 May 2011)

The premier's inner circle

The offices of the prime minister and premier often have an inner circle of ministers who hold considerable power and have the ear of the leader. For example, New Democratic Party (NDP) Premier Bob Rae (1990–1995) had a young, inexperienced Cabinet. His inner circle included Frances Lankin

(Industry), Dave Cooke (Education), and Floyd Laughren (Finance), all of whom had influence. "They (Bob, Frances, Dave, and Floyd) ran the government for all intents and purposes. They had a Wednesday breakfast group, those three or four people, and that was a very influential breakfast" (Interview, 6 June 2010). PSE policy-making in Premier McGuinty's Liberal administration went to the "blessed trinity for getting approvals for new initiatives" (Interview, 25 August 2009), a group that included the minister of training, colleges and universities; the minister of finance; and the premier himself.

Finance and Treasury

The ministers and senior staff of the federal Department of Finance are very powerful in setting policy directions given that they control the budget, which affects all other ministries (Interview, 22 May 2010). They set directives to find savings or fund initiatives that translate into policy directions. For example, in Ontario in the early 1990s, during the NDP era, Treasury officials directed civil servants to find savings in the Ontario Student Assistance Program (OSAP). Despite extraordinary resistance from the civil servants, the OSAP policy shifted to a "loans-first" policy because of Treasury insistence (Interview, 6 June 2010).

Similarly, the creation of the University of Ontario Institute of Technology (UOIT), Ontario's first new publicly funded university in 40 years, was described by a senior provincial official as a case of Minister of Finance "Flaherty exercising his power with the budget to spend funds to create a new university, after which the civil servants were left scrambling to figure out how to create an act for the institution and figure out what this thing was going to look like" (Interview, 1 August 2009). Another official commented that without Flaherty's support, it wouldn't have happened (Interview, 6 June 2010). "It was a political university created by a very political minister of finance," claims a former minister in opposition at the time (Interview, 25 August 2009). At the federal level, a non-governmental lobbyist contended that "the power centre is very much with the prime minister. Second to that would be the finance minister ... when it comes right down to it, in terms of the people that we have to lobby, there's probably only maybe three or four" (Interview, 18 May 2011).

Deputy ministers and senior advisors

The ability of civil servants and ministry bureaucrats to influence policy emerged in our data. "Absolutely, ministers are supreme in driving policy" (Interview, 20 May 2010); however, deputy ministers can also have considerable influence (Interviews, 18 November 2008, 30 November 2008, 13 November 2009, 6 June 2010). As one of our interview participants put it, "In government, if you want something to happen, you need somebody to make things happen – which usually means that you need someone lower down to do the work for a long time, and you need someone at the top who's a champion" (Interview, 10 August 2009). A university president, referring to federal government officials, concurred.

> I quickly learned that if you didn't have them on side, it probably wouldn't happen. Many of the key deputies, whether it was Peter Harder, Kevin Lynch, or David Dodge, ... they all worked together, and they worked with the PMO. So you have to bring your deputies along, there's no question.... Really, you've got to get to the deputy, and the deputy can be more important than the minister.... You look at the deputies and say, who's really making the decisions? And then you begin not just to meet with them, but develop relationships with them, so you can pick up the phone and call them, and they'll take your call. (Interview, 13 November 2009)

On the other hand, the lack of a champion inside government could be fatal to a policy initiative. With reference to the eventual closing of the CMSF by the Conservative government ten years after its founding, an interviewee noted, "There was no one on the inside arguing for the foundation. There was no champion" (Interview, 5 October 2010).

Civil servants and policy implementers

The support of key government officials, their specific interests and personalities, and the need for champions are considered central to policy-making. This applies not only to creating policy but also to the commitment – or lack of commitment – to implement it. We found examples of civil servants using their power to thwart or modify government initiatives, even those that were embedded in legislation. For example, some civil servants viewed Ontario's *Post-secondary Education Choice and Excellence Act, 2000*, which ended the "monopoly" on degree-granting by publicly funded institutions, as a heavy-handed attempt to expand the private sector presence in PSE. Consequently, they drafted the legislation in such a way that it subjected private institutions to arduous financial reporting and resource requirements.

> That was what was behind the legislation. Give the colleges degree-granting powers, unleash the private sector in the degree-granting world, challenge the universities, and get the costs down. It turns out that the legislation was drafted in a way that was too onerous for the privates, because of the ministry's [problematic] experience with the private vocational school sector, so that what the government was looking for [increasing private sector presence in PSE] never really materialized. (Interview, 1 August 2009)

Thus, it is important to recognize the power of not only political leaders but also policy implementers, who can ultimately determine the success or failure of policy initiatives.

Influential citizens

Governments also listen to people, not just organizations, because people give issues "a human face." To advance their cause, governments also recruit influential citizens, "brilliant minds" (Interview, 21 May 2010), and "strategic advisors" (Interview, 13 November 2008) from the community and from industry. Each administration may have a different pool of influential non-state actors that it consults; these people would include those who share its basic beliefs and who are experts in their fields.

In the case of the hallmark federal policy initiatives undertaken by the Chrétien government in the late 1990s, such as the Canada Research Chairs (CRC) program, the Canada Foundation for Innovation (CFI), and the CMSF, the PMO approached selected university presidents, including Martha Piper (University of British Columbia) and Robert Lacroix (University of Montreal), for their policy advice. Robert Giroux, then president of the Association of Universities and Colleges of Canada, also had considerable credibility with the government, and each of these individuals had direct access to the PMO and thus the policy process.

Similarly, Chrétien's brother, Michel, who was a research scientist at the University of Montreal, often spoke to the prime minister about the importance of university-based research. In Ontario, the first provincial bilateral exchange program with India was established as a result of a short meeting between Chris Bentley, the minister of training, colleges and universities, and Sheila Embleton, York University's vice-president academic, who spoke to the minister "on a walk to the parking lot" following his speech at a conference. Subsequently, the MTCU relied on her advice to develop a full-fledged provincial-international education strategy (Interview, 16 May 2011; see also p. 390).

Environmental determinants: external and internal

Internationalization, globalization, and the knowledge economy

Internationalization and globalization have been important direct policy determinants during the period of this study at both the federal and the provincial levels. These forces have framed several policy issues, including those in the PSE sector that were previously considered to be exclusively domestic or provincial-national issues. This has resulted in policy directives that concern multiple domains, such as trade and commerce, the labour market, education and training, the economy, and immigration, and it has led to a convergence, overlap, or collision of sectors as well as periodic tensions between federal and provincial departments. As a senior federal politician noted, "This isn't just about education. This is about the economy, immigration, our innovation, and our overall capacity to succeed as an economy" (Interview, 25 May 2011). One result of this environment has been the growing importance of the "knowledge economy" as a key policy driver for the PSE sector.

The importance of the knowledge economy was central to the federal Liberals' reforms for PSE. According to Chrétien, "Globalization is not left wing or right wing. It is simply a fact of life" (Chrétien 1992, 245; Greenspon and Wilson-Smith 1996, 98–101; Goldenberg 2006, 43). At a policy conference held by the Liberals in Aylmer, Quebec, in 1991, the party's agenda was heavily influenced by American economist Lester Thurow, who "hammered home the need to focus on government policy and investment in the promotion of innovation, knowledge and re-search ... and the priority that the Chrétien government later attached to these areas was [considered] in no small part a direct result of the Aylmer conference" (Goldenberg 2006, 42). Similarly, at the provincial level, the higher education policy document *Ontario: A Leader in Learning* (written by former premier Bob Rae) stated,

> Ontario must face up to the many and different challenges of globalization. The first is the significant internationalization of our student population.... The second is the priority to do a better job of marketing the opportunities provided in our colleges and universities to students from other countries.... Third, we need to increase the opportunities for Ontario students to study abroad. (Rae 2005, 11)

The Rae report formed the basis for the government's subsequent plan for PSE, *Reaching Higher*, published later that year.

Globalization also enables nations to learn from the policy experiences of other jurisdictions through policy borrowing, as policy discourses become internationalized in time. As Bob Rae stated, "My sense is that we aren't doing too badly, but one of the things in my report that I kept stressing was that you don't compare yourself to the guy down the street. You've got to say, 'Who's doing this best anywhere in the world, and how do we match that?'" (Unpublished interview with Bob Rae, 27 May 2011).

The integration of policy sectors as a result of globalization and inter-nationalization, especially those traditionally considered domestic and international, has had implications for the workings of Canadian federal-ism. Ontario, for example, made a significant multi-year investment in international education as a result of the Rae report (Interview, 13 May 2011), and it came to see itself as a leader in this area. However, in reality, many provinces were investing in internationalization strategies, and "provinces are all competitors too. In particular, Ontario, BC, and Alberta are all competing and often in the same markets" (Interview, 25 May 2011).

This competition among the provinces, in an area that could be deemed federal responsibility given its international nature, resulted in interprovincial tensions, and these tensions were compounded by the federal government's announcement of $2 million to establish a Canadian national education marketing brand. This initiative "caused problems," according to one federal government official, largely because the provinces felt excluded from its planning and design, although some groups, such as non-governmental organizations, were enthusiastic (Interview, 20 May 2011). As one former provincial official observed,

> a longstanding irritant in the federal-provincial-territorial relationship is the federal government's lack of engagement with provinces and territories in international issues which involve areas of provincial jurisdiction, education being the prime one. (Interview, 13 May 2011)

As seen from the above examples, globalization and internationalization have introduced a greater overlap of functions – and potential for tensions – between the two levels of government. The activities of the provinces are impinging on policy directions of the federal government and vice versa.

Economic conditions

National and regional economic contexts – the domestic market economy, deficits, and surpluses – are also key direct determinants of policy because they speak to the government's willingness and ability to develop and implement policy. Our participants emphasized that during the early 1990s, the federal deficit and the recession had an enormous impact on governments at both federal and provincial levels. As one university president stated, "In 1995, we were reeling with cuts, and I think people like Chrétien and Paul Martin needed to get our house in order" (Interview, 13 November 2009). Similarly, at the provincial level, a senior government official stated, "The drivers of the first mandate of the [Conservative] Harris Government [1995–2003] were the fiscal agenda, cumulative deficits, continually rising taxes to pay for the deficit, very much driven by the economic and fiscal agenda" (Interview, 25 January 2010).

Funding issues were thus at the core of PSE policy initiatives, with the federal government making major changes to transfer payments to the provinces and the provincial government responding with initiatives such as deregulating tuition, cutting operating funds, creating targeted and matching fund programs, and increasing the private sector presence in PSE. With these changes, student access, which was already an extremely important policy driver, became an even larger policy issue. Both levels of government responded with a range of student financial assistance programs, including the federal government's CMSF, enhanced tax incentives for PSE participation, and the Canada Education Savings grants program, among several others.

Our data also show numerous examples of PSE policy decisions being driven by real or perceived labour market trends and demands. The Access to Opportunities Program announced by the Harris Conservatives in Ontario in 1998 was a response to lobbying from the information technology and communications sector, led by the giant in the industry, Nortel Networks. The 1998 Ontario budget provided $150 million over three years to double entry-level enrolments at universities in computer science and high-demand fields of engineering by September 2000 and to increase entry-level enrolments in related college programs by 50 percent (Shanahan et al. 2005). Similarly, in the mid-2000s, Ontario passed the *Fair Access to Regulated Professions and Compulsory Trades Act* and established the Office of the Fairness Commissioner in response to reports about the demographics of the province's changing labour force presented by the business community (Interview, 21 May 2010).

Costs[5]

Another direct policy determinant closely associated with the nation's and province's economic situation is fiscal constraint. One former deputy minister bluntly stated, "If there is no money to implement an initiative, no amount of research or ideology will get it off the ground" (Interview, 22 May 2010). For example, in 1993, federal Minister of Human Resources and Skills Development Canada (HRSDC) Lloyd Axworthy proposed an income-contingent loan program to fund PSE, a proposal that was vigorously opposed by student groups and questioned by the Finance Department, which found it unaffordable in the context of government plans to reduce the federal deficit. One of our interviewees noted, "So I think that governments are going to play with [such proposals] for a while, but it's very costly ... there was concern around start-up costs.... So really, the time you want to do those things is when the economy's doing well and you're in a surplus situation and you can afford that" (Interview, 19 July 2010).

Mass media and public opinion

Our study suggests that the media is a potentially powerful direct policy determinant. The media's influence on voters concerns government as "politicians are keenly aware of polls, public sensibilities, their constituents' needs, stakeholders' wants, what is tolerable, and what is intolerable" (Interview, 21 May 2010). Public opinion translates into votes for pragmatic politicians. Salient issues driven by public opinion come to the forefront, shape policy agendas, and drive decision-making.

A clear example of one such issue is access to PSE. Public opinion in the form of parental and student pressure for accessible PSE, based on the public belief that PSE will provide personal economic benefits and positively affect an individual's ultimate financial security, has driven PSE policy across administrations over the last two decades. Recalling the 2003 "double cohort" in Ontario, when the province eliminated Grade 13, so that graduates from grades 12 and 13 were entering post-secondary schools simultaneously, an informant states,

> When the double cohort came along, Harris recognized that this was a huge political issue.... Parents were hysterical, and government committed that there would be a place for every qualified student, and they did come up with the money.... My impression is that there is one common theme that runs through history – that government cares about access, and this is where universities have some clout.... [What] resonates with voters is tuition fees, and number two is if there is a crisis about accessibility. (Interview, 16 May, 2011)

An example of the media driving policy was the newspapers' exposés of PCCs, which led the Ontario government to review the *Private Career Colleges Act* and launch an investigation into PCC institutions for allegedly violating provisions of the legislation. The government also responded to negative media coverage of the announcement by Premier McGuinty of the Ontario Trillium Scholarships program, designed to attract the best international doctoral students. Critics complained that scarce dollars would be used to lure and fund non-Canadian students instead of domestic students who had post-graduate educational aspirations and financial needs. As one official observed, the "terrible, terrible result of that [response] is that it made government gun-shy on international strategy. They don't even mention international anymore" (Interview, 16 May 2011). This example also reinforces the point that access is a visceral domestic policy issue as there is always concern about adequate space and funding for domestic students.

On the other hand, Prime Minister Stephen Harper's closure of the CMSF was an example of the government's use of the media as a political instrument to announce policy and gain the support of the electorate. The Conservatives closed the CMSF because of its very close association with the Liberal Chrétien government; but it also skillfully used federal-provincial relations to legitimize its case. According to one well-placed official,

> [the media] knew that there was a fight between [Quebec Premier] Bouchard and Chrétien, and if Harper could get a headline that he put an end to what Chrétien had started in French Quebec, that was what he was looking for. It was no accident that one of the only things that was leaked to the

Canadian press in French from the budget before budget day 2007 was the closure of the Foundation … they made sure it got coverage. (Interview, 13 November 2009)

POLICY DETERMINANTS – INDIRECT

Philosophy, platforms, and pragmatism

Policy platforms, rooted in political parties' values and ideology, have provided key roadmaps for a number of administrations since 1990, both provincially and federally (Interviews, 30 November 2009, 20 May 2010, 21 May 2010). The platforms were developed in response to several direct policy determinants, such as the priorities of the prime minister, premier, or other important individual in power; external and internal environmental drivers such as globalization and the economy; and public opinion and/or the electorate.

For example, the platform of Mike Harris's provincial Conservatives, the "Common Sense Revolution" (CSR), was crafted to respond to the dire financial situation of the province in 1995 and was imbued with a neo-conservative philosophy built on five policy pillars: lowering provincial taxes, reducing government spending, balancing the provincial budget, shrinking the size of government, and removing government "barriers" to job creation and economic growth (Ontario Progressive Conservative Caucus 1992). The CSR provided a clear agenda for the party when it took office in 1995, and within 18 months, the Conservatives had implemented every tenet (Courchene and Telmer 1998). The party's policy advisors were given the CSR and told, "Learn this. This is what you will be doing while you are here" (Interview, 20 May 2010).

When it came to adhering to platforms, both the Conservatives and McGuinty's Liberals took the view "A promise made is a promise kept" and "It makes sense for government to deliver on platform commitments as soon as possible and whenever possible" (Interview, 21 May 2010). Similarly, the federal Liberal campaign platform, *Creating Opportunity: The Liberal Plan for Canada*, subsequently dubbed "The Red Book," was effectively employed in the 1993 election campaign (Liberal Party of Canada 1993). The Red Book made a general case for the importance of research and innovation and thus for potential investment in universities. Once in power, the federal Liberals followed much of their plan, with considerable success (Axelrod et al. 2011).

However, items in a party platform are always expendable under particular circumstances. If there is deemed to be insufficient funding to implement a platform initiative, it is unlikely to get off the ground. If critical, political, or economic events, unanticipated during a campaign, emerge during a government's tenure (and this almost always happens), they will be addressed, irrespective of the campaign platform. Indeed, participants in our study cautioned that party philosophy or ideology can be overestimated as a policy-making determinant. A former provincial deputy minister observed,

> People think that governments make all of their decisions based on some set of ideological principles, when in fact they don't. They make most of their decisions based on pragmatic politics. There is an ideological overlay on that. There's a certain set of things that a political party can't possibly accept, or a certain orientation that they have. But there's a huge amount of room within that, most of which is determined by the pragmatic politics of the day. (Interview, 18 November 2009)

Thus, core values and ideology can situate policy discussions; hard political realities determine the degree to which policies are realized, modified, or discarded.

"When the stars align": timing and alignment

Timing has to be right for politicians and the public service to be receptive to ideas and adopt particular policies. This was evident in the mid-1990s, when the CRC and CFI were created. One participant from the university sector observed,

> So a lot of things were happening at once, and a lot of the ideas we floated didn't go anywhere. It was like all the stars were aligning. They [the federal government] had their fiscal house in order, they had some extra money, the knowledge economy was growing in fervour, and they had this brain-drain problem. I don't really know how real it was. I don't think there were studies done.... We all had anecdotal evidence.... But politically, with public policy, you've got to play with the politics here. (Interview, 13 November 2010)

The federal government was receptive to universities' call to compete with their American counterparts in order to attract the best and brightest researchers. This was largely a result of the alignment of three factors – the improving fiscal situation, the "one time only" nature of the invest-ment, and its presumed contribution to enhancing Canada's knowledge economy – all of which persuaded the government of the policy's virtue.

Another example was Canada's international student recruitment policy. While universities, colleges, and the non-governmental sector had been lobbying for the federal government to invest in international education for well over two decades, the government had only recently identified the marketing of Canadian higher education abroad as a priority and had committed funds to establish a Canadian brand. Here again, environmental determinants, including the combined forces of globalization, the recognition of education as an export industry, and the need for immigrants in the Canadian labour market, combined to create the right timing to enable an alignment of interests, both in the federal government – Department of Finance, the PMO, Department of Foreign Affairs and International Trade (DFAIT), Industry Canada, Citizenship and Immigration Canada, and HRSDC – and among the provinces, individual institutions, the non-governmental sector, and industry. In this instance, a constellation of environmental forces and conditions, with direct and indirect influence, came together and gave shape to the ultimate policy initiative.

The potential impact of research: the strategic use of evidence

Our data suggest that politicians are unlikely to consider research in the policy development process unless it is strategically brought to their attention. One former deputy minister stated, "There isn't a systematic approach to obtaining findings and using evidence within government" (Interview, 18 November 2009). Another policy analyst and former deputy minister remarked, "Generally speaking, the policy capacity and the re-search capacity of most governments, regardless of their political stripe, [are] not well developed" (Interview, 22 May 2010). A former provincial minister concurred.

> I would really have to think hard to be able to tell you what I would refer to as a strong research function in either of my two ministries. Even the [Ontario] Ministry of Research and Innovation [MRI] was not really about feeding government research. MRI was not there to inform government decisions. It was there to drive the economy. (Interview, 21 May 2010)

This weakness in research capacity in governments leaves them open to influence by individuals or organizations, which can suggest evidence-based arguments on particular policy directions. For example, in describing former York University president Lorna Marsden's "financial coup" (Interview, 12 August 2009) by achieving "fair funding" for universities like York, a senior government official admitted that Marsden "had a good case backed by solid data.... York's funding [per student from the provincial government] was below that of U of T[oronto]. They had great bar graphs. She went straight to the premier's office and made the case" (Interview, 1 August 2009).

Research that sheds clear light on an issue or problem, on what other comparator jurisdictions have done in response to similar problems, as well as data on what works and does not work can be meaningful and persuasive (Interviews, 18 November 2009, 30 November 2009, 21 May 2010). Research that includes "both numbers and stories" (quantitative and qualitative) may be especially useful because "politicians like to quote numbers, but people remember the stories" (Interview, 21 May 2010). Examples of this are two reports on international education published by

DFAIT in 2009, "Economic Impact of International Education in Canada" and Guhr's "Best Practices on Managing the Delivery of Canadian Educational Marketing," which were highly influential in informing Ottawa's *Advantage Canada* strategy document of 2009 and the Speech from the Throne that same year. Both of these documents described Canada's weak international comparative position while also highlighting the contribution of international students to the tune of some $6.5 billion to the Canadian economy, $291 million in government revenue, and 83,000 sustained new jobs. All of these figures have subsequently and consistently been used by various federal government departments for new policy initiatives.

Nevertheless, the influence of research on policy is, on the whole, limited. Research can inform but rarely directly determines policy because so many other factors flow into making a decision. "A good study is never going to replace powerful political arguments" (Interview, 18 November 2009). Other factors will trump research, especially, as previously mentioned, political pragmatism in response to public opinion on salient issues and/or the state of the economy and Treasury. For example, one deputy minister recounted that his minister had dismissed the research study he had presented him, saying, "I don't think [that] 'research' votes in my constituency." The evidence suggests that while research is not disregarded, it comprises only one component of the development and implementation of policy. A former deputy minister clarified the relative importance of research in the following way:

> Values are very important. The politics of process brings facts to values. Politicians do pay attention to evidence, and what they construe as evidence includes research evidence, but being very attuned to constituent preferences, stakeholders' needs, understandings, and values, and being attuned to party commitments, are all sources of evidence for the formation of public policy. The more intense the value of public commitment is to something, the less likely it is to be subject to [research] analyses and less likely that analysis is going to explain variance in the decision that is arrived at. (Interview, 22 May 2010)

Policy development structures

The legislative framework of education

The structure of Canada's federal system and the constitutional division of powers clearly affect how policy is made in PSE. One university president observed,

> We've got this bizarre structure where two of the [research] granting councils report through the [federal] Industry department, and one reports

through [federal] Health. We don't have a minister of education [at the federal level]. Because of federal-provincial issues, the vehicle that was used primarily to deliver federal policy was the research-granting councils. Then we set up these standalone foundations [which received research funding to allocate funds to universities]. I mean, these are really the main vehicles the federal government has so that the provinces don't get their noses out of joint. (Interview, 13 November 2009)

The tensions between federal and provincial governments and the impact on PSE policy-making are evident in the story of the creation and termination of the CMSF. In this instance, the federal government chose to directly control the reinvestments in PSE rather than reverse provincial funding cuts. It employed policy instruments that circumvented provincial involvement and consultation. One provincial official complained,

we have no way of establishing principles and priorities at the national level. The (CMSF) foundation model was a way of getting funds directly to students without having to go through premiers and ministers across the country, but it's too bad you have to do this. Because it implies you can't work with the provinces. (Interview, 29 March 2010)

Initiatives such as the CMSF were marked by political contention between the two levels of government and their competing visions of Canadian federalism. A number of provinces were not pleased with the new level of intrusion, and, in Quebec, it fuelled struggles between a strongly federalist prime minister (Chrétien) and the pro-independence (separatist) government of Quebec. The Ontario government, according to a highly placed official, also came to resent the sudden appearance of a new federal initiative that had been introduced without the prior knowledge of the province and would overlap with a provincial student grant program that was already under development to address rising fees (Interview, 14 June 2010).

It was clear that the federal government was interested in using the program to achieve visibility and wanted "Canadians [to be] thankful for the actions of the federal government" (Interview, 5 October 2010). Simply put, it wanted credit for supporting students. When the Conservatives came to power and Prime Minister Stephen Harper announced the termination of the CMSF program, some suggested it was a political move to "score political points in Quebec by putting an end to a legacy program from the former Liberal prime minister" (Interview, 29 March 2010). As one former university president commented, federal-provincial jurisdictional struggles "always play out. It's one of our challenges. They're like the elephant in the room" (Interview, 12 November 2009). In such an environment, with restricted constitutional jurisdiction and no federal education department, the role of the PMO emerges as potentially significant.

Provincial ministry structures and ministry organization also affect policy-making. In the early 1990s, the Ontario NDP government combined the K–12 Ministry of Education with the PSE Ministry of College and Universities and the Ministry of Skills Development to create a "super-ministry" called the Ministry of Education and Training. Various objectives explain this, including trying to generate efficiencies and Premier Rae's need to reduce the number of ministries because he had few experienced cabinet members. Response to this reorganization was mixed.

> When we [PSE] were under the same minister, we had a senior, more powerful minister, and you'd think we would have more influence, but we got less attention; when we had our own minister, we got her undivided attention, but she was more junior and had less clout. (Interview, 1 August 2009)

These remarks suggest that when PSE is part of a larger Education super-ministry, PSE priorities are overshadowed by the larger, more dominant K–12 sector priorities. By contrast, when PSE is its own ministry, albeit with a smaller budget, the minister and civil servants can focus on, and advocate for, PSE issues.

Government administrations since 1990 have created specialized or quasi-governmental structures to advance policy-making, often strategically circumventing existing structures (Cabinet committees, parliamentary committee hearings, etc.). By way of example, the Harris Conservatives in the mid-1990s set a clear agenda in their CSR platform and used traditional structures *only* when they were needed to drive policies through to implementation (Interview, 20 May 2010). By contrast, the McGuinty Liberals created new structures such as the arm's-length Higher Education Quality Council of Ontario (HEQCO), whose explicit mandate is to inform and advise on policy. Both strategies have proven effective in exploring policy innovations and carrying out new policy initiatives.

Commissions, reviews, reports

Commissions, task forces, reviews, and reports can also be used as vehicles to effect changes in policy if political conditions are favourable and the commissioner leverages them.

A good example is the Rae report, which succeeded in shaping subsequent PSE policy far more than previous similar commission reports.[6] Bob Rae, a former provincial premier, confirmed this.

> Well, that was the deal.... [I said that] I don't want to do a Royal Commission or a formal process that's outside the workings of government. I know something about the timing of budgets and ministers of finance, what

their cycle is, and what the cycle of the report is. I want my report to be in the cycle of the next budget, and I want to work closely with Mr. Sorbara [finance minister] and his staff and with everybody else to make sure that whatever we're doing is seen as being relevant and useful. I may have some things to say that you won't like, and you may decide that there are some things that you can't do, but I'm not interested in doing a three-column report that looks pretty on a shelf.

So it succeeded, and its recommendations were taken for two reasons. The first one was because there has been this growing consensus building, which my report articulated quite well. That's why it felt such resonance with the business community, the newspapers, the editorial opinion, and everybody else, saying, "Yeah, that's right. He's up to something." So I think that it did have a very positive impact from that point. But the second reason was because it was structured to succeed, and I couldn't have done it without the premier. (Unpublished interview with Bob Rae, 25 May 2011)

Here we see a number of factors contributing to the success of the Rae report: Rae's knowledge of the political environment in which the government was operating and his understanding of what was politically acceptable to the Liberals; extensive consultation between the MTCU and the commission; and system-wide consultation (Clark and Trick 2006; Interview, 20 May 2010), including a broad panel – "a good cross-section of not just people in the sector, but people who had knowledge of the sector and knowledge of the impact of the sector on life in the province of Ontario" (Interview, 21 May 2010).

Advocacy: networks, lobbying, and developing relationships with decision-makers

Lobbying and networking by constituents, if done correctly, can be effective in influencing decision-makers. However, our study has found that the influence of outside organizations on government policy varies depending on several factors. One former deputy minister remarked that external organizations need to be "powerful, smart, and strategic" in their dealings with government; otherwise, they will be dismissed (Interview, 18 November 2009). They will have the ear of the government only if they understand government priorities, what motivates government, and the political pressures the government is under (such as budget restraints). They must make persuasive, balanced arguments for their cause. They need to be able to speak to government decision-makers in language they understand and that addresses the government's pressing priorities. Finally, lobbyists need to convey their position to the media and mobilize public opinion (Interviews, 13 November 2009, 18 November 2009, 30 November 2009, 21 May 2010, 22 May 2010, 6 June 2010).

How interest groups prepare their cases for government investment is crucial. In Ontario, a senior government official described the process for awarding capital funding from the SuperBuild Growth Fund for university expansion in the early 2000s: "They [the unsuccessful universities] should have done a better job tying their proposals to [government] criteria." They had to "game their submissions" (Interview, 1 August 2009). On the other hand, successful universities were the ones that anticipated and then matched their submissions to government criteria. One university president observed, "When you work with public policy, whether it's the bureaucrats or the politicians, you have to align your arguments, lobbying, and efforts with their picture" (Interview, 13 November 2009).

Our study has cited focused, clear, persuasive, and determined advocacy, targeted at the key decision-makers, as critical to the successful influencing of policy. At the federal level, the emergence of the CRC, as explained above, was an example of university presidents making a persuasive and timely business case to Finance Minister Paul Martin. In Ontario, a senior staff member recalled the creation of UOIT.

> Gary Polonsky [a college president who led the campaign for the new university] had this vision. He used lots of different arguments to make his case – technology, science, etc. Geographically, eastern parts [of the province] are a fast-growing area with no commuting institutions within its area.… I heard that Premier Harris was coming back from an event in eastern Ontario and spoke to a Rotary Club meeting in Oshawa. Finance Minister Jim Flaherty, who was the local member of provincial Parliament, was at the meeting and got Harris together with Polonsky, who made the case. Harris said, "This sounds like a good idea. When are we going to do it?" So he evidently sent a signal [and things proceeded from there]. And the signal of putting $45 million from the budget into that area – linking investments to needs of local industry – was especially powerful. Was it more sophisticated than that? I don't think so. (Interview, 25 January 2010)

Advocacy for a new university (including a persistent campaign involving the local mayor, community, and industry), timing, and a receptive government came together, while PSE sector consultation was almost non-existent. Notably, the creation of UOIT came as a surprise to officials in MTCU, including the minister. As one senior official recalled, "It came out of the blue. The deputy minister and I were over doing budget sign-off, and when we saw the language in the budget speech … we were shocked! We had to go back and tell the [PSE] minister and the staff [who knew nothing about it]" (Interview, 1 August 2009).

Participants in our study offered examples in which organizations had taken a very adversarial tack with government and ended up rendering themselves ineffective in their objective to change policy. One policy advisor in government in the early 1990s described a difficult period during the NDP era when the COU, a lobbying association for Ontario universities, "went through a fundamental shift from a low-key advocacy group to a much more adversarial relationship with government" (Interview, 5 June 2010). The chair at the time was in the habit of sending "poison-pen letters to Premier Bob Rae ... horrific stuff ... strident, angry, telling the government what to do" (Interview, 5 June 2010). According to this advisor, COU ended up losing the premier's ear because he couldn't respond to the daily barrage of letters they sent.

One university president highlighted the importance of developing a cordial relationship with policy-makers and offered this example: "I was in a meeting recently with [former federal industry minister] John Manley, who cited the establishment of the CFI: 'The universities did it right.' Every time they [the government] did something for us, regardless of the magnitude, we made a huge, concerted effort to say 'Thank you.' Thanks, loud and clear.... [We told them] how grateful we were that they had the guts to do it and why it had made a difference. Well, I'll tell you, that was the smartest thing we ever did" (Interview, 13 November 2009). Some former PSE lobbyists indicated that knowing how to balance criticism and support of government is not only beneficial to those wanting to influence policy, but it can also improve the quality of policies as it allows the government to communicate more constructively with stakeholders (Interview, 29 March 2010).

DISTINCTIVE FEATURES OF POLICY-MAKING IN CANADIAN POST-SECONDARY EDUCATION

In researching four policy domains in higher education (funding, R&D, accessibility and student assistance, and internationalization), we have developed a conceptual framework that both illustrates the complexity of the policy-making process and identifies variables that interact in distinct and unique ways to influence policy decisions. We have differentiated these variables in terms of policy determinants that have a more direct influence versus those that have a more indirect influence on the policy-making process.

Our framework suggests that policy-making in the PSE sector in Canada is directly influenced by three main policy determinants: people (their powers and positions), external and internal environmental forces, and the media and public opinion. However, there is a much wider range of policy determinants that have indirect influences on the policy-making process. We recognize that this level of complexity does not allow for a "one size fits all" model, but suggest that the constellations of variables, their dynamics, and their influence on different policy domains can vary considerably at either the federal or provincial level.

Our study concludes that Canadian PSE policy-making has some distinguishing features. Like some other jurisdictions (such as the United

Kingdom), the federal structure and constitutional arrangements often result in higher education policy development being diffused over several departments and programs in the federal government. However, unlike other jurisdictions, this is compounded by a lack of a federal department of education and the lack of a coordinating policy mechanism, central policy focus, or clear direction.

Consequently, PSE policy-making is messy, shared responsibilities spill over and overlap, and accountability is spread out within and between federal and provincial governments (Lindquist 1999). This structure, according to an interviewee, results in a policy process that is "more serendipitous ... like who happens to be in the room at that time, or who happens to be the cousin of the prime minister" (Interview, 5 October 2010). As an example, the interviewee spoke about the federal government's announcement to increase SSHRC funding for graduate students in management and business rather than other fields in the social sciences and humanities.

> Everyone was outraged by this. [The finance minister] did not consult with people. Well, it turns out that he happened to be in Toronto at a meeting with Roger Martin, the dean of the Rotman School of Business at the University of Toronto, and Martin said to Flaherty, "What we need is a program for business students because they often don't get SSHRC funding. They fall through the cracks." So Flaherty thought it was a good idea, and he added it to the budget. It's the way you make policy ... [an] ad hoc approach because there was no place [education department] for him to go back to in the federal bureaucracy. (Interview, 19 July 2010)

In addition, the parliamentary system and the dynamics of decision-making within bureaucratic frameworks affect policy development. Canada's adoption of the British (Westminster) parliamentary system is said to have enabled centralized executive authority and a more top-down approach to governance (Brooks 1998; Brooks and Miljan 2003). Canadian PSE decision-making is often concentrated in the PMO at the federal level and the premier's office at the provincial level. Ministers of finance also enjoy tremendous influence over policy, influence that rivals that of the prime minister and premier. Financial budgets have acquired a supremacy over other policy instruments, becoming, as Savoie (2010) suggests, "the government's single most important [policy] document[s]."

Thus, in Canada, the concentration of political power in the hands of prime ministers, premiers, and ministers of finance has resulted in a largely elitist policy-making process (Bakvis and Skogstad 2007). While there is some disagreement as to how different prime ministers and premiers have used this power, there is general recognition that over the years, power is becoming more centralized within the Canadian bureaucracy and that other avenues for policy-making have been rendered far less effective.

Constituent consultation in policy-making has variably expanded and contracted over the years within and across administrations. However, the nature of government consultation (open or constrained) does not break down along party lines, and it has been far from systematic. At times, various administrations have built consensus strategically and deliberately, while at other times, they have acted unilaterally, swiftly precluding sector consultation.

Generic public policy research does not adequately capture the unique challenges of the PSE sector (in Canada or elsewhere in the world). Inherent characteristics of the PSE system resonate throughout the policy-making process. For example, the high levels of institutional autonomy enjoyed by Canadian publicly funded universities are not found in other public policy domains, and this autonomy affects policy-making and implementation. Institutional diversity also affects policy-making as the PSE sectors and institutions are not homogeneous.

Three distinct, identifiable features with implications for policy-making have emerged from our study: the binary organization of Ontario's PSE system, the lack of a system plan or coordinating body, and the development of sector-specific policy. Ontario PSE policy-making has typically been characterized by stability, the status quo, and modest adjustments; however, our data show that this approach to policy-making started to change in the early 1990s, with a shift in governance and decision-making. As the PSE system expanded, policy became increasingly complex. Without officially declaring the end of the university monopoly over granting degrees, the government opened it up, expanded the number of out-of-province and private degree-granting institutions, and allowed colleges to offer applied degrees. It created new bodies, such as HEQCO and the Postsecondary Education Quality Assessment Board, which have an arm's-length relationship with the government and yet give it crucial advice on system design and expansion.

Governments are using various policy tools and levers at their disposal to exert control over the system, including legislation, matching funds, increased regulation, and concomitant deregulation. They are becoming increasingly engaged in the PSE system, but without dramatic wholesale structural reform. This trend suggests less trust, more control, and more regulation across the public sector.

CONCLUSION

Public policy is inherently a political process as it involves a deliberate choice on the part of governments to either take action on an issue or allow for inaction (Brooks 1998), and it necessarily implicates the use of power (Simeon 1976). Universities and colleges would do well to invest in understanding the policy process and not underestimate the power of individuals. Our study reinforces this message and how policy at both levels of government is controlled from the centre; yet it also clearly indicates that there are multiple points of entry into influencing the policy-making process.

In conclusion, what might our study suggest about how public policy is made in PSE? Our research supports the perspectives offered by a number of theories, such as institutionalism, public choice theory, and environmental determinism, suggesting that they are not mutually exclusive. We find it tempting to support Savoie's observations that "soft power" is key to the policy process

> because institutions have become less important. Contacts and networks have replaced hierarchy, while personalities have gained power and influence at the expense of institutions, organizations and processes, which have become too complex, too complicated, too porous and too slow to get things done. (Savoie 2010, 193)

Yet we are reminded that formal institutions and organizations and their frameworks enable power to be distributed among individuals and structure certain processes of decision-making. Organizational structures and functions are not fixed and are themselves a result of a variety of historical, political, and environmental factors. Moving beyond traditional debates around the power of institutions over individuals and groups (or structure versus agency) in policy-making, we propose the analogy of an inverted funnel to illustrate the policy-making process. The funnel contains multiple circles of policy influence interacting with one another and ascending to the apex of power, the decision-maker – usually the prime minister or provincial premier.

In conclusion, rather than proposing a grand theory, we suggest that policy-making, a highly complex and frequently chaotic process, is affected by a number of determinants "whose general form, but not specific content, can be assumed in advance" (Howlett, Ramesh, and Perl 2009, 210). Each of these determinants is part of a cluster or policy subsystem, and each relates to or collides with the others; some are more direct, and others are more indirect, in influencing how and what policy is made in Canadian PSE.

NOTES

1. Paul Axelrod (PI), Theresa Shanahan, Roopa Desai Trilokekar, and Richard Wellen (co-investigators), *Making Policy in Post-Secondary Education since 1990*, a SSHRC project funded by a General Research Grant, 2008–11.
2. Canada's three territories – the Northwest Territories, Yukon, and Nunavut – do not have the same status and powers under the Constitution as the provinces. Consequently, in many areas of governance, including education, they are under the direct control of the federal government. However, the federal government has delegated its authority over education (including

PSE) to the territorial governments. Thus, PSE in each territory is under the control of a territorial department of education.

3. A total of 17 privately funded institutions were granted restricted legislative authority to grant degrees under the *Degree Granting Act* of 1983. By 2009, under the new *Post-secondary Education Choice and Excellence Act, 2000*, an additional nine ministerial consents had been granted to private in-province and out-of-province institutions, though six of these consents went to some of the original 17 institutions. See http://www.tcu.gov.on.ca/eng/generak/postsec/opconsents.html. See also http://www.peqab.ca/completed.html.

4. The authors conducted a number of confidential interviews for this project, and the names of the interviewees are withheld by agreement of both parties. The interview with Bob Rae was not confidential and is quoted with permission.

5. For a discussion of the cost drivers in PSE, especially faculty salaries and inflation, technology, debt servicing for capital construction, and the cost of complexity and competition, see Clark et al. (2009, 91–97).

6. See Clark and Trick (2006) for an in-depth discussion of the success of the Rae report. The authors suggest that environmental and process variables as well as political acuity contributed to its success. Environmental variables include the economy, fiscal situation, and political cycle. Process variables include reporting relationships, character of the commissioner, and stakeholders' strategies.

REFERENCES

Axelrod, P., T. Shanahan, R.D. Trilokekar, and R. Wellen. 2011. "People, Processes and Policy-Making in Canadian Post-secondary Education." *Higher Education Policy* 24 (2):143–166.

Bakvis, H., and G. Skogstad, eds. 2007. *Canadian Federalism: Performance, Effectiveness, and Legitimacy.* Toronto: Oxford University Press.

Brooks, S. 1998. *Public Policy in Canada: An Introduction,* 3rd ed. Toronto: Oxford University Press.

Brooks, S., and L. Miljan. 2003. *Public Policy in Canada: An Introduction,* 4th ed. Toronto: Oxford University Press.

Chrétien, J., ed. 1992. *Finding Common Ground: The Proceedings of the Aylmer Conference.* Hull, QC: Voyageur Publishing.

Clark, I.D., G. Moran, M.L. Skolnik, and D. Trick. 2009. *Academic Transformation: The Forces Reshaping Higher Education in Ontario.* Montreal and Kingston: Queen's Policy Studies Series, McGill-Queen's University Press.

Clark, I.D., and D. Trick. 2006. "Advising for Impact: Lessons from the Rae Review on the Use of Special-Purpose Advisory Commissions." *Canadian Public Administration* 49 (2):180–195.

Courchene, T.J., and C.R. Telmer. 1998. *From Heartland to North American Region State: The Social, Fiscal and Federal Evolution of Ontario; An Interpretive Essay.* Monograph series on Public Policy. Toronto: Centre for Public Management, Faculty of Management, University of Toronto.

Goldenberg, E. 2006. *The Way It Works: Inside Ottawa.* Toronto: McClelland and Stewart.

Greenspon, E., and A. Wilson-Smith. 1996. *Double Vision: The Inside Story of the Liberals in Power*. Toronto: Doubleday Canada.

Howlett, M., M. Ramesh, and A. Perl. 2009. *Studying Public Policy, Policy Cycles & Policy Subsystems*, 3rd ed. Toronto: Oxford University Press.

Kingdon, J.W. 1995. *Agendas, Alternatives and Public Policies*, 2nd ed. Boston: Little, Brown.

Liberal Party of Canada. 1993. *Creating Opportunity: The Liberal Plan for Canada.* Ottawa: Liberal Party of Canada.

Lindquist, E.A. 1999. "Efficiency, Reliability, or Innovation? Managing Overlap and Interdependence in Canada's Federal System of Governance." In *Stretching the Federation: The Art of the State in Canada*, ed. R. Young, 35–69. Kingston: Institute of Intergovernmental Affairs, Queen's University.

Ontario Progressive Conservative Caucus. 1992. *Common Sense Revolution.*

Rae, B. 2005. *Ontario: A Leader in Learning; Report & Recommendations*. Toronto: Ministry of Training, Colleges and Universities.

Sabatier, P. 1988. "An Advocacy Coalition Model of Policy Change and the Role of Policy-Oriented Learning Therein." *Policy Sciences* 21:129–168.

Savoie, D. 1999. *Governing from the Centre: The Concentration of Power in Canadian Politics*. Toronto: University of Toronto Press.

—. 2010. *Power: Where Is It?* Montreal and Kingston: McGill-Queen's University Press.

Shanahan, T., D. Fisher, G.A. Jones, and K. Rubenson. 2005. "The Case of Ontario: The Impact of Post-secondary Policy on Ontario's Higher Education System." New York: Alliance for International Higher Education Policy Studies.

Simeon, R. 1976. "Studying Public Policy." *Canadian Journal of Political Science* 9 (4):548–580.

CHAPTER 3

THE ROLE OF EVIDENCE AND EXPERTISE IN RESEARCH FUNDING AGENCIES

CRESO M. SÁ, MERLI TAMTIK, AND ANDREW KRETZ

INTRODUCTION

In an era of heightened expectations and constrained resources for academic research, funding agencies need to navigate a challenging policy environment. Internationally, science policy has been reconfigured around technological innovation agendas and economic goals (Lundvall and Borrás 2006). With this shift, government funding for university research has been increasingly directed toward "strategic" fields, objectives, and modes of support. The emphasis has been on the relevance and impact of research outcomes, particularly on technological applications. Such shifts in research policy have been documented across continents (e.g., Dill and van Vught 2010). Funding agencies figure prominently in the literature as vehicles for many of these new policy agendas, yet they have remained in the background as agents of policy formation and implementation.

Over the past decade, political expectations that public agencies should become more responsive and accountable are transforming the agenda and strategies of research funding agencies. In Canada, there has been a shift away from hierarchical, top-down accountability (by the federal government, granting agencies, and researchers) toward less hierarchical administration (Doern 2009). The focus is now on "clients" and "service delivery," emphasizing networks and partnerships and shared ways of funding (see also Axelrod et al. 2011). In this sort of environment, where effectiveness in public policy-making is paramount, evidence-based

Making Policy in Turbulent Times: Challenges and Prospects for Higher Education, ed. P. Axelrod, R.D. Trilokekar, T. Shanahan, and R. Wellen. Kingston: School of Policy Studies, Queen's University.

policy-making has taken on the mantle of reliable and informed decision-making (Howlett 2009). Yet for funding agencies, uncertainties around evaluating research output and impact drive a need to develop and implement new approaches and share best practices.

Since World War II, funding agencies in North America and beyond have relied on peer review as a legitimate way of making judgments about public investments in science (Geiger 1993; Doern 2009). The institution of peer review is thus deeply ingrained in the fabric of research funding systems and is an important element in the normative authority of science around the world (Drori et al. 2003). The culture of scientific expertise related to peer review pervades much of what funding agencies do, particularly adjudicating grant applications. While studies on peer review focus on the dynamics of expert judgments in science (Chubin and Hackett 1990; Lemont 2009), little is known about how or when research funding agencies employ experts and use evidence to make decisions about policy and programs. Our study addresses this gap by examining the practices of major funding agencies in Canada, the United States, and Europe.

THEORETICAL FRAMEWORK

This chapter draws on literature focusing on evidence-based policy and practice (Oakley 2000; Sanderson 2002; Nutley, Walter, and Davies 2007). Below we sketch different approaches to the use of evidence in policy; we then review relevant studies.

There are various viewpoints among scholars and policy-makers about what best counts as evidence in decision-making processes. Typically, evidence-based policy-making involves the use of the best available evidence in policy processes (Nutley 2003; Davies 2004). However, it is possible to distinguish among three main theoretical approaches to evidence use: outcome-based, methodological, and conceptual (see Table 1 below).

The *outcome-based* or *instrumental* approach is the one most often described in the public policy literature, emphasizing evidence use for producing policies that work. Davies (2004) argues that research-based evidence helps people make well-informed decisions about policies, programs, and projects to enhance policy development and implementation. By applying a process of theoretically informed empirical analysis, governments can learn from past experience, avoid repeating errors, and, as a result, better apply new techniques to resolving problems (May 1992; Sanderson 2002).

The *methodological* approach focuses on empirically rigorous ways of producing data. This approach has been promoted in literature involving medical studies and typically has a positivist focus, stressing the value of quantitative methods. Nutley, Walter, and Davies (2007) are critical of this approach and note that evidence-based policy is commonly defined

TABLE 1
Different approaches to evidence use

Approach	Type	Examples from literature
Outcome-based/ instrumental	Evidence use has a technical nature, aiming to produce policies that work. The focus is on the effectiveness and efficiency of public policies.	Nilsson et al. 2008; Davies 2004; Oakley 2000; Plewis 2000; Majone 1989
Methodological	A movement that focuses on a particular methodology for producing a specific form of evidence. It favours primarily quantitative studies, systematic reviews, and meta-analyses of experimental research.	Radaelli 2004; Chalmers 2003
Conceptual	A broad approach that focuses on the larger influence of the body of social-scientific knowledge on "policy thinking." Recognizes the tacit and experiential knowledge of the practitioner and the views of the societal actors.	Nutley, Walter, and Davies 2007; Culyer and Lomas 2006; Hammersley 2005; Bowen and Zwi 2005

Source: Authors' compilation.

in a narrow sense: as systematic reviews and meta-analysis of research studies. This relatively fixed view of evidence overshadows other sources of evidence documented in the literature.

In contrast, the *conceptual* approach frames evidence use in a broader sense, considering scientific research to be one of many possible sources of evidence (e.g., Nutley 2003; Bullock, Mountford, and Stanley 2001). Other sources of information are considered, such as evaluation studies, routine monitoring of data, expert knowledge, and information from consultations with interest groups. Bowen and Zwi (2005) differentiate among five types of evidence: empirical research (randomized control trials, observations, qualitative studies, time series analysis), knowledge and information (expert groups consultations, published reports), ideas and interests ("expert knowledge" of individuals, personal opinions, and views), politics (information relevant to the agenda of government, political risk assessment, opportunity, and crises), and economics (finance and resource implications, cost-effectiveness, opportunity costs).

The conceptual perspective of evidence use has increasingly broadened the earlier, more technical ideas that were prevalent in the 1980s. From this perspective, "evidence" incorporates deliberation, debate, and argumentation in relation to the ends of policy in addition to the ethical and moral implications of alternative courses of action. Sanderson (2006) argues that the use of evidence depends on its relevance to the "normative worlds" of policy-makers and practitioners and to the complex judgments that they must make on appropriate courses of action.

The influence of evidence on policy, then, occurs in its use of communicative learning processes to reshape or reconstruct the cognitive and normative frames of policy-makers and professionals. In this context, several authors recognize the increasing value of professional knowledge (Griew 2009; Head 2010). Griew (2009) emphasizes the need to engage with practitioners and officials who implement policies and who know particular policy contexts, proposing that such interactions lead to effective implementation of policy. In line with this viewpoint, Mullen (2004) defends the importance of educating practitioners to use evidence-based practices.

One important consideration is the point at which evidence is used in the policy process. Bowen and Zwi (2005) discuss phases in the use of evidence and relate them to the factors influencing decisions. In the introduction phase of evidence use, the framing of the problem determines what type of evidence is searched and used. Then, in the interpretation phase, evidence is synthesized and evaluated according to participants' beliefs and potential conflicts of interest. In the final, application phase, various sources of evidence are weighted, prioritized, and transformed into policy.

Other research confirms that evidence is used differently and for disparate purposes in the policy process. For instance, Whiteman (1985) differentiates among three types of evidence use: substantive, elaborative, and strategic. *Substantive* use of evidence occurs in the initial phase of decision-making, where there is no strong commitment to a specific solution. Policy-makers search broadly for evidence to help them develop a position on an issue, which must often satisfy governmental and administrative perspectives. Decision-makers employ *elaborative* use, on the other hand, to extend and refine existing policy positions. If they have already made a strong commitment to a well-defined position, they employ the third type of evidence use, *strategic*. Strategic use entails advocating or reconfirming the merit of a given policy position.

Following this line of work, Thomas (2001) identifies four stages in governments' policy formulation process – appraisal, dialogue, policy formulation, and consolidation – each involving a different emphasis on evidence use. At the appraisal stage, evidence is identified and collected in research reports, expert testimonies, and stakeholders' perspectives on a policy problem. At the dialogue stage, stakeholders engage in communication and debate, and different expert perspectives on policy issues are articulated and synthesized. In the policy formulation phase, evidence has a formal and technical nature, and studies are typically conducted to consider potential policy alternatives. In the consolidation phase, policy-makers have an opportunity to give the stakeholders feedback on the emergent policy design.

Of course, evidence use is not the only factor contributing to decision-making in policy design, implementation, and evaluation (e.g., Mulgan 2003; Davies 2004). Several authors have studied the role of knowledge in the policy-making process and have unveiled a variety of factors that potentially influence the use of evidence (e.g., Weiss and Bucuvalas 1980; Whiteman 1985; Lester and Wilds 1990; Bowen and Zwi 2005). Policy decisions may be shaped by the interactions of knowledge, environmental conditions, and political actions, among other factors (Haas 1992; Sabatier 1986; Sabatier 1988).

The literature also depicts how social contexts can influence the use of evidence in policy-making. Majone (1989) highlights how policy-making is rooted in specific institutional and organizational contexts. The general understanding of the policy-making process as a communicative process emphasizes how policy dialogue and arguments are shaped by the rules, conventions, and power structures of the policy-making context (Lindblom 1959; Bowen and Zwi 2005; Sanderson 2006). In this view, decisions are influenced by a range of actors, including legislators, public officials, other agencies, and constituents and clients (Weiss and Bucuvalas 1980). Practitioners seek to not simply deal with policy problems on a "technical" basis using pure evidence, but also to cope with ambiguity on a "practical" basis, making judgments about the appropriateness of policy action in relation to a range of technical, political, moral, and ethical concerns (Sanderson 2006). In making such judgments, practitioners need to rely on evidence (in particular, on the tacit and experiential knowledge of practitioners), but they must also address other diverse considerations. As a consequence, in the interest of consensus-building and political rationality, practitioners may overlook the best technical solutions.

Finally, conceptual models in the literature help to understand the use of evidence in public agencies. In a review of activities designed to promote research use in social care in the United Kingdom, Walter et al. (2004) identified three broad ways of thinking about and developing research-informed practice. These different approaches are encapsulated in three models: i) the research-based practitioner model, ii) the embedded research model, and iii) the organizational excellence model. The research-based practitioner model assumes that it is the responsibility of the individual practitioner to identify and remain informed about the latest research developments, then use them to influence day-to-day professional activities. In contrast, in the embedded research model, evidence use is achieved indirectly by becoming ingrained in systems, processes, and standards of practice. In the organizational excellence model, evidence use lies in the successful development of research-minded organizational structures, processes, and cultures. Moreover, there will usually be significant organizational adaptation of evidence and ongoing learning within teams and through partnerships with universities and other bodies that facilitate the creation and use of knowledge. Although these three approaches were first applied to evidence use in the social care sector, Nutley, Walter, and Davies (2009) report that they reflect much of what is happening to promote research use in other fields.

Nutley, Jung, and Walter (2008) suggest that these three models may be best suited to different circumstances. However, they note that while a combination of models is likely to be required in practice, combining them is not straightforward. One or more models may dominate another or produce tensions in an organization. For example, the assumption of professional autonomy that underpins the research-based practitioner model may clash with the constraints placed on individual practitioners in the embedded research model. Using these models to examine evidence use among research funding agencies raises interesting questions because these agencies have a historical, normative commitment to abide by expert judgment and valuations when making decisions; they often employ researchers as program officers; and they systematically interact with the scientific community on various levels.

THE STUDY: INVESTIGATING RESEARCH AGENCIES

According to the literature reviewed above, evidence-based practices involve a variety of knowledge sources, purposes, and processes that might shape decision-making in research funding agencies. Building on this literature, the following research questions guided this study:

- How are evidence and expert advice used by research funding agencies when designing and evaluating programs?
- How are decisions made about program design?
- Why is the method used perceived to be valuable?

To address these questions, we sought to obtain qualitative data from leading public funding agencies in Canada, the US, and Europe. The study was delimited to funding agencies primarily in the natural sciences and engineering fields. Agency websites were reviewed to identify potential informants, including individuals in positions relevant to program design and evaluation. Response to invitations to participate was mixed: some agency departments co-operated, while others chose not to co-operate. Agency administrators were often cautious about providing access to their staff.

Snowball sampling was used throughout the study. In most cases, our requests were mediated by the administrator of an agency well positioned to refer our team to potential informants. In all, 17 participants were interviewed[1] from the following funding agencies: in Canada, the Canadian Institutes of Health Research (CIHR) and the Natural Sciences and Engineering Research Council of Canada (NSERC); in the US, the National Institutes of Health (NIH) and the National Science Foundation (NSF); in Europe, the European Research Council (ERC). (For details about these agencies, see Table 2 below.)

TABLE 2
Characteristics of selected research funding agencies

Feature	Agency				
	CIHR	NSERC	NIH	NSF	ERC
Country	Canada	Canada	US	US	EU
Date established	2000 (after merger of two federal organizations)	1978	1950	1950	2007
2010 budget	CAN$1.03 billion	CAN$1.06 billion	US$31.2 billion	US$6.87 billion	€1.1 billion
Mission (quoted from website)	To excel, according to internationally accepted standards of scientific excellence, in the creation of new knowledge and its translation into improved health for Canadians, more effective health services and products and a strengthened Canadian health-care system	To help make Canada a country of discoverers and innovators for the benefit of all Canadians	To seek fundamental knowledge about the nature and behavior of living systems and the application of that knowledge to enhance health, lengthen life, and reduce the burdens of illness and disability	To promote the progress of science; to advance the national health, prosperity, and welfare; to secure the national defense	To encourage the highest quality research in Europe through competitive funding and to support investigator-initiated frontier research across all fields of research, on the basis of scientific excellence
Governing body	Governing Council (members drawn from private and public sectors)	Council (members drawn from private and public sectors)	Office of the Director	One director and the National Science Board	Scientific Council (made up of scientists)
Relationship with government	Federal agency	Federal agency	Federal agency	Federal agency	Autonomous body

Source: Authors' compilation.

These agencies receive different proportions of the research funding available in their countries and regions. In Canada, NSERC received approximately 20 percent, and CIHR 22 percent, of the 2010 federal research funding distributed among four funding agencies (Statistics Canada 2011; NSERC 2010; CIHR 2011). In the US, the budgets of the NIH and NSF corresponded to approximately 21 percent and 4 percent, respectively, of the total federal funding allocated to research and development in 2010 (NSF 2012). The ERC is unique as a European-level research funding body because most research is supported at the national level across the member states (van Vught 2010).

Informants had the following professional roles: members of advisory bodies (3), senior administrators (4), program directors (7), and support staff (3). Informants participated in semi-structured telephone interviews, each of which took approximately 30 minutes to conduct and was audio-recorded and transcribed. In addition to conducting interviews, we obtained publicly available policy documents and other publications from each agency's website and examined them to analyze their policies regarding program design and evaluation (see the Appendix at the end of this chapter). We used content analysis (Budd, Thorp, and Donohew 1967; Krippendorf 1980; Weber 1996) to investigate the nature, focus, and targets of these strategic documents. We then used qualitative data analysis techniques to organize, code, and analyze the interview data (Miles and Huberman 1994; Strauss 1987). For inter-rater reliability, we independently coded the transcript data and then integrated the codes into a general set of themes.

FINDINGS

The analysis points to the importance of examining evidence use in four distinct processes: agenda-setting, program design, monitoring, and evaluation. In each process, funding agencies select and use evidence in different ways. Moreover, four themes emerged from the analysis that cut across each of these processes: the role of evidence, source of expertise, motives for evidence use, and constraints on evidence use. These processes and themes are summarized in Table 3 below.

Agenda-setting

Agenda-setting is characterized by gathering ideas and input from various stakeholders. The main type of evidence includes information received from expert consultations – both within the agencies themselves and with the academic community – and information deriving from government strategies and policies. Whereas an internal approach relies on the expertise of agency staff and members of agency advisory bodies, an external approach concentrates on consultation with outside experts and

TABLE 3
Analytic categories used to assess evidence use

Analytic category	Process of evidence use in programs			
	Agenda-setting	Program design	Monitoring	Evaluation
Role of evidence	Instrumental (to promote ideas)	Operational (to finalize ideas)	Analytical/descriptive (to assess progress)	Analytical/evaluative (to analyze results)
Source of expertise	Stakeholder groups: board/council members, political stakeholders, scientists, industrial stakeholders, administrative staff	Input from administrative staff, other national and international funding agencies, board/council members, peer review	Internal/external expertise (evaluation units, statistical databases, publication databases)	Internal/external expertise (evaluation units, hired consultants, peer review)
Motives for/drivers of evidence use	Promote/interpret/resist ideas, accomplish mission, establish legitimacy, build prestige	Secure most appropriate application of ideas agreed upon	Monitor and evaluate accomplishment of program goals, relevance, and accountability	Demonstrate accountability, accomplish mission, establish legitimacy, build prestige
Constraints on evidence use	Conflict among various ideas, political pressure, government mandates, accountability	Bureaucratic requirements, predefined government mandates	Lack of short-term measurable outcomes (e.g., from fundamental/basic research)	Lack of data available for recently started grants

Source: Authors' compilation.

stakeholders from multiple sectors. Evidence has an instrumental nature as it is used for practical reasons to initiate discussions on a new scheme.

Agencies typically involve experts in their decision-making structures to facilitate consultation across fields and sectors. NSERC, for example, has a governing council composed of external experts representing industry, government, and academia. CIHR receives input from the 13 interdisciplinary "virtual" institutes whose advisory boards, likewise, draw on the contributions of a diverse group of national and international representatives of the public, private, and non-profit sectors, including the research community and healthcare practitioners. In some cases, the agencies respond to the ideas generated by their own board members or make decisions based on the information brought to them by program administrators.

At some agencies, such as the NSF, scientific experts are employed as program officers. They contribute to agenda-setting by voicing ideas and concerns regarding program creation and management. Each directorate of the NSF has a standing advisory committee composed of domestic and international experts who meet every six months to review the directorate's programs. The committee's advice is supplemented by outreach to professional organizations and by a Committee of Visitors for various areas of responsibility, and both groups examine individual programs and whole divisions. An alternate approach is to ask the members of a directorate's advisory committee to provide specific advice about future scientific priorities.

At the ERC, the Scientific Council members, all renowned scholars, provide input into new programs based on their professional expertise. The Scientific Council is the highest decision-making body in the ERC, making sure that the ideas and suggestions of the researchers are represented and accounted for in decisions.

An informant reflects on the creation of a new program based on the experts' experience.

> Nobody in the [advisory body] went away and produced six pages [of] statistics or whatever. I think it was from their knowledge of the scientific situation ... that individuals in there decided that we should develop a new scheme. (Interview, 6 October 2011)

Research funding agencies rely heavily on external consultations with the scientific community to set priorities. Many staff members in the agencies remain actively engaged as working scholars and build relationships with their disciplinary communities. Agencies employ various approaches to canvass the views of experts during agenda-setting. A common mechanism for agencies framing a new program or initiative is a workshop or set of workshops. Scholars are invited to participate in meetings and formulate consensus opinions about developments in their academic fields. Such events help to establish expert views of the research landscape. Informants suggested that this reliance on the scientific community for direction builds trust and increases the legitimacy of funding agencies in the scientific community.

> I consider it as a strength ... this recognition that even though there is internally scientific expertise, which is a big part of the agency ... the running of the program is in the hands of scientists. (Interview, 24 October 2011)

> The bottom-up input that we get is a strength, ... that we're getting the input from our ... research community to address their needs. (Interview, 14 October 2011)

There are other ways of involving experts in an agenda-setting process. Recently, the NSF's Directorate for Social, Behavioral & Economic Sciences (SBE) solicited white papers from the research community on one or more of three topics: fundamental research issues, the capacities required to pursue the research, and the infrastructure to support it. The project was announced by e-mail distributed to all NSF and SBE principal investigators and individuals associated with other federal agencies, professional societies, organizations, and academic departments. In addition, academic associations, philanthropic associations, and several boards at the National Academy of Sciences were consulted. At the same time, the SBE's Advisory Committee wrote an independent complementary report, suggesting ideas and making recommendations for the future research landscape. The SBE's final report combines the latter with the input from the academic community to outline the directorate's future strategies and priorities.

Research funding agencies also hold consultations with experts from outside academia. For instance, CIHR has an external process by which it holds workshops and conferences and invites stakeholders from several sectors in an effort to prioritize funding areas. Pressure for relevance appears to be impacting not only the evaluation of programs but also the general policies and operations of the agencies themselves. As a result, decisions about funding schemes are the result of a balancing act in which accountability to important stakeholders and relevance factors have to be taken into account. For instance, one rationale given for creating a new grant program at one agency was to increase support from industry, which was seen as being crucial to the agency's efforts to increase the budget it received from the government. As one informant noted,

> Part of the new programs can be implemented to satisfy the needs of the government as well as the needs of the community. So … that's why I would say new programs are put into place.… The [agency] took that information and went away and essentially designed the program.… It tried to satisfy the government's desire for high impact. (Interview, 22 September 2011)

Pressure for relevance has also encouraged a change in policy at the ERC. Informants referred to a debate involving the European Commission (EC) regarding the relevance of its funding programs and expected accountability. The ERC faces pressure to increase its funding of relevant research, which is measured by economic contribution and job creation, as opposed to funding basic research, where measurable indicators are not so evident.

The experience of agency staff is an important factor in agenda-setting. The interviews revealed that staff members are involved in this process by monitoring and comparing national and international research funding initiatives. Funding agencies are actively learning from one another and adapting programs to meet desired goals.

> We would compare ourselves to the US, to the UK, to Germany, France, Australia, as another ... comparable-sized economy. And depending on the particular programs or goal ... I mean, if there's programs relating to a desire to increase international collaboration ... maybe look at what's happening in emerging economies – China, India, Brazil, and so on. (Interview, 7 October 2011)

> There are many national schemes ... with [a] similar goal. And of course we also did our homework with [respect] to schemes of NSF and NIH in the States. So we looked at how these schemes [are] run by these organizations. (Interview, 24 October 2011)

Practices and lessons learned from other funding agencies provide evidence for the policies and organization of many agencies. Informants cited Canada, the US, and European countries as the main national and international reference points for benchmarking their own policies. Our findings reflect previous arguments that the US is the most strategic destination for general policy-learning for funding agencies (Balzat 2006; Dill 2010) and that agencies also look elsewhere for information.

Program design

In the process of program design, evidence is used to finalize ideas generated in the agenda-setting process to create new programs. Evidence used in this process includes mixed types of data (from evaluations and reports on similar schemes) and input from consultations with stakeholders. Political factors shape the goal and design of funding schemes as well.

Programs are usually developed over a long period of time, drawing on different sources of input and the layering of knowledge as ideas settle in. Ideas about a new funding scheme undergo several readings in the process of designing a program, and evidence from benchmarking and expert judgment is considered. Program officers often collect relevant evidence, including from similar programs operating nationally or internationally, then compare them and suggest what information should be incorporated and what should be disregarded. The following comment of an agency officer is typical:

> I wouldn't say that the origin of the scheme was strictly evidence-based, but the design of the scheme was evidence-based in terms of ... looking at examples of similar schemes with similar aims. (Interview, 6 October 2011)

In the program design phase, agency staff draw heavily on reports produced using input from scientific committees and information from stakeholders. If a program is expected to respond to government strategies, predefined program criteria are also incorporated into the design.

The main focus during this process is polishing the general ideas and distilling them into workable programs. This process can be quite lengthy. As the idea about a new program evolves, changes are made and different types of comparisons used. As an informant describes,

> I spent probably two years working, producing papers for the [advisory body] to kind of refine their ideas for this new scheme.... At different points ... it looked like it was going to be focused on a particular thing, then we would look at schemes that were like that. As the idea developed ... we would go and look at other schemes.... So we had a look at some schemes by NSF and ... [agencies] in Europe. (Interview, 6 October 2011)

In addition, the peer review panels at various funding agencies have an important influence on the design of new programs. These panels make suggestions about how programs can be improved, what criteria should be used in evaluating the proposals, and what requirements should be changed to best accomplish a program's goals. Based on the information collected from the peer review panels or evaluation reports, the need to change specific aspects of a program is brought to the attention of an agency's decision-making body.

Political imperatives also influence program design, in both formal and informal ways. Informal political influences are a result of administrative constraints and pressure to distribute awards more equally among regions, universities, and researchers. In the case of formal political influences, there are often predefined objectives shaping research funding agency agendas and actions. For example, Canada has seen an increase in the number of programs and initiatives with predefined objectives, such as the innovation and commercialization that NSERC is expected to deliver.

This increased pressure for inter-government agency collaboration is also apparent at the NSF, where a core strategy is to promote partnerships with academic institutions, private industry, and state and local governments. Pressures for relevance at the NSF have since the 1980s, in fact, influenced the design of a series of programs (Geiger and Sá 2009). Recently, in part to pre-empt governmental influence on program design, the Scientific Council of the ERC created the Proof of Concept funding scheme, which funds researchers previously supported by the ERC so that they can take their ideas to the marketplace.

The main constraints on using evidence and expertise in program design are bureaucratic requirements resulting from agencies' interdependent relationship with governments. These requirements involve setting dates for budget cycles, creating technical procedures for hiring people, and submitting reports. Agencies view the bureaucratic constraints on this process as potentially influencing the overall quality of a program. One informant provides an example that, although atypical, illustrates these issues.

The bureaucracy demanded that the person whom we want to appoint as an expert should send in a letter from the institute that the person is good enough for the job. Now, can you imagine? That is a Nobel Prize winner being invited, and he has to bring a letter from the director of the institute that he is good enough for the job. (Interview, 18 October 2011)

During program design, the conceptual ideas of the agenda-setting process are refined by the input received from administrative research and the information retrieved from the peer-review expert panels. This process is technical and operational, requiring more expertise and evidence about program design and administration, as agency staff seek to make the program cycle work as smoothly as possible.

Monitoring

The monitoring process starts after research projects have been funded, when agencies start collecting information about the early impact of grants. This process continues through the lifespan of sponsored programs. In this process, evidence is used as agencies track and review programs, assess researcher performance, and identify potential areas in which policies will need to change in the future. The evidence that agencies collect in this phase concerns both program administration (e.g., grant application data) and research results and performance.

During the monitoring process, agency decision-makers note that information about programs is considered together with agency priorities and their own expertise. Selected information from both the application data and research productivity indicators is reportedly used in discussions with governments and external stakeholders. For instance, the NSF uses information from its annual reports when demonstrating its performance to Congress, as mandated by the *Government Performance and Results Act* of 1993. Similarly, key informants from NSERC report an increasing trend in accounting to government and stakeholders, and the ERC must submit a budget each year to the EC – an example of how evidence directly supports the agency's requests.

Agencies tend to collect information from applications for internal circulation and to inform the administration of their own programs. This includes information on applicant pools, which agencies use to identify potential gaps or opportunities in their support of academic investigators. Application data, including application rates, applicants' demographics, proposed topics, and grant success rates, are collected, then used to inform policy decisions about the direction and scope of current funding programs.

[A] very good example in this respect is the low participation of women researchers in the call.... When we see these numbers, we go and look at the population, the potential population that could apply.... So we try to see whether this low percentage of participation is representative of the presence of women in senior positions. (Interview, 24 October 2011)

Program monitoring also involves collecting evidence of research productivity and "excellence" in funded projects. All agencies have policies regarding the collection of scientific reports from funded investigators to keep them up to date on the progress of research. For example, the ERC collects mid-term reports, and the NSF collects technical project reports for all funded projects every year. Agencies also perform a bibliographic analysis of papers resulting from sponsored programs. In addition to researching publications, the ERC looks for awards connected to funded research, how much a funded project has contributed to the career of a researcher (in the case of certain grants), and any evidence of international collaboration. The following quotes expand on this:

We do our own monitoring [through] international databases ... we are monitoring also the award of various scientific prizes, and we see whether [our] grantees are being included in [the] list of awardees. (Interview, 24 October 2011)

We would expect from our grantees that ... their research is published in the highest-level journals, and this is essentially evidence [of] successful projects. (Interview, 13 October 2011)

The data collected in the monitoring process is used to inform agency decision-makers about the progress of individual programs. Program data give program officers and administrative offices information on the progress of funded projects and the way funds are being used. Depending on the agency, these decision-makers are program officers, division directors, or scientific councils.

Evaluation

The evaluation of programs provides a significant source of evidence for making decisions about their sustainability and whether they are meeting accountability requirements. Agency staff appear to consider the first step in program evaluation as occurring during the panel review of submitted grant applications. Subsequently, agencies conduct program evaluations at various points in the life cycle of sponsored programs. The evidence collected in this process depends largely on the goal of a program and the expected outcomes. In general, agencies face mounting pressure to demonstrate the effectiveness and impact of their investments in research, and this creates challenges for evaluating programs.

When asked to discuss the use of evidence, agency officials usually referred to their practices regarding peer review. Funding agencies' historical reliance on peer review is commonly used to demonstrate their commitment to expert judgment. When agencies are adjudicating proposals, experts assess the merit and promise of grant applications as individuals or as members of review panels. Agency staff often take the approval of a proposal as evidence of excellent research and a wise investment of agency funds. In this way, the peer review process is seen as part and parcel of agency efforts at evaluation.

Agencies use formative and summative evaluations across programs. In addition to annual or mid-term reports, they use final project reports to collect evidence of funded projects. Output indicators (e.g., publications, citations, patents) are usually then used to assess programs. There are growing pressures on agencies to evaluate the success of programs in terms of the impact of the research results; indicators include the number of jobs or products created as a direct result of a funded research project. One informant referred to such indicators as evidence of a research project's relevance or impact, which evaluators seek as evidence of an agency's investment in economic development and the social good. The apparent connection between the grant awards for research and the benefit to society provided by the research serves as evidence to justify the agency's decisions.

> Internationally, agencies are really striving to develop the metrics that allow you to say that these are the socio-economic benefits that came out of a particular program of research. (Interview, 31 October 2011)

This trend toward evaluating and measuring research has led to an ongoing search for methodologies, indicators, and standards. For instance, Canada's minister of industry, on behalf of NSERC, requested in 2011 that an international panel of experts be formed; its mandate was to conduct an assessment of approaches used nationally and internationally to evaluate research performance and the indicators that enable comparisons across areas of research in the natural sciences and engineering. Using this information, NSERC expects to develop a methodology, in consultation with key stakeholders, that will enable it to make objective budgetary allocations based on performance assessments.

Heightened accountability has also increased funding agencies' reporting requirements. One informant described the challenges flowing from the pressures described above when capturing the economic benefits of research.

> Assessing at a dollar level the impact of a particular program of research is extraordinarily hard for everyone. This is a socio-economic impact, and it's exceedingly difficult [to measure]. Thirty years later you can say, look

at the impact that it had. Look at the dollars that just saved us. Just look at the lives it has saved. That, that's often hard to assess in the short term. (Interview, 31 October 2011)

Funding agencies are being confronted with demands to provide objective, quantifiable metrics for processes that are complex and that current assessment models do not measure. While traditional scholarly contributions such as publications remain the primary indicators of success, indicators of technology transfer and economic impacts are increasingly being used. Agencies are including the number of patents, licences, and spinoffs created as a result of funded research as evidence when evaluating the impact of funded research projects that are more applied in nature.

The emphasis that agency evaluations are now placing on the academic, social, and economic impact of research as an indicator of excellence and success demonstrates the larger shift in accountability. Several participants observed that their respective agencies were "under [a] great deal of pressure to spend public money wisely and responsibly" (Interview, 6 October 2011). Participants were quick to point out that the scientific merit of grant proposals was the only consideration in decisions to fund research. Still, when reflecting on political and accountability pressures, one participant commented,

> We are under immense pressure to … account for things that are political, like how many grants there are in each jurisdiction and why it is [not] equally balanced. (Interview, 6 October 2011)

Another participant at a different agency noted,

> You know, we *do* focus on excellence. And if, in competitions, that means that there is less money going to [region], that is likely something that we might come under criticism for. (Interview, 7 October 2011)

Evaluation reports and analyses of output indicators all have an essential role to play in the decisions affecting program design. It is suggested that their impact varies, from terminating an existing funding program to establishing a new one. Informants reflected as follows:

> Well, it's resulted in the termination of programs. And it's also resulted in the expansion of programs … or in a pilot being, you know, made permanent. I mean, it has everything in between. (Interview, 7 October 2011)

> We will then monitor the results. And if it is sort of positive, we will continue, and otherwise, we will discontinue this type of grants. (Interview, 11 October 2011)

I would say there's a very high use of evaluation [reports]. I have … program directors and VPs who come looking, and the president, who comes looking for data. (Interview, 7 October 2011)

Program evaluations and reviews are performed routinely and address particular concerns. For example, NSERC recently established an International Review Committee to address concerns that the Discovery Grants Program – its largest program – inefficiently supports researchers to world-class standards. The committee's subsequent report constitutes one part of NSERC's review of the program.

Overall, it is apparent that the evaluation process is crucial to improving funding schemes. By synthesizing the various streams of evidence collected from panel reviews, program evaluations, and project reports, agency staff learn about the strengths and weaknesses of their programs. Incorporating the best available evidence into program design is seen as crucial to establishing the agencies' legitimacy because it demonstrates the tangible results and value added by the grants they distribute. By providing evidence on socio-economic impact and scientific contributions, agencies are able to prove the relevance of their programs.

CONCLUSION

Funding agencies have historically relied on the expertise of the academic community to make important decisions about how to allocate research funding. Researchers, usually guided by the principles of trust, informality, and discretionary decision-making, have collectively decided the direction of research fields and financial support for research projects (Dill and van Vught 2010; Henkel and Kogan 2010). In recent decades, however, attempts by governments to enlist university research in national innovation agendas, alongside heightened expectations for public agencies to demonstrate relevancy and accountability, have changed the policy environment. There is greater pressure on research funding agencies to respond to the needs of politically defined priority areas and produce public benefits such as jobs, local economic growth, and socially useful products (Dill and van Vught 2010; Greenberg 2007).

These trends have sparked debate and criticism. It is believed that the greater pressure being placed on funding agencies and research institutions to generate prescribed outcomes is having negative impacts on academic science, including limiting the originality of research and de-emphasizing interdisciplinary research (Dill 1998). The emphasis on having performance information drive resource allocation can also have unintended consequences that are detrimental to the health of research systems. A study conducted by the Organisation for Economic Co-operation and Development (OECD) indicates that performance-based research funding systems in OECD countries decrease institutional equity, reduce the diversity of research, and do not necessarily enhance economic relevance (OECD 2010).

Our findings reflect contemporary policy change and show that although the academic community continues to play an important role in setting priorities, funding agencies regularly interact with a variety of stakeholders to generate policy ideas and gather input. With the expectation to be responsive to stakeholders' needs and support relevant research, funding agencies serve as "intermediary organizations" (Bielak et al. 2008), connecting their commitment to scientific excellence with various government agendas and the interests of various professional groups and industry associations. In a measurement-driven context, these multi-faceted interactions increase expectations for shared decision-making and drive efforts to monitor and evaluate sponsored research.

The matrix that emerges from our analysis – differentiating among the role of evidence, source of expertise, motive for evidence use, and constraints on evidence use in each process related to funding programs – is consistent with previous studies. Klein (2003), for one, suggests that different stages of the policy process call for different types of evidence. As discussed above, research funding agencies use a large variety of evidence sources, and they relate to the distinct needs of each process in the funding cycle. Professional knowledge and expertise are typically prevalent in the agenda-setting process. The program design process further uses professional knowledge, in addition to evidence from efforts to benchmark best practices, evaluations, and reports on the respective schemes. The evaluation process, similar to the monitoring process, focuses on output indicators gathered from project reports. Throughout the life cycle of agency funding programs, various evidence sources interact with political pressures and organizational issues to generate decisions about program design, administration, and assessment.

Consistent with the literature (e.g., Bowen and Zwi 2005), funding agencies use evidence and expert advice for different reasons and disparate purposes. Our findings show that evidence and expertise are used for instrumental, operational, and analytical purposes. Evidence is used for instrumental reasons to turn policy ideas into practices being promoted by stakeholders in government, the scientific community, and industry. Funding agencies play the role of mediators that articulate and translate policy ideas into practice. In the decision-making process, decisions about promoting, interpreting, or negotiating ideas based on the specific rationale or interest of a stakeholder are made based on evidence and expertise. Evidence is also used for operational and technical reasons when decisions about the most appropriate strategies for delivering policy ideas need to be made. It is often agency staff who use evidence for operational reasons to establish specific program requirements. Evidence is used to demonstrate or predict the result of a specific strategy or program design by reporting what works or has worked in similar funding schemes and convincing decision-makers to take a specific course of action. Finally, evidence and expert advice are used for analytical reasons to monitor and evaluate the results of programs.

In using the various practices discussed above, funding agencies embody elements of the three models identified by Walter et al. (2004) as broad ways of thinking about and developing research-informed practice: the research-based practitioner model, the embedded research model, and the organizational excellence model. At some agencies, program officers or administrators are expected to be experts in their fields (the research-based practitioner model); agencies remain accountable to governments for collecting and reporting internal data (the embedded research model); and agencies themselves are responsible for collecting and disseminating evidence (the organizational excellence model).

Some have suggested that the presence of these three models in an organization may produce tensions (Nutley, Jung, and Walter 2008). However, contrary to such suggestions, these models appear to peacefully coexist in research funding agencies. Many of the practices of these agencies are well described by an interactive perspective on research use (Nutley, Jung, and Walter 2008). Agency officials need to continually adapt input from the scientific community to different contexts and situations. The preferences of stakeholders (i.e., the scientific community, industry, government) interact with the experiences and expertise of agency staff as they consider different forms of evidence. Moreover, the research community, program managers (often members of the research community), and stakeholders engage in ongoing relationships that lead to the development of protocols and programs that influence agency management (as described in the embedded research model). Finally, agencies experiment, evaluate, and develop programs and projects based on evidence and partnerships with stakeholders (as in the organizational excellence model). The composition of research funding agencies – embedded as they are in communities of research and practice – and their interactive use of evidence seem to reduce any tensions that might otherwise arise in employing different models of evidence use.

Our analysis is consistent with the literature emphasizing the broad, conceptual approach to understanding the use of evidence in policy and practice, including the important role of professional expertise (Nutley, Walter, and Davies 2007; Hammersley 2005). It also builds on studies showing the various means by which evidence is used in public agencies (Walter et al. 2004) by detailing the use of evidence across multiple organizational processes in research funding agencies. By doing so, this work takes another step toward clarifying the role of funding agencies in developing research policy.

NOTE

1. All interviews conducted for our study were confidential, as per research ethics requirements. The names of the interviewees are therefore withheld.

REFERENCES

Axelrod, P., R.D. Trilokekar, T. Shanahan, and R. Wellen. 2011. "People, Processes, and Policy-Making in Canadian Post-secondary Education, 1999–2000." *Higher Education Policy* 24 (2):143–166.

Balzat, M. 2006. *An Economic Analysis of Innovation: Extending the Concept of National Innovation Systems*. Northhampton, MA: Edward Elgar.

Bielak, A.T., A. Campbell, S. Pope, K. Schaefer, and L. Shaxson. 2008. "From Science Communications to Knowledge Brokering: The Shift from Science Push to Policy Pull." In *Communicating Science in Social Contexts: New Models, New Practices*, ed. D. Cheng, M. Claessens, T. Gascoigne, J. Metcalfe, B. Schiele, and S. Shi, 201–226. Dordrecht: Springer.

Bowen, S., and A.B. Zwi. 2005. "Pathways to 'Evidence-Informed' Policy and Practice: A Framework for Action." *PLoS Medicine* 2 (7):e166.

Budd, R.W., R.K. Thorp, and L. Donohew. 1967. *Content Analysis of Communications*. New York: Macmillan.

Bullock, H., J. Mountford, and R. Stanley. 2001. *Better Policy Making*. London: Centre for Management and Policy Studies.

Chubin, D., and E. Hackett. 1990. *Peerless Science: Peer Review and U.S. Science Policy*. Albany: State University of New York Press.

CIHR (Canadian Institutes of Health Research). 2011. Budget 2010. At http://www.cihr-irsc.gc.ca/e/41352.html (accessed 11 June 2013).

Davies, P. 2004. "Is Evidence-Based Government Possible?" Paper presented at the Campbell Collaboration Colloquium, Washington, DC, February. At http://www. nationalschool.gov.uk/policyhub/downloads/JerryLeeLecture1202041.pdf (accessed 11 June 2013).

Dill, D.D. 1998. "Evaluating the 'Evaluative State': Implications for Research in Higher Education." *European Journal of Education* 33 (3):361–377.

—. 2010. "The United States." In *National Innovation and the Academic Research Enterprise: Public Policy in Global Perspective*, ed. D. Dill and F. van Vught, 387–437. Baltimore: Johns Hopkins University Press.

Dill, D.D., and F. van Vught. 2010. *National Innovation and the Academic Research Enterprise: Public Policy in Global Perspective*. Baltimore: Johns Hopkins University Press.

Doern, B.G. 2009. "The Granting Councils and the Research Granting Process: Core Values in Federal Government–University Interactions." In *Research and Innovation Policy: Changing Federal Government–University Relations*, ed. B.G. Doern and C. Stoney, 89–122. Toronto: University of Toronto Press.

Drori, G., J. Meyer, F. Ramirez, and E. Schofer. 2003. *Science in the Modern World Polity: Institutionalization and Globalization*. Stanford, CA: Stanford University Press.

Geiger, R.L. 1993. *Research and Relevant Knowledge*. New York: Oxford University Press.

Geiger, R.L., and C.M. Sá. 2009. *Tapping the Riches of Science: Universities and the Promise of Economic Growth*. Cambridge, MA: Harvard University Press.

Greenberg, D.S. 2007. *Science for Sale: The Perils, Rewards, and Delusions of Campus Capitalism.* Chicago: University of Chicago Press.

Griew, R. 2009. "Drawing on Powerful Practitioner-Based Knowledge to Drive Policy Development, Implementation and Evaluation." Paper presented at the roundtable of the Productivity Commission, Canberra, Australia, 17–18 August. At http://www.pc.gov.au/__data/assets/pdf_file/0020/96221/16-chapter12.pdf (accessed 11 June 2013).

Haas, P.M. 1992. "Introduction: Epistemic Communities and International Policy Coordination." *International Organization* 46:1–36.

Hammersley, M. 2005. "Is the Evidence-Based Practice Movement Doing More Good Than Harm? Reflections on Iain Chalmers' Case for Research-Based Policy Making and Practice." *Evidence and Policy* 1 (1):85–100.

Head, B.W. 2010. "Reconsidering Evidence-Based Policy: Key Issues and Challenges." *Policy Society* 29 (2):77–94.

Henkel, M., and M. Kogan. 2010. "The United Kingdom." In *National Innovation and the Academic Research Enterprise: Public Policy in Global Perspective*, ed. D. Dill and F. van Vught, 337–386. Baltimore: Johns Hopkins University Press.

Howlett, M. 2009. "Policy Analytical Capacity and Evidence-Based Policy-Making: Lessons from Canada." *Canadian Public Administration* 52 (2):153–175.

Klein, R. 2003. "Evidence and Policy: Interpreting the Delphic Oracle." *Journal of the Royal Society of Medicine* 96:429–431.

Krippendorf, K. 1980. *Content Analysis: An Introduction to Its Methodology.* Thousand Oaks, CA: Sage Publications.

Lemont, M. 2009. *How Professors Think: Inside the Curious World of Academic Judgment.* Cambridge, MA: Harvard University Press.

Lester, J.P., and L.J. Wilds. 1990. "The Utilization of Public Policy Analysis: A Conceptual Framework." *Evaluation and Program Planning* 13:313–319.

Lindblom, C. 1959. "The Science of 'Muddling Through.'" *Public Administration Review* 19 (2):79–88.

Lundvall, B., and S. Borrás. 2006. "Science, Technology, and Innovation Policy." In *The Oxford Handbook of Innovation*, ed. J. Fargerberg, D.C. Mowery, and R.R. Nelson, 559–621. Oxford: Oxford University Press.

Majone, G. 1989. *Evidence, Argument, and Persuasion in the Policy Process.* New Haven, CT: Yale University Press.

May, P. 1992. "Policy Learning and Failure." *Journal of Public Policy* 12 (4):331–354.

Miles, M., and A. Huberman. 1994. *Qualitative Data Analysis: An Expanded Sourcebook.* Thousand Oaks, CA: Sage Publications.

Mulgan, G. 2003. "Government, Knowledge and the Business of Policy Making." *Canberra Bulletin of Public Administration* 108:1–5.

Mullen, E.J. 2004. "Facilitating Practitioner Use of Evidence-Based Practice." In *Desk Reference for Evidence-Based Practice in Healthcare and Human Services*, ed. A.R. Roberts and K. Yeager, 152–159. New York: Oxford University Press.

NSERC. 2011. Quick Facts on Funding. At http://www.nserc-crsng.gc.ca/_doc/FactsFigures-TableauxDetailles/QuickFactsonFunding_eng.pdf (accessed 11 June 2013).

NSF, National Center for Science and Engineering Statistics. 2012. Federal R&D Funding by Budget Function: Fiscal Years 2010–12. Detailed Statistical Tables NSF 12–322. Arlington, VA. At http://www.nsf.gov/statistics/nsf12322/ (accessed 11 June 2013).

Nutley, S. 2003. "Bridging the Policy/Research Divide: Reflections and Lessons from the UK." Keynote paper presented at the National Institute of Governance Conference, Canberra, Australia, April.

Nutley, S.M., T. Jung, and I. Walter. 2008. "The Many Forms of Research-Informed Practice: A Framework for Mapping Diversity." *Cambridge Journal of Education* 38 (1):53–71.

Nutley, S.M., I. Walter, and H.T.O. Davies. 2007. *Using Evidence: How Research Can Inform Public Services*. Bristol: Policy Press.

—. 2009. "Promoting Evidence-Based Practice: Models and Mechanisms from Cross-Sector Review." *Research on Social Work Practice* 19 (5):552–559.

Oakley, A. 2000. *Experiments in Knowing*. Cambridge: Polity Press.

OECD. 2010. *Performance-Based Funding for Public Research in Tertiary Education Institutions: Workshop Proceedings*. OECD Publishing. At http://dx.doi.org/10.1787/9789264094611-en (accessed 11 June 2013).

Sabatier, P.A. 1986. "Top-Down and Bottom-Up Approaches to Implementation Research: A Critical Analysis and Suggested Synthesis." *Journal of Public Policy* 6:21–48.

—. 1988. "An Advocacy Coalition Framework of Policy Change and the Role of Policy-Oriented Learning Therein." *Policy Sciences* 21:129–168.

Sanderson, I. 2002. "Evaluation, Learning and Evidence-Based Policy Making." *Public Administration* 80 (1):1–22.

—. 2006. "Complexity, 'Practical Rationality' and Evidence-Based Policy Making." *Policy and Politics* 34 (1):115–132.

Statistics Canada. 2011. Canada Year Book. R&D Funding in Higher Education. At http://www.statcan.gc.ca/pub/11-402-x/2011000/chap/science/science 02-eng.htm (accessed 11 June 2013).

Strauss, A. 1987. *Qualitative Analysis for Social Scientists*. Cambridge: Cambridge University Press.

Thomas, H.G. 2001. "Towards a New Higher Education Law in Lithuania: Reflections on the Process of Policy Formulation." *Higher Education Policy* 14 (3):213–223.

van Vught, F.A. 2010. "The European Union." In *National Innovation and the Academic Research Enterprise: Public Policy in Global Perspective*, ed. D. Dill and F. van Vught, 148–207. Baltimore: Johns Hopkins University Press.

Walter, I., S. Nutley, J. Percy-Smith, D. McNeish, and S. Frost. 2004. *Knowledge Review 7: Improving the Use of Research in Social Care*. London: Social Care Institute for Excellence / Policy Press.

Weber, R. 1996. *Basic Content Analysis*, 6th ed. Newbury Park, CA: Sage Publications.

Weiss, C.H., and M. Bucuvalas. 1980. *Social Science Research and Decision-Making*. New York: Columbia University Press.

Whiteman, D. 1985. "The Fate of Policy Analysis in Congressional Decision Making: Three Types of Use in Committees." *Political Research Quarterly* 38 (2):294–311.

APPENDIX

Publications and documents reviewed by agency

Agency	Publications and documents reviewed
CIHR	Strategic plan (2011–14); annual reports (2009–10, 2010–11); financial plans (quarterly, 2011, budget 2008)
NSERC	Guidelines for application reviews (engineering and applied sciences, interdisciplinary research); plans for financial grant distribution (2009, 2010, 2011)
NIH	Grants Policy Statement (2011); grants process overview; biennial reports of the director (fiscal years 2008 and 2009)
NSF	Proposal and Award Policies and Procedures Guide (2011); Rebuilding the Mosaic (2011); Budget Request to Congress (fiscal year 2012); strategic plan (2011–16)
ERC	Annual reports (2009, 2010); minutes of council meetings (nine sets, October 2009 to June 2011); organizational reviews (2005, 2009), guides for peer reviews: Starting Grants and Advanced Grants, Proof of Concept (2011)

II

AGENDA-SETTING: THE ROLE OF POLICY ACTORS

CHAPTER 4

HOW DO GOVERNMENTS REALLY MAKE HIGHER EDUCATION POLICY, AND HOW CAN UNIVERSITIES INFLUENCE THE POLICIES GOVERNMENTS MAKE? AN EXPERIENCE-BASED ANALYSIS

HARVEY P. WEINGARTEN

INTRODUCTION

Students, the public, and society are best served when governments adopt a sensible, purposeful and effective set of higher education policies and when they maintain a harmonious, respectful, and mutually informed relationship with universities. Based on years of experience as a university administrator and then as a government advisor, I present a perspective on the reality of how governments form higher education policy and how the behaviour of universities influences their decisions and actions.

The discussion suggests that governments' higher education policies are not always fully informed by evidence, are influenced by political considerations, take a long time to get right, and are typically conservative and incremental. It also suggests that these attributes are thoroughly understandable given cognitive processes that affect everyone's decision-making and the dynamic within which governments now operate. To have greater influence on government action and policies, universities are advised to think less about themselves, to be consistent in their messaging, to rely less on the media and more on their president, and to

Making Policy in Turbulent Times: Challenges and Prospects for Higher Education, ed. P. Axelrod, R.D. Trilokekar, T. Shanahan, and R. Wellen. Kingston: School of Policy Studies, Queen's University.

demonstrate a tangible commitment through a priori resource allocation to a project before approaching government for support. Finally, I make the observation that it is in turbulent times that the biggest changes in higher education policy are formed and therefore when the observations above may be most relevant.

OVERVIEW

The higher education sector in Canada is highly controlled by government through an extensive suite of policies, regulations, and processes. For example, governments determine the two major revenue sources, grant and tuition, that form the bulk of a university's[1] operating budget. Even when governments allow some latitude (deregulation) in the setting of tuition, they still typically impose a regulatory framework that limits the flexibility of institutions. On the capital side, even in a world where large philanthropic gifts are more common, governments still provide the lion's share of funding for the construction of new buildings or other major facilities. Either directly or indirectly, government policy, regulation, and practices also control a university's major expenditure – salaries.[2]

Given this reality, it is to the great benefit of a public post-secondary system that governments create a purposeful, effective, and user-friendly higher education policy regime. Since the experts on higher education more typically reside in institutions than in governments, it is also of the greatest public benefit if institutions have a harmonious and productive dynamic with government so that they will have the capacity to influence the policies governments impose on their public post-secondary systems. A positive relationship between government and post-secondary institutions is particularly important in turbulent and economically re-strained times because it is precisely in this environment when changes, sometimes significant ones, are most likely to happen.

Regrettably, in my experience and in the opinion of others, the relationships between governments and post-secondary institutions are far from optimal and may, by some accounts, be deteriorating. Governments appear increasingly frustrated at the lack of responsiveness of post-secondary institutions, their slow pace of change, and, in the view of some, their resistance to accountability. An example is provided by comments made by then premier Dalton McGuinty of Ontario, perhaps one of Canada's staunchest promoters of education, to the *Globe and Mail* editorial board when he provided the following assessment of the impact of the substantial investments his government had made in universities.

> Can I honestly say that I have got qualitative improvement as a result of these investments? I don't think so, and we need to talk about that.… We have not demanded the same kinds of accountability that we have with our hospitals and elementary and secondary schools. (*Globe and Mail*, 9 April 2010)

Post-secondary institutions, in contrast, are frustrated by government policies that appear to be capricious, ill-informed, or politically driven. Many in the post-secondary sector are vexed by their sense that governments fail to appreciate the consequences and impact of chronic underfunding. The government-university dynamic is strained further by the fact that when universities approach governments for money, their pleas are often accompanied by a passionate reminder of institutional autonomy. Universities see this as a traditional given, but governments see this as an entitlement mentality – i.e., institutions deserve more money, but governments, the suppliers of these public funds, cannot tell them what to do with it.

We could all agree, I imagine, that there is an imperative for change in Canada's higher education sector and that we will have better, more positive change if we have a sensible, meaningful, respectful, and productive dialogue between governments and post-secondary institutions. This chapter offers personal views on how we might achieve this better state.

In the spirit of full disclosure, I admit that I have never taken a course in public policy, higher education policy, or political science (although some of my best friends are political scientists and political junkies). Rather, the views and ideas expressed here reflect about 15 years of experience as a senior university administrator in two of Canada's large public research universities in two provinces – one year as dean of science and five years as provost and vice-president academic at McMaster University in Ontario and eight and a half years as president and vice-chancellor of the University of Calgary in Alberta – as well as the last two years as president of the Higher Education Quality Council of Ontario (HEQCO). During this time, I have had innumerable opportunities to observe how governments form higher education policies and how universities can, or cannot, influence these decisions. Consider the arguments made in this chapter, therefore, as a tribute to experiential learning.[3]

As with any commentary that relies on personal experiences, the reader is justified in questioning the credibility of the writer. I could point out that the discipline in which I have been immersed for over three decades, psychology, prides itself on cultivating keen observers of behaviour and experts at behavioural change – be the organism under observation a rat, human, government, or institution. But even I would be underwhelmed by this alone as a serious reason to motivate you to read further. So I offer two other considerations to establish my bona fides as a commentator on government higher education policy-making and the strategies universities may use to influence them.

First, I have had the opportunity to observe and experience a lot of turbulence in government higher education policy. As dean of science in 1995, I shepherded the faculty through the budget cuts of Ontario's Conservative government under then premier Mike Harris, negotiating the early retirement of about 40 percent of the faculty complement. As provost, for the next five years I dealt with government often to fashion policies appropriate to operate in this new environment and to prepare for expected challenges, such as the double cohort. In Alberta, I interacted with a provincial government and a government–civil service–university trilogy that was culturally and operationally different from Ontario's.

For completeness, I had the experience of living through a full boom-bust cycle characteristic of Alberta's economy and the policy correlates of that: policies of austerity and cuts in the deficit-slashing early-to-mid-Klein years, policies of spending and surpluses in the heady boom years of the mid-2000s, and the return to austerity and cuts in the 2009 economic recession. In addition, my years as a senior university administrator co-incided with significant changes in the policy regime between the federal government and Canada's universities, highlighted by significant federal investments in higher education (e.g., creation of the Canada Foundation for Innovation, Canada Research Chairs program, Centres of Excellence for Commercialization and Research program, funding of the indirect costs of research, etc.).

To further establish bona fides, and although I appreciate the difficulties associated with self-evaluation, we[4] seem to have had some success in influencing and dealing with government. Over the time I was at the University of Calgary, government relations improved considerably, and we enjoyed significant community support, both rhetorically and financially. More important, we were quite successful in extracting significant decisions[5] and funding[6] from the government. All of that said, the reader is reminded that the opinions expressed in this chapter are based on experiential learning and therefore are personal ones. With these caveats and qualifications, how do governments really make higher education policy? Here is what I think based on the experiences I have had.

HOW DO GOVERNMENTS REALLY MAKE HIGHER EDUCATION POLICY?

Policies are based on stories, anecdotes, stereotypes, intuitions, ideologies, and personal experiences as much as they are on evidence

We would like to think that governments fashion policy based solely on considered and scholarly analyses, a deep appreciation of best practices, data, evidence, and a full and informed appreciation of the implications and consequences of the various policy options available. This is not necessarily the case. This is not to suggest that governments do not consider evidence in forming policy. They do, when it is available. However, the higher education policies they adopt are also influenced by stories, anecdotes, stereotypes, intuitions, ideologies, and personal experiences, and, in some cases, these influences may dominate evidence.

We should not be surprised by this. These are the bases on which most humans make decisions. Even economics, a field that had as one of its underpinnings the idea of decisions made by the "rational person," is distancing itself from this view in light of the impressive findings of irrational decision-making coming from the discoveries of behavioural economics (Ariely 2008; Brafman and Brafman 2008). Similarly, even other presumably science-based fields, such as medicine, are struggling with the problem of how to encourage practitioners to make medical and treatment decisions based on scientific evidence. So the cognitive processes of politicians and civil servants are no different from those of anyone else. They are just like you and me and everyone else.

The opportunity to make decisions about higher education on the basis of their personal experiences or stories is exacerbated by the fact that, in contrast to the situation 40 years ago, many of the decision-makers in governments today attended university.[7] It is also enabled by the paucity of rigorous scholarship that has been applied to the post-secondary sector itself. The need for and merit of independent scholarly research and evidence-based policy advice (i.e., not conducted by lobby or advocacy groups) in higher education keeps places like HEQCO in business.

Perhaps one of the best examples of the absence of evidence and scholarship influencing higher education policies is current-day discussions, policies, and decisions about tuition.

The idea that higher education policies made by government are not as evidence-based or as informed as they should be is particularly galling for an academic community that prides itself on the importance of critical thinking, scholarship, and evidence in decision-making.[8] This is not to say that evidence and rigorous analyses are not important. They are. They should form the foundation and context for any serious government policy or decision in higher education. As a rule, informed public policy is better public policy. And, for completeness, when evidence is available, it sometimes, but not always, does contribute to the policies governments adopt.

However, even when good and reliable information is available, universities and many academics make the common mistake of believing that a rigorous, scholarly, well-developed rational argument is sufficient to sway the government's views and to convince them to do the right thing. It may be necessary, but it is not sufficient. Rather, this evidence, research, and analysis must then be packaged, communicated, and infused into the political and government dynamic in ways that make it accessible and useable by government. This is a task that requires a very different set of skills than those required to do the research and analysis. Some of these required skills, the domain of communicators and marketers, are discussed later.

Policies are made on the basis of political considerations

A common and angst-inducing lament of those in higher education is that governments make policy decisions on political grounds – i.e., to achieve desired political outcomes (usually votes in an election). Of course they do. This is what politicians are supposed to do! Politicians make political decisions – that's why they are called politicians. To ask them to do otherwise is akin to suggesting that a physicist can violate a law of thermodynamics.

The increasing influence of political considerations in government policy-making may also be related to two other governance trends. The first is the tendency for the political side of government to exert greater influence than the civil service over the policies the government adopts. The second is a shift for more policy control by central offices (e.g., the prime minister's and premier's offices) relative to line ministries.

The more sophisticated form of the lament that governments make political decisions is that politicians are biased toward making short-term policy, tied to the election cycle, rather than doing things that are good in the long term even if unpopular in the short term. This is a reasonable complaint; it is not restricted to policies around higher education. I believe there would be general agreement that we would be better served if politicians and governments thought more long term.

Many political commentators have identified why governments today tend to be more attuned to the short term. I will not replay the arguments here. However, I admit to having some sympathy for and understanding of the tendency of politicians to think in the short term. Every three to five years, politicians do a remarkably difficult thing. They stand up in front of their constituency, and in a very public arena they ask them, "Do you want me around for another three to five years?" They also know that the judgments of many of those deciding their fate is ill-informed – fuelled by superficial media reports, sound bites, confrontational positions by political opponents, and considerations (such as the popularity of the party leader) over which they have no control. I suspect that if I were put into that position, I might also be inclined to be biased toward decisions that would serve me well in the next election. Can you imagine how the behaviour of professors would change if they did not have tenure but rather, every five years, their continuing appointment was subject to a vote by their students?

Politicians and governments today will make political and short-term decisions.[9] To suggest otherwise is naïve. The task for universities is to figure out how to weave their needs and goals within these constraints.

Good government policies have long gestation periods

This principle crystallized for me during a speech I heard David Dodge, former deputy minister of finance in the federal government, give at a dinner celebrating the Early Child Development Program at the Canadian Institutes for Advanced Research. In his talk, he pointed out the success that program had had in influencing federal government policy and expenditures. But, in that same speech, he noted that although the government was convinced of the need and value of these policies and expenditures from the very first discussion, it took almost five years for the government to allocate the first dollars.

The behaviour of governments during this gestation period is described by many government relations specialists as "hurry up and wait." It is an apt description, and, although sometimes frustrating, it is a good sign because at least it shows that the policy issue is still under consideration.

It is not clear why it takes governments so long to execute sound policy, but it does. Typically, from the first time a university approaches a government with the request for a new building or program, it will take three to five years for that funding to be realized. There are times when governments can articulate and implement policy very quickly. However, in my experience, these are often occasions when policies are crafted by politicians without adequate consultation or during the election frenzy, two situations that do not necessarily lead to the best outcomes.

Given the long gestation period, the reader may be left wondering how to gauge whether a particular policy under consideration during this period will result in a live birth. A seasoned, but perhaps overly cynical, government relations expert (at least I was told they were an expert) once told me that when governments speak, "yes means maybe; maybe means no." In my experience, however, "maybe" sometimes really means "maybe." The best way of gleaning what policies the government will ultimately adopt may depend on the nature of the relationship between the university president and the key decision-makers in government. More on this later.

The lesson for universities? Be patient! Good policy takes time. There are certain university behaviours that can shorten the policy-making time constant of governments; these are discussed in the next section.

Governments today have difficulty making bold or innovative policy

There is good reason for the risk aversion in government policy-making. Taking risks and being innovative necessarily mean that some things will fail, and the political dynamic today is highly intolerant of any government failure, no matter how reasonable, sound, or sensible the original idea might have been. Government failures are subject to auditor examination and criticism, howls of indignant protestation from opposition parties, and screaming headlines in the media – all things that do not serve a government well when the next election comes along.

Sometimes, governments will speak as if they are prepared to make bold or innovative policy changes.[10] This is especially true in turbulent and financially difficult times. However, the historian will conclude that when push comes to shove, governments often, but not always, and for the understandable reasons noted above, retreat from bold and innovative policy directions. The conservative nature of government policy-making is inextricably linked to the next principle.

Governments don't start a parade, but once it forms, they try to jump to the front to lead it

No one understood this better than Ralph Klein, former premier of Alberta, who revealed this trait to me in the colourful and candid manner of which he was a master. This attribute is related in obvious ways to the general hesitancy of current governments to be bold or innovative. A tangible manifestation of this tendency is that present-day politicians and political parties spend considerable sums of money on public opinion polls and surveys that tell them what the public wants. Once the public position (i.e., the parade) is identified, governments will move in that direction and develop policies and projects consistent with public opinion (i.e., lead the parade).

The existence of a parade influences government policy. Statements by university officials, even in eloquent speeches or op-eds, do not constitute a parade. Governments recognize a parade when they repeatedly hear the same advice from different groups of people in different venues. The obvious implication for universities is that they will need to engage others to start a parade that ultimately will be helpful to guide government policies.

HOW CAN UNIVERSITIES INFLUENCE THE POLICIES GOVERNMENTS MAKE?

Given the nature of Canada's public higher education system, good government relations are necessary for any university that wishes to be successful. Just as there are principles and characteristics of how governments form higher education policy, there are principles and best practices for institutions of higher education that wish to influence the policies governments adopt. Here are some guidelines for effective practices for universities that wish to influence government policy.

Remember – nobody is thinking about you

In a brilliant book, Rosenblatt provides 58 rules for successful aging.[11] Rule Number 2 is: Nobody is thinking about you. To quote the author: "Nobody is thinking about you. They are thinking about themselves – just like you" (Rosenblatt 2000, 3).

Universities are often unaware (or at least act as if they are unaware) of this important rule. Rather, universities often act as if it is all about them – their issues, their problems, their needs, their desires, and their challenges. This trait of self-absorption is not conducive to good government relations. Why? Because, as predicted by Rosenblatt's rule, governments are also thinking about themselves. So if you want to influence what governments do, it is most effective to use their language, address their issues, and indicate interest in solving their problems.

Some university people see this advice as a sellout. It is not; it is just smart. The trick is to figure out how to weave the institution's needs, desires, and wants into something that also solves the problems or challenges that governments face. This is not that difficult, and it can lead to highly collaborative and purposeful engagements with government. The only thing it requires is to stop thinking about oneself and spend a little time thinking and seeing the issues from the perspective of government.[12]

Consistency of message is critical

As noted above, it may take a long time between the initial discussion with government and the actual decision by government to adopt a particular policy, make a particular decision, or allocate resources to a particular project – a time frame of perhaps three to five years. The critical point is that if a university changes its key messages or priorities during this period, the clock can (and often does) reset to zero. Changing priorities, or different messages sent to government from members of the same university, are a recipe for government inaction or inattention, and rightfully so.

This guideline extends to the system level as well. Post-secondary systems make it easy for governments to ignore them when they present a fragmented face to government. Presenting a consistent, united message to a government in a system as large and as diverse as Ontario's university system is not easy.[13] But, in its absence, governments may have no choice but to follow policies and actions that reflect their own agenda and thinking, rather than ones effectively guided by the sector itself.

On an optimistic note, one should be encouraged by the flip side of the observations above. Governments, like nature, abhor a vacuum. So, when a policy vacuum exists, politicians will fill it with something. In my experience, if they receive strong and consistent policy advice from a unified sector, they are likely to follow it.

The president is the point person for government relations

In Canada, governments expect the president to be the point person for government relations. It is an obligation presidents shirk at their (and their institution's) peril. It is understood that the best government relations occur when the efforts of the president are supported, instructed, and guided by people in the institution who are experts in these matters.[14]

As presidents discharge their government relations obligations, they are advised to remember that government relations are a contact sport. As one highly successful politician once told me when I was president at the University of Calgary, "You and I are in the same business. Ninety percent of our success is just showing up." Politicians remember who shows up, and they are especially sensitive to situations in which they perceive that they are doing the unpopular but right thing (e.g., permitting a larger than expected tuition increase) and no one from the sector shows up to support them. It violates human nature to think that you can influence people if you support them only when you want something from them.

I do not minimize how difficult this can be for university presidents. One of the surest and fastest ways for a university president to increase his or her popularity on campus is to buy a megaphone, stand on the stairs of the legislature, and scream at the government. However, that is also the day the president should resign because any effectiveness with government after that cathartic act is greatly minimized. Presidents navigate this difficult, delicate, and complex relationship between their institutions and governments every day. Occasional praise of government goes a long way. Achieving the right creative tension in the university-government relationship is more art than science. It depends heavily on the human relationship between the university president and the relevant government officials. This relationship is a critical variable in determining the amount of influence a university will enjoy.

You can't be too far ahead of government

Because governments are so often immersed in putting out fires and solving immediate problems, it is difficult for them to think too far ahead. It is very hard to get traction with government if one puts something in front of them that is too far ahead of what they, the sector, or the public are currently thinking. Many a progressive, bold idea got lost in government by failing to heed this advice.

Researchers are aware of this attribute. It is often difficult to convince a granting agency to give you funds if the project you are promoting is too bold or too much of a departure from the *Zeitgeist*. The best grant proposal I ever submitted was written with a collaborator unknown to the field, and it proposed an innovative way of assessing the involvement of some biological signals in appetite control. It was rejected as being too "way out." We did the work anyway, published a bunch of papers in respected journals, and even convinced some others to follow the approach. Three years later, we submitted essentially the same proposal, which was now acceptable because, as some of the referees were willing to admit, it was more conventional. Obviously, this episode made an impression on me.

You can't rely on the media to tell your story

Universities spend an inordinate amount of time working the media to present their stories in an effort to influence government. It seems at times that having an op-ed piece in a national newspaper is, for some academics, the pinnacle of their career. But, as an accomplished communications guru once told me, "Media are in the failure business ... they expect us to fail, they need us to fail...." This opinion aligns with the other comment often heard about the media: "If it bleeds, it leads."

What is most influential with governments is when people they are inclined to listen to – business leaders, donors to the party, opinion leaders at arm's length from university – advocate for a university's position. Politicians are also disproportionately influenced by calls to their constituency offices. So good public relations, community engagement, and strategic alliances with non-university opinion leaders are the substrate for good government relations.

Have skin in the game

Since governments are so used to people approaching them with their hands out, they are inordinately influenced when you start a conversation by telling them that you do not want their money (of course, governments are also savvy enough to know that at some point, you *will want* their money). As with any other reasonable person, politicians are far more likely to affiliate with and support a university's policy direction or request if the proponent has shown a commitment to a project. Eloquent position papers and lofty rhetoric do not constitute a commitment. A commitment is demonstrated by something tangible – like the a priori allocation of institutional resources to the project.

In my experience, a university allocating dollars to a project in advance of any government commitment is one of the strongest influencers of a government's thinking and willingness to follow suit. It is all the better if the university allocation is accompanied by a significant philanthropic donation because it shows that someone else is also prepared to make a very tangible commitment to the idea or project. Again, all of this is quite understandable. If a university truly believes in the importance of some project, it should be willing to allocate dollars to this priority initiative. If it is unwilling to do so, why should anyone else, including government, invest in it?

CONCLUSION

It is a time of turbulence in public higher education, and for all the reasons contributing to this environment, it is likely that we will see more extensive policy development and changes than usual in Canada's public higher education system. If nothing else, there is a growing sense of urgency about higher education, an attribute that is a prerequisite and motivator for change (Kotter 1996; Kotter 2008). The nature of the public sector in Canada suggests that governments will be inextricably involved in changes in higher education. This is appropriate; remember that governments were elected for their policies and ideas. The best higher education policies will be fashioned when governments work sensibly and productively with those in higher education institutions. The engagement of those in the sector is important because they are experts in the business and instrumental in implementing any policies that may be adopted. For those reluctant to engage the sector because they fear that institutions of higher learning operate on self-interest, let me say that I have seen many examples of universities rising above institutional self-interest and advocating for the good of the system, students, and the public.

There are varying opinions about the respective roles of governments and institutions in the formation of policy. In a previous analysis of Ontario's higher education sector, Fiona Deller and I advised that the primary role of government was to establish public policy goals (understanding that these decisions should be informed, guided, and shaped by experts in the higher education sector) and desired outcomes. We suggested further, though, that governments should not be too prescriptive in telling institutions how those policy goals and outcomes were to be achieved (Weingarten and Deller 2010).

We increase our chances of navigating these turbulent waters and landing in safe and desirable harbours if we fashion and maintain a productive, harmonious policy discussion between governments and the institutions of higher education they regulate. In the end, the students, public, and country benefit from this desirable state, and perhaps some of the suggestions and observations made in this chapter can contribute to moving us closer to it.

NOTES

1.   The public post-secondary sector in Canada is composed of both universities and colleges. The relationship between governments and the college and university sectors is different, particularly in provinces like Ontario, which grant universities far more autonomy and independence than colleges. This chapter is biased toward universities because this sector occupies more of the attention of governments and the media, it is where the majority of students choose to pursue post-secondary studies, and it is the sector that I know best. That said, many of the arguments made here apply equally to colleges and universities.
2.   For a fuller description of the regulatory control of universities by government, see Weingarten (2011).

3.   There appears to be a great tradition of former university presidents writing about the nature and state of higher education systems and institutions based upon their experiences. If you are inclined to read only one such experience-based publication, try Kennedy (1997).

4.   This is a real "we," not the royal "we." Whatever successes we had reflected the contribution and efforts of a talented cabal of colleagues.

5.   For example, the University of Alberta and the University of Calgary competed for the Alberta School of Veterinary Medicine. The U of C prevailed, not the usual result when the U of C and the U of A competed for significant government attention and resources.

6.   At one of my "retirement" events, the minister related the story of his bemusement when I presented him with a $1 billion capital plan to renew the University of Calgary facilities and then updated him several months later with the news that the cost was really closer to $1.5 billion. The next speaker, the president of the University of Alberta, reminded the minister that he had failed to deliver the punch line to the story, which was, "And then you gave him the money."

7.   I recall a conversation with former Reform Party leader, and son of an ex–Alberta premier, Preston Manning, when he expressed his puzzlement that politicians of his father's era, even though they had typically not gone to university, seemed to him to be more supportive of higher education funding than current-day politicians. The cynic might suggest that current-day politicians may be generally less supportive precisely because they had attended colleges and universities.

8.   Notwithstanding the fact that, in my experience, many decisions in universities about significant matters may also be made with little evidence or data and are influenced by stories, anecdotes, stereotypes, intuitions, ideologies, and personal experiences.

9.   This tendency is not unknown in university circles either. It is not unheard of for a university administration to adopt a policy that works in the short term but may not be advisable in the long term because it thinks that any deleterious consequences, if they became apparent, would arise only after the terms of the current slate of administrators had ended.

10. This is a good thing because in many areas of the public sector – think higher education, health care, financing of infrastructure and pensions – we need some bold and innovative thinking.

11. I thank Seymour Schulich for making me aware of this informative manual.

12. Some will argue that this arrangement should be symmetrical and that governments should spend a little more time trying to appreciate the context, issues, and challenges faced by the universities. In an ideal world, this would be the case. However, the world of university-government relations is not an exercise in creating an ideal world, and it is not symmetrical. Rather, it is an exercise in pragmatics. Anyway, when the university-government interaction is one where the institution is asking for something from government (as is so often the case), remember the general rule that the one holding the cash is king and therefore is also the one who makes the rules.

13. This is where the reader's mind gravitates to visions of "herding cats."

14. For some interesting reading on the critical role of the president, the reader might wish to consult Fisher and Koch (1996), Bowen (2010), and Paul (2012).

REFERENCES

Ariely, D. 2008. *Predictably Irrational: The Hidden Faces That Shape Our Decisions.* New York: Harper Collins.

Bowen, W.G. 2010. *Lessons Learned: Reflections of a University President.* Princeton, NJ: Princeton University Press.

Brafman, O., and R. Brafman. 2008. *Sway: The Irresistible Pull of Irrational Behavior.* New York: Crown Business.

Fisher, J.L., and J.V. Koch. 1996. *Presidential Leadership: Making a Difference.* Lanham, MD: Rowman and Littlefield.

Kennedy, D. 1997. *Academic Duty.* Cambridge, MA: Harvard University Press.

Kotter, J.P. 1996. *Leading Change.* Boston, MA: Harvard Business Press.

—. 2008. *A Sense of Urgency.* Boston, MA: Harvard Business Press.

Paul, R. 2012. *Leadership under Fire: The Challenging Role of the Canadian University President.* Montreal and Kingston: McGill-Queen's University Press.

Rosenblatt, R. 2001. *Rules for Aging: A Wry and Witty Guide to Life.* Orlando, FL: Harcourt Books.

Weingarten, H.P. 2011. "The Diminishing Quality of Ontario's Universities: Can the System Be Fixed?" *It'snotacademic* (blog), 31 October. At http://heqco.ca/en-CA/blog/archive/2011/10/31/the-diminishing-quality-of-ontario%E2%80%99s-universities-can-the-system-be-fixed.aspx (accessed 12 June 2013).

Weingarten, H.P., and F. Deller. 2010. "The Benefits of a Greater Differentiation of Ontario's University Sector." At http://www.heqco.ca/siteCollection Documents?DifferentiationENG.pdf (accessed 12 June 2013).

CHAPTER 5

LINEATION AND LOBBYING: POLICY NETWORKS AND HIGHER EDUCATION POLICY IN ONTARIO

GLEN A. JONES

Three dogs are sitting on the corner outside a restaurant when a meat truck pulls up. As the driver steps out to deliver the meat, the dogs begin strategizing about how to get some for themselves. One dog says, "I used to be a lawyer. Let me negotiate with the driver and talk him into giving us the meat." The second dog says, "I used to be an architect. I know a secret passageway to the kitchen. I can lead us to the meat." The third dog says, "I used to be a college president. I'm sure they will give us all the meat we want if we just sit here on the corner and whine and beg." (Cook 1998, xi)

While one might argue that the leaders of Canada's publicly supported universities and community colleges have always lobbied government, in the sense of articulating the needs and interests of their institutions, there is considerable evidence that the nature and importance of these activities have increased exponentially over the last four decades (Charles 2011; Constantinou 2010; Paul 2011). While the "whining and begging" approach alluded to in the anecdote above may well have described the lobbying activities of higher education leaders in the 1970s and 1980s, many universities have adopted somewhat more sophisticated approaches, often employing dedicated staff or external consultants. As policy issues have become increasingly complex and technical, university and college leaders, at least in the province of Ontario, have come to rely on the advocacy efforts of their sector associations: the Council of Ontario

Making Policy in Turbulent Times: Challenges and Prospects for Higher Education, ed. P. Axelrod, R.D. Trilokekar, T. Shanahan, and R. Wellen. Kingston: School of Policy Studies, Queen's University.

Universities (COU; for the university sector) and Colleges Ontario (for the college sector).

The most consistent and enduring focus of university and college efforts to lobby government has been money – particularly the total operating grant or annual increase in the total operating grant, but also at times the allocation formula, capital funding, and tuition regulation or re-regulation (a long and quite interesting story on its own). The set of issues other than those directly pertaining to money that have perhaps been the next largest focus of lobbying have been those pertaining to mission.

In the university sector, at least since 1981, there have been periodic calls for greater institutional differentiation, which have meant a diminution of the mission of some institutions toward a greater emphasis and concentration on teaching relative to research. Universities have generally shown solidarity in resisting this type of change, though there have been exceptions. While the universities have lobbied to resist changes in mission, the Ontario colleges have lobbied for the opportunity to expand their mission, which, if some colleges expanded their mission more than others, would lead to greater differentiation among them. While there has been some solidarity among the colleges in this type of lobbying (such as for degree-granting and for the new charter), there has been less solidarity than in the university sector as individual and small groups of colleges have advocated for special treatment. What is certainly true for both sectors is that there has been a great deal of lobbying about lineation, that is, about the line boundaries that define and differentiate post-secondary sectors and institutional missions.

While arguments to increase the level of what Birnbaum (1983) has referred to as systemic diversity within the Ontario system are far from new, this policy issue now appears to be receiving greater political traction. Using pluralist political theory and policy networks as a foundation, the objective of this chapter is to analyze some key elements and challenges associated with the intersection between lobbying, or what is more commonly referred to as government relations at the institutional and system level, and contemporary debates over the boundary lines surrounding current institutional types. The chapter will begin by introducing a number of relevant theoretical concepts before turning to an analysis of the intersection between lineation and lobbying in the Ontario higher education context.[1]

PLURALISM AND POLICY NETWORKS

Pluralist political theory begins with the assumption that individuals and organizations have interests and that they will take action to further their interests. Pross suggests that "the essence of pluralism is the unorchestrated interaction of individual citizens, each striving through political action to improve or defend his or her position and lot in life"

(1986, 227). Given the time, energy, and resources necessary to become actively involved in the political process, most individual interests remain latent, but pluralism assumes that individuals will become politically active if they see ways of furthering their interests, or if they believe that their interests are being threatened.

One obvious way of furthering one's interests is to join an advocacy group or coalition of individuals or organizations that share common interests. Pressure groups have come to play a quite important role in contemporary politics in terms of keeping government informed of the views of group members, as well as shaping and influencing government policy. Since some organizations, groups, and coalitions have more resources than others,[2] governments have often taken steps to make lobbying activity somewhat more transparent. In Ontario, the *Lobbyists Registration Act, 1998* provides a formal definition of lobbyists and lobbying and requires all individuals who engage in these activities to be registered (Lobbyists Registration Office 2012). The assumption underscoring the act is that the legislature should monitor lobbying activity through the receipt of regular reports from the Lobbyists Registration Office, and that citizens should have access to information on lobbying activity so that these processes become more public and transparent.

While there are certainly exceptions, government policy-making has tended to become increasingly specialized and decentralized. Relatively few issues are dealt with at the macro level of the political system and receive broad public attention; instead, most policy issues are addressed at the meso level, where *policy communities*, composed of individuals and groups who are interested in the policy area, discuss and shape policy outcomes. Pross, in his classic work on group politics in Canada (1986), defines policy communities quite broadly to include the government agency assigned responsibility for the policy area, as well as other agencies, pressure groups, individuals, and members of the media. The term *policy network* refers to

> the relationship among policy actors around a policy issue of importance to the policy community. Policy networks account for informal relations in policy-making and are created in the "gray" area between state and civil society in response to new or failed governmental policies; they may emerge as a consequence of political pressure from the civic society or as an initiative of governmental and intergovernmental organizations. (Padure and Jones 2009, 108)

The image of the political system that emerges from these basic concepts is of a community of interest in a particular policy area – for example, higher education, which includes a lead government department assigned responsibility for this policy area – for example, the Ontario Ministry of Training, Colleges and Universities, as well as a range of individuals and organizations and media. Policy networks can be seen as a much smaller subset of this community, which emerges around specific policy issues and includes both formal and informal interactions that shape policy decisions and directions.

THE ONTARIO HIGHER EDUCATION SYSTEM

While the history of higher education in Ontario can be traced back to the early 19th century, the provincial government's involvement in higher education policy was extremely limited until the period of post-WWII expansion. The government did not create an office or agency with responsibility for higher education until 1951, when a part-time consultant was employed by the Ministry of Education. In 1956, the premier asked a small group of senior civil servants from different departments to provide advice on the expansion and funding of the Ontario system. The University Committee, as this interdepartmental group became known, was replaced by the Advisory Committee on University Affairs in 1961. The government's need to plan and develop policy in this sector continued to increase as the system expanded; in 1964, the Government of Ontario created a distinct Department of University Affairs, with William G. Davis as the first minister, and a new advisory agency called the Committee on University Affairs (Beard 1983; Jones 1997).

The institutional autonomy of universities was regarded as a key principle within the system even as government involvement in the sector increased. The new Committee on University Affairs was, at least in part, designed to be a "buffer" agency that would provide "neutral" advice to government rather than functioning as an arm of the department. The committee included individuals nominated by the sector, and early suggestions that the province develop some form of system plan, or even move toward an integrated University of Ontario model, were rejected in favour of supporting a network of autonomous institutions (Jones 1997).

The presidents of these autonomous institutions began meeting in 1962 as the Committee of Presidents of Provincially-Assisted Universities and Colleges of Ontario, a title that reflected the view that the universities were independent rather than "public" institutions that were supported by government grants. The committee later evolved into the more formal COU.[3] The COU was essentially a coalition of university presidents; it charged membership fees that supported a secretariat and council research and advocacy activities. Like other political pressure groups, the COU provided a forum for determining the shared interests of member institutions and articulating those interests to government, but it is also important to note that the internal organization of the COU also served to link institutions on multiple levels. In addition to functioning as a committee of presidents, each institution also appointed an "academic colleague" and these colleagues discussed sector-wide academic issues, and the council facilitated interaction between institutions in a wide range of academic and administrative areas through, for example, supporting the creation of provincial associations of deans of medicine, law, and other specific areas, associations of librarians, etc. This internal structure obviously promoted the sharing of information among institutions in a range of specialized areas of activity, but in political terms it also meant that the COU secretariat, which facilitated these interactions, was kept informed of university interests across areas of government activity, and this strengthened the integrated nature of its government relations activities.

Other provincial pressure groups also emerged during this time period. The Ontario Council (and later Confederation) of University Faculty Associations (OCUFA), a coalition of institution-based faculty associations, was formed in 1963. Student interests were represented by a coalition of university student associations called the Ontario Union of Students (which went through a number of organizational changes, later emerging as the Ontario Federation of Students in the 1970s) (Fleming 1972; Jones 1997).

While the expansion of higher education led to the creation of new universities, these new institutions essentially took on the characteristics of the existing ones. Universities had both teaching and research functions, similar governance structures, and were essentially treated the same by government. By the late 1960s, decisions on government funding allocations were made using a common formula. Even the newest universities moved quickly to become comprehensive institutions with some combination of undergraduate, graduate, and professional programs. While there were clearly differences by institution in program mix and areas of emphasis (the University of Waterloo's focus on co-operative education, for example), there was little systemic diversity (Birnbaum 1983) in that all universities shared a roughly common mission and relationship to government.

Systemic diversity within the higher education system emerged with the creation of the Ontario Colleges of Applied Arts and Technology (CAATs) through legislation introduced in 1965. The new CAATs would have a very different mission and relationship to government than the universities. While the universities were created as autonomous, not-for-profit, private corporations, the CAATs were established as Crown corporations under an act of the provincial parliament that assigned tremendous regulatory authority to the minister. The mission of the colleges was also quite different from the universities; they were to be highly accessible institutions offering a comprehensive range of technical and vocational programs to address the needs of industry, but, unlike the American community college model, the new CAATs were not designed to be feeder institutions to the university sector. They would not provide university-transfer courses, a decision that would lead to recurring discussions of how to facilitate student mobility between sectors. The universities would retain a public monopoly on degree-granting, a principle that would be enshrined in the *Degree Granting Act* of 1983 (Skolnik 1987), while the colleges would offer a wide range of one-, two-, and three-year programs leading to a certificate or diploma.

The core systemic differences between the sectors were paralleled by distinct regulatory arrangements. Institutional autonomy continued to be a central theme within the university sector. While the legislation introduced to create a new Ontario Council on University Affairs (OCUA) envisioned an intermediary body with some regulatory authority, there was resistance from within the sector. The proposed legislation was never approved, and OCUA was eventually created by Order-in-Council in 1974 with an advisory role quite similar to that of the former Committee on University Affairs. OCUA became an agency within the sub-government of the Ontario university sector. It received input from the community through a process of annual consultations held in different geographic regions of the province, and then provided advice to government in the form of advisory memoranda that would, following a response from government, become public, and both the advice and the government response were published in its annual reports.

Almost every government commission or task force that has reviewed the university sector has recommended some form of rationalization or institutional differentiation within the sector (for example, Committee on the Future Role of Universities in Ontario 1981; Commission on the Future Development of the Universities of Ontario 1984), but these proposals were strongly opposed by the COU and individual institutions. In her study of the various committees and task forces that had reviewed Ontario universities, Royce noted both the consistent argument that the Ontario system could be improved through institutional differentiation, and the consistent unwillingness, in the face of lobbying from within the policy community, or inability, in the face of other practical issues, of the government to actually reform the system (Royce 1997). I will return to this point in more detail below. In the absence of reform, the university sector continued to be characterized by high levels of institutional autonomy and minimal government regulation, an era that I have previously defined as "modest modifications and structural stability" where government policy changes took the form of minor tinkering within a stable structural arrangement (Jones 1991; Jones 1994).

Minor tinkering also characterized the level of policy change in the CAAT sector, but this was in the context of a quite different authority relationship with government. Most major CAAT initiatives, such as the creation of new programs, or capital projects, required government approval. Each college had its own governing board and each was encouraged to respond to the changing needs of industry and the labour market, but the government regulated the boundaries of CAAT activity, and the fact that labour unions in the sector were provincial (rather than institutional as in the university sector), with the provincial Council of Regents for the CAATs negotiating on behalf of management, further decreased institutional flexibility. The college sector quickly established a reputation for being highly responsive, in part because, in the absence of statutory requirements for, or a tradition of, academic self-government, college presidents could steer their institutions in ways that would be unheard of in the university sector (Jones 1997).

The key elements of the Ontario higher education system had emerged by the beginning of the 1970s, and these characteristics largely defined the system into the 1990s. The university sector was composed of a network of autonomous institutions that received grants under a common funding formula and were generally treated as equals by government. There was little systemic diversity within the sector, except perhaps for the existence of several hybrid institutions that were largely treated as universities, such as Ryerson Polytechnic Institute and the Ontario College of Art and Design (OCAD). The Ontario CAATs were Crown corporations that were subject to higher levels of regulation than their university peers and had a more restrictive mandate.

GOVERNMENT RELATIONS

The expansion of the Ontario higher education system in the 1960s took place during a time period when the provincial coffers were full, but, in the early years of the 1970s, a global recession and major changes in tax revenues forced the government to reconsider the pace of its expenditures. While government relations might have once taken the form of a simple exchange between president and minister over the magnitude of the annual grant, the changing fiscal environment meant that governments had to be more careful. The rules of the game began to change.[4]

A funding formula had been used in the university sector since 1967, but in its earliest form, the formula actually determined the level of government support to the system since the total level of the government grant was influenced by the number of students enrolled in the sector as well as a calculation of inflation. The formula was quickly amended to become only an allocative mechanism: the government would determine the level of total funding that was to be distributed to the sector, and the formula would determine the share of funding that would be given to each institution based on enrolment and program mix. The question of determining the appropriate mechanism for calculating the level of year-over-year increase in grant was assigned to OCUA. After consulting with the policy community, OCUA developed a mechanism for calculating inflation in the sector and made annual recommendations to government on the level of grant increase required by the sector. The government accepted this advice for a few years, but beginning in

1977–78, it decided that it would provide universities a smaller increase than the level recommended by OCUA. The decision on the total level of funding moved inside government, and the era of complaining about government underfunding began.

The notion that government relations were characterized by the "whining and begging" suggested by the anecdote at the beginning of this chapter may be an exaggeration, but perhaps only a modest one. University presidents, given their academic training, believed that governments would listen and provide more funding if the argument could be made more convincing, with all of the appropriate evidence, and with great clarity, a key theme underscoring a book by Michael Skolnik and Norman Rowen (1984) entitled *"Please, sir, I want some more": Canadian Universities and Financial Restraint*.

The COU played a central role in lobbying for increased government funding on behalf of its members, and it devoted considerable attention to preparing public reports on the financial needs of the system, though these efforts seemed to have little impact on the ministry. In a move that illustrates the council's approach to government relations as well as its frustration, in 1982 the council updated the detailed materials that it had submitted the previous year and renamed its report "Once More With Feeling" (1982). Levin and Sullivan described the relationship between universities and governments in Canada as a political context in which "the two parties peer balefully at each other across a wide and apparently widening gulf" (1988, 1).

Convinced that the university sector was underfunded, OCUA continued to produce an annual advisory memorandum on the financial needs of the system, even though its work seemed to have little impact on the level of government grants. In the early years, these calculations discussed both the historical gap in total funding tracing back to 1977–78 (when the government began to provide less than OCUA had requested) as well as a precise calculation of recent inflation. The size of the total funding gap since 1977–78 became so large that OCUA concluded that it was unrealistic (and politically embarrassing) to continue with its traditional calculations, and so it modified its approach in order to reduce the size of the total gap to a level that would be less unfathomable, while still attempting to make its point that government funding needed to increase to address the "real" inflationary needs of the system.

While the government may not have been convinced by OCUA's advice on funding increases, it did listen to its recommendations on modifications to the funding formula. In response to its consultations with the policy community, OCUA recommended changes designed to stabilize funding levels, decrease the impact of sudden changes in enrolment, and create an environment that would support longer-range university planning. Rolling average calculations were added, and eventually an enrolment corridor was introduced so that a university's share of funding would not be impacted unless the institution's enrolment moved above or below its corridor enrolment. With little ability to influence the level of institutional grants in the context of a stable, formulaic grant allocation system, university presidents worked closely with the COU to create a common front in arguing that the entire system needed more government support.

Convinced that the university sector should be reformed to increase the level of institutional differentiation, and that the most powerful mechanism to promote differentiation was a redesigned funding system, in the early 1990s the New Democratic Party (NDP) Government asked OCUA to provide advice on reforming the approach to allocating resources in the sector. OCUA took its new role in recommending major system reforms quite seriously and, with the support of the government, was moving toward a model that would differentiate the system by separating funding support for teaching and research. There was little support for these possible changes within the COU or the institutional leadership. As Royce (1997) notes, the stage was set for a major reform to the university system under a government minister who was convinced that change was necessary even in the face of bitter opposition from the institutions themselves, with the reasonably clear, workable plan proposed by the intermediary body. The only thing missing was time.

An election was called in 1995, and the NDP Government was soundly defeated. The Conservative Party, under Mike Harris, was elected, and its "Common Sense Revolution" became the agenda for the new government. The government moved quickly to address the provincial deficit; operating grants to universities and colleges were cut, and tuition fees were substantially increased.

In an attempt to further reduce expenditures and simplify government processes, a large number of advisory bodies and government agencies were eliminated. OCUA became one of the agencies slated to go, and with its reputation severely tarnished in the eyes of the university establishment by its role in supporting major reforms to the funding system, neither the COU nor the university presidents lobbied strongly on its behalf. With the elimination of the intermediary body, the relationships among government, the COU, and the university presidents became more important and more direct. The nature of government relations changed, especially in the context of a government that encouraged competition.

In his study of government relations in both the university and the college sectors in Ontario, Peter Constantinou (2010) found that most of the university and college presidents he interviewed believed that the government relations function had increased in importance during this period, in part because the stakes had increased. With the creation of new targeted funding programs and the government's interest in increasing market-like competition in the sector, it became extremely important to ensure that the government was aware of the interests of individual institutions, as well as the interests of the sector as a whole, through the advocacy work of the COU. It is also important to note that there was no formal government plan or strategy and no clear mechanism for making strategic decisions. With the demise of OCUA and in the absence of a formal mechanism for system-wide planning or strategic development, lobbying became the logical response from higher education institutions and pressure groups. This was particularly important when final decisions for some major capital projects, especially under the SuperBuild initiative, were discretionary, and government relations became essential in order to lobby for specific projects (Constantinou 2010).

The evolution of government relations in the Ontario college sector is a quite different story, in large part because the ground rules in the two sectors were quite different in the first place. As Crown corporations, the CAATs were more clearly positioned as instruments of government policy related to addressing the skilled human resource needs of industry. They had far less autonomy than the universities and required government approval for a wide range of academic program and financial (including capital construction and real estate) initiatives. These regulatory requirements meant that the CAATs were used to working independently with the college branch of the ministry, and the funding formula arrangements in the college sector encouraged competition among institutions.

While the university funding formula had been modified to provide a level of stability within the sector to facilitate planning, allocations in the college sector were far more responsive to changes in enrolment. The government determined the amount of funding that would be made available to allocation, and these funds were allocated to each institution based on its share of total enrolment (weighted by program). The CAATs could increase their share of government funding only by increasing their share of enrolment, and they were soon competing for a larger share of the pie. In the 1990s, the net effect of the funding arrangement was that the colleges were competing to expand faster than their peers and consistently receiving lower government support on a per-student basis.

The provincial umbrella association, the Association of Colleges of Applied Arts and Technology of Ontario (ACAATO), provided a forum for the exchange of views through the Committee of Presidents, but, unlike the COU in the university sector,[5] ACAATO provided little support for research on the colleges, and its advocacy activities were considered quite basic. According to Anne Charles (2011), who conducted an extremely detailed analysis of policy development in the college sector, the importance of strengthening the advocacy activities of ACAATO became clear in the early 1990s, when tensions began to emerge between the NDP Government and the college presidents, and it was reinforced during the Harris era. ACAATO thus developed a much more strategic approach to its government relations activities, and this strategic approach to advocacy played an important role in the government's decision to authorize degree-granting by the college sector (through the *Post-secondary Education Choice and Excellence Act, 2000*) and modestly increase the level of college independence (through the *Ontario Colleges of Applied Arts and Technology Act, 2002*).

The importance of government relations in both the college and the university sectors was reinforced during the Harris era. With the dissolution of OCUA, the relationships between universities and government became more direct, and the COU began to work closely with the government on a range of policy issues. Government reforms led to a reorganization and reduction of staff in the ministry, a change that reduced the government's policy research capacity, as well as its historical memory, in this area (Jones 2004). In the college sector, the advocacy activities of ACAATO, which would be rebranded as Colleges Ontario, were strengthened. New government initiatives, such as the massive investment in capital construction under SuperBuild, meant that government relations were now viewed as essential since lobbying could influence the allocation of resources or new policy directions (Constantinou 2010).

According to Constantinou (2010), while lobbying has become quite important in both sectors, there are subtle differences in how college and university presidents describe these functions. College presidents report devoting much more time to these activities than university presidents. There were differences in how college and university presidents defined the boundaries of their political activities. For example, all of the college presidents whom he interviewed indicated that college funds were sometimes used to purchase tickets for political fundraising dinners or events, while all university presidents felt uncomfortable participating in such functions and either did not attend, or attended but either arranged for the tickets to be sponsored by a third party (such as a supportive alumnus), or paid for the tickets with personal (not university) funds.

Generally speaking, college presidents believed that university presidents had much greater political influence than they did. While there were differences in approach by sector, presidents from both colleges and universities reported that their respective advocacy organizations were becoming more sophisticated in their lobbying activities; college presidents noted that the decision to appoint David Lindsay, the former principal secretary to Premier Mike Harris and president of SuperBuild, as president of Colleges Ontario in 2006 had played a key role in strengthening the organization's capacity for effective government relations.

It is also important to note that the lobbying activities of public sector institutions became a political issue in Ontario in 2010. In October of that year, the auditor general of Ontario (2010) released a report that was very critical of the use of consultants by Ontario hospitals, but the auditor general also noted that half of the health service agencies that were reviewed also employed private lobbyists to lobby government over specific public funding issues. The fact that public sector agencies were using public funds to hire private lobbyists to lobby government for public funds received considerable attention in the media. Peter Constantinou's thesis (2010), which focused on the government relations activities of Ontario's colleges and universities and contributed important findings for this chapter, provided evidence that at least some universities and colleges were also employing public lobbyists to lobby the Ontario government. The result of these conclusions was a brief firestorm of media interest leading to the decision on the part of the Liberal Government of Dalton McGuinty to quickly introduce the *Broader Public Service Accountability Act*, which received royal assent in December 2010. The act prevents broader public sector institutions from using public funds to hire private lobbyists, which largely means that universities and colleges will continue to lobby about differentiation and boundary lines, but only by using staff employed directly by these institutions and the related sector organizations.

OBSERVATIONS ON LINEATION AND LOBBYING IN ONTARIO

As already noted, there is nothing new about the suggestion that there would be benefits and efficiencies associated with increasing the level of institutional differentiation in the Ontario higher education system. Numerous task forces focusing on the university sector have recommended reforms designed to rationalize the system through differentiation, and the review of resource allocation conducted by OCUA led to recommendations designed to increase differentiation through major adjustments to the government funding mechanism. Advocating for greater institutional differentiation in the college sector has been a major preoccupation of a number of its leaders, and these lobbying activities played an important role in the creation of new legislation that allowed for the expansion of degree-granting beyond the existing universities and, subject to review and government approval, provided colleges with the possibility of offering degrees in applied areas. These efforts also led to an attempt to provide some formal recognition of institutional differentiation in the college sector through the renaming of selected colleges as Institutes of Technology and Applied Learning (ITALs), though this was far from the notion of creating a truly distinctive sector that had been advocated by selected presidents and Polytechnics Ontario.

In some respects, the level of institutional diversity in the university sector had actually declined over time. Distinctive institutions such as the Ontario Institute for Studies in Education (OISE), Ryerson Polytechnic Institute, and the OCAD would evolve to become members of the broader club of comprehensive universities. OISE abandoned its independent status to become a component faculty of the University of Toronto.

Ryerson became Ryerson Polytechnic University and then Ryerson University. The OCAD would become OCAD University.

A number of quite recent events have reinforced the importance of institutional differentiation as a policy issue in the Ontario system. In July 2010, the deputy minister of training, colleges and universities asked the Higher Education Quality Council of Ontario (HEQCO) to review the issue of whether increased differentiation in the university sector might be advantageous, and HEQCO responded by creating a working group of senior officials, including the deputy minister, selected university presidents, and the president of Colleges Ontario. The working group's final report, released in October of 2010, provided strong arguments for increased differentiation (Weingarten and Deller 2010). More recently, Clark, Trick, and Van Loon's (2011) book on academic reform in Ontario has received considerable press coverage, especially their recommendation for the creation of a new sector of undergraduate universities that would be primarily focused on teaching. Finally, in February of 2012, the report of the Commission on the Reform of Ontario's Public Services (Drummond 2012) recommended a series of changes to the Ontario higher education system with institutional differentiation as a key theme. In short, there seems to be considerable interest in redrawing the lines that define the two sectors in order to allow for greater differentiation, though, as in the past, it is far from clear whether the government will act on these recommendations or, if it decides to act, what it will do.

At the same time, the analysis of the history of government relations and system structure presented above lays the foundation for a number of important observations on the relationship between lobbying and institutional differentiation that may assist in explaining how this complicated issue is taken up in the higher education policy network.

The first, and most important, observation is that there are substantial differences in the implications of furthering institutional differentiation between the college and university sectors. A key characteristic of the legislation under which the colleges function is that considerable authority over the sector is assigned to the minister. While the 2002 charter provides colleges with slightly more independence over selected matters, the colleges continue to be heavily regulated institutions. Institutional differentiation in the college sector is synonymous with forms of deregulation and expanding the missions of selected institutions, in that any policy designed to increase systemic diversity requires that the government take a step back from its control of one or more institutions in the sector. For example, the expansion of degree-granting in 2000 essentially redrew the boundary lines of the sector to provide institutions with an expanded mission, and some level of programmatic differentiation has taken place since effectively only a handful of institutions have taken up this expanded mission. Furthering institutional differentiation in the college sector implies expanding roles and deregulating (or re-regulating) elements of the relationship between institutions and government.

In contrast, the university sector is characterized by uniformly inclusive missions (almost all universities offer some combination of undergraduate, graduate, and professional programs operating under charters that provide institutions with considerable flexibility to pursue a teaching, research, and service mission of their choosing) and high levels of institutional autonomy. Increasing institutional differentiation in the university sector means either restricting the mission or objectives of selected institutions (implied by the recommendations of the recent Drummond report) through regulation or targeted or performance-related funding, or creating new institutions with limited missions operating under more restrictive legislation than existing institutions. In other words, institutional differentiation within the college sector involves expanding missions through deregulation, while institutional differentiation within the university sector means restricting missions through regulation.

The second observation is that institutional differentiation has quite different implications in terms of the politics of advocacy within the pressure groups of the two sectors. Pressure groups advocate on behalf of the interests of their members, and there are differences in how interests related to institutional differentiation are understood in the two sectors. While there have clearly been differences of opinion among colleges on the need to stray from the original mission and expand the role of the sector (Charles 2011), all of the colleges have shared a common interest in decreasing regulation and increasing administrative flexibility (that is, to obtain some of the freedoms that universities already have). In other words, it is in the interests of all institutions to support some elements of deregulation associated with institutional differentiation even if there is limited consensus on specific modifications to the mission of the sector. Colleges Ontario can advocate for expanding the mission of the sector and deregulation because it is in the self-interest of the sector.

On the other hand, there can be little consensus in the university sector over restricting the mandate of existing institutions or providing the government with additional regulatory tools. Given that the COU can only effectively advocate on issues where there is a consensus on a position among members, the whole issue of institutional differentiation becomes problematic because there are no member institutions that support the restriction of their own missions (though there are institutions that support the notion that government should restrict the mandate of selected peers). The issue of creating new undergraduate universities is equally troublesome for the COU because there are members that have a vested interest in alternative proposals (for example, creating satellite campuses), there are members that fear that the creation of new institutional types will be a step toward restricting the mandate of existing institutions that are less comprehensive and research-oriented, and there are members that are concerned that "academic drift" will eventually lead primarily teaching institutions to evolve into new comprehensive institutions, thus expanding the size and level of future competition in the sector. The structure of the policy community and the existing structural and authority arrangements within the system have direct implications for how the issue of institutional differentiation is taken up within the sectoral pressure groups.

The third observation is that the lobbying activities of individual institutions advocating for differentiated missions are perceived differently in the two sectors. When five university presidents attempted to lobby for special recognition as Canada's most research-intensive universities, the reaction was almost uniformly negative; it was generally argued that the initiative was elitist and designed to provide a rationale for additional resources. Jack Lightstone (2010), the president of Brock University, argued that instead of focusing resources on a limited number of institutions, governments should ensure that all Canadian universities are research universities. In other words, institutional lobbying for a differentiated role that positions one institution above its peers is bitterly resisted within the sector. In contrast, when a collection of colleges took steps to rebrand themselves as differentiated institutions under the umbrella of Polytechnics Canada, the opposition from other colleges was comparatively muted. There were certainly differences of opinion on the degree to which colleges should be allowed to stray from their original mission, but there was general support for the position that colleges should have an applied research mandate and some other elements of the polytechnics initiative.

The fourth observation is that in the long history of this issue in both sectors, there is little evidence that the government of Ontario has a clear picture of what sort of institutional differentiation it would like to facilitate. As Royce notes (1997), the resource allocation exercise in the early 1990s may have been the only time when almost all of the various pieces were in place for a major reform of the university sector – but then the government fell. The reaction to most recommendations for institutional differentiation in the university sector, even from task forces and commissions created by the government, has been silence. While there currently appears to be considerable interest in differentiation, there is little clarity on the goals associated with differentiation or the form that it would take within the university sector (for example, see Drummond 2012). The government's attempt to differentiate the college sector by designating selected colleges as ITALs has accomplished little; the designation refers only to a modest form of programmatic diversity (see Birnbaum 1983) since the ITALs can have a slightly larger ratio of degree students, but there is no clear difference in mandate associated with the new title. Not all of the colleges that have the designation have chosen to use the title. The Drummond report (2012) suggests taking a step backward; the commission argues in favour of institutional differentiation in the university sector, but recommends that no new degree programs be approved in the college sector.

Taken together, these observations suggest that there will continue to be strong resistance to any attempt to increase the level of systemic diversity within the Ontario university sector. From the perspective of most of the institutions and their pressure group, there is more to be gained by protecting institutional autonomy, and the current broad mandates of all institutions, than in supporting a move to rationalize the system that might limit the autonomy and mission of selected peers.[6] On the other hand, there continues to be considerable interest in institutional differentiation within the college sector, with at least one college (Sheridan) already explicitly advocating for some form of special university status, and several others planning and advocating for a new status in more subtle ways. This analysis suggests that (focusing only on the politics of the two sectors rather than other substantive issues) it may actually be easier for the government to increase institutional differentiation in the Ontario higher education system by repositioning and re-regulating institutions in the college sector rather than by attempting to rationalize the university sector.

NOTES

1.   Acknowledgement: The author is grateful for the comments and suggestions provided by Michael Skolnik on an earlier draft of this chapter. The chapter draws heavily on the original research conducted by two of my former doctoral students, Anne Charles and Peter Constantinou. I want to acknowledge the tremendous contribution that these two individuals have made to my understanding of these issues; it is a good example of how teachers often learn more from their students than the other way around.

2.   Differences in the power, influence, resources, and real or perceived legitimacy of individuals and groups participating in the political arena are key assumptions underscoring both post-pluralist and neo-pluralist theory.

3.   For a detailed history of the COU, see Monahan (2004).

4.   A detailed historical analysis of the politics and economics of higher education in Ontario during this period is provided by Axelrod (1982).

5.   In reviewing a draft of this manuscript, Michael Skolnik reminded me that at one point, the COU was second only to Statistics Canada in terms of producing data and research on universities. While this function was never abandoned, there is little doubt that the COU began to devote more attention to advocacy and less attention to research during this time.

6.   Ian Clark makes a quite similar argument from a government perspective in his 2007 paper for the Higher Education Quality Council of Ontario.

REFERENCES

Auditor General of Ontario. 2010. *Consultant Use in Selected Health Organizations* (Special Report, October). Toronto: Queen's Printer.

Axelrod, P. 1982. *Scholars and Dollars: Politics, Economics, and the Universities of Ontario, 1945–1980*. Toronto: University of Toronto Press.

Beard, P. 1983. *The Ontario Council on University Affairs: What, Why and How*. Toronto: Ontario Council on University Affairs.

Birnbaum, R. 1983. *Maintaining Diversity in Higher Education*. San Francisco: Jossey-Bass.

Charles, A.C. 2011. "Policy Windows and Changing Arrangements: An Analysis of the Policy Process Leading to the Colleges of Applied Arts and Technology Act, 2002." PhD diss., University of Toronto, Toronto.

Clark, I.D. 2007. "A Jurisdictional Competitiveness Framework for Thinking about System Capacity in Higher Education." Paper presented at the first retreat of the Higher Education Quality Council of Ontario, 9 November. At http://ww2.publicpolicy.utoronto.ca/FacultyandContacts/IanClarkWebPageatUofT/Documents/A%20Jurisdictional%20Competitiveness%20Framework%20for%20Higher%20Education.pdf (accessed 22 June 2013).

Clark, I.D., D. Trick, and R. Van Loon. 2011. *Academic Reform: Policy Options for Improving the Quality and Cost-Effectiveness of Undergraduate Education in Ontario*. Queen's Policy Studies Series. Montreal and Kingston: McGill-Queen's University Press.

Commission on the Future Development of the Universities of Ontario. 1984. *Ontario Universities: Options and Futures*. Toronto: The Commission.

Committee on the Future Role of Universities in Ontario. 1981. *The Report*. Toronto: The Committee.

Constantinou, P.P. 2010. "Government Relations in the Post-secondary Education Sector in Ontario." PhD diss., University of Toronto, Toronto.

Cook, C.E. 1998. *Lobbying for Higher Education: How Colleges and Universities Influence Federal Policy*. Nashville, TN: Vanderbilt University Press.

Council of Ontario Universities. 1982. *Once More with Feeling*. Brief to the Ontario Council on University Affairs. Toronto: Council of Ontario Universities.

Drummond, D. 2012. *Public Services for Ontarians: A Path to Sustainability and Excellence*. Toronto: Commission on the Reform of Ontario's Public Services.

Fleming, W.G. 1972. *Educational Contributions of Associations*. Toronto: University of Toronto Press.

Jones, G.A. 1991. "Modest Modifications and Structural Stability: Higher Education in Ontario." *Higher Education* 21:573–587.

—. 1994. "Higher Education Policy in Ontario." In *Higher Education Policy: An International Comparative Perspective*, ed. L. Goedegebuure et al., 214–238. Oxford: Pergamon.

—. 1997. "Higher Education in Ontario." In *Higher Education in Canada: Different Systems, Different Perspectives*, ed. G.A. Jones, 137–158. New York: Garland.

—. 2004. "Ontario Higher Education Reform, 1995–2003: From Modest Modifications to Policy Reform." *Canadian Journal of Higher Education* 34 (3):39–54.

Levin, B., and N. Sullivan. 1988. "Governments and Universities." *Canadian Journal of Higher Education* 18 (1):1–12.

Lightstone, J. 2010. "Comment: Canada Needs All Universities to Do Research." GlobeCampus (*Globe and Mail*). At http://www.globecampus.ca/in-the-news/globecampusreport/comment-canada-needs-all-universities-to-do-research/ (accessed 27 February 2012).

Lobbyists Registration Office. 2012. "A Guide to the *Lobbyists Registration Act*." Toronto: Lobbyists Registration Office, Office of the Integrity Commissioner.

Monahan, E.J. 2004. *Collective Autonomy: A History of the Council of Ontario Universities, 1962–2000*. Waterloo, ON: Wilfrid Laurier University Press.

Padure, L., and G.A. Jones. 2009. "Policy Networks and Research on Higher Education Governance and Policy." In *International Perspectives on the Governance of Higher Education: Alternative Frameworks for Coordination*, ed. J. Huisman, 107–125. New York: Routledge.

Paul, R.H. 2011. *Leadership under Fire: The Challenging Role of the Canadian University President*. Montreal and Kingston: McGill-Queen's University Press.

Pross, A.P. 1986. *Group Politics and Public Policy*. Toronto: Oxford University Press.

Royce, D. 1997. "University System Planning and Coordination in Ontario, 1945–1996." PhD diss., University of Toronto, Toronto.

Skolnik, M.L. 1987. "State Control of Degree Granting: The Establishment of a Public Monopoly in Canada." In *Governments and Higher Education – The Legitimacy of Intervention*, ed. C. Watson, 56–83. Toronto: Higher Education Group, Ontario Institute for Studies in Education.

Skolnik, M.L., and N.S. Rowen. 1984. *"Please, sir, I want some more"*: Canadian Universities and Financial Restraint. Toronto: OISE Press.

Weingarten, H.P., and F. Deller. 2010. *The Benefits of Greater Differentiation of Ontario's University Sector*. Toronto: Higher Education Quality Council of Ontario.

CHAPTER 6

SETTING STRATEGIC DIRECTION FROM THE PRESIDENTIAL SUITE: HURDLES AND SUCCESSES

JUDITH WOODSWORTH

INTRODUCTION: A LEADERSHIP INDUSTRY

Being the head of a post-secondary institution has never been an easy task. However, in recent years, the job of university president has been rendered particularly daunting, for, as the title of this book suggests, these are turbulent times. Economic volatility; intense competition for students, faculty, and resources; and ever greater demands from a diverse and complex set of stakeholders all place an increased burden on the shoulders of those selected to head universities (Fisher 1984; Brown 2006).

It takes leaders with exceptional capabilities to face these extraordinary challenges. Leadership development, therefore, has become a critical topic (Madsen 2007), reflected not only in thousands of scholarly and practitioner-oriented articles (Madsen 2008) but also in professional development sessions designed to address the needs of executive heads (Brown 2006) – although perhaps to a lesser degree in Canada than in the United States. Taking on a university presidency has become a "precarious option," as Nigel Thrift, vice-chancellor of the University of Warwick, has suggested, pointing out that the "perils of presidency" have given rise to a "leadership industry" (2011).

While there is general agreement on the severity of the challenges facing university presidents, around the world and in Canada (Paul 2011), as well as on the requirement for corresponding talents to take

Making Policy in Turbulent Times: Challenges and Prospects for Higher Education, ed. P. Axelrod, R.D. Trilokekar, T. Shanahan, and R. Wellen. Kingston: School of Policy Studies, Queen's University.

up these challenges, there is no consensus on the particular attributes required of an institutional leader. Much literature has focused on corporate leadership, but less has been said about the leadership styles of university presidents, particularly women (Madsen 2008). There has been insufficient research, moreover, on the causes of their success or failure, or on their actual impact or positional power (Birnbaum 1989; Bryman 2007; Cutright 2007; Paul 2011).

In this chapter, I offer my personal observations, based on three decades of administrative experience in positions ranging from program director to department chair, vice-dean, and provost, including over eight years as a president of two universities – anecdotal, to be sure, but with some remarks, questions, and conclusions that could pave the way for further examination and empirical research.

The appointment of a new president is an opportunity for a university community to stand back, take stock, and re-evaluate the direction it is taking. It is relatively common for the appointing body – the board of directors, governors, or trustees – to expect that the incoming executive head will carve out a new path for the institution in order to give it fresh direction, often in the context of a fundraising campaign or new initiatives.

As difficult as it might seem in an organization like a university, where the constituents exhibit more loyalty to their disciplines and departments than to the organization as a whole (Brown 2006), it is important for a leader to articulate a vision and, through her own commitment and passion, to inspire the organization to pursue common goals. It is generally agreed that the most important role of a president is to formulate and promote the mission, vision, and long-term goals of the institution – in other words, to manage the "big picture" (Paul 2011).

This takes the form of strategic planning, which guides the institution over a certain period of time and which, in principle, drives a series of other processes such as academic planning and budgeting. It is tantamount, therefore, to setting overarching policy for that organization. This chapter will examine how the strategic planning process unfolds under the direction of the president and then how it can be influenced by external factors: government policy decisions, the vicissitudes of the economy, and pressures from community groups or other influential stakeholders, for example. Also addressed are the internal controversies: the debate around balancing teaching and research, the critique of a market-driven approach to promotional activities and student recruitment, and the opposition to various forms of revenue generation. The chapter will provide examples of successful outcomes of strategic planning, along with examples of some of the constraints on or obstacles to the achievement of presidential goals and targets. It concludes with an overview of the characteristics of female leaders, the relevance of location, and the changing nature of board relations and the university presidency itself.

CHARTING A COURSE OR NAVIGATING TROUBLED WATERS?

In the language of strategic plans, navigational metaphors ("charting a course for the future") appear as frequently as construction ones ("building on strengths," "building on excellence," "blueprint"), denoting the perceived importance of these plans in effecting positive change.

Even if the predecessor has been a huge success, there is an expectation that a new president will bring about change (Shaw 2002). In cases where the previous leader is perceived to have been less successful, or where there are urgent problems to resolve, the need for new strategic direction is particularly acute.

My own experience falls into the second category. I have twice taken the helm of an institution in crisis, following the premature departure of a predecessor, with resulting reputational challenges, financial instability, and a general state of demoralization, discontent, and even cynicism among staff and faculty. It was anticipated – even before I took office – that I would develop a strategic plan that would somehow solve all problems and cure all ills. In the first case, very shortly after confirming my appointment as president of Laurentian University in Sudbury, Ontario, in early 2002, the board of governors sent me a copy of a resolution calling on me to undertake a strategic planning process and submit a plan for its approval within the first academic year. Six years later, when I was recruited for the position of president and vice-chancellor of Concordia University in Montreal, the task of developing a strategic plan was explicitly included in the job description and then in my goals for the first year.

Designing a process and setting the stage

To complicate matters for this newbie president, not only were there disparate views about a common direction the university might follow, there was no consensus around what constituted a "strategic plan" in the first place. Instead, my experience at three universities – which included Mount Saint Vincent University in Halifax, where I had also participated in strategic planning as vice-president – revealed a divergence of opinions: at one extreme were those who rejected the idea of planning, preferring to keep on doing what they had always done, and who viewed all administrators with suspicion as "bean-counters," and, at the other end of the spectrum, were those who viewed a strategic plan as a way to cut the "money losers" and concentrate on the most profitable "product lines." What form was the plan to take: were we seeking to define a vision and high-level goals or, instead, an action plan or "to do" list?

While I was kept busy with administrative tasks as well as symbolic and ceremonial functions, it was my primary responsibility to define the vision and strategic directions that would be grounded in the institutional culture, but that would also likely lead to actions and successful, measurable outcomes. Strategic planning is a process of formulating a set of goals in response to a specific environment, taking into account documented strengths and weaknesses as well as a means of developing a set of actions based on institutional priorities. The strategic plan would set direction, point to a clearly articulated destination, and guide the allocation of the resources required to get there.

The initial stumbling block can be resistance to authoritarian leadership, in a culture that has been described as an "intellectual free-for-all," necessary nonetheless for the protection of self-expression (Brown 2006). However, this climate can also bring with it a resistance to planning itself, a kind of allergy in some quarters to the very word and concept. Occasionally, some long-serving member of the university community would appear at a meeting, having found a yellowed, dog-eared copy of some former plan buried deep in a filing cabinet, and draw the conclusion that all former attempts at planning had been futile. To counter push-back from sceptical and sometimes quite vocal colleagues, it was important to begin earning trust in relatively short order.

Consultation is of the essence, especially in a university, which is a community of intellectuals trained in debate and steeped in a tradition of free expression. Designing a consultation process that is open, transparent, helpful yet effective, and not overly drawn out is therefore paramount. I used a variety of consultation tools. I held open or town hall meetings, and I encouraged individuals to drop in to one-on-one "meet the president" sessions. At Laurentian, I organized a series of focus groups on a variety of topics, with the assistance of professional facilitators; at Concordia, I appointed "presidential panels" or ad hoc task forces to discuss, solicit feedback, and report back on the student experience, employee relations, and community engagement. Particularly fruitful at Concordia were the "world cafés," an innovative mechanism for sharing ideas in a relaxed setting similar to that of a café, which brought together a mix of staff, students, and faculty in small groups to brainstorm about issues facing the university. At every step of the consultation process at both universities, members of the university were invited to send comments in by mail or e-mail, and responses were sent to all. The university senate was the forum in which a draft version of the plan was first discussed in a committee-of-the-whole format and then brought back for approval at a subsequent meeting once suggestions had been taken into account. A similar process was carried out with board committees and the whole board. At Laurentian, a joint meeting of the senate and board executive committees proved to be a productive means of reaching consensus.

Throughout this period of consulting the community, during which I was learning while doing, I solicited the views and support of those who stood out as the opinion leaders within the organization, beginning at both Laurentian and Concordia with members of the presidential search committee who I believed could act as knowledgeable insiders, with expertise on the immediate challenges and pitfalls (Smerek 2011). Their initial reservations notwithstanding, faculty and staff reacted well. By giving a wide range of stakeholders – including alumni and community members – an opportunity to be heard, I was able to achieve a sense of buy-in, and the eventual plan was more nuanced and robust. While I am satisfied with both the process and the final outcome, the reaction of volunteer board members was not always positive to such broad-ranging consultation, particularly in the case of those from the private sector who were more accustomed to the chief executive officer (CEO) model and a hierarchical, top-down decision-making process.

However protracted and complex this process may appear, I did manage to complete the task in a timely fashion while generating goodwill and improving morale considerably. I began both presidencies as an outsider. I was totally new to Laurentian and had not lived in Ontario for some years. When I returned to Concordia as president, it was after an absence of 11 years; much had changed, and I was thus in many respects just as "new." It was critical, therefore, to do a lot of listening before putting my own stamp on the place, although I also realized that it would be my job, ultimately, to create the plan that would move each of the institutions forward. This double process has been described as one of "sensemaking" and "sensegiving," which involve finding out about the organization while already giving direction and influencing others, or simultaneously "being" the president and "learning about being the president" (Smerek 2011).

Sensegiving: developing the plan

While making sense of the university, through and throughout the consultation phase, I was already beginning to give shape to a strategic plan. In public and private meetings, I listened to the stories of current and past faculty members, current and former students, and community members and friends of the institution. From them, I got a feel for the deep-rooted values and distinguishing features of each of the universities – in other words, what people were most proud of or attached to and what, therefore, could not change. At the same time, I learned about their aspirations, about the pockets of strength and innovation, and about the road to a brighter future.

The two places were not dissimilar: in both cases, it was clear that academic quality needed to improve, and performance – on a variety of levels – needed to be boosted so that the universities could overcome their reputational hurdles. Academic quality needs to be central to any strategic plan, all the more so at these two schools, and it includes a range of sub-themes revolving around program quality, teaching standards, research activity, and so on. Beyond that, each university had a job to do to improve its flagging reputation. It is not enough to be good: you need to be recognized for your strengths. At Laurentian, just as at Concordia, there were areas of strength that were well-kept secrets.

But there needed to be something more that could galvanize a community. I was looking for a big idea, something that could be used internally and externally to encapsulate the essence of the institution and act as a leitmotif to underpin many of the other strategic initiatives. What I articulated as these defining strategic directions were "quality of life" at Laurentian and "community engagement" at Concordia.

My earliest conversations in Sudbury were very revealing, particularly in light of the negative, albeit polite, reactions I had had to my going there in the first place – the most blunt of which was, "Isn't it ... well, ugly?" Because of the adverse effects of the mining industry on the environment, Sudbury had earned an unfortunate reputation. It was known as the place where the Apollo astronauts went to train because the devastated landscape so closely resembled that of the moon. I learned, first of all, that the astronauts had not gone there because of the moonscape, but because of Sudbury's geological features – namely, the large crater formed by a meteorite. While I detected defensiveness in conversations, an apparent collective sense of inferiority, members of the community were also intensely proud of the fact that they had reclaimed the landscape. Eleven million trees had been planted in 25 years; the city's 300 lakes, once dead, were now teeming with life.

Very soon after arriving, I accepted an invitation to have lunch with retired faculty. I asked a group of about 20 of them how many were original Sudburians. Not a one. Their stories were all quite similar: they had come to work at the university, in its earliest days, for a year or two, and then had stayed a lifetime. Their reason: the quality of life that they and their families could enjoy there.

What began to gel in my mind was, first, that the quality of life in Sudbury, and at Laurentian University, was a factor in attracting and retaining people and, second, that the university, through its faculty and their teaching and research, had contributed to enhanced quality of life in the city and the region.

Sudbury would have been just another mining town without its university, which brought world-class research to bear on environmental remediation (through work on forests and lakes), on the mining industry (for example, in designing methods for mining deeper but more safely), and on health research (with a focus on cancer) – added to which was a new medical school with a mandate to train physicians to work in northern communities.

Thus "quality of life" became one of the four pillars of the strategic plan, *Building on Excellence*, approved in the spring of 2003. Added to the other directions – academic excellence, competing for people and resources, and enhancing image and reputation – that could be found in any number of university plans, this particular focus became a distinctive feature of the university. It enabled me to position new programming and unique research to obtain support. In particular, I secured joint funding from industry, governments, and private donors in support of two major initiatives: a freshwater ecology research centre and a centre for excellence in mining innovation.

Laurentian had faced severe enrolment challenges just before I arrived. Enrolment patterns changed drastically, in part owing to the "double cohort"[1] phenomenon in Ontario that resulted in an enrolment bulge throughout the system. However, Laurentian outpaced its sister institutions, notably as a result of an exercise in rebranding, which was driven in large part by the "quality of life" factor. In print and electronic materials, we highlighted the beautiful lakes and woods, and we showed images of athletic people running, mountain biking, and paddling. The tagline we developed – "Learning, it's in our nature. Apprendre, naturellement." – conveys the interrelation between the healthy environment and the areas of academic focus. It remains in effect to this day.

At Concordia, the theme of "community engagement" was similarly written into the strategic plan as one of three overarching goals, alongside academic quality and an outstanding student experience. At first, it was not clear how such a concept, which was difficult to quantify or measure, could be used as a strategic direction or goal. Since our plan was written and adopted, however, there have been similar strategic plans across the country in which "community engagement" figures prominently.

In speaking with a wide range of Concordia alumni, I was struck by the tremendous impact of our tradition of openness and accessibility. Alumni of both founding institutions (Sir George Williams University and Loyola College), many of whom became successful and prominent in later life, were profoundly grateful for the opportunity they had been given to get an education. Consistently open to a diverse student population, with flexibility in timetabling, Concordia continued to attract both international students and new Canadians in significant numbers, as it had done for decades. In addition, the university had played a part in urban development and had become a catalyst for the revitalization of an otherwise rundown neighbourhood. New, sustainable buildings improved the use of space and promoted the use of public transport – for example, by providing a tunnel to the metro instead of an underground parking garage. Outreach to the community was the hallmark of the university, as reflected in student volunteerism and the action-oriented research of faculty. Taken together, this justified a focus on "community engagement," which, in turn, allowed further resources to be directed to initiatives such as the establishment of a student volunteer centre, and external funding to be sought for the support and promotion of research and teaching in areas such as sustainability and genocide and human rights study, for example.

Once a strategic plan is approved, it takes on a new life, fulfilling multiple functions both internally and externally and guiding subsequent planning at various levels of the organization. In the best of scenarios, each faculty, and each administrative and academic department, will formulate its own strategic and operational plans consistent with the broader institutional goals and objectives. Action plans that make provisions for resources, oversight, and metrics are developed on an annual basis. Reporting is imperative – to the internal community and to external stakeholders such as governments, funders, alumni, and parents. The strategic plan is also a promotional tool that can help the president frame the stories she tells to her constituents for various purposes: to enlist external support, including financial resources; to attract high-quality students, staff, and faculty; and, not insignificantly, to boost the morale of the internal community by making them more conscious of the strengths and successes within their own walls.

After direction has been set in the form of a sound plan, with specific objectives, actions, targets, and indicators of success, what can happen to jeopardize or even derail this policy or, conversely, to ensure its successful implementation and hence the success of the organization? External forces can test strategic directions and bring about unforeseen changes to institutional priorities; yet in some cases, this can be a good thing, and institutions must be nimble enough to take advantage of new possibilities. Internal clashes or simple differences of opinion, too, can surface or resurface to challenge underlying assumptions. The lines between success and failure, between opportunities and hurdles, are sometimes blurred, and it is for this reason that the strategic plan must, in fact, be a living document, adjusted from time to time.

External influences: opportunities, hurdles, and roadblocks

Government policy decisions are formulated to some extent in response to lobbying on the part of universities. Lobbying can occur collectively, through the national body, the Association of Universities and Colleges of Canada (AUCC), or through a provincial one, such as the Council of Ontario Universities or the Conférence des recteurs et des principaux des universités du Québec. It can occur in response to specific groups within the collective, such as the group of research-intensive universities established in Canada as the G10, then the G13, now the U15, or even in response to particularly strong voices within that elite group (Axelrod et al. 2011).[2] But these policy decisions can be at odds with the aspirations and strategic goals of a particular institution. I have some examples.

Shortly after I took office as president of Laurentian, the Liberal Government of Dalton McGuinty was elected in Ontario. Wanting to be seen as the Education Premier, Mr. McGuinty commissioned an extensive review of higher education by Bob Rae, who later became the interim leader of the federal Liberal Party. Following the review, during which universities, students, and the general public were consulted, the government came up with its so-called Reaching Higher Plan, which aimed to inject $6.2 billion into higher education. The executive heads of Ontario universities would have liked nothing better than to have the money allocated across the system according to some reasonable formula, for us to use as we saw fit. Things are never so simple, however, and instead we were burdened with complicated funding envelopes and accountability agreements.

Targeted funding was made available to achieve what government saw as priorities. There were provisions, for example, for assisting disadvantaged groups of students such as francophones, Aboriginal peoples, or students who were the first in their families to attend post-secondary institutions. Laurentian University was well served as it had a "bilingual and tricultural" mandate, along with a large number of students who attended part-time and who were indeed the first in their families to go to university. On the other hand, a government decision to fund graduate student expansion did not help us, despite the priority we accorded in the strategic plan to the growth of graduate programs. Ironically, at a time when Laurentian was implementing its first doctoral programs in areas of particular strength and relevance to the region – six in the time I was president – along with a number of master's programs, we were penalized by the criteria established and were allocated funding for only a very small number of graduate students based, unfairly in our view, on the fact that we had not previously had any graduate programs.

A 2010 report issued by the Higher Education Quality Council of Ontario (HEQCO), established in 2005 as an arm's-length agency of the government of Ontario, is a further example of how public policy can intervene to alter the mission and planned course of an individual institution. A HEQCO paper (Weingarten and Deller 2010) advocated greater differentiation of Ontario universities, sparking a debate in Ontario and beyond about the value of assigning specific missions to universities and, in particular, of differentiating between undergraduate, teaching universities and larger, research universities. (I will return to the issue of the teaching and research functions below.)

At a time when we can no longer afford to be all things to all people, universities are acting responsibly by defining what they are good at and in which areas they would like to grow. Their stated priorities, however, may be trumped by public policy. In the government of Canada's 2007 report, *Mobilizing Science and Technology to Canada's Advantage*, for example, then minister of industry Maxime Bernier writes, "Let's create a new culture of scientific and technological achievement in our country, and bring new ideas and innovations to the world" (Industry Canada 2007, 4). The national science and technology agenda lists four research priorities: environmental science and technologies, natural resources and energy, health and related life sciences and technologies, and information and communications technologies. Other areas of science and technology and, most notably, the social sciences and humanities, are excluded from a national research agenda. When questioned in a recent meeting with AUCC representatives, officials at the Ministry of State for Science and Technology said that of course "science" was to be taken in its broadest sense to include the social sciences. Yet, while the social sciences and humanities are funded through a federal granting council, their place in the minds of our elected and non-elected officials is precarious. In the absence of a national ministry of education and corresponding national post-secondary education policy (Axelrod et al. 2011), there is no national strategy for safeguarding or indeed strengthening one of the historic foundations of the university, the liberal arts (Axelrod 2002).

Internationalization is discussed by other authors in this anthology, but I will touch on it briefly as it has been high on my agenda since my time serving as a provost and through two presidencies. I refer to internationalization on all fronts: recruiting students and ensuring that they are successful in the Canadian academic system; sending Canadian students abroad for study, internships, and volunteer placements; and forging international partnerships for development and research. Even when these efforts were well integrated into the policy directions of specific universities, they were for some years stymied by decisions made by governments or bureaucracies. Just obtaining a visa, for example, was a major hindrance to student recruitment, as it was to inviting foreign academics for short or longer-term visits.

This has changed, for two different kinds of reasons. Some provinces, as well as the federal government since the report on the economic impact of international education in Canada (Roslyn Kunin & Associates 2009) was released by then minister of international trade Stockwell Day, have acknowledged the benefits to the economy of having large numbers of foreign students. Consequently, there has been an interest in recruiting foreign students and a willingness to provide funding to assist universities in marketing Canadian education overseas. At the same time, there has been an openness to welcoming foreign students as potential new Canadians to fill anticipated gaps in the labour market. This is the case in Quebec, which has signified its interest in fast-tracking international students wishing to become citizens (along with a parallel interest in ensuring that they have good French-language skills). On a trade and education mission to India in February 2010 in which I took part, then premier Jean Charest openly recruited potential citizens for Quebec. Governments, both federal and some provincial, are now providing financial incentives to Canadian students for study-abroad programs. But I would say that these government initiatives have followed rather than preceded the policy decisions in the more forward-looking educational institutions.

Universities were hard hit by the economic downturn of 2008, which had serious implications for the best-laid institutional plans. Endowments, in particular, with a significant percentage of funds invested in the stock market, were affected. While this had less of an impact in Canada than in the US, where colleges and universities are more likely to use endowment income to fund operations, it did impede our ability to fund financial aid programs for students, something that is typically done by paying out 4 to 5 percent in endowment interest. This occurred at precisely the time we had identified the objective of enhancing the student experience through more adequate financial support. In a province where operational funding is directly tied to student enrolment, we could not afford to lose students who might be in financial need, and therefore we needed to take money from other sources to be able to continue paying out the student awards. Through sound financial management, as well as a slight increase in enrolment, we were able to meet this objective without compromising other objectives, such as faculty hiring, which was tied to the other overall goal of enhancing academic quality. But there had been a significant risk of derailing our plans.

Another external force that can affect the course of the university is community pressure, particularly in a smaller city such as Sudbury, where there is just one university to serve the city and surrounding area. When I arrived, the community was enjoying the success of the recently announced Northern Ontario School of Medicine, the first new medical school in Canada in over 30 years. The community had lobbied for the establishment of a medical school in the North ever since the last new medical school in Ontario had opened in Hamilton, at McMaster University. The combined efforts of community groups, the municipality, and the university had resulted in a promise from the government that there would be a new school in Sudbury, housed at Laurentian. This changed, following some pressure from the city of Thunder Bay, to a joint Laurentian-Lakehead school of medicine, with teaching sites across the North. The school opened with great fanfare in 2005 and would graduate its first MD students in the spring of 2009.

With the wind in their sails, community groups in Sudbury looked to other projects they might advance, the most significant of which were a law school and a school of architecture. However, neither law nor architecture figured anywhere in Laurentian University's strategic plan, which did envisage the implementation of the medical school, six PhD programs, a mining research centre, and other projects. By the spring of 2008, the architecture school and law school had in fact found their way into the next strategic plan I drafted for Laurentian in the form of a commitment to explore their feasibility.[3] The School of Architecture has in fact come to fruition under the leadership of my successor, with government funding, and it shows how an idea from left field can become an opportunity.

Internal controversy

Striking the right balance between teaching and research has been a particular challenge over the past decades, particularly in those institutions that have traditionally characterized themselves as primarily undergraduate teaching institutions. The debate has been both internal to specific institutions and generalized across the country – and indeed in other parts of the world. While teaching is fundamental to what we do, research imparts a certain status. Research also brings resources: money from government-sponsored granting councils, from corporations, and from private donors. Despite the long-standing argument in favour of increased indirect costs of research to make research activities less of a drain on each university's individual resources, there is a perception, at least, that research brings wealth and prosperity to research-intensive institutions. There is no doubt that research intensity is a factor in the recruitment of a new brand of faculty: well before would-be professors complete their doctoral, and post-doctoral, studies, they are productive researchers, in the sciences as well as the social sciences and humanities. When they are hired into junior positions, they come with relatively well-developed research programs. This has consequences for the hiring institutions: to be competitive, they need to foster a climate in which research is valued and supported and in which graduate programs exist so that the new faculty can teach courses that interest them and have access to students who will participate in their research.

The consequence of this climate is that there has been a move, enshrined in strategic plans – strategic research plans required to qualify for the Canada Research Chairs program and the strategic plans of individual universities – to enhance the research and graduate studies missions of institutions that were previously more concerned with undergraduate teaching.

This was my experience in Laurentian and Concordia, both previously known for their "accessibility," for famously giving students a "second chance," but then ensuring their unqualified success through personalized attention and excellent teaching. In the wider university community in Canada, the splitting off of the so-called G13 (U15) universities, and the public debate around differentiation, have contributed to the widely held view that there should be a two-tiered approach to higher education – a separation of research-intensive universities from mainly teaching undergraduate ones. Internally as well, the balance between teaching and research has been a sensitive topic. There has been a critique of the newer aspirations of the university in general, of the ambitions of younger faculty, and in a context of reduced teaching loads that accompany proven research productivity, a perception that the teaching function has been devalued. It has been important, therefore, to emphasize a continued student-centred focus and to reward good teaching through a variety of approaches and mechanisms.

Another internal force is the opposition to a range of revenue-generation efforts, often perceived to fall into the broad category of neo-liberalism. Universities are criticized of late for becoming increasingly "corporatized" or "privatized," with the result that a market-driven approach to promotional activities and student recruitment may be frowned upon. This is sometimes accompanied by opposition to some aspects of internationalization: given differential fees for international students, internationalization can be perceived as a money grab as well as an exploitation of less privileged students from overseas.

Student protests against rising tuition fees, which are part of the land-scape across Canada and indeed many parts of the world, have become particularly virulent in Quebec since spring 2012. The tuition debate was accompanied by opposition to many types of spending – even on faculty research, for example – as well as to various forms of fundraising. Boards, despite their interest in fundraising and attention to balanced budgets, are sometimes sympathetic to the fee-increase protests, as are faculty members, who nonetheless demand salary increases on par with colleagues elsewhere in Canada and the US. At a time when governments are contributing less, not more, and when costs are rising at a rate that exceeds that of inflation and that of tuition increases, presidents face a complex set of problems: how can they maintain academic standards, keep faculty salaries competitive, raise funds, keep the university afloat financially, meet the moral expectations of the internal community, and serve as public intellectuals in the broader community – all the while remaining true to the vision, mission, values, and goals articulated in their strategic plans?

GLASS CEILING OR FEMALE ADVANTAGE?

In recent years, various reports have highlighted the under-representation of women in arenas such as business, politics, and academia, identifying the characteristics of female leaders and pointing out the extent to which women have the potential to make a positive contribution to their specific fields and society in general.

According to a report issued by the Conference Board of Canada, *Women on Boards: Not Just the Right Thing ... But the "Bright" Thing*, women directors bring perspectives that balance the views of their male col-leagues, that contribute to improved decision-making, and that lead to greater attention to ethics and corporate social responsibility (Brown, Brown, and Anastasopoulos 2002). Companies that have women on their boards, research shows, outperform those that do not. A decade has elapsed since the report was published, however, and boardroom doors are scarcely more open to women than they once were. Academia is no different. Women are seen as an "untapped resource," as under-represented as trustees and directors on governing boards as they are in the upper echelons of administration and policy-making, a situation that becomes increasingly inappropriate with the proportion of women students now outweighing the proportion of men (Glazer-Raymo 2008).

A series titled Groundbreakers, first issued in 2009 by the firm Ernst & Young, has emphasized the economic advantages of promoting gender equality and increasing the participation of women in business. Women executives and managers bring a distinctive leadership style that works well in businesses where communication and teamwork are called for, particularly in firms pursuing innovation; an ability to attract and de-velop female managerial talent may therefore be a source of competitive advantage (Dezső and Ross 2011).

It is said that women are team-oriented and consultative. They take a collaborative approach to leadership and try to build consensus. Women are thought to be better than men at empowering teams and staff; they are more willing to see all sides of a situation and to solicit other people's opinions. Once they have done so, women leaders are able to be more persuasive than their male counterparts, according to a study done by a Princeton-based consulting firm (Caliper Corporation 2005).

With so few women heading up universities, there have been no significant or conclusive studies about the particular characteristics of female university leaders. It has been argued that there are as many dif-ferences among women university leaders as there are between women and men (Marsden 2004). There is some consensus, however, particularly with respect to the consultative approach, which can have both pluses and minuses. It is a drawback in that it takes time and can slow down decision-making, but it is also more welcome in an academic setting. Women encourage openness and are more accessible. They are considered more tolerant of differences and hence more skilled at managing diversity. Women leaders can also be more sensitive to the emotions and moods of those on their team and, what is perhaps more important, empathetic to today's students, who tend to face increasing pressures and personal challenges.

It is critical to listen to various constituencies and to respect the spirit of debate that must prevail in a university, while at the same time strik-ing a balance between process and action. It is important, as well, to form alliances, build trust, and establish legitimacy. While these and the previous observations about women in the corporate world have yet to be validated through more thorough research with a larger sampling of women leaders, they are consistent with my own approach to leadership and match the style evoked by other women presidents (Bornstein 2003; Wolverton, Bower, and Hyle 2009; Woodsworth 2009).

LOCATION, LOCATION …

All universities are in competition with one another. There are big universities and small ones, ones located in large urban centres and others in small towns or remote regions. Both Mount Saint Vincent and Laurentian have had to deal with being "small" in a "smaller" city or at least less central location, competing for students, faculty, and resources with larger or better-known institutions. Concordia is among the largest universities in the country in terms of its student body and number of employees. Its location in one of Canada's biggest and most dynamic cities makes it a natural draw for both students and staff. On the other hand, as a more recent, less traditional institution, accessible to a diverse student population, it has been in the shadow of its well-established, world-renowned, and well-endowed sister university, and in competition with a number of other post-secondary institutions, in Montreal. Not unlike the two other universities mentioned, its challenge has been to maximize and showcase its competitive features and build on its strengths through effective planning and leadership.

In a small community, being the president of the only university, albeit in the company of two community college presidents, was a privilege and a unique opportunity. The president was in demand at almost all social, cultural, and political events, expected to be an ambassador for the university, but also an active participant in the life of the community. It was a challenging position because your time and private life were never your own. Still, if you performed this role with dedication, commitment, and enthusiasm, it was easy to earn the loyalty of your constituents. In a large community like Montreal, you are one university president among several others, not to mention the heads of other types of schools and cultural institutions, all of whom are vying for a voice, influence, and resources. Consequently, you have a harder time making inroads into the community or feeling that you are making an impact. It was helpful to have cut my teeth in Sudbury because much of my experience could be applied even in a much larger city: for example, I could make myself available to serve on community organizations on both sides of the linguistic divide, like the United Way or Chambre de Commerce, speak to groups like the Canadian Club, or reach out to schoolchildren on campus or in their own schools. In contrast, the time constraints and political and economic pressures in a big city are more acute, making it more difficult to manage your activities, to be both ubiquitous and generous, while tending effectively to core duties on and off campus.

CLASHES OF CULTURE: BOARD RELATIONS

Much has been written about the role of boards generally and the need for greater responsibility and accountability in a post-Enron, post–Sarbanes-Oxley era (Hansell 2003). Sophisticated training in corporate governance is being offered to current and prospective directors.[4] Members of both corporate and not-for-profit boards are taking their roles more seriously, and rightly so.

Among board responsibilities, the most important are hiring (and firing) the CEO, providing financial oversight, and offering strategic guidance. The difficulty arises when board members overstep the bounds and begin delving into operational matters. Hence the long-standing rule of thumb: "Nose in, fingers out," which may well be easier said than done. Clashes arise in an academic setting when external board members used to a top-down management style feel frustrated by the apparently endless consultative processes related to strategic planning or search committees, for example. Board members may also become impatient with the way in which fiscal challenges are dealt with and will want to advocate dealing with scarce resources through aggressive business-style practices and cuts to less profitable activities. There may be ambiguity around the notion of accountability: accountable to whom? Unlike the corporate world, in which a board of directors is accountable to the shareholders, who are primarily interested in profitability, university boards are accountable to multiple stakeholders – faculty, students, and the public at large – who have an interest in maintaining quality of education and upholding a range of seemingly vague academic and ethical values. In this context, it is critical to allow management – that is, the president and his or her executive team – to actually run the university, while steadfastly asking probing questions and providing responsible oversight and valuable guidance.

Not surprisingly, board education is very helpful and should be as systematically provided in the academic world as it is in the corporate one. Academic boards should have rigorous orientation sessions, ongoing training opportunities, and regular evaluation procedures for its members. This process works best when collaboratively designed and implemented by both the board and management. Information regarding good governance is available and should be disseminated freely. As an example, the University of Alberta published a series in its magazine, *Folio*, on the complex issue of university governance: the board of governors, it points out, has senior oversight of the institution in that it is concerned with "the long-range planning and the business affairs of the institution" while remaining "non-operational" (Brown 2010, n.p.).

In Canada, the National Association of University Board Chairs and Secretaries holds an annual conference that provides information sessions and technical support to professional staff assisting boards and to board chairs themselves, with considerable input from university presidents as well. The Association of Governing Boards, a US-based organization, publishes a useful magazine and also holds institutes for board chairs and presidents. While president of Laurentian, I attended a seminar in the US with a newly appointed board chair. Designed for CEOs and chairs of a range of not-for-profit organizations by the American Society of Association Executives' Center for Association Leadership, the sessions were extremely informative and gave us invaluable preparation for renewing the university's strategic plan collaboratively and effectively. Training of this kind would be a welcome addition in Canada. If both parties were open to this kind of opportunity for joint learning, board-president relations would be greatly enhanced.

THE CHANGING NATURE OF THE PRESIDENCY

I served as Laurentian's president for six years. The review of my first term had been decisively positive, and I had begun a second term when approached about taking on a new presidency at Concordia University, where I had spent the first 17 years of my career as a faculty member and where I had also occupied various administrative posts. It is public knowledge that I stepped down from the presidency at Concordia halfway through a first term. There is not a lot I am able to say about it, except that this turn of events was neither expected nor pleasant. I loved being a president and had thrown myself into the role with passion, integrity, and deep commitment to each institution I served. As one magazine article pointed out, I was in "good company," among a wave of about a dozen Canadian university presidents who had exited prematurely in the previous five years (Patriquin 2011).

While that remains cold comfort, I do feel gratified, nevertheless, that *Reaching Up, Reaching Out: A Strategic Framework for Concordia University* is still on the university website.[5] Unanimously approved by the senate and the board of governors in the spring of 2009, it has resulted in a number of new initiatives and continues to drive the planning and operations of the university. Since my departure, for example, the university has adopted an academic plan, which professes to be "guided by the sense of mission, vision, and values articulated in *Reaching Up, Reaching Out*, our strategic framework."[6] It has been said that changes in the presidential ranks have little bearing on the development of an institution (Birnbaum 1989). Individuals do come and go, but – despite the push and pull of outside influences and internal differences of opinion – good policy, perhaps, does endure.

A president's role is to provide vision, craft a plan, and establish direction for the university – all of which should be not only consistent with its past tradition and mission, but also innovative enough to allow the institution to distinguish itself in a crowded, competitive marketplace. The president is both the face of the university and the interface between the external community and the academy as well as between the board and the professoriate. Like the translator, the president is a go-between, communicating between cultures and across borders, conveying the sense of the academic enterprise to external stakeholders and board members, and interpreting the business-related concerns and preoccupations of a responsible board to the internal community.

In the current context of political turmoil and economic challenges, this is no easy task. Following the leadership crisis at the University of Virginia in the spring of 2012,[7] Moody's Investors Service forecast increased conflict between governance and leadership, attributing these clashes to the need for new sources of revenue and operating efficiencies. According to Moody's, the situation would only get worse in the coming years "as the sector's ability to grow revenues dwindles, and its emphasis shifts to new operating efficiencies and cost containment" (Moody's Investors Service 2012). The University of Virginia debacle has prompted others to observe that governing boards will demand that "their presidents perform more like corporate chief executives, much to the chagrin of academics who say treating colleges as businesses doesn't fit the mission of higher education" (Sampson 2012). Another US-based report points out that the average presidential tenure dropped from 8.5 years in 2006 to seven years in 2011 and that more college and university presidents are being hired from outside academia, while fewer academics are aspiring to the presidential suite (Zagier 2012).

While these events and the contexts that spawned them occurred south of the border, the situation in Canada is not dissimilar, and it is clear that the nature of presidential leadership is changing here too.[8] With extremely difficult waters to navigate, it is inevitable that there will be casualties. The best that can be hoped for is that sound policy will guide good practice and continued movement toward the achievement of common academic goals.

NOTES

1. The government of Ontario decided to eliminate the fifth year of secondary school, or Grade 13, effective 2003. That year, Grade 12 and Grade 13 graduates were eligible to enter university at the same time, creating a spike in enrolment referred to as the "double cohort" for which universities had to make accommodation.
2. Also the subject of one of the chapters in this book: "Lineation and Lobbying: Policy Networks and Higher Education Policy in Ontario" by Glen A. Jones.
3. From the second strategic plan *Building on Success: A Strategic Plan for Laurentian University 2008–2011*: "Investigate the feasibility of responding to the community's interest in a school of architecture and/or law school; explore the possibility of implementing additional health programs such as a school of pharmacy." As Laurentian has recently adopted a new strategic plan, the 2008 version is no longer available on the university site.
4. For example, the Directors Education Program offered by the Institute for Corporate Directors in collaboration with Canadian business schools such as the Rotman School of Management at the University of Toronto.
5. At the time of writing, at least, at http://www.concordia.ca/content/dam/concordia/docs/strategic-framework-eng.pdf.

6. On Concordia University's academic planning website at http://www. concordia.ca/about/strategic-framework/academic-plan.html.
7. President Teresa Sullivan was forced to resign because her board thought she wasn't doing enough to address funding challenges; she was reinstated after faculty and students protested.
8. These matters are beginning to attract attention in Canada. Former University of Victoria president David Turpin has been studying the unexpected departures of presidents in Canada as well as the changing nature of the presidency; the preliminary results of his Canadian University Presidents Project were presented to AUCC in April 2012. Turpin also makes reference to a research project on Canadian university governance, being carried out under the leadership of Glen Jones, at http://web.uvic.ca/president/ speeches/pdfs/Turpin_CUPP_AUCC_2012-04-23.pdf.

REFERENCES

Axelrod, P. 2002. *Values in Conflict: The University, the Marketplace, and the Trials of Liberal Education*. Montreal and Kingston: McGill-Queen's University Press.

Axelrod, P., T. Shanahan, R.D. Trilokekar, and R. Wellen. 2011. "People, Processes, and Policy-Making in Canadian Post-Secondary Education, 1990–2000." *Higher Education Policy* 24 (2):143–166.

Birnbaum, R. 1989. "Presidential Succession and Institutional Functioning in Higher Education." *The Journal of Higher Education* 60 (2):123–135.

Bornstein, R. 2003. *Legitimacy in the Academic Presidency: From Entrance to Exit*. ACE/Praeger Series on Higher Education. Westport, CT: Praeger Publishers.

Brown, D.A.H., D.L. Brown, and V. Anastasopoulos. 2002. *Women on Boards: Not Just the Right Thing ... But the "Bright" Thing*. Conference Board of Canada. At http://www.conferenceboard.ca/temp/3814c437-fd91-4905-afc9-54807e 98e4cc/341-02rpt.pdf (accessed 23 August 2013).

Brown, D.G., ed. 2006. *University Presidents as Moral Leaders*. ACE/Praeger Series on Higher Education. Westport, CT: Praeger Publishers.

Brown, M. 2010. "University 101: Board of Governors: 'Nose in, Fingers out.'" *Folio* 49 (3). At http://www.folio.ualberta.ca/article.cfm?v=103346&i=100742&a=6 (accessed July 2012).

Bryman, A. 2007. "Effective Leadership in Higher Education: A Literature Review." *Studies in Higher Education* 32 (6):693–710.

Caliper Corporation. 2005. *The Qualities That Distinguish Women Leaders*. At http:// www.caliper.com.cn/en/brochures/WomenLeaderWhitePaper.pdf (accessed July 2012).

Cutright, M. 2007. "University Presidents as Moral Leaders." (Review of Brown 2006.) *The Review of Higher Education* 30 (2):201–202.

Dezső, C.L., and D.G. Ross. 2011. "Does Female Representation in Top Management Improve Firm Performance? A Panel Data Investigation." Robert H. Smith School Research Paper No. RHS 06-104. At http://ssrn.com/abstract=1088182 (accessed July 2012).

Fisher, J.L. 1984. *Power of the Presidency*. New York: American Council on Higher Education / Macmillan.

Glazer-Raymo, J. 2008. "Women Trustees: An Untapped Resource." *Trusteeship Magazine* 16 (6):21–24.

Hansell, C. 2003. *What Directors Need to Know: Corporate Governance*. Toronto: Carswell.

Industry Canada. 2007. *Mobilizing Science and Technology to Canada's Advantage.* At http://www.ic.gc.ca/eic/site/ic1.nsf/vwapj/SandTstrategy.pdf/$file/SandTstrategy.pdf (accessed February 2012).

Madsen, S.R. 2007. "Learning to Lead in Higher Education: Insights into the Family Backgrounds of Women University Presidents." *Journal of Women in Educational Leadership* 5 (3):183–200.

—. 2008. *On Becoming a Woman Leader: Learning from the Experiences of University Presidents*. San Francisco: Jossey-Bass.

Marsden, L. 2004. "Canada's Women University Presidents: Social Change in Canada." The Canada House Lecture, Canadian High Commission, London.

Moody's Investors Service. 2012. "Virginia Dispute Highlights Governance Stress and Economic Threats Facing US Higher Education." At http://chronicle.com/blogs/ticker/files/2012/07/UVA.pdf (accessed July 2012).

Patriquin, M. 2011. "The Very Short Goodbye." *Maclean's on campus*, 31 December. At http://oncampus.macleans.ca/education/2011/01/31/the-very-short-goodbye (accessed 21 June 2013).

Paul, R. 2011. *Leadership Under Fire: The Challenging Role of the Canadian University President*. Montreal and Kingston: McGill-Queen's University Press.

Roslyn Kunin and Associates. 2009. *Economic Impact of International Education in Canada*. Final Report. Prepared for Foreign Affairs and International Trade Canada. At http://www.international.gc.ca/education/assets/pdfs/RKA_Int Ed_Report_eng.pdf (accessed February 2012).

Sampson, Z.C. 2012. "College Boards Turn to Business-Style Approaches." *Detroit News*, 27 June. At http://www.detroitnews.com/article/20120627/SCHOOLS/206270376#ixzz20tfA16hL (accessed July 2012).

Shaw, K.A. 2002. "Creating Change: Suggestions for the New President." In *Field Guide to Academic Leadership*, ed. R.M. Diamond, 389–400. San Francisco: Jossey-Bass.

Smerek, R. 2011. "Sensemaking and Sensegiving: An Exploratory Study of the Simultaneous 'Being and Learning' of New College and University Presidents." *Journal of Leadership & Organizational Studies* 18 (1):80–94.

Thrift, N. 2011. "The Perils of Presidency." *The Chronicle of Higher Education* (blog), 30 November. At http://chronicle.com/blogs/worldwise/the-perils-of-presidency/28922 (accessed 2 July 2013).

Weingarten, H.P., and F. Deller. 2010. "The Benefits of Greater Differentiation of Ontario's University Sector." Higher Education Quality Council of Ontario. At http://www.heqco.ca/siteCollectionDocuments/DifferentiationENG.pdf (accessed 22 June 2013).

Wolverton, M., B.L. Bower, and A.E. Hyle. 2009. *Women at the Top: What Women University and College Presidents Say about Effective Leadership*. Sterling, VA: Stylus.

Woodsworth, J. 2009. "Strategic Leadership: Spearheading Social Change and Environmental Sustainability." Keynote presentation at the 4th World Women University Presidents Forum, Nanjing, China, September.

Zagier, A.S. 2012. "Big Rewards, Less Job Security for College Leaders." *Boston Globe*, 5 July. At http://articles.boston.com/2012-07-05/news/32553569_1_job-of-college-president-independent-colleges-richard-ekman (accessed July 2012).

III

POLICY ISSUES: ACCESS, QUALITY, AND AFFORDABILITY

CHAPTER 7

HIGHER EDUCATION AND STUDENT FINANCIAL SUPPORT IN ENGLAND: ALL CHANGE OR NO CHANGE?

Claire Callender

INTRODUCTION

The expansion and growing importance of higher education in England since the 1980s have prompted numerous reforms aimed at reshaping and restructuring the sector and its funding, reflecting the changing ideological, economic, and social functions of higher education. The reforms introduced in 2012–13 in England are by far the most radical and those concerning higher education funding and student finances the most far-reaching. They seek to make higher education financially sustainable, improve the student experience, and increase social mobility. This chapter aims to "unpack" the drivers for these reforms, locating them in a broader historical and policy context. It describes the 2012–13 higher education changes and analyzes their initial and potential impact while questioning the policy objectives and whether the policy goals are achievable.

It is argued that the reforms herald a fundamental change in the role of the state in higher education provision and in the balance of public and private contributions toward its costs. In turn, they reflect changes in beliefs about higher education, its purpose and role in society, and who should have access to it and pay for it. The reforms are both driven and shaped by ideological, political, and economic factors, which together are leading to deleterious policy change. The new policies are untested. They

Making Policy in Turbulent Times: Challenges and Prospects for Higher Education, ed. P. Axelrod, R.D. Trilokekar, T. Shanahan, and R. Wellen. Kingston: School of Policy Studies, Queen's University.

represent a big experiment with unknown consequences and unforeseen unintended consequences. It is unclear, therefore, whether the reforms are achievable and will meet their stated aims or whether they will stand the test of time. We will not know for sure for several years to come. However, they are having a destabilizing effect on the higher education sector in the short term and are likely to polarize higher education in the longer term, exacerbating existing social divisions and inequalities within and across the sector.

The chapter starts by examining the contradictory roles and purpose of universities and how these are reflected in the changing nature of undergraduate student finances in England. This, alongside the legacy of earlier policies, is key to understanding the proposed 2012–13 reforms. Next, the chapter explores the lead-up to the 2012–13 reforms and the recommendations of the 2010 Independent Review of Higher Education Funding and Student Finance – chaired by Lord Browne of Madingley – which informed the coalition government's proposals. Then it will discuss the government's response to Browne, encapsulated in its November 2010 announcement and its subsequent 2011 white paper, *Higher Education: Students at the Heart of the System*. Finally, the changes will be critiqued and assessed against the stated aims of the white paper. The discussion throughout focuses on England[1] and primarily on full-time undergraduates domiciled in the United Kingdom.[2]

THE CONTEXT FOR THE REFORMS OF FINANCIAL SUPPORT

Student funding and financial support policies reflect the ideological, economic, and social functions of higher education. These policies, therefore, encapsulate several different models for the purpose of higher education, the importance of which change over time. The first model encapsulates the notion of increasing international competitiveness: Britain can compete in a globalized knowledge economy only if its workforce has high-level skills and if it can produce certain types of knowledge, and universities are central to both providing such skills and generating this knowledge. The second model emphasizes the significance of human capital[3] and the economic returns of higher education from individual investment. The third model focuses on social mobility and individual advancement in a social hierarchy. Here higher education is seen as an engine for greater equality and, in turn, social justice. Finally, there is a social development model of higher education, which views higher education as being of value to society as a whole, beyond those who receive it, and in terms of national culture or democratic decision-making and citizenship.

These models incorporate Castells' (2001) four major functions of universities. First, universities play a key role as ideological apparatuses, expressing the ideological struggles present in all societies. Second, they are mechanisms for selecting and socializing elites and for setting off these elites from the rest of society. Third, universities generate and apply knowledge. Finally, universities train the labour force, especially those members requiring high-level skills. These functions change over time, depending on a given society's prevailing history, culture, ideology, or politics. In addition, they are not always congruent; hence, Castells refers to universities as "dynamic systems of contradictory functions." Moreover, he observes that

> the critical element in the structure and dynamics of university systems is their ability to combine and make compatible seemingly contradictory functions. The fact that because universities are social systems and histor-ically produced institutions, all their functions take place simultaneously within the same structure, although with different emphases is probably the most complex analytical element to convey to policymakers. (2001, 211)

Castells goes on to suggest that universities are also subject to more implicit pressures from the host society and that this combination – of implicit and explicit pressures and of local and universal functions – results in a "complex and contradictory reality" (2001, 211). This chapter will show how these contradictions and implicit and external pressures have played out in the higher education student funding system and are reflected in the nature of student funding policies that have been introduced in the past two decades, including the most recent reforms.

To understand the precise nature of the 2012–13 student funding re-forms, it is imperative to locate them within a historical context, particu-larly earlier changes to student finances. Three major shifts in student funding policies in England can be identified with the introduction of student loans, tuition fees paid up front, and variable tuition fees repaid through student loans. First, government-funded student loans were established for all students to help pay for their living costs follow-ing the 1988 white paper, *Top-Up Loans for Students* (DES 1988), and the subsequent 1990 *Education (Student Loans) Act*. This was a new form of student financial assistance in Britain: its mortgage-style, income-related loan repayments were to be paid on graduation, with the loans available at a zero real rate of interest. All students, irrespective of their families' income, were eligible for these new loans. In parallel, the cash value of existing means-tested maintenance grants for low-income students, and of the assumed parental contribution, was frozen.

The 1988 white paper outlined the following six objectives of the government's student loans scheme: to share the cost of supporting a student more equitably among students, their parents, and the taxpayer; to increase the amount of money students received (because of the falling real value of grants); to decrease the parental contribution to students' living costs; to reduce public expenditure; to reduce student dependence on the social security benefits system; and to increase students' economic awareness and self-reliance. These objectives were a response to the Conservative Government's desire for a centralized, government-driven higher education expansion, as set out in its 1987 white paper, *Higher Education: Meeting the Challenge*, and an aspiration to widen higher education participation. These dual aims reflected an unresolved battle within government.

> The Department of Education and Science (DES) wants access and expansion; in contrast, it is increasingly clear that the Treasury is not concerned with either aim, but almost exclusively with meeting the nation's need for skilled personnel through central control of higher education and manpower planning. The DES and Treasury aims are wholly incompatible ... and a scheme (the result of Treasury pressure) which does virtually nothing for access and expansion. (Barr 1989, 141)

Others (Winn and Stevenson 1997) claim that the prime purpose of these reforms was to increase students' economic awareness by altering their attitudes toward their financial responsibilities. The government argued that student loans would rid students of their dependency on the state (and their parents), make them more aware of the costs of their education, and promote a sense of self-reliance and responsibility. In other words, they were part of a larger Thatcherite agenda to tackle "the dependency culture" and its efforts to "roll back the welfare state." Some commentators (Farrell and Tapper 1992) suggest that this desire to influence student culture through student loans was an attempt to use the student maintenance system as a mechanism for reshaping the character of higher education itself, to make it more accountable to government, in line with the overall aim of its 1987 white paper.

The second shift in student financial support was the introduction of a flat–rate, means-tested tuition fee of £1,000 paid up front by students and/or their families, following the publication of the Dearing Report (NCIHE 1997) and the Labour Government's 1998 *Teaching and Higher Education Act*. At the same time, the government abolished means-tested grants for low-income students. Instead, support for living costs was provided exclusively by new, restructured, "income-contingent" student loans, to be repaid on graduation. This reform signalled that students as well as taxpayers should contribute toward the costs of higher education, and for those from higher-income families, higher education was no longer free at the point of access.

The context for these reforms was first one of "a real sense of crisis in UK higher education" (Watson and Amoah 2007, 7) and, above all, the strains of underfunding. There had been up to this time a massively underfunded and unmanaged expansion of higher education. Student numbers had risen from 777,800 students in 1979 to 1,659,400 in 1996, while the unit of funding per student had fallen by just over 40 per cent between 1976 and 1996 (NCIHE 1997). And with this expansion, the costs to the state of providing maintenance grants had soared from £503 million in 1987 to £1.2 billion in 1993, then down to £932 million in 1997 because of the Conservatives' cuts in the value of grants.

The second significant context was the newly elected Labour Government. Labour positioned both economic prosperity and social inclusion as key goals of their higher education policies through expanding and widening participation, as symbolized by their goal of increasing higher education participation to 50 percent by 2010. Labour's economic arguments for widening access were integrated with liberal ideas of the functions of higher education, and they were seen as a means of overcoming social exclusion (Naidoo and Callender 2000). This, along with its stress on social cohesion and justice, distinguished Labour's vision from that of past governments, which had emphasized economic development and individual competitiveness. The minister responsible for these student funding changes, David Blunkett, when introducing the 1998 *Teaching and Higher Education Act*, proclaimed,

> The Act puts in place new funding arrangements for higher education designed to address the funding crisis we inherited. It modernizes student support in higher education in a way that is fair to individual students and their families. Savings from the new arrangements will be used to improve quality, standards and opportunities for all in further and higher education. (DfEE 1998)

Central to these "savings" was the principle underlying the Dearing Report's recommendations,[4] that those who benefit from higher education should share the cost. The social and economic returns of higher education were, therefore, employed as a justification for the introduction of the fees, and the income raised from fees would help fund wider participation.

The final shift in student funding was heralded by the 2004 *Higher Education Act*, which came into force in 2006. It launched variable tuition fees, capped by the government at £3,000.[5] These tuition fees were to be paid by graduates through income-contingent student loans. These changes meant that all students, even the poorest, had to pay tuition fees and that all students were automatically eligible for loans to cover all their fees. The interest paid on the student loans for tuition, and on the maintenance loans for living costs that predated the 2004 act, was equal to inflation, so it was in effect a zero real interest rate. At the same time, a package of financial support was introduced for low-income students. This included the reintroduction of government-funded maintenance grants that Labour had abolished in 1998 and the establishment of bursaries paid in cash and funded by universities from their additional tuition fee income. Consequently, low-income students qualified for grants, loans, and bursaries toward their living costs, while their more affluent students were eligible just for loans.

These 2006 changes aimed to promote a more marketized system of higher education through variable tuition fees on the one hand and bursaries and scholarships on the other. Thus, they abandoned the general principle that all students, irrespective of where and what they studied, should be treated the same, pay the same tuition fees, and, if they met universal and fixed government-set national eligibility criteria, receive the same types and amount of financial support. The 2004 act also established the idea that universities should provide students with financial support but that universities, not the state, should select the beneficiaries and what they receive; for the first time, discretionary rather than universal financial support became widespread (Callender 2010).

The context for these reforms was articulated in the 2003 white paper, *The Future of Higher Education* (DfES 2003). They encompassed concerns about competing in a globalized knowledge economy, harnessing knowledge for wealth creation, and meeting the high-level skills required in such an economy. Higher education had to expand to meet these rising skill needs and to widen participation to exploit "the talented and best from all backgrounds" (DfES 2003, 2). However, universities needed "the freedoms and resources to compete on the world stage ... to undo the years of under-investment" (2). Universities' new freedom to set their own tuition fees "will allow them to fund their plans, and unleash their power to drive world-class research, innovative knowledge transfer, excellent teaching, high-quality, greater and more flexible provision, and fair access" (DfES 2003, 76). The white paper continued, "As we are asking new students to pay for the benefits they receive from higher education, to build sustainable funding freedoms for the future, we believe that it is also right that those who have already benefited from higher education should be able to contribute" (76).

The changes in student financial support and finances since the 1988 white paper reflect gradual transformations in beliefs about higher education, its role in society, who benefits from higher education, and so who should pay for higher education. Central to this are the balance of private and public contributions toward the costs of higher education and what proportion of these costs should be borne by students and/or their families, employers, and the government or taxpayer. Since 1988, all of the reforms to higher education student funding in England have adopted a "cost-sharing agenda" (Johnstone and Marcucci 2010). They have attempted both to reduce public expenditure and to shift the costs of higher education away from government and taxpayers so that more of these costs are borne by students and/or their families. The 2012–13 reforms continue this trend and encourage another form of cost-sharing – private providers who bear most of the costs of provision rather than the state.

This cost-sharing agenda is a global policy, not restricted to England. According to Johnstone and Marcucci (2010), higher education needs a more robust stream of non-governmental revenue because of the growing importance of, and demand for, higher education; the increasing costs of higher education, driven by higher education expansion and rising per-student costs; the inability of governments to meet these costs; and the inadequacy of cost-side solutions to solve these problems. Their answer is more money from tuition fees paid for by students and/or their families alongside financial assistance in the form of student loans, grants, and other public subsidies. Johnstone and Marcucci insist that cost-sharing for "almost all countries ... is an imperative for the financial health of their colleges and universities" but warn that cost-sharing must "always ... supplement and augment government revenue, never replace it" (2010, 283).

Figure 1 illustrates the consequences of the cost-sharing agenda in England and the impact of the policy changes discussed above. It shows how full-time students' sources of income have changed over time, calling on data derived from the government's Student Income and Expenditure Survey. Figure 1 highlights the movements in the private and public contributions to higher education. Specifically, it shows how the costs of higher education have shifted away from the state and taxpayers to individual students and their families. This has been achieved through, first, the replacement of grants with loans and, second, the replacement

FIGURE 1
The changing composition of students' income from 1992–1993 to 2007–2008

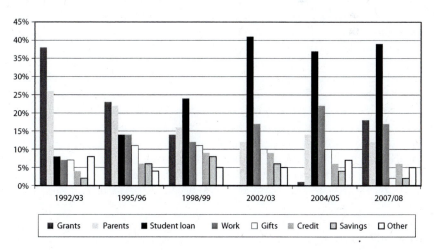

Source: Author's compilation from the Student Income and Expenditure Survey, various years.
© 2010 C. Callender

of parental contributions with loans, resulting in rising student loan debt and falling parental contributions. This latter strategy has been regressive as those who have benefited most both from the introduction of loans for living costs, and then tuition fees, have been parents from middle-class backgrounds.

REVIEW OF HIGHER EDUCATION FUNDING AND STUDENT FINANCE, 2009

The Independent Review of Higher Education Funding and Student Finance, chaired by Lord Browne, was launched on 9 November 2009 with the support of all political parties. It arose from the previous Labour Government's commitment to review the operation of variable tuition fees for full-time students after three years. It was "tasked with making rec-ommendations to Government on the future of fees policy and financial support for full and part-time undergraduate and postgraduate students" (BIS 2009a) and was to report after the May 2010 general election. So the highly contentious (and vote-losing) issue of resolving student finances was wiped off the election agenda and left to the incoming government – the Conservative–Liberal Democratic coalition.

The economic context within which the review operated was one of the global recession and unprecedented cuts in public expenditure (HM Treasury 2010). This is paramount for understanding the review's recom-mendations and the coalition's response to them. So too is the political context and the coalition's ideology. This political environment was not exceptional. As Johnstone and Marcucci (2010, 102) remind us in their global review of funding, tuition fees are the "political and ideological flashpoint for debates over the need for, and the propriety of, cost-sharing in all its forms." They continue, "tuition fees are almost everywhere con-tested" (23), reflecting the cultural and historical acceptability of tuition fees as well as prevailing political ideologies.

Consequently, to understand tuition fee and financial support poli-cies in England and elsewhere, we have to acknowledge the political and ideological context in which they are formulated and implemented, and how these shape the nature of the provision. Hence, whatever way forward economic or cost-sharing theory or research evidence may suggest, that direction will be both determined and compromised by political considerations. This is true of earlier student funding reforms in England[6] and of Browne's recommendations and the government's response to them.

"The case for reform"

The Browne Review's final report – *Securing a Sustainable Future for Higher Education: An Independent Review of Higher Education Funding and Student*

Finance – was published on 12 October 2010. The report's case for reform focused on three issues (IRHEFSF 2010, 23). First, higher education participation needed to increase because demand exceeded supply; low-income students and under-represented groups were not going to the most prestigious universities, so "fair access" had not been achieved; and access to part-time study was being hampered by a lack of government financial support. Second, quality needed to be improved because students lacked the skills employers want to improve productivity, higher education institutions needed more money to upgrade their courses, and higher education institutions lacked incentives to enhance the "student experience." Third, a sustainable system of higher education funding needed to be created because the balance of private and public contributions to the sector had not changed since 2006. Tuition fees of £3,000 had generated more income for universities, but the government was spending more on student financial support. Consequently, higher education remained overly reliant on public funding, and if subject to public expenditure cuts, the sector would be unable to attract additional funds.

Browne's diagnosis of higher education's problems are contestable. The report is devoid of research evidence. Unlike previous inquiries into higher education funding, the committee commissioned no research, bar an opinion poll, to inform its deliberations. At the committee's public hearings, only 9 of the 31 witnesses were academic specialists – the rest were higher education stakeholder representatives. The report is limited in its scope and vision. Its approach is narrow economic instrumentalism. It valorizes the private benefits of higher education at the expense of the public benefits and does not question the private subsidy of public benefits. It is an exemplar of the prioritizing of private gain over public good. By positioning higher education purely as a private investment, there is no space, either in the report or in the government's response to it, of higher education as a public good (Reay 2012).

Undoubtedly, Browne's recommendations were driven by the coalition's desire to reduce both the costs of student support and higher education public expenditure, in line with their broader strategy to cut the fiscal deficit and stimulate economic growth. By 2010–11 (before any cuts), over half of the total higher education annual expenditure of the Department for Business, Innovation and Skills (BIS) was to be devoted to financing student aid, compared with 38 percent in 2003–04. Such costs arose from the 2006 reforms, particularly the large government subsidy on student loans. For every £100 a student borrowed, it cost the government £28. This was because the interest rate on these loans was linked to inflation, which was lower than the government's costs of borrowing, and some graduates never repaid their loans in full because repayments depended on graduates' earnings. These high costs limited the number of students who could receive loans and restricted the number of student places. Since 2009–10, higher education institutions had been prohibited from expanding to meet increasing demand. Money spent on student support also diverted funding from universities' other activities, yet they wanted more money to compete in an international, globalized, higher education market.

It is beyond the bounds of this paper to discuss all of the Browne Report's recommendations, but the major ones were as follows:

A. Most of the money universities received from the government for teaching undergraduate courses should be withdrawn, but government subsidies for science, technology, engineering, and mathematics courses should continue at a reduced level. This lost income would be replaced by higher tuition fees.

    Consequently, there would be no, or limited, taxpayer support for teaching because these costs would be met by students paying higher fees with the help of student loans. Government support for undergraduates, therefore, would shift from teaching grants to student loans – from a block grant to individual students.

B. The government-set cap of £3,290 on undergraduate tuition fees should be removed.

C. All full-time students would continue to receive student loans to pay all of their tuition fees, including those attending private higher education institutions, and for the first time, part-time students should also be eligible for fee loans.

D. The terms and conditions of student loans repayment should change. The point at which graduates start to repay their loans should increase from £15,000 to £21,000 and all outstanding debt forgiven after 30 years; previously it was 25 years. Consequently, graduates would pay 9 percent (unchanged) of their income above £21,000 until they had repaid all of their student loan debt, with any outstanding debt written off after 30 years.

E. The interest paid on the loans for graduates earning above £21,000 should be equal to the government's cost of borrowing (inflation plus 2.2 percent) and no longer rise in line with inflation.

Browne's recommendations were an attempt to develop a quasi-market in higher education. His vision was of a sector whose purpose and role was defined by the market. As Le Grand reminds us in relation to other public services, markets are considered a means for delivering "high-quality services efficiently, equitably and in a responsive fashion" (Le Grand 2007, 38). For choice and competition to operate effectively, "competition must be real" – that is, the money must follow users' choice, there must be a variety of types of provision and providers, with new providers entering the market and failing ones exiting, while "users must be properly informed" (76–77).

One of the six principles guiding Browne's report is increasing student choice by putting "students at the heart of the system" (IRHEFSF 2010, 25) and "relying on student choice to drive up quality" (29). Other recommendations aim to increase competition among higher education institutions by abolishing the cap on tuition fees, so that universities charge different fees, and by giving students loans that, in effect, are like an educational voucher that students redeem at the institution of their choice. Consequently, the bulk of universities' money will follow students' choices, while, theoretically, consumer demand will determine what higher education institutions offer. To survive, institutions will have to become more responsive to student needs. Those with high student demand will be able to charge higher fees and expand, while those that cannot recruit enough students will fail and potentially close down.

Browne's proposals also seek to provide greater student choice and provider competition by enabling the development of a more diverse and flexible higher education sector with more variety in the range and nature of higher education provision, including part-time study. Essential to this is allowing new providers, including private universities and further education colleges, to enter the higher education market and encouraging providers to compete by driving up teaching quality and driving down price through efficiency gains.

The promotion of a market in public services, characterized by user choice and provider competition, is not new. It was central to the previous Labour Government's modernization agenda and public services reforms, with the consumer at its heart (Clarke et al. 2007). This steered Labour's higher education policies too and was most pronounced in its final higher education document – *Higher Ambitions: The Future of Universities in a Knowledge Economy* (BIS 2009b). But, as we have seen, it was crucial to Labour's introduction of variable tuition fees and bursaries in 2006, which together would establish price differentials among providers. Yet, by 2010–11, all higher education institutions were charging the maximum tuition fee for bachelor's degrees. Any competitive advantage of charging lower fees was outweighed by the benefits of higher fee income. Consequently, contrary to Labour's intentions, the new maximum fee had become a new flat rate. So the Browne Report, and the coalition government's response to it, could be seen as an attempt to complete Labour's unfinished higher education agenda.

THE COALITION GOVERNMENT'S RESPONSE TO THE BROWNE REPORT

The coalition government's formal response to the Browne Report came in two stages. The first was in a statement by David Willetts, Minister for Universities and Science, in the House of Commons on 3 November

2010 (*Hansard* 2010, cols. 924–946). The second came in the government's publication on 28 June 2011 of the white paper *Higher Education: Students at the Heart of the System* (BIS 2011a), which reiterated the November 2010 announcement. Unsurprisingly, the government accepted some of Browne's proposals while rejecting others, and it introduced some new mechanisms in the white paper while supporting the notion of a higher education market and students as consumers.

Announcement by David Willetts in the House of Commons on 3 November 2010

All the changes Willetts pronounced on 3 November 2010 came into force in 2012–13 for new higher education entrants.

1. The government endorsed Browne's recommendation to withdraw most of the universities' teaching funds (see recommendation A above); this represents a cut of 80 percent in higher education's teaching budget.
2. It rejected Browne's suggestion that the tuition fees cap should be abolished (see recommendation B above). Instead, the existing cap of £3,290 per annum rose to a maximum of £9,000.
3. The government concurred with the extension of tuition fee loans for part-time undergraduates (see recommendation C above).
4. It agreed with Browne's earnings threshold for loan repayments and the extended period of debt forgiveness (see recommendation D above). However, the government is charging higher interest rates on loans than those proposed by Browne (see recommendation E above). Graduates from both part-time and full-time study do not start repaying their loans until they are earning £21,000 a year, when the interest on their loans is limited to inflation. Graduates earning between £21,000 and £41,000 are charged interest on a sliding scale, up to a maximum of inflation plus 3 percent, once their annual earnings exceed £41,000. Consequently, loan repayments are now more progressive.
5. Finally, the government backed the continuation of student maintenance loans for all students and increased maintenance grants for low-income students, but eligibility for partial grants is limited to students whose families' annual income is between £25,000 and £42,000, down from £50,000. Also, universities will continue to give these and other students discretionary cash bursaries, merit-based scholarships, and fee waivers, with the latter being particularly encouraged by government to help reduce the student loan bill.

Significantly, both Browne and the government recognized the importance of a comprehensive student support system to safeguard higher education participation. Without it, fee increases could lead to substantial falls in participation (Dearden, Fitzsimons, and Wyness 2010). And the overall structure and type of student financial support for full-time students remained largely unchanged, compared with provisions introduced in 2006 (see Figure 2). As a result of the reforms, during university, low-income students are now slightly better off due to increased up-front support. But after university, graduates will have much higher student loan debt, and it will take them far longer to pay it off – on average, around 29 years for women and 25 for men, although the loan repayment system will be more progressive (Chowdry et al. 2012). Overall, the new system is more complex and less transparent, with greater variability in fees and in institutional aid.

FIGURE 2
Student financial support for full-time undergraduates from 2012–2013

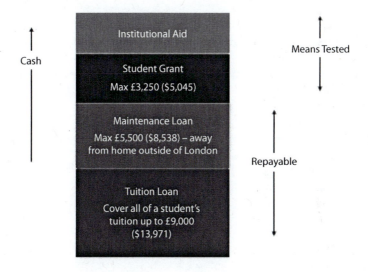

Source: Author's compilation. © C. Callender

For these announcements to be implemented by 2012–13, universities had to respond rapidly. They had to set their tuition fees, fee waivers, and other financial support offered to students *before* some changes outlined by the government had reached the statute book and *before* the publication of its white paper in June 2011. In July 2011, the majority of universities declared their intention to charge at or within £1,000 of the full £9,000-per-year tuition fee come 2012–13, while the average fee was £8,509 and £8,267 after fee waivers – hardly a differentiated market (OFFA 2011).[7] These fee levels were well above the average of £7,500 anticipated by the Treasury.

2011 white paper – *Higher Education: Students at the Heart of the System*

The 2011 white paper, unlike previous higher education white papers, was very narrowly drawn. It focused exclusively on the undergraduate economy, especially student funding, while failing to locate higher education within a broader context or addressing other higher education concerns such as research, knowledge exchange, postgraduate study, teaching, and learning. It primarily repeated, in more detail, Willetts' November 2010 statement, but it also sought to deal with the universities' responses to that announcement, especially the higher-than-expected fees that institutions planned to charge.

The white paper mirrors the Browne Report's case for reform.

> Our reforms tackle three challenges. First, putting higher education on a sustainable footing. We inherited the largest budget deficit in post-war history, requiring spending cuts across government. By shifting public spending away from teaching grants and toward repayable tuition loans, we have ensured that higher education receives the funding it needs even as substantial savings are made to public expenditure. Second, institutions must deliver a better student experience; improving teaching, assessment, feedback and preparation for the world of work. Third, they must take more responsibility for increasing social mobility. (BIS 2011a, 4)

The overall number of student places has not been increased. However, the white paper established mechanisms to reduce the tuition fees charged by universities (and the government's student loan bill) and to create more competition among providers in an environment of constrained student numbers by "liberating student number controls" (BIS 2011a, 48). It introduced "core and margin" student places. In 2012–13, universities were allowed to recruit as many students as they liked who scored at A Level[8] the equivalent of grades AAB or above, while 20,000 places were reserved for higher education providers whose average tuition fee (after fee waivers) was £7,500 or below. These places were removed from the national pot of government-allocated student places and a higher education institution's core allocation. This led to at least a 9 percent reduction in core allocations in 2012–13, but the impact on institutions varied considerably. With no increase in total student numbers, there were winners and losers: higher education institutions with few AAB students charging fees over £7,500 were particularly badly affected. The policy intention is that over time, the number of "core" places will decline, while the number of competitive "margin" places will increase. Indeed, in 2013–14, there will be no restrictions on the number of students that universities can recruit who gain grades ABB at A Level, while the number of lower-fee numbers have been reduced to 5,000.

AN ASSESSMENT OF THE 2012–13 REFORMS

The rest of the chapter assesses the government's reforms against the white paper's three stated aims regarding higher education funding, the "student experience," and social mobility. It questions both the policy objectives and whether the policy goals are achievable. The reforms are untested, and, at the time of writing, there is limited evidence of their initial impact. Some argue that the changes are so radical that we cannot even learn from earlier funding reforms (Chowdry et al. 2012) or from other countries' experiences to gauge their effects.

"Putting higher education on a sustainable financial footing"

The 2012–13 reforms aimed to reduce public expenditure on higher education while maintaining the sector's income. The most costly component is student financial support, specifically the government subsidy on student loans – the part of loans written off by the government that will never be fully recovered from graduate loan repayments. Significantly, *only* this subsidy counts as public spending (as measured by the Public Sector Borrowing Requirement) and is a cost to the taxpayer. The money raised to provide student loans is not. However, any part of a loan not repaid by graduates appears in the BIS budget as current spending. Have the reforms reduced this level of subsidy and hence public expenditure?

The simple answer is no, certainly not in the short to medium term. The rise in student-loan interest rates has eradicated one element of the government subsidy on student loans. But other 2012–13 changes mean that loans will remain highly subsidized because increasing proportions of graduates will never fully repay their loans. First, the high level of average tuition fees means larger average tuition fee loans. The face value of loans increases, and therefore their total value increases. Having larger loans means that graduates are less likely to pay them off in full. The combined effect is that public spending becomes a bigger share of a larger total loan amount.

The second reason for the continued government subsidy on loans relates to the rise in the loan repayment threshold (see 4. above), which will be up-rated annually. This is expensive because it reduces the monthly repayments of all graduates (not just low-earning graduates), means that a large number of graduates make no repayments because they are earning less than £21,000, and makes it more likely that graduates will not fully repay their loans. Barr and Shephard (2010) use the problem of moral hazard to argue that this threshold acts as an incentive for all higher education institutions to charge higher fees because the cost of non-repayment falls on the taxpayer, not higher education institutions.

The net result is that under the new system, an estimated 50 to 60 percent of graduates will have some, or all, of their student loan written off, compared with around 15 percent under the previous system (*Hansard* 2011, c156W). The government estimates that the student loan subsidy will rise to £32 for every £100 a student borrows, up from £28 (BIS 2011b, 57). This could increase public spending by around £300 million in steady state (OFFA 2011). Others believe that the subsidy will be higher, a situation that would increase government spending and reduce any savings (Thompson and Berkhradnia 2011). The exact costs are unknown, and they will arguably not be fully known until 2046, at the end of the 30-year loan period for the first cohort of students graduating under the 2012–13 funding regime. Over time, universities may reduce their fees, students may opt for less expensive courses, student numbers may fall, and previous patterns in graduate earnings may change – all of which will impact on these costs. As David Willetts, Minister for Universities and Science, admitted, "No one can be certain. This is a set of big changes. I am not claiming that we can be absolutely certain" (House of Commons BIS Committee 2011, 19, para. 72).

The problems are of the government's own making. It is right and proper for the government to provide income-contingent loans and subsidies to low-earning graduates to safeguard equity, affordability, and widening participation, although, as Barr and Shephard (2010) suggest, they do encourage price gouging. However, if the government had not withdrawn most of the universities' teaching grant for most university courses (see 1. above), the cap on tuition fees would arguably have been lower. In turn, student debt would also be lower, and this would reduce the amount of student loan write-off. Consequently, greater direct subsidies to universities and lower tuition fees could have offset some of these issues.

Will other elements of the 2012–13 reforms reduce public expenditure and public sector debt? The shift in funding away from direct public support for teaching undergraduate courses (see 1. above) to student loans means that public expenditure on higher education will fall. The money the government provided to higher education institutions for teaching was counted as public expenditure, but most spending on student loans, which replaces these teaching funds, is not – apart from the loan subsidy. As Barr (2011, 1, para. 2) observes, "Though little has changed in cash terms (since the government has to finance the upfront cost of loans), there is an apparent reduction in the BIS budget; it is not unfair to say that an accounting trick is driving deleterious policy change." The cash needed to provide loans will add to the stock of public sector debt. Government spending on higher education could increase by around 10 percent between 2010–11 and 2014–15; thus, the net impact of the changes in funding will increase public sector debt in the short to medium term, possibly by around £1 billion in 2014–15. In the longer term, however, the loan repayments are expected to reduce the size of the debt. It is estimated that student loan payments will increase net government debt and will peak around 2030 at 6.1 per cent of gross domestic product (GDP), or £94 billion in today's money, before declining to 4.4 percent of GDP by 2061–62 as repayments begin to outweigh the new loans (OBR 2011).

It is, therefore, highly questionable whether the new funding system is sustainable in the longer term. Not only is it expensive, but the expense means that student places are capped.

Delivering "a better student experience"

The main driver in the 2012–13 reforms for improving the "student experience" (whatever this term really means)[9] is the development of a higher education market that, in theory, will lead to better quality provision, drive down prices, and put "students at the heart of the system." It is debatable whether a market in higher education will lead to falling costs. The United States has a well-established market, but there, tuition fees have consistently grown at a much faster pace than inflation or average earnings[10] (College Board 2011). It is questionable how much of a market will actually develop in England, for the reasons discussed below.

First, there will be no free market because fees are capped and, most importantly, so are student numbers because of the continuing high costs of student financial support. Consequently, admissions are a zero-sum game: if some universities expand, others must contract, and if the number of institutions increases with new entrants, the average size of each must fall (Barr 2011, 2, para. 5). Without an increase in student numbers, participation is unlikely to increase even if more providers enter the market or new types of more flexible and diverse provision are offered. Providers will be unable to respond to a growth in demand. In a competitive market, if a university's quality dropped, we would expect reduced demand and a downward pressure on price, but excess demand largely negates these pressures. Without higher student numbers, demand will continue to outstrip supply, and this will constrain competition for quality and limit student choice. Where demand exceeds supply, universities select students, and there will be little incentive to invest in an improved "student experience."

Second, even before these reforms, universities' income from teaching depended on student preferences and universities' success in recruiting students. Students have always been able to choose where and what to study, but their choices rarely followed the logic of economic orthodoxy. And it is not clear that they will in the future, especially given the limited price differences in tuition fees (Chowdry et al. 2012) to signal variations in quality and a system of institutional aid that is overly complex and so fails to operate as a market signal. A myriad of social, economic, and cultural factors influence student higher education decision-making and choices (Bates et al. 2009; Reay, David, and Ball 2005). Financial concerns and material constraints play a major role, but costs and finances are just one set of factors that explains patterns of higher education participation and why students select a particular higher education institution (Usher et al. 2010). Indeed, US research (Baum, McPherson, and Steele 2008) shows that price has a greater impact on low-income students' decision to enter higher education than on their choice of institution.

Finally, quality at some higher education institutions may fall rather than improve because not all higher education institutions are charging fees high enough to replace their lost income from government-funded teaching grants. Indeed, the 2011 white paper specifically aimed to put a downward pressure on tuition fees by reserving 20,000 student places for institutions charging less than £7,500. However, Browne estimated that universities would need to charge £7,000 to replace their lost teaching funds. Consequently, some institutions are unlikely to have the additional funds to improve the "student experience," while efficiency savings are likely to be made at the expense of "the student experience" and an investment in teaching. Universities with extra income may not invest it in students – the additional fee income they have gained since 2006 has gone into improving their surpluses and the salaries of academic staff rather than into areas that directly affect the "student experience" (UUK 2011).

One of the most significant impediments to competition is the restriction on student numbers arising from the costs of student financial support. The other is the cap on student fees. Unregulated tuition fees might drive greater investment in the student experience in some institutions. However, greater price competition without a tuition fee cap would lead to other problems, particularly escalating costs, including a higher student loan bill. As US experience shows, the "arms race" has contributed to ever-increasing university costs and tuition fees. To attract good students, universities have to provide better and better facilities (e.g., sports, dormitories) commensurate with those of their competitors. These facilities have little to do with students' learning or teaching or their educational attainment, yet they push up the cost of tuition. Moreover, in the US, price competition has also led to price competition for student quality, with colleges paying more in student aid to attract the best undergraduates. This is to the advantage of low-income students at the wealthiest colleges and universities, but to the detriment of those universities and colleges without the resources (primarily endowments) to fund high student institutional aid; thus, their prices rise at the same time that expenditures per student fall. Universities with less accumulated wealth, therefore, are particularly vulnerable to price competition (Winston and Zimmerman 2000).

A cap on student fees helps to contain some of these costs, although wealthier universities will always be able to pay their students higher levels of institutional aid. On the other hand, even with a cap on price, some of these developments are emerging in England. For instance, some middle- and lower-ranking universities are investing considerable sums in bursaries and scholarships to attract AAB students and take advantage of these uncontrolled places. Such merit-based student aid tends to advantage those students least in need of financial help – those from middle- and higher-income families (Callender 2010).

The UK government could attempt to deal with the rising costs associated with uncapped (or capped) fees by limiting the amount of student loans that students can borrow for their tuition fees. For instance, it could restrict student loans to, say, £X, whereby individual students would then have to meet the difference between the value of the loans (£X) and the fees charged by a university (£Y) out of their own pocket. In such circumstances, only those from wealthier families could attend the best universities, which are the institutions charging the highest fees. Such a move would undermine the government's purported commitment to social mobility and fair access, unless universities substantially increased their institutional aid to make up the difference between the value of the loans and the fees charged.

Alternatively, the amount of tuition loan that a student would be eligible for could be pegged to the family's income so that students from the poorest families would receive a loan for the full amount of fees. The proportion of fees covered could be reduced as one moved up the income ladder, with the wealthiest families being asked to fund the tuition fees themselves. This would stem some of the continuing decrease in parental contributions toward the cost of higher education (as shown in Figure 1 above) and potentially mitigate against a rising student loan bill. Both strategies would potentially challenge issues of equity, affordability, and widening participation. Just as significantly, they would contest a basic tenet underpinning the UK Welfare State: that services are free at the point of access. Moreover, they would eliminate a defining feature of the UK higher education system – that higher education remains one of the only positional goods that, currently, cannot be purchased by the wealthy (Collini 2012).

"Increasing social mobility"

Just as constraints on student places limit improvements in the "student experience," so they undermine efforts to increase social mobility and widen participation. The prospective students least likely to find a university place are those from the most disadvantaged backgrounds, who up till now have benefited, albeit to a limited extent, from higher education expansion (HEFCE 2010). Yet there is little in the 2011 white paper to help eradicate the large social-class inequalities in higher education access and participation that widening participation aims to tackle. The coalition abandoned Labour's target to increase participation to 50 percent, and its student funding reforms alongside other policy changes might exacerbate these inequalities.

First, the white paper subtly redefines both the parameter and scope of debate and its policy focus. Gone is the notion of widening participation and improving access for under-represented groups – of opening up the doors to higher education and thus reducing inequalities. Widening participation is trumped by "relative social mobility" defined in terms of fairness. "For any given level of skill and ambition, regardless of an individual's background, everyone should have a fair chance of getting the job they want or reaching a higher income bracket" (BIS 2011a, 54). So fairness rather than disadvantage or inequalities are to steer policy. Hence the white paper's focus on the "fair access" agenda – of trying to steer more disadvantaged students toward the most selective universities rather than opening university doors to a wider cross-section of students. The issue, therefore, is one of social mobility within a system of widening inequalities rather than an attempt to tackle poverty and inequality, which limit opportunities and aspirations.

Overall, to avert these negative effects, the government needs to revert to the principles underpinning widening participation and move away from notions of social mobility. Above all, it would require policies aimed at tackling poverty and inequality – policies that go well beyond the remit of higher education. A start would be a stronger policy focus on underperforming public secondary schools because it is the low levels of educational attainment among the most disadvantaged who populate these schools that largely explains their under-representation within higher education. Of late, such policies, in the name of greater parental choice, have focused on the overall structure of public secondary schooling, with the development of new types of schools (free schools, academies, etc.), rather than on policies concentrating on what happens inside schools and on improving pupils' attainment and aspirations.

Second, in an environment of limited university places, there is a tension in the white paper between the "core and margin" places and widening access and participation. As discussed, universities were allowed to recruit as many students as they liked who scored grades of AAB or above in their A-Levels in 2012–13 and who score ABB in 2013–14. The AAB/ABB policy potentially undermines the "fair access" agenda. To help meet this agenda, some universities offer places to bright disadvantaged students with potentially lower A-Level entry grades rather than to students from more advantaged backgrounds. However, such universities may be reluctant to offer places below AAB/ABB.

Furthermore, under-represented students are the least likely to benefit from the unlimited AAB/ABB places because of the strong links between high A-Level grades and socio-economic advantage. As is well-established, academic attainment, as measured by examination performance, is highly correlated with students' socio-economic characteristics. And those students attaining these high A-Level grades are overrepresented among students from wealthy backgrounds and those educated in private secondary schools. For instance, a quarter of students from the highest socio-economic status quintile achieve the top A-Level grades, compared with 3 percent from the lowest quintile. Disadvantaged students are also less likely to have the qualifications to access the reduced number of "core" university places, especially at universities with a low proportion of AAB students. According to the government, a squeeze on places at these "universities will impact disproportionately on opportunities for widening participation students, many of whom apply to [these] universities.... A shift in the availability of sub-AAB places from [these] universities towards FE [further education] colleges will not necessarily provide greater social mobility or better returns for any widening participation students displaced" from higher education institutions to higher education in FE (BIS 2011b, 71).

Third, responsibility for driving social mobility has shifted away from the state to the efforts of individual universities and students, as evidenced by the coalition's other post-compulsory education reforms. First, the coalition abolished the Educational Maintenance Allowance, designed to incentivize low-income pupils to stay on in post-compulsory education and gain the qualifications needed to enter higher education. Second, the coalition withdrew funding from Aimhigher – a national collaborative outreach program, established to encourage progression to higher education, that encompassed a wide range of activities to engage and motivate school and college learners who had the potential to enter higher education, but who were underachieving, undecided, or lacking in confidence. Aimhigher, albeit through a deficit discourse of under-represented groups that lacked certain skills or competences or appropriate attitudes and aspirations, did encourage them to apply to university, and to the most prestigious ones. Third, the government, in effect, has curtailed important routes into higher education for many adults, especially women wanting to improve their qualifications and skills to climb onto the higher education ladder, by withdrawing funding from access courses and from Level 3 courses (equivalent to A-Levels) for those over 24 years old. In future, adults will have to pay much higher fees themselves and take out student loans. Given these students' backgrounds, and the way the education system has failed many of them, will they be willing to take the risk and make the financial commitment demanded by loans and to speculate financially on an uncertain future – especially given the limited financial returns to these qualifications? And will they be willing to accumulate additional student loan debt to progress to a full-time degree?

Finally, tuition fees have tripled for most students in 2012–13, as will student loan debt. It is impossible, at this stage, to predict the longer-term impact of the reforms and increases in tuition fees and debt on individuals' higher education aspirations, their participation rates, and higher education choices in the medium and long term. The 2006 higher education finance reforms did not lead to a sustained fall in participation, but their full effects are unknown because we do not know what would have happened to participation in the absence of the reforms (Crawford and Dearden 2010). Yet the 2012–13 reforms are more extreme. In 2012–13, full-time UK and EU undergraduate entrants to universities and colleges in England fell by 12 per cent compared with 2011–12. However, full-time applications are up for 2013–14.

Significantly for widening participation, higher education entry rates for 18-year-olds from the most disadvantaged backgrounds studying full time seemed relatively unaffected by the 2012–13 changes in student funding (HEFCE 2013). This suggests that poorer students have been protected from some of the reforms, not least by the continued access to means-tested support while studying for a degree. But this should not mask the slow progress in narrowing the socio-economic gap in access to higher education. There remain large gaps in entry rates between those from more and those from less advantaged backgrounds. Young people from the most advantaged areas are three times more likely to enter university than those from the most disadvantaged areas, and they are between six and nine times more likely to go to the most prestigious, research-intensive universities.

However, the goal of widening participation and social mobility is still at risk from these 2012–13 reforms. They have particularly affected mature and part-time student enrolments, characteristics that are inter-linked given that the vast majority of part-time students are over the age of 25 years. Among full-time undergraduates, acceptances among UK applicants aged 18 and under fell by 1.7 percent between 2011 and 2012, but among those aged 20 and over, they fell by 7.1 percent despite the increase in the total number of people in their twenties and thirties in the general population. In addition, for those aged 30 and over, there have been further falls in applications for 2013–14 (HEFCE 2013).

By far the most dramatic decline in enrolments since the 2012–13 re-forms has been among part-time undergraduate students. Their numbers fell by a third between 2011–12 and 2012–13 and by 40 per cent between 2010–11 and 2012–13. These students are more likely than their full-time peers to be non-traditional learners and mature, entering part-time higher education either with lower-level qualifications or higher-level qualifi-cations. Young students from the most disadvantaged backgrounds are twice as likely as the most advantaged young people to study part time (HEFCE 2013). So these falls in part-time enrolments are likely to have implications for equity and diversity.

It is unclear at this stage whether the sharp decline in part-time student enrolments is a direct result of the new tuition fee loans for part-timers, the increased fees, or the limitations of the financial help available. Student financial support for part-time students is far less generous than the aid provided to their full-time peers. Part-time undergraduates are eligible only for tuition fee loans and do not qualify for any help toward other study costs or maintenance. Moreover, eligibility for these tuition loans is restricted to those who do not already hold a degree, and consequently, two-thirds of part-timers do not qualify for them. As a result, the majority of part-time students still have to pay for their much higher tuition fees up front and out of their own pocket (Callender, forthcoming). Alternatively, the fall in demand may be attributable, in part, to other factors such as the recession; employers' inability or willingness to finance students, especially in the public sector, resulting from public expenditure cuts; and/or pressures on household budgets.

Overall, it remains unclear whether the new student financial support will adequately offset rising higher education costs as well as concerns about them and escalating student loan debt in the longer term. Research suggests that those most likely to be affected will be low-income students, who are more price sensitive, price elastic (Baum, McPherson, and Steele 2008), and debt averse (Callender and Jackson 2005) than their wealthier peers – the very target of social mobility. Taken together, all of these government policies are likely to reduce rather than enhance the chances of those from disadvantaged backgrounds entering higher education to improve their job prospects and earning capacity. It is hard to imagine how these students are at the heart of any of these changes.

Yet the new student financial support system, particularly income-contingent loans and grants, do have equity dimensions, as does the shift away from a system in which most direct institutional subsidies and teaching grants went to fund the participation of the well-off. As a result of the reforms, during university, low-income students are slightly better off due to increased up-front support. After university, all graduates will be worse off because of the increase in fees. However, the revised structuring of the loan repayments is more progressive than under the previous repayment system, with greater subsidies going to the lowest-earning graduates (Chowdry et al. 2012).

In theory, if students are well informed, those from poor backgrounds may not be dissuaded by higher fees and debt. But asymmetries in information remain an issue and are exacerbated by the reforms. This is because the system is more complex and less transparent due to greater variability in tuition fees and especially more university-specific and course-specific support packages. Beyond the greater competition for the restricted number of university places, the extent to which the reforms will affect higher education participation, especially among the poorest, and therefore social mobility, will largely depend on the degree of debt aversion among students from the poorest backgrounds, the ability of government and universities to provide clear information about student financial support and the actual costs and benefits of going to each institution, and the graduate wage premium holding up.

CONCLUSION

As the 2011 white paper acknowledges, the changes represent a radical reform of the higher education system. Arguably, they herald a retreat of the state's financial responsibility for higher education, with a shift toward individual universities and especially students carrying most of this responsibility and the risks. Implicit in this strategy is a fundamental, ideological revision of the purpose of higher education, driven by economic competition and the dominance of financial values. Higher education is no longer seen by government as a public good, of value to society as a whole beyond those who receive it, and so worthy of public funding, but instead as a private good with private economic returns from individual investment. Higher education's private-good functions are pitted against its public-good functions and reveal a policy mindset and political ideology that consider the public and private benefits of higher education a zero-sum game. The direct non-market benefits of higher education, which McMahon (2009) argues exceeds the market benefits, are ignored.

The policies are unproven, with unknown consequences and unforeseen unintended consequences. It is highly questionable whether the reforms will meet their stated aims of putting higher education on a sustainable financial footing, improving the "student experience," and increasing social mobility, or whether they will stand the test of time. We will not know for sure for several years to come.

In the short term, the changes are having a destabilizing effect on the higher education sector. There may be some fiscal savings, but will these be at the expense of the longer-term effects on quality, social equity, and universities as public, civic, and cultural institutions? The concern is that the reforms will entrench elitism in higher education and perpetuate existing inequalities within and across the sector so that universities revert to one of Castells' (2001) key functions – as mechanisms for selecting and socializing elites, and for setting off these elites from the rest of society, at the expense of higher education's other functions. There is a danger that higher education will become more segmented, polarized, and elitist, while equality of opportunity is fractured, with bright and wealthy students being concentrated in a few "traditional" well-resourced universities, while other financially constrained students are confined to poorly resourced, low-cost alternatives.

Privileged students who populate the top universities will pay more but receive a high-quality education and highly valued degrees. Low-income students who populate institutions at the bottom of the hierarchy will pay less and receive less, but still have large student loan debts. Others may be excluded completely. Will these divisions among institutions and among students reinforce both social class and disadvantage so that higher education becomes more socially and ethnically differentiated and polarized than ever before, rather than higher education institutions being cherished centres of teaching, learning, and knowledge creation for all to benefit?

NOTES

1. Higher education policy in the UK is devolved – that is, England, Northern Ireland, Wales, and Scotland have jurisdiction over their own higher education policies, including student funding. The reforms discussed relate only to students who live in England and who study in England. They do have implications for other UK and EU students, but it is beyond the scope of this chapter to discuss these complicated cross-border arrangements.
2. For an examination of the impact of the 2012–13 reforms on part-time undergraduates, see Callender (forthcoming).
3. Human capital is defined as "the knowledge, skills and competences and other attributes embodied in individuals that are relevant to economic activity" (OECD 1998, 9).
4. The changes introduced by Labour were at odds with Dearing's actual recommendations on the student funding changes. Dearing proposed a £1,000 contribution from all students, to be repaid on an income-contingent basis, and the retention of means-tested grants.
5. The cap was to rise in line with inflation each academic year.
6. The reader may recall that former prime minister Tony Blair staked his career on the successful passage of the 2004 *Higher Education Act*, which was passed in Parliament by just five votes.
7. Of the universities whose fees were published by OFFA in 2011, 72 out of 87 have a maximum fee at or over £8,500 per year; 58 have an average fee at or over £8,500 per year.
8. A-Levels are a national General Certificate of Education qualification usually taken in the optional final two years of secondary schooling (years 12 and 13) and are traditionally a prerequisite for university entry. Unlike in other countries, the subjects that students study in these final two optional years have a high degree of specialization. Students usually take A-Levels in only three or four subjects, and they sit a separate examination for each one. Each A- Level examination taken is graded from A* (highest) to E rather than being given a percentage grade. (Thus, unlike in the US, students are not given a grade point average.) Students' grades are based on the A-Level examination result in each subject and are represented alphabetically (e.g., AAB) rather than as a numerical percentage. University courses have a minimum entry requirement of A-Level grades, and students are offered a university place based on their predicted A-Level grades.
9. Given the diversity of the student population, it is highly questionable whether we can really talk about a monolithic "student experience."
10. Over the decade from 2001–02 to 2011–12, published tuition and fees for in-state students at public four-year colleges and universities increased at an average rate of 5.6 percent per year beyond the rate of general inflation. This rate of increase compares to 4.5 percent per year in the 1980s and 3.2 percent per year in the 1990s.

REFERENCES

Barr, N. 1989. "The White Paper on Student Loans." *Journal of Social Policy* 18 (3):409–417.

—. 2011. "Assessing the White Paper on Higher Education." Supplementary Submission to the Business, Innovation and Skills Committee, The Future of Higher Education. Session 2011–12, HC 885.

Barr, N., and N. Shephard. 2010. *Towards Setting Student Numbers Free.* At http://econ.lse.ac.uk/staff/nb/Barr_Setting_numbers_free_101217.pdf (accessed 29 October 2011).

Bates, P., E. Pollard, T. Usher, and J. Oakley. 2009. "Who Is Heading for HE? Young People's Perceptions of, and Decisions about, Higher Education." BIS Research Paper 3. London: Department for Business, Innovation and Skills.

Baum, S., M. McPherson, and P. Steele, eds. 2008. *The Effectiveness of Student Aid Policies: What the Research Tells Us.* New York: College Board.

BIS. 2009a. Press release. At http://hereview.independent.gov.uk/hereview/press-release-9-november-2009/ (accessed 9 November 2009).

—. 2009b. *Higher Ambitions: The Future of Universities in a Knowledge Economy.* London: Stationery Office.

—. 2011a. *Higher Education: Students at the Heart of the System.* Cm. 8122. London: Stationery Office.

—. 2011b. "Impact Assessment – Higher Education: Students at the Heart of the System." London: Department for Business, Innovation and Skills.

Callender, C. 2010. "Bursaries and Institutional Aid in Higher Education in England: Do They Safeguard Access and Promote Fair Access?" *Oxford Review of Education* 36 (1):45–62.

Callender, C. Forthcoming. "Part-Time Undergraduate Student Funding and Financial Support and the 2012/13 Higher Education Funding Reforms." In *Browne and Beyond: Modernising Higher Education in England*, ed. C. Callender and P. Scott. London: Bedford Way Papers.

Callender, C., and J. Jackson. 2005. "Does Fear of Debt Deter Students from Higher Education?" *Journal of Social Policy* 34 (4):509–540.

Castells, M. 2001. "Universities as Dynamic Systems of Contradictory Functions." In *Challenges of Globalisation: South African Debates with Manuel Castells,* ed. J. Müller, N. Cloete, and S. Badat. Cape Town: Maskew Miller Longman.

Chowdry, H., L. Dearden, A. Goodman, and J. Wenchao. 2012. "The Distributional Impact of the 2012–13 Higher Education Funding Reforms in England." *Fiscal Studies* 33 (2):211–236.

Clarke, J., J. Newman, N. Smith, E. Vindler, and L. Westerland. 2007. *Creating Citizen-Consumers: Changing Publics and Changing Public Services.* London: Paul Chapman.

College Board. 2011. *Trends in College Pricing 2011.* New York: College Board.

Collini, S. 2012. *What Are Universities For?* London: Penguin Books.

Crawford, C., and L. Dearden. 2010. "The Impact of the 2006–07 HE Finance Reforms on HE Participation." BIS Research Paper Number 13. London: Department for Business, Innovation and Skills.

Dearden, L., E. Fitzsimons, and G. Wyness. 2010. "The Impact of Higher Education Finance on University Participation in the UK." BIS Research Paper Number 11. London: Department for Business, Innovation and Skills.

DES. 1988. *Top-Up Loans for Students.* Cm. 520. London: HMSO.

DfEE. 1998. "Blunkett Welcomes Teaching and Higher Education Act." Press release, 17 July.
DfES. 2003. *The Future of Higher Education*. Cm. 5735. London: Stationery Office.
Farrell, S., and E. Tapper. 1992. "Student Loans: The Failure to Consolidate an Emerging Political Consensus." *Higher Education Quarterly* 46 (3):269–285.
Hansard. House of Commons Debates. 3 November 2010. Vol. No. 517. Part No. 64.
—. 10 January 2011.
HEFCE. 2010. *Trends in Young Participation in Higher Education: Core Results for England*. Bristol: Higher Education Funding Council for England.
—. 2013. *Higher Education in England: Impact of the 2012 Reforms*. 2013/03. Bristol: Higher Education Funding Council for England.
HM Treasury. 2010. *Spending Review 2010*. Cm. 7942. London: Stationery Office.
House of Commons Business, Innovation and Skills Committee. 2011. *Government Reform of Higher Education*. Twelfth Report of Session 2010–12. HC 885. London: Stationery Office.
IRHEFSF. 2010. *Securing a Sustainable Future for Higher Education: An Independent Review of Higher Education Funding and Student Finance*. At http://www.independent.gov.uk/browne-report (accessed 12 October 2010).
Johnstone, D.B., and P. Marcucci. 2010. *Financing Higher Education Worldwide: Who Pays? Who Should Pay?* Baltimore: Johns Hopkins University Press.
Le Grand, J. 2007. *The Other Invisible Hand: Delivering Public Services through Choice and Competition*. Princeton, NJ: Princeton University Press.
McMahon, W. 2009. *Higher Learning, Greater Good: The Private and Social Benefits of Higher Education*. Baltimore: Johns Hopkins University Press.
Naidoo, R., and C. Callender. 2000. "Towards a More Inclusive System? Contemporary Policy Reform in Higher Education." *Social Policy Review* 12:224–249.
National Committee of Inquiry into Higher Education. 1997. *Higher Education in the Learning Society*. Main Report. London: HMSO.
OBR. 2011. *Fiscal Sustainability Report*. London: Stationery Office.
OFFA. 2011. Access Agreement Data Tables for 2012–13. Bristol: Office for Fair Access. At http://www.offa.org.uk/publications/.
Reay, D. 2012. "Universities and the Reproduction of Inequality." In *A Manifesto for the Public University*, ed. J. Holmwood, 112–116. London: Bloomsbury Academic.
Reay, D., M.E. David, and S. Ball. 2005. *Degrees of Choice: Social Class, Race and Gender in Higher Education*. Stoke on Trent: Trentham Books.
Thompson, J., and B. Berkhradnia. 2011. *"Higher Education: Students at the Heart of the System": An Analysis of the Higher Education White Paper*. Oxford: HEPI.
UCAS. 2011. 2012 Application Figures – January 2012. At http://www.ucas.com/about_us/media_enquiries/media_releases/2012/20120130.
Usher, T., S. Baldwin, M. Munro, E. Pollard, and F. Sumption. 2010. "The Role of Finance in the Decision-Making of Higher Education Applicants and Students." Research Paper No. 9. London: BIS.
UUK. 2011. *Patterns and Trends in UK Higher Education 2011*. London: Universities UK.
Watson, D., and M. Amoah. 2007. *The Dearing Report: Ten Years On*. London: Institute of Education / Bedford Way Papers.
Winn, S., and R. Stevenson. 1997. "Student Loans: Are the Policy Objectives Being Achieved?" *Higher Education Quarterly* 51 (2):144–163.
Winston, G., and D. Zimmerman. 2000. "Where Is Aggressive Price Competition Taking Higher Education?" *Change* July/August 32 (4):10–18.

CHAPTER 8

BALANCING QUALITY AND EQUITY IN HIGHER EDUCATION POLICY AGENDAS? GLOBAL TO LOCAL TENSIONS

LESLEY VIDOVICH

INTRODUCTION: A CONTEXT OF GLOBALIZATION

Quality and equity discourses are capturing education policy agendas on a global scale. Here the focus is on the Australian higher education sector[1] as a case of quality and equity policies being used to drive national competitiveness in the global marketplace. While there is no intention to extrapolate directly from the Australian case to other countries, issues surrounding quality and equity policies and global-national-local[2] tensions are arguably also reflected and refracted through university-sector policies in many other jurisdictions. Therefore, this chapter is also offered as food for thought in those contexts where engagement with a competitive global knowledge era is receiving policy priority.

Rizvi and Lingard characterize globalization in three main ways:

> as an empirical fact that describes the profound shifts that are currently taking place in the world; as an ideology that masks various expressions of power and a range of political interests; and as a social imaginary that expresses the sense people have of their own identity and how it relates to the rest of the world, and how it implicitly shapes their aspirations and expectations. (2010, 24)

Making Policy in Turbulent Times: Challenges and Prospects for Higher Education, ed. P. Axelrod, R.D. Trilokekar, T. Shanahan, and R. Wellen. Kingston: School of Policy Studies, Queen's University.

They also make a distinction between *space* and *place* that is relevant to this analysis, defining *space* as a more abstract concept associated with compression of distance in an era of globalization and *place* as a more specific construct relating to a core of personal and community experiences. This distinction is useful in highlighting global-national-local policy dynamics. Marginson suggests that it is the concept of *place* that is "the platform on which human agency is erected" (2010a, 124).

As globalization accelerates, the degree of agency by which policy actors can produce and practise policy in ways that are nationally and locally relevant is of deep interest and concern. However, it is important to avoid reification of globalization as a force that sweeps all before it, impacting in the same ways on different jurisdictions to create global policy convergence. Identifying both common global discourses as well as national and local variations in education policy facilitates more nuanced understandings of globalization processes and focuses attention on the need to develop policies that are suited to place. That is, examining situated cases (Marginson 2007), such as offered here, helps to avoid reification of globalization.

This chapter is divided into four main sections. The first section reviews the definitions of quality and equity in higher education presented by the Organisation for Economic Co-operation and Development (OECD) in its landmark report, *Tertiary Education for the Knowledge Society* (2008). This chapter also draws from a number of other policy domains featured in the report to highlight broader policy interactions and construct an analytic framework (see Figure 1 below).

The second section focuses on Australia in 2008–09 and the call by the minister for education, employment and workplace relations and social inclusion for a "revolution" to enhance both quality and equity in higher education and, in turn, national competitive positioning in the global knowledge economy. The third section examines the evolution of quality policy in Australian higher education in both research and teaching-learning in the period 2009–12, highlighting the themes that have emerged for measuring quality. The fourth section uses the analytic framework in Figure 1 to characterize the dynamics of quality and equity policies in contemporary Australian higher education. The chapter concludes by highlighting global-national-local policy dynamics and the potential implications for other countries.

THE OECD, QUALITY, EQUITY, AND DYNAMIC POLICY INTERACTIONS

The OECD has become a central node in globalized education policy networks (Rizvi and Lingard 2010). Its power of discursive closure has enabled it to set global education agendas that have become a taken-for-granted "rule of ideas" (Rubenson 2008, 257), especially through its national thematic reviews and its statistics and indicators programs. Lingard and Rawolle have argued that the OECD plays an increasingly active role in creating a global field of comparison in education, one that has become central to contemporary forms of governance: "[It] has established a niche as the centre for technical excellence for international educational indicators and for international comparative measures of student performance [and has forged] a globalised approach to policy as numbers" (2009, 215).

The OECD identified its 2008 report, *Tertiary Education for the Knowledge Society*, as "the most comprehensive analysis ever undertaken of tertiary education policy issues at international level" (2008, 3). This report highlighted tertiary education as "a major driver of economic competitiveness in an increasingly knowledge-driven global economy" (13) as well as the central concepts of *quality* and *equity*: "substantial reforms are taking place in tertiary education systems [that are] expected to contribute to *equity*, ensure *quality* and operate efficiently" (14; emphasis added).

How, then, has the OECD defined *quality* and *equity*? Chapter 5 of the report ("Assuring and Improving Quality") focused on assessing quality in teaching and learning rather than in research. It noted the multiple interpretations of *quality* but defined it as follows: "In abstract terms quality can be defined as the distance between an objective and a result, with the implicit assumption that quality improves as this distance shrinks" (OECD 2008, 262). Such a definition implies that the objectives and results can be readily measured and compared. The OECD cited the seminal work of Harvey and Green (1993), who distinguished five key aspects of quality as exception (excellence), perfection (zero defect), fitness for purpose (defined by the provider), value for money (efficiency and effectiveness), and transformation (enhancement). It then presented Sachs' (1994) distillation of Harvey and Green's five categories into two broad types of quality assurance – accountability and improvement – and noted that these dual requirements "are tackled quite differently across countries" (OECD 2008, 265).

That chapter identified and described the three main approaches to assuring quality as accreditation, assessment (evaluation), and audit (review). It concluded with seven pages of pointers for future policy development to "help countries achieve their goal of ensuring high *quality* provision in tertiary education and adequately preparing their populations for participation in the knowledge economy" (OECD 2008, 309; emphasis added). Here, and throughout the report, narrower discourses of a knowledge *economy* dominated despite the report title featuring the broader construct of a knowledge *society*.

In a separate volume of the report, Chapter 6 ("Achieving Equity") began by noting that "equity is increasingly prominent in countries' tertiary education policies [and that] the chapter focuses on equity *in* tertiary education and only briefly addresses equity *through* tertiary education (or the social mobility effects of tertiary education)" (OECD 2008, 13). With regard to the latter, it focused on equal opportunities in the labour market, suggesting an economic rationale for equity policies. It offered a comprehensive definition of *equity* to include inputs, processes, and outcomes.

Equitable tertiary systems are those that ensure that access to, participation in, and outcomes of tertiary education are based only on individuals' innate abilities and study efforts. They ensure that achieving educational potential at the tertiary level is not the result of personal or social circumstances, including factors such as socio-economic status, gender, ethnic origin, immigrant status, place of residence, age, or disability (OECD 2008, 14).

That chapter reviewed trends in equity and factors affecting equity in tertiary education. It noted that "socio-economic background impacts on the aspirations for tertiary studies of secondary students" (OECD 2008, 25), citing the OECD's Programme for International Student Assessment (PISA) data from 15-year-olds. It also noted that "in most countries, there is little emphasis on equity of outcomes [such as] completion rates by under-represented groups" (35). As with the chapter on quality, it finished with seven pages of pointers for future policy development.

It is evident from the OECD's overview that both quality and equity are multifaceted. In earlier work, I have described *quality* as being like a chameleon[3] (Vidovich 2001), and this label might also be applied to *equity*. Both concepts are thus "in the eye of the beholder." However, I argue here that the OECD report has paid insufficient attention to the ideological underpinnings of these constructs, the way they might interact with each other, and the way they might play out differently in different contexts (both nationally and sub-nationally). In addition, the OECD's pointers for future policy development are of concern given their propensity to suggest that these are generic policy solutions equally applicable across different countries.

I attempt to tackle these issues in the remainder of this chapter, and I begin with Figure 1.

Figure 1 has been constructed with a view to locating quality and equity within broader higher education policy parameters and facilitating a more holistic examination of dynamic policy interactions. It draws on the policy themes in the OECD report. (However, that report contains a separate chapter on each policy theme, each written by different authors, with little consideration of the potential interactions among them.) At the apex of the triangle sits the policy contexts, including globalization and internationalization. Inside the triangle is the primary focus of policies on quality and equity in research and teaching-learning. The base of the triangle is represented by the governance structures and processes as well as funding mechanisms – the major policy parameters for achieving quality and equity (or not).

I will return to this figure later in this chapter.

FIGURE 1
Quality and equity policy dynamics

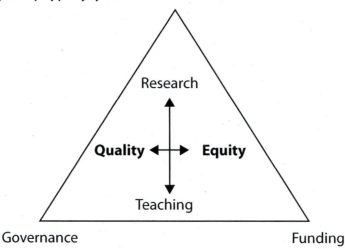

Source: Author's compilation.

"REVOLUTION" IN AUSTRALIAN HIGHER EDUCATION TO IMPROVE QUALITY AND EQUITY (2008–09)

By way of context, Australia is one of the six federations in the OECD. Higher education has been under central Commonwealth Government control since the 1970s, facilitated by a vertical fiscal imbalance in which the Commonwealth's income tax yields a much higher level of financial resources than the states can muster. There are 39 universities across the country, and major groupings with a secretariat are the Group of Eight (research-intensive), Australian Technology Network (former institutes of technology), and Innovative Research Universities (established in the 1960s and 1970s). In addition, there are ungrouped universities (largely former colleges) and an increasing number of private providers and branch campuses of international universities.

A significant turning point in contemporary higher education policy was the election of a Labor Government in late 2007, on the platform of an "education revolution," after more than a decade of the conservative Coalition Government. This education revolution was to be founded on a quality-equity policy couplet. The minister for education, employment and workplace relations and social inclusion (later prime minister) asserted, "The Education Revolution ... must improve *equity* and *quality* because we're falling behind in both" (Gillard 2008, n.p.; emphasis added). The sense of urgency in lifting Australia's education performance – compared to other developed countries – was palpable. The Labor Government initiated two reviews focused on universities in early 2008, and the reports, *Venturous Australia: Building Strength in Innovation* (Cutler 2008) and *Review of Australian Higher Education* (Bradley 2008), were released the same year, just months after the OECD report.

The Cutler report highlighted policy discourses of quality and excellence in research. It asserted that "high *quality* human capital is critical to innovation" (2008, xi; emphasis added) and recommended building "concentrations of excellence" (167) as well as allocating an increasing amount of research funding based on evidence of excellence in research. There was no reference to equity in the report; its recommendations about further concentrating research among the highest-performing researchers represents the antithesis of equity.

However, the Bradley report identified both quality and equity as the underlying rationales for its recommendations.

> There is an international consensus that the reach, *quality*, and performance of a nation's higher education system will be key determinants of its economic and social progress. If we are to maintain our high standard of living, underpinned by a robust democracy and civil and *just society*, we need an outstanding, internationally competitive higher education system. (2008, xi; emphasis added)

The Bradley report set specific targets for 2020 to align with quality and equity goals, respectively: 40 percent of all 25-to-34-year-olds should graduate with a bachelor's degree, and 20 percent of undergraduate enrolments should come from low socio-economic backgrounds. In relation to the quality target of increasing the number of graduates to service the global knowledge economy, international comparisons were clearly a driving force: "Australia is losing ground. Within the OECD we are now ninth out of 30 in the proportion of our population aged 25 to 34 years with such [degree-level] qualifications, down from seventh a decade ago" (2008, xi). The equity target of increasing the number of disadvantaged students enrolling at universities could also assist with achieving the quality target because if more graduates were to be produced, intakes would have to draw on new groups of students who had not historically been well represented in universities, such as those from low socio-economic backgrounds.

It is notable that the Bradley report expressed the equity target in terms of more enrolments of disadvantaged groups (inputs), whereas the quality target was expressed as more graduations (outcomes). The quality target was more consistent with the outcomes discourses of contemporary education policy and suggests that equity was marginalized from the outset. Many commentators (e.g., Allport 2009; Gale cited in

Rowbotham 2009) welcomed the more explicit equity recommendations, but concerns were expressed about how quality and equity would be balanced, especially with the proposed market-style funding allocations driven by student demand: markets in education have a long history of exacerbating inequalities.

The government endorsed most of the Bradley report's recommendations in its 2009 policy, *Transforming Australia's Higher Education System*. It emphasized that the policy was "essential to enable Australia to participate fully in, and benefit from, the global knowledge economy" (Australian Government 2009, 5). Quality assurance was to be the responsibility of a new national regulator, which was enshrined in legislation in 2011 as the Tertiary Education Quality and Standards Agency (TEQSA). TEQSA would begin operation in 2012 by registering and evaluating the performance of higher education providers against a Higher Education Standards Framework, which would consist of the five domains of Provider Standards, Qualification Standards, Teaching and Learning Standards, Information Standards, and Research Standards. TEQSA would have a dual focus of "ensuring that higher education providers meet minimum standards, as well as promoting best practice and improving the *quality* of the higher education sector as a whole" (Australian Government 2012, n.p.; emphasis added).

But on having TEQSA monitor equity there was silence, suggesting that equity was slipping further off the agenda. Equity policy was not significantly developed beyond the initial target set in 2008 of 20 percent of students from low socio-economic backgrounds being enrolled by 2020. In fact, this target was subsequently delayed by five years, and even then the chair of TEQSA, who had conducted the *Review of Australian Higher Education* (Bradley 2008), publicly acknowledged that equity targets would be the biggest challenge.

The next section focuses on the high level of policy attention, since 2009, to developing quality in research and teaching-learning in Australian universities and enhancing the country's international competitiveness. The lack of policy development in the equity domain means that a parallel discussion on equity is not possible, although it does speak volumes about the relative priorities of quality and equity in higher education.

EVOLUTION OF QUALITY POLICY IN AUSTRALIAN HIGHER EDUCATION: POLICY REVERSALS (2009–12)

The development of policy on quality in Australian higher education was both rapid and marked by dramatic policy reversals; this is described in the following two subsections, which focus on policy examples in research and teaching-learning. The final subsection focuses on key themes that emerged from attempts to measure quality in both domains.

Australian policy on quality in research

The centrepiece of the Australian government's strategy to forge inter-national competitiveness by enhancing research quality is the *Excellence in Research for Australia* (ERA) initiative, which was announced in 2009; the first research assessment was carried out in 2010, and performance funding began to flow after the subsequent assessment in 2012. The ERA further shifted the focus in research assessment from quantity to quality of publications, and it further accelerated research concentration, which was deemed to be in Australia's strategic interest. According to the minister for innovation and research, the ERA would "revolutionise Australia's research performance" (Carr 2009, 36) and also allow research assessment to be more transparent.

For the 2010 ERA, journal rankings were a proxy measure of research quality, based on the assumption that the quality of a paper can be as-sessed from the quality of the journal in which it is published. Journals across eight discipline groupings were ranked on a scale of A*, A, B, and C, with the latter being the bottom 50 percent (classified as "below international standard"). These competitive journal rankings were highly contentious, and by early 2011, strong negative reactions from the sector were building. The minister initially indicated that the 2012 ERA assess-ment would be largely unchanged, with only some minor reshuffling of the journals, after much lobbying by academics to have the journals repositioned. However, criticism from the sector continued to mount.

The most common criticisms of the 2010 ERA were its methodological weaknesses; the time wasted in both preparing submissions and ob-taining peer evaluations; the undervaluing of interdisciplinary research; the undermining of collaborative research by such a competitive process; the associated use of performance management in universities to set publication targets for individual academics based on journal rankings; a reduction in locally relevant research, especially in the social sciences; and, finally, a diminution of the number of Australian journals and researchers given that the highest-ranked journals were internationally based (Cooper and Poletti 2011; Martin 2011; Young, Peetz, and Marais 2011; Vidovich and Currie 2013).

In mid-2011, there was a dramatic reversal in policy. Taking the sector by surprise, the minister – seemingly acting alone – decided to scrap the journal rankings altogether for the 2012 ERA. He explained his decision: "There is clear and consistent evidence that the rankings were being deployed inappropriately within some quarters of the sector in ways that could produce harmful outcomes and based on a poor understand-ing of the actual role of rankings. One common example was setting targets for publication in 'A' and 'A*' journals by institutional research managers" (Carr cited in Dobson 2011, 28). The minister's explanation for the problems with the ERA journal rankings appears to place the blame on university practices rather than on the government's poor design of the policy in the first place. For the 2012 ERA, a "journal quality profile" was one component of the evaluation committees' assessment in research quality on a scale of 1 to 5. Arguably, such an approach is even less transparent than the controversial journal rankings, despite the minister's original contention that enhanced transparency was one of the main rationales for the ERA.

In addition to the controversy about journal rankings, there was much debate about including research impact as a dimension of quality in the 2010 ERA. After a great deal of uncertainty about how to measure the impact of research, the minister for innovation and research excluded it from the first ERA in 2010. Then, a year later, the same minister resurrected it from the government's "too hard basket" (Rowbotham 2011, 23), this time to propose that it be a separate assessment from the ERA. The Australian Technology Network universities had led the push to include research impact, understandably, given the more applied nature of their research output and therefore the relative ease of documenting evidence of research impact, especially in the short term. The Australian Technology Network, as well as the Group of Eight universities (where a large portion of the medical research is located), proceeded to conduct trials on the measurement of research impact in 2012. Issues surrounding a definition of *quality*, which includes research impact, point to sector lobbying and political contestation over the relative value placed on pure and applied research as well as more pragmatic issues of appropriate measures of impact.

The above examples of policy reversals demonstrate the fluid nature of defining research quality of an international standard. There have also been examples of policy reversals in the push to achieve an international standard of quality in teaching-learning, as outlined below.

Australian policy on quality in teaching-learning

The context for university teaching-learning is changing in Australia (and in many other countries) in the face of globalization, especially with demands to better prepare students for a global knowledge economy. The changing nature of student populations – in particular, massification and internationalization – have resulted in more heterogeneous student groupings as well as larger class sizes (although budgets have seldom grown in concert with enrolments). Furthermore, because students are more mobile and/or more internationally connected, they increasingly select their higher education institution from a global "menu." Universities are now competing to attract and retain the best and the brightest students locally, nationally, and internationally (de Wit 2009). Sophisticated markets have developed for higher education, in which quality is paramount. Equity has also been a concern with more heterogeneous student populations, and issues around inclusivity in the classroom are emerging (Arnesen, Mietola, and Lahelma 2007). All of these changes bring potential challenges for university teaching-learning.

In Australia, national policy on teaching-learning in universities has been progressing on two main fronts: that focused on supporting the development of teachers and that focused on measuring student learning outcomes. The development of university teachers had been the mission of the Australian Learning and Teaching Council (ALTC); however, the prime minister suddenly abolished it in February 2011 to fund reconstruction after extensive floods the month before. The speed with which the ALTC was sacrificed for small financial savings astonished the sector. After an uproar from universities, a review by a British higher education expert later in the same year led to a reversal of the policy, and the Office for Learning and Teaching (OLT) was established "in an attempt to retain an independent identity for the functions of the ALTC" (Trounson 2011b, 28).

The OLT "promotes and supports change in higher education institutions for the enhancement of learning and teaching" (2012, n.p.). Its key responsibilities include awarding grants to implement innovations, commissioning work of strategic significance to inform policy development, managing a suite of awards to celebrate excellence, and disseminating and embedding good practice. It has an advisory committee with representatives from senior university leadership, staff, and student unions to maintain a sense of ownership by the sector (Trounson 2011b, 28). However, one might argue that such sector "ownership" of the OLT represents a rather token gesture toward recognizing academic autonomy in the face of the parallel development of the government's harder-nosed drive to measure student learning outcomes and publicly compare them, both nationally and internationally.

The Bradley review had recommended constructing "a set of indicators and instruments to directly assess and compare learning outcomes and a set of formal statements of academic standards by discipline along with processes for applying those standards" (2008, xxii). Furthermore, incentive funding would be attached to teaching-learning performance, and although marginal (2.5 percent of teaching-learning funds), it symbolized the government's intention to raise quality. The search was then on to find valid and reliable instruments to measure student learning outcomes, and the OECD's Assessment of Higher Education Learning Outcomes (AHELO) project became a significant source of influence.

Ultimately, international comparisons in higher education forged by the OECD may well take on a similar role to PISA in the schooling sector because that program has become a powerful instrument for driving quality and equity agendas around the world. In addition to being influenced by the OECD, by 2010 the Australian policy elite was seeking to adopt the Collegiate Learning Assessment (CLA), a test that measures a graduate's generic skills, from the United States. However, this move drew strong negative reactions from the sector in Australia as being inappropriate, evidenced by headlines in the higher education press: "No End to Row over Standards" (Trounson 2010, 29) and "US Test of Skills a Poor Fit Here" (Lane 2010a, 25). And a government spokesperson claimed that the "CLA would allow international benchmarking and pointed to OECD endorsement of the test" (Lane 2010b, 24).

By 2011, the government had decreed that an Australian version of the CLA would form part of an ensemble of performance indicators for measuring the quality of university teaching and learning (Australian Government 2011). This ensemble would also include performance data from individual universities, published on the MyUniversity website for "consumers" to compare. But by early 2013, there was silence on CLA developments, and the final report on the OECD's AHELO feasibility study was imminent, so an instrument to measure student learning outcomes remained elusive. Notably, there was also a reversal of policy on performance funding for teaching-learning, although, I would suggest, only temporarily, until measures of student learning outcomes are further developed, both in Australia and internationally.

TEQSA has operated since 2012, and the assessment of learning and teaching standards has come under the Higher Education Standards Framework, giving TEQSA the power to de-register a university if it does not meet the standards. The foundation chair of the Higher Education Standards Panel, a well-respected former vice-chancellor, indicated that he would "seek to balance the need to reassure the public on *quality* while ensuring that standards were not excessively intrusive on universities" (Robson cited in Trounson 2011a, 31; emphasis added). He further commented that he was personally keen on peer review for maintaining standards.

Robson's appointment will likely ease the way for the standards agenda in the sector, bridging the often deep government-universities divide. However, one might argue that despite the "ownership" value of peer review, it will require a further investment of academics' time when they are already being stretched to produce world-class outcomes in both research and teaching-learning. The standards agenda also risks criticism of standardization, which may assure minimum quality but act as a barrier to achieving the high level of quality improvement required to attain world-class status and thereby attract the best and brightest students. In all, developing measures of quality in teaching-learning is still evolving rapidly, and the stakes are becoming higher.

Measuring quality: emergent themes

The discussion in the previous two subsections on the evolution of quality policy in Australian higher education over the period 2009 to 2012 in research and teaching-learning has revealed a number of emergent themes. Measuring quality has been highly contested, and a series of backlashes from the sector have been somewhat successful in bringing a number of dramatic reversals in policy, demonstrating that definitions of quality are arbitrary. The level of ministerial involvement in both policy announcements and reversals also suggests that quality is politically malleable. The desire of the policy elite to measure finer and finer degrees of quality has outstripped the development of valid and reliable measurement instruments.

Arguably, it is not just a matter of trying harder to find the "right" measures – those that can claim validity and reliability – but acknowledging that some of the most valuable outcomes of university research and teaching-learning are the most difficult to measure and that attempts to impose narrow and reductionist conceptualizations of quality may well be counterproductive. Put another way, moves by the policy elite to narrow the definitions of quality to those dimensions that are most easily measured undermine developing an authentic, bottom-up approach to quality, whereas academics conduct their work with a high degree of agency based on their expert knowledge, and this in turn would better foster the essence of creativity and innovation that purportedly characterizes a global knowledge era.

This policy problem of how to measure quality is revealed in the tension between peer review (qualitative judgments by academics) and metrics (quantitative data collected by bureaucrats), which has percolated through the evolution of quality policy. A detailed examination of the strengths and weaknesses of employing peer review and metrics is beyond the scope of this chapter, but the point to be made here is that the metrics–peer review alternatives reflect different conceptualizations of quality, and they direct academic work in different ways, again demonstrating the chameleon-like nature of quality. However, the bigger question remains: does the drive for more sophisticated accountability mechanisms in university research and teaching-learning actually improve quality? I don't believe it does, as the title of one of my earlier publications suggests: "You Don't Fatten the Pig by Weighting It" (Vidovich 2009).

DYNAMICS OF QUALITY AND EQUITY POLICIES IN AUSTRALIAN HIGHER EDUCATION

Here I return to the framework provided in Figure 1 in an attempt to characterize contemporary Australian higher education policy on quality and equity in research and teaching-learning. The subsections below draw together the relevant policy domains and focus on the interactions among them.

Global and international influences

Marginson maintains that "global flows constitute lines of communication and lines of effect that are relatively visible" (2010b, 202). The analysis in that chapter points to visible flows of quality and equity policy in higher education through international "policy borrowing" (Dale 1999; Phillips and Schweisfurth 2007). Powerful influences from the OECD are evident – for example, Australian higher education policy discourses on quality and equity rose to prominence later in the same year as the OECD's 2008 report *Tertiary Education for the Knowledge Society*. In teaching and learning, the OECD's AHELO project has been influential in placing the measurement of student learning outcomes firmly on higher education policy agendas.

It is interesting to note another, more personal, conduit of policy transfer from the OECD to the Australian policy elite. Barry McGaw, a former head of the Directorate of Education at the OECD, returned to Australia not long before the change to a Labor government in 2007, and, while his impact was perhaps more visible in the schooling sector as chair of Australia's first National Curriculum Board, he was instrumental in raising the profile of quality and equity discourses in education. He argued that while Australia is ranked above average compared to other countries in the quality of its educational outcomes, as measured by the OECD's PISA, "Our main equity problem is that differences in students' backgrounds have a greater influence on educational results in Australia than in some other high-performing countries such as Canada" (McGaw 2007, 25; see also McGaw 2008). In general, though, global and international influences have been less visible for equity policies than for quality policies in Australian higher education.

The United Kingdom has been a source of policy borrowing for Australian education policy since colonial times. For example, its Research Assessment Exercise (RAE) was a model for research assessment in Australia (the ERA and its predecessor, the Research Quality Framework), in principle if not in detail. It is apparent, though, that Australian policy on research quality has been significantly less stable than that in the UK, being subject to more rapid policy changes and complete policy reversals and with a shorter lead time between policy announcements and assessments. In 2009, the UK announced that from 2014, its RAE would be replaced by the Research Excellence Framework, which would make greater use of quantitative indicators of research quality and also assess the economic and social impact of research, giving it a 20 percent weighting (Corbyn 2009). So watch this space for continued evolution of Australian policy along these lines.

The significant influence of the UK on Australian research quality assessments is ironic given that US universities dominate the top of international league tables, a position to which Australian universities aspire. Thus, while the US provides the "gold standard" for research outcomes, the UK appears to remain powerful in providing mechanisms for achieving quality in Australian research. This is possibly due to the highly centralized nature of higher education policy in both the UK and Australia compared with the greater autonomy of universities in the US. Surely there should be a message in this for the Australian policy elite about the link between autonomy and quality in research. The American CLA initiative in teaching-learning has also been influential, despite a backlash from the Australian sector that it is inappropriate. The policy "solution" in Australia is to produce its own version of the CLA, although in early 2013, its use remains unclear.

In all, there is clear evidence of strong global and international influences on quality policy and, to a lesser extent, on equity policy in Australian higher education. However, the Australian government has not directly imported such policies, unmodified, from international sources; it has experimented and adapted specific policy details in both research and teaching-learning. Overall, though, the primary locus of influence on higher education reform agendas is global. The prevailing (near hegemonic) global economic ideology is a powerful policy stimulus. In particular, the underlying rationale for new quality and equity policies has been the need to improve Australia's competitive positioning in comparison with other OECD countries. This demonstrates the phenomenon of international comparisons as a significant new form of governance (Lingard and Rawolle 2009).

Governance and funding policies

Australian policies on governance and funding in higher education have been key vehicles for enacting policy priorities for quality and equity. Over the last three decades, Australian higher education governance and funding have been affected by tightening centralized control and the "power of the purse" in dictating and embedding new policies. Over time, the leverage of relatively small amounts of performance funding has been effective in steering cash-strapped universities rapidly toward government priorities. The OECD has highlighted the effective use that the Australian government makes of financial policy levers in higher education: "The most common use of financial tools to support policy implementation is in the form of incentives. This steering mechanism has been successfully used in Australia for nearly two decades already" (2008, 332). However, there have been growing tensions between, on the one hand, highly centralized control, including increasing interest at the ministerial level in policy and attenuated performance funding, and, on the other, reduced autonomy or agency of both universities and academics to steer their own paths in the so-called global knowledge era.

In 2009, the Labor Government's policy response to the Bradley and Cutler reviews of 2008 brought further reforms to governance and funding to support higher education policies on quality and, to a lesser extent, equity. The Bradley report noted the effect of underfunding during the previous decade of the Coalition Government, especially on the quality of Australian higher education: "Australia is the only OECD country where the public contribution to higher education remained at the same level in 2005 as it had been in 1995" (2008, xv). It noted further that funds for research infrastructure were so low that there was a "pattern of quite unacceptable levels of cross-subsidy from funds for teaching, adversely affecting the *quality* of the student experience" (xii; emphasis added).

Funding has been significantly increased to attempt to bring it up to OECD levels (A\$5.4 billion over four years). However, it is clear that the price to be paid for more funding is more accountability, especially with the establishment of TEQSA as a powerful national regulator – a significant new governance mechanism in Australian higher education. TEQSA accredits universities and conducts quality audits of standards, more firmly entrenching an audit culture in Australian higher education. Increased performance funding is a key policy lever for rapidly embedding quality policy in research and teaching-learning (although proposed performance funding in teaching-learning was suspended in 2011).

Despite clear evidence of increasing Australian government control over higher education, it is also evident that lobbying by universities and academics has been able to achieve reversals of some quality policy details, suggesting at least a limited degree of localized agency in Australian higher education policy processes. Overall, though, I would argue that politicians and bureaucrats are too powerful in relation to the marginalized voices of academics in Australian policy on quality and equity (and other policy domains). Top-down policy processes overwhelm bottom-up input into decision-making. Furthermore, tight national government steerage has been justified by and reinforced with discourses on the imperatives of globalization and the global knowledge economy.

One interesting point to note about governance style in Australian higher education is the growing role played by several former vice-chancellors in mediating the accelerating control by the national government, especially the "spools of red tape" (Craven 2010, 28) threatening to strangle the sector. In particular, Denise Bradley – former vice-chancellor, chair of the *Review of Australian Higher Education* and chair of TEQSA – has been instrumental in bridging the gap between the national government and the universities as well as managing the control-autonomy tension.

This governance strategy of co-opting well-respected former university leaders into the government's policy processes has arguably increased the likelihood of translating national government policy intent into workable policy parameters that will enhance acceptance by universities. Such key personalities can provide a conduit for the government to appear to be listening to feedback from the sector, although policy modifications may be only marginal when set against the overarching thrust of the government holding universities to greater account for achieving "world class" outcomes.

In all, the financial power of the Australian government in higher education continues to give it the leverage to tightly control quality and equity policies, purportedly in the national interest.

Quality and equity policies

In Australia, a quality-equity policy couplet has been highlighted from the time of the Labor Government's election in late 2007, and it was translated into new higher education policy in 2009. However, quality consistently dominates equity in both national- and university-level policies and practices. Equity has remained underdeveloped – aspirational at best – and has not received the sustained policy attention of quality. Quality and equity policies can be in sharp tension, especially when they are competing for limited resources. The OECD's 2008 report pointed to the challenges for national policy-makers presented by "policy paradoxes" or "tradeoffs" that reduce policy coherence and "create tensions between policy initiatives which may end up being mutually contradictory" (OECD 2008, 136). Arguably, the quality-equity policy couplet in Australian higher education exemplifies such a policy paradox. That is, quality might well be achieved at the expense of equity or vice versa, although when they are in competition, it is most likely that quality targets will prevail.

It is important to highlight the fact that quality and equity targets have been constructed using different frames of reference. In Australian higher education, the reference points for judging quality are quite decisively global in scale, economic in orientation, and based on outcomes measures; that is, they aim to enhance competitiveness in a global knowledge economy, and they reflect the dominant neo-liberal ideology that has prevailed in public policy over the last 30 years.

For equity, these reference points appear to be more national in scale, social in orientation, and based on inputs. The OECD has noted that "in most countries, equity policies have traditionally emphasized equity of access over equity of outcomes" (2008, 35) and that little data is available on outcomes such as completion rates of disadvantaged students. This is true in Australia. With the current Labor Government, equity policies are couched in the discourses of social inclusion and social cohesion. Green (2006) describes the latter in terms of a high level of educational and income equality as well as trust. However, equity policies can also be viewed as a tool for enhancing global economic standing if they result in less waste of human capital by "pulling up the tail" and raising national averages on international comparative performance measures;

that is, equity can also be seen to represent economic efficiency. Equity, then, is possibly even more chameleon-like in nature than quality as it has both economic and social rationales that may not always be in sync.

However, equity is at least appearing more often on higher education policy agendas (OECD 2008) now that the economistic discourses accompanying globalization have become more prevalent over the last three decades. As the discourses change from the narrow construct of a knowledge economy to the wider construct of a knowledge society (as evidenced in the OECD report), we may be witnessing a nascent shift toward what has been referred to as *inclusive liberalism* (Craig and Porter 2005; Rubenson 2008).

This concept points to a potential hybridization of neo-liberal and social democratic governing ideologies, and it may herald a greater hybridization of quality and equity policies. Such a shift would warrant closer examination of the interplay between economic and social discourses in higher education reform agendas. In this regard, the framework shown in Figure 1 is useful for thinking about contemporary higher education quality and equity policy priorities, and highlighting the interactions between them, as well as their relationships to other policy domains. The triangle allows a more holistic examination of the interplay among them.

In all, quality and equity are not necessarily comfortable bedfellows, as is suggested in agendas articulated by the policy elite in Australian higher education. Quality discourses are significantly more powerful, and they are constructed in terms of enhancing comparative economic performance on the global stage. Equity discourses have remained marginal. Governance and funding structures and processes in Australian higher education have targeted improving the quality of outcomes, but equity policy remains underdeveloped and under-supported, with a focus on access (inputs) rather than outcomes. There is, however, some (limited) evidence of an ideological shift by which social discourses may begin to feature more prominently.

CONCLUSION

To conclude, this chapter returns to the issue of global-national-local policy dynamics with which it began. In Australian higher education, just as there is evidence of powerful global and international influences on quality policies, and to a lesser extent equity policies, there is evidence of national government mediation of globalized policy discourses, as well as some localized inputs from universities and academics, into the development of national policy. Thus, there is at least a limited sense of place (Rizvi and Lingard 2010) and localized agency in Australian quality and equity policy processes. Altogether, this creates networks of dynamic global-national-local policy interactions (Marginson and Rhoades 2002).

It is important, though, that policy-makers at the national and local (university) levels step back to critique globalizing discourses on global knowledge economy and global knowledge society and ask to what extent current higher education policy directions are supporting or undermining the knowledge, skills, and attitudes appropriate for the new times in Century 21. Furthermore, policy-makers need to ask whether policy solutions are necessarily equally relevant in different national and sub-national jurisdictions. This should include critically examining the role of the OECD in increasing the pressure to create global "policy pandemics" (Vidovich 2009) and convergence with its comparative statistics and reports such as *Tertiary Education for the Knowledge Society*, which offers long lists of pointers for future policy development directed at national governments. That report states that "OECD work helps countries to learn from one another" (OECD 2008, 3), but it may well be that its pointers for future policy development delimit alternative ways of viewing policy problems and solutions that are, or should be, context-specific. Mac Ruairc, among others, has criticized "the OECD way ... [of] one size fits all" (2010, 233) across different jurisdictions.

As always, further research would help illuminate issues raised in this chapter. It should not remain unstated that despite the prevalence of discourses of evidence-based policy, the Australian government has not provided an evidence base for its policy choices on quality in research or teaching-learning, and this has probably contributed to the dramatic policy reversals in recent years. There has been a significant amount of uncritical policy-borrowing from international sources such as the OECD, UK, and US. Research in other countries could provide the basis for informative and critical comparative analysis, and for this, the schema in Figure 1 may be helpful. For example, how does the balance among the policy domains in the triangle vary across different jurisdictions? International comparative research can be very useful for active *policy learning* (Lange and Alexiadou 2010; Vidovich 2009) – a more dialectic concept than passive *policy borrowing* – to develop and sustain context-relevant policies and preserve localized place and agency to support creativity and innovation in a global knowledge era.

NOTES

1. *Higher education* is used in this chapter as it is the term used in the Australian context, although *tertiary education* and *post-secondary education* are used in other contexts.
2. For the purposes of this chapter, *local* refers to the institutional level of individual universities.
3. A chameleon is a reptile that is able to suddenly and dramatically change its colour to suit its environment, thereby achieving camouflage and enhancing its survival.

REFERENCES

Allport, C. 2009. "Not All Institutions Can Be Treated Equally." *Australian Higher Education Supplement* 14 January:28.

Arnesen, A.L., R. Mietola, and E. Lahelma. 2007. "Language of Inclusion and Diversity: Policy Discourses and Social Practices in Finnish and Norwegian Schools." *International Journal of Inclusive Education* 11 (1):97–110.

Australian Government. 2009. *Transforming Australia's Higher Education System*. Canberra: Department of Education, Employment, Workplace Relations and Social Inclusion.

—. 2011. Advancing Quality in Higher Education Information Sheet: An Australian Version of the Collegiate Learning Assessment. At http://www.innovation.gov.au/HigherEducation/Policy/Documents/Collegiate_Learning_Assessment.pdf (accessed 4 June 2013).

—. 2012. About TEQSA. At http://www.teqsa.gov.au/about (accessed 4 June 2013).

Bradley, D. 2008. *Review of Australian Higher Education: Final Report*. Canberra: Commonwealth of Australia.

Carr, K. 2009. "Research Impact Hard to Quantify." *Australian Higher Education Supplement* 15 July:36.

Cooper, S., and A. Poletti. 2011. "The New ERA Journal Ranking: The Consequences of Australia's Fraught Encounter with 'Quality.'" *Australian Universities' Review* 53 (1):57–65.

Corbyn, Z. 2009. "UK Focuses on Benefits of Research." *Australian Higher Education Supplement* 1 July:29.

Craig, D., and D. Porter. 2005. "The Third Way and the Third World: Poverty Reduction and Social Inclusion Strategies in the Rise of 'Inclusive Liberalism.'" *Review of International Political Economy* 12 (2): 226–223.

Craven, G. 2010. "Taking the Toxic Out of TEQSA." *Australian Higher Education Supplement* 23 June:28.

Cutler. T. 2008. *Venturous Australia: Building Strength in Innovation*. Melbourne: Cutler.

Dale, R. 1999. "Specifying Globalization Effects on National Policy: A Focus on the Mechanisms." *Journal of Education Policy* 14 (1):1–17.

de Wit, H. 2009. "Internationalisation, Teaching and Learning and Strategic Partnerships." Keynote address at the Internationalising Learning and Teaching in Academic Settings Conference, Sydney, Australia, 23–26 November.

Dobson, I. 2011. "Victory in a Battle That Need Not Have Been Fought." *Advocate* 18 (2):28.

Gillard, J. 2008. "The Sir Robert Menzies Oration 2008." Given at the University of Melbourne, Melbourne, Australia, 6 November. At http://www.unimelb.edu.au/speeches/transcripts/gillard_menzies_oration_2008.doc (accessed 4 June 2013).

Green, A. 2006. "Models of Lifelong Learning and the Knowledge Society." *Compare* 36 (3):307–325.

Lane, B. 2010a. "US Test of Skills a Poor Fit Here." *Australian Higher Education Supplement* 1 December:25.

—. 2010b. "Performance Funding Queried." *Australian Higher Education Supplement* 8 December:24.

Lange, B., and N. Alexiadou. 2010. "Policy Learning and Governance of Education Policy in the EU." *Journal of Education Policy* 25 (4):443–463.

Lingard, B., and S. Rawolle. 2009. "Rescaling and Reconstituting Education Policy." In *Re-reading Education Policies: A Handbook Studying the Policy Agenda of the 21st Century*, ed. M. Simons, M. Olssen, and M.A. Peters, 205–219. Rotterdam: Sense Publishers.

Mac Ruairc, G. 2010. "This Way Please! Improving School Leadership: The OECD Way." *Journal of Educational Administration and History* 42 (3):223–246.

Marginson, S. 2007. "Global Position and Position Taking: The Case of Australia." *Journal of Studies in International Education* 11 (1):5–32.

—. 2010a. "Space, Mobility and Synchrony in the Knowledge Economy." In *Global Creation: Space, Mobility and Synchrony in the Age of the Knowledge Economy*, ed. S. Marginson, P. Murphy, and M. Peters, 117–149. New York: Peter Lang.

—. 2010b. "Higher Education as a Global Field." In *Global Creation: Space, Mobility and Synchrony in the Age of the Knowledge Economy*, ed. S. Marginson, P. Murphy, and M. Peters, 201–228. New York: Peter Lang.

Marginson, S., and G. Rhoades. 2002. "Beyond National States, Markets, and Systems of Higher Education: A Glonacal Agency Heuristic." *Higher Education* 43 (3):281–309.

Martin, B. 2011. "ERA: Adverse Consequences." *Australian Universities' Review* 53 (2):99–102.

McGaw, B. 2007. "Resourced for a World of Difference." *Australian Higher Education Supplement* 1 August:25.

—. 2008. "How Good Is Australian School Education?" In *Education, Science and Public Policy: Ideas for an Education Revolution*, ed. S. Marginson and R. James, 53–77. Melbourne: Melbourne University Press.

OECD. 2008. *Tertiary Education for the Knowledge Society*. (Authored by P. Santiago, K. Tremblay, E. Basri, and E. Arnal.) 2 volumes. Paris: OECD.

OLT. 2012. About the Office for Learning and Teaching. At http://www.olt.gov.au/about-olt (accessed 25 January 2012).

Phillips, D., and M. Schweisfurth. 2007. *Comparative and International Education*. New York: Continuum.

Rizvi, F., and B. Lingard. 2010. *Globalizing Education Policy*. London: Taylor and Francis.

Rowbotham, J. 2009. "Gale Raises Equity Fears." *Australian Higher Education Supplement* 21 January:30.

—. 2011. "Research Impact Hard to Quantify." *Australian Higher Education Supplement* 9 November:23, 25.

Rubenson, K. 2008. "OECD Education Policies and World Hegemony." In *The OECD and Transnational Governance*, ed. R. Mahon and S. McBride, 285–298. Vancouver: UBC Press.

Trounson, A. 2010. "No End to Row over Standards." *Australian Higher Education Supplement* 1 December:29.

—. 2011a. "Robson to Chair Standards Panel." *Australian Higher Education Supplement* 9 November:31.

—. 2011b. "Independent Overview of Learning, Teaching." *Australian Higher Education Supplement* 16 November:28.

Vidovich, L. 2001. "That Chameleon 'Quality': The Multiple and Contradictory Discourses of 'Quality' Policy in Australian Higher Education." *Discourse: Studies in the Cultural Politics of Education* 22 (2):249–261.

—. 2009. "'You Don't Fatten the Pig by Weighting It': Contradictory Tensions in the 'Policy Pandemic' of Accountability Infecting Education." In *Re-reading Education Policies: A Handbook Studying the Policy Agenda of the 21st Century*, ed. M. Simons, M. Olssen, and M. Peters, 549–567. Rotterdam: Sense Publishers.

Vidovich, L., and J. Currie. 2013. "Aspiring to 'World Class' Universities in Australia: A Global Trend with Intended and Unintended Consequences." In *The Forefront of International Higher Education: A Festschrift in Honour of Philip G. Altbach*, ed. R.M. Bassett and A. Maldonado-Maldonado. Dordrecht: Springer.

Young, S., D. Peetz, and M. Marais. 2011. "The Impact of Journal Ranking Fetishism on Australian Policy-Related Research." *Australian Universities' Review* 53 (2):77–87.

CHAPTER 9

RESEARCH AND RELUCTANCE IN IMPROVING CANADIAN HIGHER EDUCATION

IAN D. CLARK AND KEN NORRIE

INTRODUCTION

Higher education paradoxes and outline of this chapter

One of higher education's many paradoxes is that the sector values research but devotes little effort to scholarly inquiry about how to improve its performance. A second paradox is that the higher education sector values evidence but is reluctant to act when evidence calls for change in core practices.

This chapter examines these two paradoxes as they apply to Canadian universities. We begin with a look at recent studies of the performance of Canadian higher education and then propose an improvement-oriented research agenda for the next decade. We believe that scholarly work on this agenda would generate compelling propositions for changing the way Canadian higher education is organized and how academic work is assigned and conducted. We introduce a thought experiment of imagining the titles of research chairs that could be created in Canada if each university devoted 1 percent of its operating budget to inquiry into improving higher education. We then examine some of the reasons why Canadian universities place such low priority on research into self-improvement in the face of mounting evidence that their performance is declining and why Canadian universities appear so reluctant to act on research-based

Making Policy in Turbulent Times: Challenges and Prospects for Higher Education, ed. P. Axelrod, R.D. Trilokekar, T. Shanahan, and R. Wellen. Kingston: School of Policy Studies, Queen's University.
© 2013 The School of Policy Studies, Queen's University at Kingston. All rights reserved.

evidence about how their performance could be improved. We look at the general incentives and cultural issues in the academic world and at some specific Canadian issues associated with system homogeneity, attitudes toward differentiation, governance processes, and the roles of faculty and university associations. We end the chapter with suggestions for encouraging higher education research and for overcoming the reluctance to act on its findings.

Proposals for improving Canadian higher education performance

Many recent studies suggest that the quality of education in Canadian universities has been falling even when the resources per student have kept pace with general inflation.

Concern about the resources devoted to teaching in Canadian universities goes back at least two decades. Stuart Smith (1991) aimed to generate a national debate on the quality of teaching and learning with his *Commission of Inquiry on Canadian University Education*, but the commission's report had relatively little impact on scholarship in this area (Halliwell 2008, 11), and there was no follow-through on Smith's recommendation for a fund for practical research into improving teaching. Pocklington and Tupper's book, *No Place to Learn* (2002), has been followed by works by Côté and Allahar (2007), Clark et al. (2009), Côté and Allahar (2011), Coates and Morrison (2011), and Clark, Trick, and Van Loon (2011). Although these studies document how class sizes have been increasing and student contact with full-time professors has been decreasing, higher education leaders in universities and government have, until very recently, been reluctant to publicly admit the increasingly obvious: that the quality of education that our institutions are providing most students has been declining.

One of the first to state this conclusion in a relatively public forum was Robert Campbell, president of Mount Allison University in Sackville, New Brunswick, at a workshop co-sponsored by the Association of Universities and Colleges of Canada (AUCC) and the Centre for Higher Education Research and Development entitled "Transforming Canadian University Undergraduate Education," held in Halifax, Nova Scotia, on 6–8 March 2011. Campbell said, "We all feel and know that the character of the undergraduate experience has deteriorated in our lifetimes, especially so in the last decades. And we know in our heart of hearts that this experience can and should be much better" (AUCC 2011, 1). In October 2011, Harvey Weingarten, the president of the Higher Education Quality Council of Ontario (HEQCO) and former president of the University of Calgary in Alberta, was more explicit, as suggested in the title of his lecture, "The Diminishing Quality of Ontario's Universities: Can the System Be Fixed?"

So, what happens when revenues are not sufficient to cover incremental costs? You continue to take more students because that is the imperative and they are a source of revenue. Inflation is a reality. Compensation changes are a contractual obligation. So, the only place to compromise is on quality. In short, the sad but inevitable consequence of the way we now manage and fund public postsecondary education in Canada is an erosion of quality. (Weingarten 2011, n.p.)

Over the last five years, there has been substantial research commissioned with the object of improving higher education in Ontario, and many of the insights from this work have national application. These studies have been described in HEQCO's first three *Review and Research Plan* documents (HEQCO 2007, 2009, 2010) and in two monographs, *Academic Transformation* (Clark et al. 2009) and *Academic Reform* (Clark, Trick, and Van Loon 2011).

The HEQCO documents organize the research topics under the three pillars of the agency's mandate: accessibility, educational quality, and accountability. The two monographs examine the forces transforming higher education and policy options for improving the quality and cost-effectiveness of undergraduate education.

These studies suggest broad lines of reform. The authors propose that the first step is to acknowledge that there is a problem. They call on governments and universities to focus on student learning and commit to measuring and improving it. Provinces should project demand for post-secondary spaces – college, undergraduate, and graduate – over the next 20 years and develop affordable plans to meet this demand. Provinces that have not already done so could mandate the creation of a two-year academic credential offered at colleges, designed so that students who pass with high marks can go directly into third-year university. Where enrolment is projected to grow, provinces should create teaching-oriented undergraduate universities rather than relying on the high-cost model of research universities, where faculty are expected to do as much research as teaching. Universities could redesign and make more attractive the three-year bachelor's degree, which is becoming the standard across Europe.

The reformers propose that provinces should change their funding formulas to fund university teaching and research separately so that governments wishing, for example, to generate 20 percent more teaching could do so without paying for 20 percent more scholarly publications. They suggest that provincial funding of the costs of research could be linked to performance measures such as the number of publications and citations, and success with federal granting councils. Provinces could provide targeted funding for initiatives that Canadian universities associate with better teaching and learning. And provinces could follow the lead of Australia and the United Kingdom in collecting and publishing better information on the use of full- and part-time faculty, student course satisfaction, and student success in finding employment that makes use of their education. Governments could encourage all institutions to conduct, as some universities in the United States are starting to do, standardized tests of what students actually learn during their undergraduate years. The government of Canada could support these efforts by maintaining a rigorously merit-based system of research grants and by fully funding the costs of federally supported research so that universities do not have to pay for research out of their teaching budgets (Clark et al. 2009; Clark, Trick, and Van Loon 2011).

The fiscal crunch

Policy reforms of this magnitude do not usually happen in the absence of an overwhelming need to change. This is especially true in the post-secondary education sector, with its ancient traditions and reverence for the ideal of institutional autonomy. It is likely that reforms in Canadian higher education, a sector that has enjoyed a long period of budget growth, will in the next 10 to 20 years be driven mostly by fiscal necessity in the face of continual pressure to make public spending more productive. A look at the underlying numbers suggests that over the next two decades, Canadian governments will face pressures to reduce spending comparable to those in the early 1990s. *Restoring Public Finances*, the 2011 report of the Organisation for European Co-operation and Development (OECD), projects the sum of expenditure reductions and revenue increases needed for national and state-level governments combined, as a percentage of gross domestic product (GDP), to reduce gross general government debt to 60 percent of GDP by 2025. For Canada, the number is 4.5 percent. While this is lower than in the UK, where the number is close to 12 percent, and the US, where it is over 14 percent, the target is still demanding because, over the same 15-year period, Canada will have to find another 2.5 percent of GDP to deal with age-related spending on health and pensions, for a total adjustment of about 7 percent of GDP (OECD 2011, 19–20).

The last major period of fiscal consolidation in Canada, from 1983 to 1997, produced a change of 10 percent of GDP in revenues minus expenditures (IMF 2010, 62). But in the coming period, Canada's economic growth is unlikely to match that of the 1990s, when the world economy was growing rapidly and interest rates were falling. It will be harder to reduce the deficit-to-GDP ratio when growth in other countries is constrained by fiscal consolidation and once interest rates begin to rise. These pressures are already being felt in the US public higher education system, where state expenditures on higher education in 2011–12 were 7.6 percent lower than the previous year and 3.8 percent lower than they were five years earlier, even without accounting for inflation. In some states with historically strong public university systems, the declines over the five-year period have been dramatic (e.g., California, 12.5 percent; Michigan, 19.3 percent; Ohio, 8.8 percent).

AN IMPROVEMENT-ORIENTED RESEARCH AGENDA

This brief look at the broad lines of potential higher education reforms demonstrates how contestable are the policy conclusions that can be drawn from what appear to be relatively incontestable facts, and it suggests how valuable it would be to have ongoing, Canada-specific research to help refine the theory, assumptions, and evidence to support improvement initiatives. This section sets out an improvement-oriented research agenda for the next decade, with topics nested into three broad categories of quality, accessibility, and bringing about change.

Research topics on quality

Two issues have framed much of the international research in higher education in the last two decades: i) what students are learning in their higher education programs, and ii) what can they do with this knowledge. There is a clear sequence in how the research has advanced, although understandably, there is considerable overlap among the steps.

The first step is to identify and articulate expected learning outcomes and competencies. At the credential level, these statements take the form of qualification frameworks. These frameworks, with associated quality assurance processes, are now common in Europe, Canada, the US, and other OECD countries. The Tuning exercise (Wagenaar 2012) is an attempt to develop comparable statements at the program or discipline level. Tuning has spread widely from its European roots to involve nearly 150 universities in more than 30 countries. To date, Canada's involvement in Tuning is limited to a pilot project currently underway in Ontario, led by HEQCO.

There are a number of initiatives that would bring Canada to the forefront of this research.

- A survey and evaluation of qualification frameworks and quality assurance processes among provinces. Is there a "best" model, or will frameworks and processes necessarily reflect disparate provincial economies and post-secondary education systems?
- A survey and evaluation of how these frameworks and processes have been integrated into degree and program development at Canadian colleges and universities. Is there a "best" model, or will adoption patterns necessarily reflect disparate provincial post-secondary education systems? As part of this exercise, surveys could be conducted

of senior administrators and grassroots faculty along the lines of those conducted by the National Institute for Learning Outcomes Assessment (Kinzie 2012).

- Depending on the results of the HEQCO pilot in Ontario, conduct more Tuning exercises. These might usefully be coordinated by the U15 group (the recently created group of 15 research-intensive Canadian universities).

The second step in the quality research is to determine the extent to which expected outcomes and competencies are being achieved. Measurement is sought for two reasons: accountability and improvement. As Jillian Kinzie notes (Kinzie 2012), these motives have very different implications for how measurement is carried out and how the results are used.

Research on measuring learning outcomes is still very much a work in progress. There are two approaches: indirect and direct measures. The National Survey of Student Engagement (NSSE) is the most prominent indirect approach. The NSSE is widely used in the US and Canada and is spreading outside North America.

To date in Canada, most NSSE research has been conducted in house, for internal academic planning purposes, and is not publicly available. The exceptions are four HEQCO-supported projects (Conway 2010; Conway, Zhao, and Montgomery 2011; Conway and Zhao, 2012; Mancuso et al. 2010). These exploratory studies were sufficiently instructive to warrant further NSSE research.

- A new and expanded NSSE national project, building on the initial HEQCO-supported initiative, to include more institutions with more attention to sample sizes and more specific research questions.
- More projects testing the ability of the NSSE and the Classroom Survey of Student Engagement to evaluate the effectiveness of program and course-level interventions designed to improve learning effectiveness.

There are a number of direct measures of learning outcomes, of which the Collegiate Learning Assessment (CLA) is the most prominent (Benjamin 2008). The CLA tests a student's ability to apply generic skills in simulated real-life exercises. The measure is value-added: the difference in performance between the beginning and the end of a credential or program. The CLA can track individual students over time (longitudinal) or compare first- and final-year students (cross-sectional).

The Assessment of Higher Education Learning Outcomes (AHELO) is a major international effort to develop measures of learning that can be used to compare learning outcomes in countries with different languages and cultures (Lalancette 2012). AHELO is developing and piloting tests for generic skills and for specific skills in two disciplines – civil engineering and economics. Canada is participating in the civil engineering component through a project sponsored by the Ontario government and led by HEQCO.

There is considerable scope for additional research on direct measures of learning outcomes.

- Exploring the power of the CLA to measure learning outcomes. This would use more pilots, building on the Ontario experiments and a proposed U15 project.
- Exploring the merits of designing a version of the CLA specific to Canada.
- Considering further involvement with AHELO based on what we learn from the Ontario pilot.
- Comparing the explanatory power of NSSE with that of the CLA or other direct measures.

The third step is to identify and disseminate promising practices in teaching and learning. The scholarship of teaching and learning has advanced significantly in recent years, and the research is receiving increasing attention from administrators and practitioners. This work is generally a bottom-up activity, with instructors introducing innovations in program and course design and course delivery, and assessing the effectiveness. There is an obvious overlap here with the measurement issues discussed above.

The list of potential topics is large. A few examples:

- Innovative ways to teach large classes.
- Use of technology.
- Blended learning approaches.
- Use of teaching-stream professors.
- Evaluating student performance.
- Evaluating instructor performance.
- Link between teaching and research excellence.
- Finding ways to mobilize what we already know about effective teaching and learning but do not use commonly or effectively.

Another research area that falls generally under quality is the link between higher education attainment and labour market outcomes. Does the supply of graduates, in terms of both credentials and specialization, match the demand? One view is that we should expect an alignment.

- Labour markets signal excess demand and excess supply through relative changes in wages and employment rates.

- Entering students, or at least some of them, note these trends and choose programs of study accordingly.
- College and university officers, or at least some of them, adjust admissions to reflect application trends.

That is, the system adjusts as needed, albeit not without some lag.

Sceptics would argue that at least one of these tenets must be incorrect because we appear to have significant structural imbalances in the number of graduates and in their profiles, notably a shortage of skilled trades and an oversupply of humanities and social science graduates.

Research to date on this topic has tended to show no significant change in the higher education premium over time or in the relative returns by credential level of field of study. But this conclusion needs to be examined very thoroughly given the apparent widespread public conviction that the higher education system is not sufficiently aligned with current and emerging labour market needs. Some possible topics:

- Fully exploiting the National Graduate Survey and Follow-up of Graduates survey data.
- Using census (and National Household Survey) data to look at the distribution of returns within cohorts; most work to date focuses on cohort averages.
- Case studies of government attempts to promote specific credentials or programs (e.g., computer science).
- Particular focus on labour market outcomes for holders of graduate degrees.
- Participation and completion rates for apprenticeship programs.

Research topics on accessibility

Canada shares with most other nations the goal to raise higher education and graduation rates. Given current patterns, this goal largely means increasing these rates for traditionally under-represented groups. We know who the under-represented groups are, thanks to extensive and innovative research using the Youth in Transition Survey and other data (Finnie et al. 2009). Patterns are remarkably consistent among provinces and, indeed, among countries.

There is certainly more to learn about the determinants of accessibility by demographic and socio-economic group. With limited resources, the focus should be on projects that link secondary school, application, and college and university data sets to follow patterns and trends into and through higher education. These detailed data are already being generated as part of annual administrative activity, and they can be used to assess effects on participation of changes in key policy parameters, such as tuition rates and student assistance policies.

The pressing accessibility research priority, however, should be to identify and evaluate promising policies to increase the representation of traditionally under-represented groups. What has worked and why? What has failed and why? Suggestions are:

- Take lessons from the Canada Millennium Scholarship Foundation experiments.
- Compare provincial experiences with respect to policies to encourage participation of specific groups.
- Examine international experiences with encouraging participation of under-represented groups.

A second priority in this area is to add to our understanding of graduation rates:

- Identify the significant differences among demographic and socio-economic groups.
- Define the determinants of decisions to drop out (financial and non-financial) and the role of student support services.

A third area is tuition and other fees. This is well-tilled ground, and there is as close to consensus on the findings as one finds in social science research: tuition fees do not appear to be an important determinant of higher education participation and continuation decisions, given the federal and provincial financial assistance policies in place. Yet the demand for lower or even zero tuition persists, leading the Ontario government to reduce tuition fees significantly even for relatively high-income families, and to protests and street violence in Quebec. This leads to the following questions:

- Why does the empirical evidence on the role of tuition fees fail to convince policy-makers and much of the public more generally?
- Is the evidence wrong or incomplete?
- Or is it correct and complete but poorly presented?
- Does it fail to consider broader social issues?

A fourth topic in this area is student financial aid policies and student debt. Again, this is well-tilled ground, yet it continues to generate considerable heated discussion and debate. We need:

- A clear and comprehensive picture of student debt, not just simple averages.
- A comparative analysis of student financial-assistance policies among provinces. Is there a "best" system?

- A survey of financial assistance policies in other nations, particularly those where repayment is linked to income upon graduation.

Research topics on bringing about change

Research on quality or accessibility, however productive, is obviously only useful if the recommendations are actually implemented. It is certainly safe to say that this aspect – bringing about change – is one of the least explored topics of higher education research in Canada.

What changes to the higher education system are we seeking? We suggest the following:

- Greater attention to learning quality.
- Increased participation and graduation rates of under-represented groups.
- Neither should come at the expense of research capacity.
- Both should be affordable in a fiscally tight environment.

Bringing about change has two components: institutions need to be committed to reform, and individuals need to be committed to their institution's reform priorities. The former suggests a role for innovative government policy, while the latter puts the focus on internal policies and procedures.

System-level change

Two logical questions guide system-level research.

- What are the incentives (carrots and sticks) in the current funding and regulatory arrangements, and how well do they align the system-wide goals noted above? In particular, what are the incentives for enhanced educational quality?
- How might these arrangements be altered so that there is more incentive to bring about the desired changes?

This is a natural topic for comparative analysis. Funding and regulatory systems vary significantly among Canadian provinces, and considering those in other nations as well adds to the variety. The task, as usual in comparative studies, is to identify promising practices that could be adopted and adapted in other jurisdictions.

Four features of higher education systems are worth serious comparative analysis.

- System design: mix of non-university and university institutions; differences in missions within each type (e.g., research-intensive versus primarily undergraduate); and credit transfer within and among types.

- Performance measures: indicators of performance in teaching and research that can be used for the purposes of accountability and resource allocation.
- Accountability frameworks: annual or multi-year reporting requirements to government and the public; scorecards.
- Funding formulas: sustainable and predictable funding and/or funding tied to performance.

Institution-level change

There is relatively little public research on how higher education institutions operate, yet this information is essential for structuring policies for reform. Do decisions vary widely among units, as institutional autonomy might suggest, or is there a predictable pattern of behaviour? Some interesting issues:

- How do institutions develop strategic priorities? In particular, how closely do they attempt to align these with government priorities more generally? This could include case studies of specific policies, with and without financial incentives, to study responsiveness.
- How do institutions ensure that internal policies and procedures are aligned with these priorities?
- How do institutions allocate resources internally among faculties and departments, and between teaching and research activity?
- What incentive systems do they use to promote excellence in teaching, research, and service?

With respect to enhancing learning quality specifically, research could take the following forms:

- Conduct case studies of institutions with missions for excellent undergraduate education, such as the University of British Columbia's Okanagan campus; the British Columbia teaching universities; Mount Royal University in Calgary, Alberta; Grant MacEwan University in Edmonton, Alberta; and the undergraduate institutions in the Maritime provinces. These case studies would look at incentive structures, resource allocation mechanisms, and the pressure for mission creep.
- As already noted, further work on the link between teaching and research excellence.

COULD SUFFICIENT RESEARCH CAPACITY BE MOBILIZED?

The paucity of higher education research centres in Canada relative to the UK, US, and Australia

This is a big research agenda. In Canada, the number of faculty doing serious research into ways to improve university education is low relative to the task at hand – perhaps a dozen or so researchers out of 42,000 full-time faculty[1] – and appears to be low relative to the number of faculty engaged in such research in Australian, UK, and US universities.

Let us look briefly at centres that specialize in higher education. In the UK, the Centre for Higher Education Research and Information was operated by the Open University until mid-2011, and it generated several publicly available reports every year and a steady stream of journal articles and book chapters. It created the web-searchable Higher Education Empirical Research database, which was transferred to the Quality Assurance Agency of Higher Education. In Australia, the University of Melbourne's Centre for the Study of Higher Education is one of the longest-established centres of its kind in the world. The Griffith Institute for Higher Education in Brisbane is both the Griffith University's academic development unit and a centre for research on teaching and learning. The websites of the directors of these two institutions, Richard James and Kerri-Lee Krause (who collaborate on many projects), provide a good deal of useful material on teaching improvement and measurement.

In the US, Berkeley's Center for Studies in Higher Education, established in 1956 to study systems, institutions, and processes of higher education, has among its many resources a marvellous Research and Occasional Papers Series, with all of its material publicly downloadable. Boston College's Center for International Higher Education, directed by Philip Altbach, a prominent writer on international trends in higher education, publishes the quarterly *International Higher Education* and maintains a database of international publications on higher education. Other well-established centres include the University of Southern California's Center for Higher Education Policy Analysis; Pennsylvania State University's Center for the Study of Higher Education, publisher of *Higher Education in Review*; the University of Michigan's Center for the Study of Higher and Postsecondary Education; and Indiana University's Center for Postsecondary Research, which hosts the NSSE. And there are many more centres associated with US universities that publish research on higher education.

There are only three long-standing research centres in Canadian universities that focus on higher education. The University of British Columbia's Centre for Policy Studies in Higher Education and Training was established in 1984 with a focus on the relationship between higher education and the economy. The University of Manitoba's Centre for Higher Education Research and Development was established in 1987 and is particularly focused on the professional development of faculty and administration in post-secondary education. The University of Toronto's Higher Education Group was founded in 1969 within the Ontario Institute for Studies in Education. Although many of the scholars associated with these centres are active researchers, their work is typically not published in working paper series or other publicly accessible materials on their centres' websites, as is the case in some of the UK, Australian, and US university-based centres.

A perusal of recent publications by some of Australia's higher education scholars reveals how dynamic the scholarship of higher education is in that country. A cursory comparison of institutional and personal websites suggests that Australia does several times more applied higher education research than Canada to serve many fewer students. This is also reflected in the publication record of government agencies. For example, Ontario has recently created HEQCO, an agency that has conducted an impressive research program for the last five years. But Australia has the Australian Council for Educational Research, which has been operating since 1930 and has 41 current higher education research projects. The Australian Universities Quality Agency has frequent workshops and an active occasional paper series. The Higher Education section of the Department of Education, Employment and Workplace Relations produces a wealth of statistics in its annual reports on staff, students, and finances, and it has a substantial list of publications on higher education, much longer than can be found on any Canadian federal or provincial government site.

Higher education research generally does not require expensive laboratories and equipment. The main cost is in faculty salaries for research time. Canadian governments and students are already paying faculty salaries for research time, so the issue is essentially one of academic research priorities.

A thought experiment: imagine that Canadian universities committed 1 percent of revenues to research on improving higher education

Imagine that each university were to devote 1 percent of its operating revenues to research on how it could improve the product that it delivers.

This may sound like a radical idea, but it is not the first time that spending 1 percent of operating revenues on efforts to improve university teaching and learning has been suggested. The government of Ontario introduced the Ontario Universities Program for Instructional Development (OUPID) in the 1970s, which was intended to "assist individual Faculty members in Ontario Universities and the Universities themselves in improving the effectiveness and efficiency of their instructional processes" (Elrick 1990,

65). Funding was $250,000 to $500,000 per year from 1973–74 until it was wound up in June 1980. The review of the program, conducted after its first two and a half years of operation (Main, Berland, and Morand 1975), suggested that funding be substantially increased. Main, Berland, and Morand recommended that "the Ministry of Colleges and Universities make available an annual sum of money which is additional to normal disbursements to universities and which is clearly earmarked for the purposes of instructional development in the universities" and that the sum "rise over a period of three years to a maximum of 1 percent of the total education expenditures in the universities" (56).

Since total university spending in those days was close to $1 billion annually, this was effectively a recommendation to increase OUPID's budget to $10 million per year.[2] OUPID's aims were not exactly the same as the research initiative proposed in this chapter. They were narrower in that they focused on the instructional element of education improvement, but they were also broader in that they included developmental and training elements that go beyond the research function.

In the present fiscal climate, one could imagine some of the 1 percent for education-improvement research coming as net new revenue from external sources (government or private donors), but it is more realistic to imagine that most of the research money would come from internal re-allocation of existing university expenditures. For example, the proposed 1 percent could be financed by reallocating approximately 2 percent of annual operating grants to this purpose or by employees forgoing a 1.3 percent compensation increase. Given current compensation levels[3] and the number of qualified applicants for faculty positions,[4] it is unlikely that this would affect institutions' ability to attract and retain excellent faculty.

To facilitate this thought experiment, let us imagine that each university would create a number of research chairs, modelled on the Ontario Research Chairs in Public Policy.

Let us imagine that $1 million per year is allocated for each of these research chairs to cover full compensation and benefits for the chair, support staff, and research assistants; the full contribution to indirect costs; and adequate funds for travel and conferences.[5] How many such chairs would 1 percent of operating budgets support? Total revenues are approximately $20 billion per year, so this would imply 200 research chairs. For example, York University in Toronto, with operating expenses of $927 million in 2011, would commit to funding nine research chairs.

Using the topics outlined in the previous section, one could imagine that large universities (those with revenues of over $500 million) would each have a number of chairs with common fields of research, focused on the application to the particular university. For example, each university could have five chairs with names like:

• Research Chair in Academic Quality Assurance

- Research Chair in Learning and Assessment
- Research Chair in Teaching Technologies and Innovation
- Research Chair in Academic Curriculum and Standards
- Research Chair in Academic Training and Development

The incumbents in these positions would be internationally recognized experts in their fields and be particularly knowledgeable about the specific environment of their own university.

There are several fields in which it would be useful to have at least one chair per province, although not necessarily at every university. These might include:

- Research Chair in Academic Freedom and Accountability
- Research Chair in Academic Management and Governance
- Research Chair in Academic Productivity
- Research Chair in Academic Performance Measurement
- Research Chair in Academic Compensation and Performance Management
- Research Chair in Higher Education System Design
- Research Chair in Higher Education Funding
- Research Chair in Student Fees and Financial Support

Many of these titles would seem alien in a Canadian university today. Why?

IMPEDIMENTS TO HIGHER EDUCATION RESEARCH AND REFORM

This section looks at the principal factors that impede the allocation of appropriate efforts to perform improvement-oriented research and to act on the results of such research. They are as follows: faculty incentives that privilege research over teaching, a university culture that encourages extreme specialization and a preference for theory over practice, the role of faculty associations, the design of governance systems, an institutional aversion to differentiation, and lack of interest in higher education research by university associations.

Faculty incentives for research over teaching

The list of potential reforms that opened this chapter reveals the nature of the challenges to increasing faculty interest in research on education improvement and to acting on the findings of such research. At one level, the challenges can all be found in the title of Harold Lasswell's 1936 classic: *Politics: Who Gets What, When, How*, especially if this is supplemented with who *does* what, when, how.

Whether because of an inherent love of scholarly work or because of incentives placed upon them by their disciplines and institutions, it seems clear that most faculty feel compelled to devote more time to research – to conduct "scholarship at gunpoint," in Jacques Barzun's memorable phrase,[6] on subjects generally unrelated to education improvement – and less time to teaching. The incentives, including the prestige differential between faculty teaching and research, have been discussed in dozens of articles and books, such as those by Ernest Boyer (1990), Jacques Barzun (1991), Christopher Lucas (1996), Derek Bok (2005), and Louis Menand (2010).

It seems obvious that improvements in undergraduate education will require a greater priority to be placed on teaching at the system level. Clark, Trick, and Van Loon (2011) are explicit in their objectives of increasing the time that most faculty members devote to undergraduate education, and of increasing the proportion of students and government resources going to institutions that focus on undergraduate education, without diminishing the ability to attract and retain the highest-performing university researchers.

Why do universities not organize themselves so that the most productive researchers focus on research and other faculty focus on teaching, when logic would suggest that such specialization could produce both more research and more teaching from the same population of faculty members?

As noted at the outset, the chief reason is the set of incentives that privileges research. US sociologists Richard Arum and Josipa Roksa (2011) suggest that many faculty believe that "one of the few remaining moral bases for academic life is a quasi-religious commitment to embracing research as a vocational calling."

> For many faculty, commitment to their own individual research programs is thus understood not as an act of self-aggrandizement or personal selfishness, but rather as a moral imperative that one must pursue and struggle to achieve regardless of institutional obstacles. (Arum and Roksa 2011, 10)

University culture: specialization and a preference for theory over practice

There are clearly strong incentives for faculty to focus on research and scholarship over teaching. But what kinds of research and scholarship? Might one expect that research on practical ways to improve the quality and cost-effectiveness of higher education would emerge as an important field of inquiry? Unfortunately, the answer is no – because of two strong elements of academic culture: the pressure to specialize in narrow subdisciplines and the preference to focus on theoretical and conceptual questions rather than practical solutions.

Louis Menand, a professor of English at Harvard University, has demonstrated in his compact book, *The Marketplace of Ideas: Reform and Resistance in the American University* (2010), that almost all disciplines have become more specialized and more theoretical. The work of faculty is becoming increasingly removed from the practical problems in which citizens and government are immersed. Faculty see a higher academic payoff in making a small, non-jurisdiction–specific, theoretical advance than in applying established precepts of the discipline to a specific policy in a particular place. One hears Canadian economists in their 30s and 40s say that they have been advised by colleagues to "leave that policy stuff" until they get older so they can devote their most productive years to getting articles published in the discipline's most respected international journals.

A similar tendency seems to be apparent in the field of education studies. A review of titles in the *Canadian Journal of Higher Education* suggests that many Canadian higher education scholars are more comfortable writing theoretical critiques on topics such as "The Scholarship of Teaching and Learning and the Neo-Liberalization of Higher Education" (Servage 2009) than they are conducting empirical studies in Canadian universities aimed at improving learning outcomes.

Indeed, throughout the North American academy, there is no shortage of professors ready to apply theoretical constructs to critiquing proposals for improving teaching practice. A revealing example is the recent paper in the new *Journal of Academic Integrity* in response to a thoughtful article by Stanley Katz, president emeritus of the American Council of Learned Societies, on the role that faculty members should play in assessing learning outcomes. Katz wrote,

> Why should faculty members support efforts on their campuses to assess student learning outcomes?... Most often, legislators and bureaucrats bluster and then do little to implement assessment strategies, while the universities dodge and weave in response to perceived threats, and then do little or nothing to carry out their boasts that they are fully capable of self-evaluation.... Student learning outcome assessment is a particularly delicate area, however, since it constitutes an intersection between individual faculty prerogative (the right to evaluate one's own students) and the institutional interest in promoting learning across the curriculum and over the span of students' college attendance.... This faculty attitude probably has to change if we are to take seriously the emerging conception of institutional responsibility for overall student learning outcomes.... Assessment instruments such as NSSE and the CLA have attracted wide interest because they attempt to evaluate the entirety of students' collegiate learning. Is there any reason why the professoriate should be suspicious of (or opposed to) this new mode of evaluation?... I can well imagine university teachers who oppose even formative assessment on the grounds that no one should be

able to tell them how to teach, but we have all submitted to student course evaluations for many years, no matter how dismissive we may be of the current forms of that technology. It is hard to imagine a principled objection to careful evaluation of learning outcomes or to thoughtful suggestions for improvement in pedagogical strategies. (Katz 2010, n.p.)

John Champagne responded to Katz,

It is highly ironic that writers who would pose critical thinking as the outcome of education cannot seem to think critically about the relationship between power and knowledge, a relationship that critical theorists have been interrogating since at least the end of the Second World War. The critique of instrumental reason; the insight that "there is never interpretation, understanding, and then knowledge where there is no interest" (Said 1997, 165); the suggestion that there is something named the unconscious that might interrupt our best efforts to produce knowledge of the social world in particular; the realization that any mode of cultural explanation necessarily silences alternative explanations, and that it is crucial to contemplate the itinerary of this silencing (Pierre Macherey, cited in Spivak 1990, 32); the proposition that truth, knowledge, and power are intertwined in ways we have an ethical obligation to try and understand (Foucault 1990). (Champagne 2011, 10)

The preference for specialization over interdisciplinarity and for theoretical critique over practical empiricism adds to the challenge of mounting a research agenda directed at improving higher education in Canada.

The role of faculty associations

Given that one of the roles of faculty associations is to advance the profession,[7] one might expect Canadian faculty associations to be strong proponents of research in the matter of improving the quality and cost-effectiveness of higher education. The active support of faculty associations for such research would be valuable because on most Canadian campuses, faculty associations are very influential; faculty have a more significant role in managing the production activities of their enterprise than do unionized employees in most other settings.

Harry Arthurs, former president of York University and an authority on Canadian labour law, has noted that although faculty unions and university administrations are similar to other unions and employers in some ways, they are also different in certain important respects. Because the professoriate has actual as well as formal control over some or all aspects of important decisions (recruitment, hiring, tenure, promotion, curriculum, research priorities, pedagogy, etc.), it controls many features of the "productive process" in ways that other workers do not. Because the professoriate has a voice (and sometimes a veto) in the appointment of senior university administrators, it has the ability to influence management values and perceptions in ways that are denied to other workers; this influence is enhanced to the extent that academic administrators continue to participate in or identify with the social and intellectual life of the professoriate – to which they formally and symbolically belong and sometimes actually return (Harry Arthurs, personal communication, 2011).

Despite faculty associations' commitment to teaching excellence, they have not to date been major sources of ideas for improving university education. Typically, they have called for additional government funding to support the hiring of more full-time faculty whose teaching and research responsibilities would be based on the current model. One should nevertheless note the potential for new ideas and vigorous discussion within the labour movement about how to defend members' interests while at the same time maintaining the financial viability of the organizations for which they work. In the North American auto sector, for example, union concerns for the long-term viability of employers in the 1970s and 1980s inspired union-led proposals for improving productivity and quality in the face of increased competition from overseas automakers. The prospect of exogenously driven policy changes to address escalating per-student costs and concerns about quality could lead to similar proposals from faculty associations. A recent proposal from the vice-president of the Ontario Confederation of University Faculty Associations to establish principles for teaching-stream appointments may be a promising sign.[8]

University governance

Governance in higher education refers to the formal structures through which stakeholders interact with each other and exert influence on the policies and practices of universities and colleges.[9] Historically, a major focus of interest in governance has been on the problem of balancing the interests and views of internal stakeholders, particularly faculty, with those of external stakeholders, especially those deemed to represent the interests of the community or state.

For the purposes of this chapter, the question is whether governance structures and practices in most Canadian universities constitute impediments to the allocation of appropriate resources to research on education improvement and to action on the findings of such research. If it would be in the public interest for more such research to be conducted and acted upon, another way of expressing the question is: Who speaks for the public interest within the university governance system?

Governance systems have been designed to provide universities with considerable autonomy from government. This autonomy is desirable for several reasons: universities' activities are presumed to be only partly in the service of explicit societal objectives, although increasingly so in recent years; it is widely thought that their work would not be as productive if conducted under the supervision of government; some of their roles, such as social criticism and innovative thinking, require independence from government; the risk or appearance of intrusion of political influence into some of the kinds of decisions made by universities, such as admissions into professional programs, is unseemly in a democracy; and it has been argued that institutional autonomy is important for protecting academic freedom, though whether the former is a necessity for the latter is quite contentious.

The most common governance model, which dates back to the 16th century in Europe (Kerr and Gade 1989), is the bicameral structure, in which the ultimate responsibility for managing the affairs of the institution is divided between two chambers, typically referred to as a governing board and an academic senate. Of course, balancing the interests and views of different participants within each of these broad categories is often at issue as well. Thus, in the process of the governance reform at the University of Toronto that was spurred by campus unrest in the 1960s, one of the focal points of controversy was how to fine-tune the precise numbers of representatives from different internal constituencies (Bissell 1974). In regard to external members, a number of jurisdictions have issued guidelines or requirements for the representation of different social groups.

It is widely accepted that within universities, academic staff should have primary responsibility for decisions concerning academic matters, such as admission and graduation requirements, curriculum, and academic standards. The rationale for assigning this responsibility to academics is that they, rather than laypersons from the community, have the requisite expertise in academic matters, they are closest to the academic action, and they have a particular stake in the academic reputation of the institution that is determined at least in part by the academic policies of the institution. On the other hand, most if not all jurisdictions have taken the view that the financial management and larger administrative control of the institution should be the responsibility of a body that contains a majority of external members – i.e., the governing board.

The advent of faculty collective bargaining has added a third nexus: faculty associations representing the interests of those who do the teaching and research. Much has been written about the uneasy relationship among the three groups. Canadian faculty associations have been very effective in advancing their members' interests, but they have been very conservative forces on matters related to the organization and delivery of academic work. Similarly, Birnbaum (1989, 235) notes that senates have traditionally been a force for organizational conservatism. They have generally been effective in maintaining traditional disciplinary standards and resisting changes that might undermine academic freedom and established operating procedures.

This leaves the governing board as the forum in which the public interest in conducting and acting on improvement-focused research is expected to be voiced. So have university boards been effective in exercising their fiduciary responsibilities to ensure their institutions' financial sustainability and to represent the public interest in maximizing the amount of teaching and research that is produced for each taxpayer and student dollar? Given that many universities are not operating on a financially sustainable basis (Clark, Trick, and Van Loon 2011, 16–17), given the acknowledged decline in teaching quality, and given the widespread and easily understood inefficiencies from the reluctance to capture economies of specialization, it would be easy to conclude that university boards have been unwilling or unable to act unambiguously in the public interest.

Institutional aversion to differentiation

At the institutional level, the resistance to reform – and to research that might lead to reform proposals – is largely driven by concerns over status. Status-seeking behaviours by institutions lead to an almost universal propensity for mission creep and to political resistance to policies that encourage institutional differentiation. Clark and Eisen (2010) observe that although the application of division of labour, specialization, and economies of scale are among the cornerstones of economic theory, policies based on them are resisted by those who do not wish to see differential government treatment of individuals or institutions. When Canadians think about the values that should animate the actions of their governments, equality is among the first to come to mind. Equality leads to a preference for uniformity in the treatment of groups, institutions, and individuals in most areas of public management and reluctance to embrace policy options that call for explicit differentiation. It is usually easier to invoke Canada's egalitarian tradition and defend uniformity as an extension of that tradition than it is to take more efficient and equitable policy measures that would require data, evidence, imagination, and willingness to defend criteria that lead to explicitly differential treatment.

There are many areas of the university system where there are clearly benefits to be captured by more concentration and specialization. This occurs in areas such as research and graduate education, where the average cost falls as scale increases, where efficiencies can be gained through specialization, and where benefits can be obtained from working in proximity to those performing related activities. Clark (2013) has developed an illustrative model showing that if the research productivity among faculty follows a 70–30 distribution (whereby 70 percent of the output is produced by 30 percent of the faculty), then a modest reallocation of teaching loads could produce substantial increases in both teaching and research output for the system as a whole.

Virtually all countries face similar challenges, and most are responding by permitting, even encouraging, greater differentiation. Encouraging differentiation in a public system requires that government deal with the "essential problem of isomorphism" (where all universities aim to look alike) driven by "unbridled competition among academic institutions pursuing the same goals" (Altbach, Reisberg, and Rumbley 2009, 19). The authors further note:

> Academic staff often press the university to emphasize research as its key mission, knowing that a research orientation and productivity in this area promise the highest prestige and (often) the best salaries for academics. If the universities remain the sole decision makers, many more academic institutions would seek to improve their status by becoming research intensive. In most cases, this strategy does not serve the interests of academe in general nor is it widely achievable. Often, it takes governmental "steering" to keep the academic system diversified and institutions within the system serving larger national goals. (18–19)

Lack of higher education research interest on the part of associations in Canada relative to the UK, the US, and Australia

The final factor we look at in regard to the reluctance to conduct or act on improvement-oriented research is the role of university associations. Relative to their counterparts in Australia, the UK, and the US, Canadian associations of higher education appear to devote relatively little attention to exploring ways to improve the quality and cost-effectiveness of undergraduate education.

Universities Australia is the body that represents all 39 universities, and it produces regular public submissions and reports, primarily directed at the national government. The Group of Eight represents the research-intensive universities (Western Australia, Monash, Australian National, Adelaide, Melbourne, New South Wales, Queensland, Sydney). It produces one to two dozen substantial papers every year, many of which address issues in addition to enhanced government funding that are pertinent to the quality of teaching and research.

The university system in the UK is highly differentiated, and the constituent institutions have organized themselves into four non-overlapping groups. Some of them produce analytical work that does more than simply advocate for more public resources for their members. For example, the 1994 Group (the association of 19 of the largest universities not part of the self-selected Russell Group) has a policy group on the student experience that produces substantial papers, such as the 2007 *Enhancing the Student Experience* report.

In the US, there are hundreds of regional and national associations of university administrators and functional experts. There are six so-called presidential higher education associations. The American Council on Education (ACE), which "represents presidents and chancellors of all types of U.S. accredited, degree-granting institutions: community colleges and four-year institutions, private and public universities, and non-profit and for-profit colleges," has a Policy & Research Links section of its website that provides an excellent list of resources, including most of the journals, institutes, and associations in the higher education field.

The other five associations, with somewhat overlapping membership, represent the interests of different types of higher education institutions. Most members of all of these associations – from Harvard University to Kalamazoo College – are also members of the Association of American Colleges and Universities (AAC&U), an association "dedicated to ensuring that the advantages of a liberal education are available to all students regardless of background, enrollment path, academic specialization, or intended career." The AAC&U publishes four periodicals (*Liberal Education, Peer Review, On Campus with Women,* and *Diversity & Democracy*). One of its signature projects is Liberal Education and America's Promise (LEAP), a national initiative that champions the importance of a 21st-century liberal education and that promotes essential learning outcomes, high-impact educational practices, authentic assessments, and inclusive excellence. The AAC&U website has voluminous resources on topics like curriculum development, assessment, and institutional and systemic change.

The titles of two monographs published by the AAC&U give a flavour of the seriousness of this research effort: *The LEAP Vision for Learning: Outcomes, Practices, Impact, and Employers' Views* (2011) and *High-Impact Educational Practices: What They Are, Who Has Access to Them, and Why They Matter* (2008) by George D. Kuh. The whole Winter 2010 issue of *Peer Review* was devoted to the theme of "Engaging Departments: Assessing Student Learning." ACE, in conjunction with the Association for Institutional Research and the National Institute for Learning Outcomes Assessment, has developed the website Measuring Quality in Higher Education: An Inventory of Instruments, Tools and Resources, which provides links to resources on Accountability; Accreditation; Assessment; Educational Evaluation, Testing and Measurement; Higher Education Benchmarking Data; and Search Engines and Resource Compendia.

The Australian, UK, and particularly the US associations have more useful and more plentiful public resources than their Canadian counterparts on the question of improving the quality and cost-effectiveness of undergraduate education.

ENCOURAGING RESEARCH AND OVERCOMING RELUCTANCE

The books *Academic Transformation* and *Academic Reform* contain numerous proposals for systemic change. This chapter has suggested that good research, broadly communicated, can help. Here are four process suggestions for moving the research agenda forward.

Encouraging a serious discussion between government and the academy

Provincial governments should make much more explicit their expectations of the post-secondary education sector and their projections of the resources that will be available from the sources they control: provincial grants and regulated tuition revenues. Where there is a clear gap between what is being produced with the resources and what is expected to be produced, the government should initiate a serious discussion with institutional leaders, with input from associations representing students and faculty, about the nature of the change required and how it will be conducted. The discussions should include how substantial institutional autonomy can be preserved in a more system-focused approach. Although one could not expect unanimity on all the details of a reform program, it may be possible to reach a reasonable consensus on the areas where careful research would help improve the understanding of what should be done.

Strengthening the ability of university boards to represent the public interest in cost-effectiveness

It seems clear that governing boards of universities need to exercise stronger roles in bringing issues of productivity and cost-effectiveness to institutional decision-making. But how should this be done? In the long term, it will probably be necessary to rethink university governance structures – on the basis, of course, of solid research – and to pass provincial legislation to give stronger voice to those who represent the public interest. In the short term, efforts could be made by the government to ensure that board members are better briefed on their responsibilities, on the incentives and behaviours within the academy, and on instruments for improving quality and cost-effectiveness within their institutions. Ideally, several members of every board would become highly interested in how the results of higher education research can assist them in these duties.

Creating a HEQCO-like national institution

Canada does not have the impressive tradition of education research funding by private donors that exists in the US. In that country, major foundations such as Ford, Pew Charitable Trusts, and Carnegie have for decades funded research in higher education.

Following the windup of the Canada Millennium Scholarship Foundation and the Canadian Council on Learning, HEQCO is far and away Canada's leading sponsor of research on higher education issues. The council and principal staff members were appointed in fiscal year 2006–07. The budget for 2010–11 was $5 million. HEQCO conducts research in its three mandate areas of accessibility, educational quality, and accountability. HEQCO has produced an impressive body of research in the last five years. Much of it is applicable to post-secondary education policy throughout Canada. A strong case could be made for creating some sort of national body to do such work with a broader geographical mandate. In his independent review of HEQCO, Lorne Whitehead suggests that other interested provinces could "create their own provincial versions of HEQCO's advisory role, and to collaborate with one another in supporting what might eventually be described as the "Canadian Higher Education Research Council" – presumably with networked branch offices in participating provinces" (Whitehead 2011, 13).

Improving academic transparency in an online world

Recent developments in information and communications technology can have profound effects on the relationship between the academy and the public, and on the way research is used. For those who work in public institutions and whose scholarship is supported by public funds, making their scholarly work publicly available is encouraged by freedom of information legislation: in most Canadian provinces, universities are obligated to respond to a request for information in university document collections and e-mail systems.

The Internet is now the main source of information for people interested in what goes on in universities, particularly in the research conducted by faculty. It is possible to find almost any document that a faculty member has presented at a conference by Googling the professor's name and a rough description of the subject because most conferences retain materials on a website. Almost all university departments now have websites that list the recent publications of faculty members, and many departments encourage faculty members to post their full academic résumés. If they do, the full content comes up on a Google search (Clark 2010).

The effort to make scholarship publicly available on the Internet in a manner consistent with intellectual property laws will increasingly be seen to be part of every faculty member's service responsibilities to contribute to public knowledge. Such information will provide an excellent resource for students (and parents) in selecting universities and departments. Universities should embrace this by encouraging (and providing technical support for) every single faculty member to have a public website with up-to-date descriptions of his or her teaching, research, and service contributions.

Over time, it could be expected that more and more citizens will develop an interest in the topics that higher education researchers are pursuing and an interest in how the findings are being implemented by governments and academic leaders to improve the quality and cost-effectiveness of public university systems.

NOTES

1. The first number is the authors' assessment; the second is from the AUCC's *Facts at a Glance* (2011), at http://www.aucc.ca/canadian-universities/facts-and-stats/, accessed 8 January 2012.
2. In 1980, the total operating grant revenues of Ontario universities were $788,525,000 in government operating grants and $142,318,000 in tuition revenues. The sum of these two sources ($930,843,000) constituted 94 percent of university operating revenues that year (David Trick, personal communication, January 2012).
3. Canadian university faculty are very well compensated by international standards. A recent international survey of faculty salaries, using purchasing power parity, found that among the 28 countries surveyed (including the US, UK, Germany, France, and Australia), Canadian faculty were the highest paid at all faculty ranks (Altbach et al. 2012). The data for the project are available at http://acarem.hse.ru/.
4. For example, *Academic Reform* examined the number of assistant professors from 1971 to 2009 compared with the Ontario population aged 25–44, which is the age range into which almost all assistant professors fall. The increase in supply of PhDs has vastly outstripped the increase in demand for new full-time professors. The number of assistant professorships has grown, but the number of people who meet the minimum academic qualifications for these positions has grown faster. The ratio of people in Ontario aged 25–64 who hold an earned doctorate to the total population in that age range almost doubled in the period 1986 to 2006. For every full-time professorship that exists at an Ontario university, there are five PhDs in the population. Every year, about 2,100 new PhDs graduate from Ontario universities, about 80 percent of whom will remain in Canada after graduation. Another 1,400 PhDs immigrate to Ontario each year. Meanwhile, only about 800 full-time university faculty reach the normal retirement age – a figure that will rise to about 1,000 per year a decade from now. The large stock of PhDs outside of the university and the large inflow of new PhDs each year guarantee that there will be heavy competition for full-time university positions with any plausible level of faculty compensation.
5. This is a more generous funding model than the endowment-based model used for the Ontario Research Chairs in Public Policy, which were funded by a one-time capital contribution of about $2.5 million to the university.
6. Skolnik (2000) notes that a variety of motivations are at play. On the one hand, some faculty are likely driven by the coercive forces described by Barzun (1991) and elaborated by Lucas (1996, 189–99), who goes on to say of the effects of the pressure, "the sadness of it all, critics claim, is that so

many academics have allowed themselves to become part of a system that forces them to write when, as is painfully obvious, they have nothing of any great importance to say" (84). On the other hand, as Skolnik says (2000, 24), "Many academics have a genuine passion for writing and would try to continue to find a way to keep writing regardless of changes in the academic reward structure."

7.   The constitution of the Canadian Association of University Teachers states that the purpose of the association is "to promote the interests of academic staff, including but not limited to professors, professional librarians and researchers, to advance the standards of their professions, and to seek to improve the quality of post-secondary education in Canada."

8.   See http://ocufa.on.ca/2011/any-discussion-of-expanding-teaching-stream-faculty-should-adhere-to-certain-principles-says-ocufa%E2%80%99 s-lawson/, accessed 22 January 2012.

9.   We are indebted to Michael Skolnik for assistance with this section, which draws heavily from material that he provided for an internal paper that he and Ian Clark jointly produced at the request of a university board.

REFERENCES

AAC&U. 2011. *The LEAP Vision for Learning: Outcomes, Practices, Impact, and Employers' Views*. Washington, DC: AAC&U.

Altbach, P.G., L. Reisberg, and L.E. Rumbley. 2009. *Trends in Global Higher Education*. A Report Prepared for the UNESCO 2009 World Conference on Higher Education. At http://unesdoc.unesco.org/images/0018/001832/183219e.pdf (accessed 1 June 2011).

Altbach, P.G., L. Reisberg, M. Yudkevich, G. Androushchak, and I. Pacheco, eds. 2012. *Paying the Professoriate: A Global Comparison of Compensation and Contracts*. New York: Routledge.

Arum, R., and J. Roksa. 2011. *Academically Adrift: Limited Learning on College Campuses*. Chicago: Chicago University Press.

AUCC. 2011. *The Revitalization of Undergraduate Education in Canada*. At http://www.aucc.ca/wp-content/uploads/2011/09/the-revitalization-of-undergraduate-education-in-canada-2011.pdf (accessed 5 December 2011).

Barzun, J. 1991. *Begin Here: The Forgotten Conditions of Teaching and Learning*. Chicago: University of Chicago Press.

Benjamin, R. 2008. *The Contribution of the Collegiate Learning Assessment to Teaching and Learning*. At http://www.cae.org/content/pdf/The_Contribution_of_ the_%20Collegiate_Learning_Assessment_to_Teaching_and_Learning.pdf (accessed 17 May 2012).

Birnbaum, R. 1989. "The Latent Organizational Functions of the Academic Senate: Why Senates Do Not Work but Will Not Go Away." *The Journal of Higher Education* 60 (4):423–443.

Bissell, C. 1974. *Halfway up Parnassus: A Personal Account of the University of Toronto 1932–1971*. Toronto: University of Toronto Press.

Bok, D. 2005. *Our Underachieving Colleges: A Candid Look at How Much Students Learn and Why They Should Be Learning More*. Princeton, NJ: Princeton University Press.

Boyer, E.L. 1990. *Scholarship Reconsidered: Priorities of the Professoriate*. San Francisco: Jossey-Bass.

Champagne, J. 2011. "Teaching in the Corporate University: Assessment as a Labor Issue." *JAF – AAUP Journal of Academic Integrity*, Volume Two.

Clark, I.D. 2010. "A Taxpayer View of University Funding, or, Steve and Di's Evening on the Internet." *University Affairs*, 8 March. At http://www.universityaffairs.ca/a-taxpayers-view-of-university-funding.aspx (accessed 15 January 2012).

—. 2013. "How to Get Better Research – and Teaching – from Universities." *Policy Options* December 2012–January:48–50.

Clark, I.D., and B. Eisen. 2010. "Frugal Public Management Principles for an Age of Austerity." *Policy Options* October:67–71.

Clark, I.D., G. Moran, M.L. Skolnik, and D. Trick. 2009. *Academic Transformation: The Forces Reshaping Higher Education in Ontario*. Queen's Policy Studies Series. Montreal and Kingston: McGill-Queen's University Press.

Clark, I.D., D. Trick, and R. Van Loon. 2011. *Academic Reform: Policy Options for Improving the Quality and Cost-Effectiveness of Undergraduate Education in Ontario*. Queen's Policy Studies Series. Montreal and Kingston: McGill-Queen's University Press.

Coates, K.S., and W.R. Morrison. 2011. *Campus Confidential: 100 Startling Things You Don't Know about Canadian Universities*. Toronto: James Lorimer.

Conway, C. 2010. *Implementing Engagement Improvements through Targeted Interventions: Final Report; Intervention Processes, Impacts and Implications*. Toronto: Higher Education Quality Council of Ontario.

Conway, C., and H. Zhao. 2012. *The NSSE National Data Project: Phase Two*. Toronto: Higher Education Quality Council of Ontario.

Conway, C., H. Zhao, and S. Montgomery. 2011. *The NSSE National Data Project Report*. Toronto: Higher Education Quality Council of Ontario.

Côté, J.E., and A.L. Allahar. 2007. *Ivory Tower Blues: A University System in Crisis*. Toronto: University of Toronto Press.

—. 2011. *Lowering Higher Education: The Rise of Corporate Universities and the Fall of Liberal Education*. Toronto: University of Toronto Press.

Elrick, M.-F. 1990. "Improving Instruction in Universities: A Case Study of the Ontario Universities Program for Instructional Development (OUPID)." *Canadian Journal of Higher Education* 20 (2):61–79.

Finnie, R., R.E. Mueller, A. Sweetman, and A. Usher, eds. 2009. *Who Goes, Who Stays, What Matters: Accessing and Persisting in Post-secondary Education in Canada*. Kingston and Montreal: McGill-Queen's University Press.

Halliwell, J. 2008. *The Nexus of Teaching and Research: Evidence and Insights from the Literature*. Toronto: Higher Education Quality Council of Ontario.

HEQCO. 2007. *Review and Research Plan 2007*. Toronto. At http://www.heqco.ca/SiteCollectionDocuments/101_EN.pdf (accessed 14 January 2012).

—. 2009. *Second Annual Review and Research Plan*. Toronto. At http://www.heqco.ca/SiteCollectionDocuments/Second%20Annual%20Review%20and%20Research%20Plan.pdf (accessed 10 January 2012).

—. 2010. *Third Annual Review and Research Plan*. Toronto. At http://www.heqco.ca/SiteCollectionDocuments/TARRP.pdf (accessed 10 July 2011).

IMF. 2010. *From Stimulus to Consolidation: Revenue and Expenditure Policies in Advanced and Emerging Economies*. At http://www.imf.org/external/np/pp/eng/2010/043010a.pdf (accessed 29 June 2013).

8

8 23 content

Katz, S.N. 2010. "Beyond Crude Measurement and Consumerism." *Academe* September–October. At http://www.aaup.org/AAUP/pubsres/academe/2010/SO/feat/katz.htm (accessed 24 May 2011).

Kerr, C., and M. Gade. 1989. *The Guardians: Boards of Trustees of American Colleges and Universities*. Washington, DC: Association of Governing Boards of Universities and Colleges.

Kinzie, J.D. 2012. *Carnegie Mellon University: Fostering Assessment for Improvement and Teaching Excellence*. NILOA Examples of Good Assessment Practice. Urbana, IL: University of Illinois and Indiana University, National Institute for Learning Outcomes Assessment.

Kuh, F.D. 2008. *High-Impact Educational Practices: What They Are, Who Has Access to Them, and Why They Matter*. Washington, DC: AAC&U.

Lalancette, D. 2012. "OECD Assessment of Higher Education Learning Outcomes (AHELO): Rationale, Challenges and Initial Insights from the Feasibility Study." In *Measuring the Value of a Postsecondary Education*, ed. K. Norrie and M.C. Lennon. Queen's Policy Studies Series. Montreal and Kingston: McGill-Queen's University Press.

Lucas, C.J. 1996. *Crisis in the Academy: Rethinking Higher Education in America*. New York: St. Martin's Press.

Main, A., A. Berland, and P. Morand. 1975. *Teaching and Learning*. Toronto: Council of Ontario Universities.

Mancuso, M., S. Desmarais, K. Parkinson, and B. Pettigrew. 2010. *Disappointment, Misunderstanding and Expectations: A Gap Analysis of NSSE, BCSSE and FSSE*. Toronto: Higher Education Quality Council of Ontario.

Menand, L. 2010. *The Marketplace of Ideas: Reform and Resistance in the American University*. New York: W.W. Norton.

OECD. 2011. *Restoring Public Finances*. Special Issue of the *OECD Journal on Budgeting*. Volume 2011/2. Paris: OECD Publishing.

Pocklington, T.C., and A. Tupper. 2002. *No Place to Learn: Why Universities Aren't Working*. Vancouver: University of British Columbia Press.

Servage, L. 2009. "The Scholarship of Teaching and Learning and the Neo-Liberalization of Higher Education: Constructing the 'Entrepreneurial Learner.'" *Canadian Journal of Higher Education* 39 (2):25-44.

Skolnik, M. 2000. "Does Counting Publications Provide Any Useful Information about Academic Performance?" *Teacher Education Quarterly* Spring:15-25.

Smith, S. 1991. *Commission of Inquiry on Canadian University Education*. Ottawa: Association of Universities and Colleges of Canada.

Wagenaar, R. 2012. "Modernization of Higher Education Programs in Europe: Student-Centred and Learning Outcomes Based." In *Measuring the Value of a Postsecondary Education*, ed. K. Norrie and M.C. Lennon. Queen's Policy Studies Series. Montreal and Kingston: McGill-Queen's University Press.

Weingarten, H. 2011. "The Diminishing Quality of Ontario's Universities: Can the System Be Fixed?" *It'snotacademic* (blog), 31 October. At http://www.heqco.ca/en-CA/blog/archive/2011/10/31/the-diminishing-quality-of-ontario's-universities-can-the-system-be-fixed.aspx (accessed 5 December 2011).

Whitehead, L. 2011. *Review of the Higher Education Quality Council of Ontario*. At http://www.heqco.ca/SiteCollectionDocuments/Whitehead%20Review.pdf (accessed 23 May 2012).

IV

THE POLICY-MAKING CONTEXT: GLOBAL DIMENSIONS

CHAPTER 10

GLOBALIZATION AND "POLICYSCAPES": RUPTURES AND CONTINUITIES IN HIGHER EDUCATION

Nelly P. Stromquist

INTRODUCTION

Dramatic changes are transforming the landscape of higher education. Its institutions are undergoing comprehensive change in their organizational structure, identity, and social mission and in the composition of their faculty and students. The university, a site of advanced knowledge creation and diffusion, is facing demands for responsiveness to its environment – a responsiveness it cannot avoid if it is to survive. Many of these changes, intensified by competition for rank among rivals, are underscored by the emergence of the "knowledge society," for which advanced learning and skills are indispensable. While many countries are not active parts of the knowledge society, as Meyer et al. (2006) observe, what is more important than its actual form is the set of assumptions and cultural claims underlying it.[1]

Universities throughout the world see themselves facing global economic and cultural change, which they internalize as a drive to "bring themselves into the 21st century." At present, these transformations are conspicuous and pervasive.

Making Policy in Turbulent Times: Challenges and Prospects for Higher Education, ed. P. Axelrod, R.D. Trilokekar, T. Shanahan, and R. Wellen. Kingston: School of Policy Studies, Queen's University.

Explaining institutional change

Three theoretical perspectives can be invoked: one linked to world culture theory, also termed world polity theory (Meyer et al. 2006), another tied to the notion of institutional isomorphism (DiMaggio and Powell 1983), and a third connected to contemporary globalization and market ideologies (Carney 2009). The first focuses on the dissemination of norms and values compatible with high modernity; it "stresses the dependence of local social organizations on wider environmental meanings, definitions, rules, and models" (Meyer et al. 2006, 3). The second emphasizes changes at the organizational level, contending that the process of change, paradoxically, engenders similar responses among institutions. The third looks at the diffusion of ideas that cut across countries as a phenomenon propelled by information and communications technologies (ICTs) as well as by economic ideology and survival. These three perspectives are related in that they seek to explain the change process through factors external to the institution, but they differ significantly in the attribution of change to particular social actors.

The world culture perspective assumes a relatively conflict-free process of diffusion in which new ideas and practices are adopted because they advance human peace and progress; in other words, whatever is adopted is for the good of society. The notion of organizational isomorphism proposed by DiMaggio and Powell moves the concept of diffusion to a more concrete level – focusing on institutions – and hypothesizes that this diffusion is due to three possible forces: coercion (where the strongest organizations dominate the environment), mimetic (by which institutions imitate those perceived to perform at high levels of excellence), and normative (by which the circulation of professional values and standards brings institutions into compliance with similar procedures).

In contrast with the world culture and the organizational isomorphism perspectives is the notion of "policyscape," proposed by Carney (2009)[2] to signal the circulation of educational policies and how local sites connect to national and international policy formulation processes. Policyscape highlights the global spread of policy ideas and pedagogical practices across highly diverse national school systems and locates their driving force in ongoing processes of neo-liberalism. This perspective, therefore, recognizes the role of ideology and economic power in the diffusion of educational policies and maintains that a nation-focused analysis fails to capture how these ideas both affect and surpass national territories. Carney holds that a cornerstone of the current policyscape is the ideology of neo-liberalism, with its focus on economic relations and liberalism, in which individualism is held as the strongest value.[3] Similarly, Stromquist (2002) considers that globalization and neo-liberalism go hand in hand, but which gave rise to the other is a matter of debate.

Some observers of globalization, and education in particular (Anderson-Levitt 2012; Soudien 2012), argue that while we are seeing a tendency toward isomorphism in the academic landscape, there are also clear local responses, affected by history and particular contingencies. A question of importance then becomes, what are the relative degrees of transformation and preservation occurring in universities today?

This chapter explores changes in universities by examining institutional policies and practices at four levels: resource competition – the deployment of energies toward increasing revenues, in which rankings and research loom high; management and governance – new forms of leadership and thus decision-making; professional identity – faculty moving away from stable academic affiliation; and internationalization – strategies for work in settings beyond the universities' domestic environments. As Cowen (2009) has noted, exploring the occurrence of change implies attention to acts of rupture, tension, conflict, and resistance (cited in Carney 2009). Therefore, the proposed stock-taking considers forces and instances of action in unexpected, even contrary, directions. I seek to assess the balance of the breaks and continuities in institutional identity, norms, and practices.

Analytically, I rely on the concept of policyscape while modifying it slightly. I use it to mean a package or constellation of policy prescriptions that are legitimized through institutional "emitters" with power and world recognition. Policyscapes circulate widely as processes that cut across national boundaries without dissolving the nation-state and provide symbolic models of what is suitable for contemporary society. They occupy societal spaces rather than a particular society or country. At the same time, because these ideas are not spelled out in detail, substantial translation goes on in their name. The configurations of new policies are exported and/or imported in no particular order or sequence, nor are they felt with identical consequences. I further hold that policyscapes are a notion that may be applied not only internationally but also across institutions *within* a given country, for decontextualized and standardized change can also take place at national levels, especially in large countries such as the United States. This is quite compatible with Carney's observation that educational policies and practices in one institution should be seen as an ongoing relationship with other institutions.

The study relies primarily on data about recent developments in US research universities. Whenever data are available for other countries, I refer to university developments in those settings. In all, the evidence I muster brings together a number of important developments; it does so in the form of a collage and thus is neither comprehensive nor exhaustive but rather indicative of prevailing trends. The unit of analysis in this exploration is not the country or the institution but rather the set of dimensions that comprises a particular policyscape (Pries 2007).

Sources of change

Change is multi-causal, although some forces are obviously stronger than others. Among university leaders, there is consensus that economic and technological globalization is a significant force that has both created new environments and accelerated our response to them (IAU 2003).

Two of the core features of economic neo-liberalism affecting higher education are deregulation and privatization. These two features tend to be mutually supportive because easing the rules favours the emergence of private business. Privatization is further fostered by the reduced state sought by neo-liberalism: with smaller public budgets, private provision becomes a substitute for public services, including universities. The nature of change is shaped by those who foster it. Mechanisms such as privatization and deregulation bring changes in rules that incorporate market values. A number of scholars consider that this leads to an erosion of the common good (Brown 2009).

Most of the expansion of higher education in the past two decades has occurred through private provision, except in the case of Canada, a country that has one of the highest levels of public funding for higher education among countries in the Organisation for European Co-operation and Development (OECD) (CCL 2011), although even there, a trend has been detected toward privatization and a reduction of state support (Fisher and Rubenson 1998).

The disinvestment of governments in higher education is a phenomenon observed throughout the world, with a few exceptions. This is particularly the case in the US and other countries where the balance of the political economy is tipped firmly in the direction of neo-liberalism. In 1999, for example, the state of California paid 70 percent of higher education costs; ten years later, it paid less than 25 percent (Reich 2009). And this is happening with the University of California system too, one of the most prestigious expressions of public higher education in the country. At the aggregate level, all 50 states together were spending US$4 billion less on higher education in 2011 than they did in 2008, while enrolments had increased in most states (Kiley 2011d).[4]

Not surprisingly, the most pressing problems of US universities, according to their leaders, are changes in state support and inadequate budgets (Kiley 2011d). Equal problems have been identified by European universities (EHEA 2010). Previously Communist countries, such as Russia and Poland, are also facing drastically reduced university budgets. Japan constitutes perhaps the most dramatic example of privatization, as in 2004 the government initiated a process of turning all national universities into semi-autonomous public corporations, now run by executive councils with limited institutional guidance by faculty members (Kaneko 2012). In this global panorama, Canada emerges as an exception in the degree of autonomy its provinces grant to their public institutions (CCL 2011).

Ideas have always circulated throughout the world, even if in earlier eras circulation was cumbersome and it might have taken months and years for such ideas to become known, let alone adopted and adapted. In those times, the role of intellectuals, through their writings and physical visits to different places, was essential. With globalization, we have readily mobile expressions of technology and expertise and instant access to information about new institutional practices and strategies. As is well recognized, professional associations and conferences, institutional analyses and reports, and individual experiences in university life introduce rapid exposure to university models being tried out elsewhere and reproduce around the globe those that appear to have merit (Appadurai 1996; Meyer et al. 2006; Carney 2009).

While multiple actors today engage in the dissemination of innovations in the functions and practices of universities, we have seen the development of institutional centres immensely more powerful than just the mobility of free-floating intellectuals. This is particularly true of universities in developing countries, where what makes certain policies and practices transnational and others not depends on their sponsorship by certain powerful institutions: the World Bank; the OECD; and the regional development banks for Asia, Africa, and Latin America. Most of these institutions endorse an instrumental view of education, one that links knowledge to the needs of the economy (Rizvi and Lingard 2006). While the trend toward convergence of educational ideas and practices can have normative dimensions, as Mundy (2009) observes, the leverage of financial institutions (international and regional banks, and supranational institutions such as the OECD) vastly exceeds the normative power of more sensitive agencies such as the United Nations Educational, Scientific and Cultural Organization and international non-governmental organizations (Anh and Marginson 2010; Klees, Samoff, and Stromquist 2012).

Across the globe, one powerful institution, the World Bank, is promoting the establishment of world-class universities, arguing that countries need such institutions in order to join "globally competitive economies by developing a skilled, productive, and flexible labor force and by creating, applying, and spreading new ideas and technologies" (Salmi 2009, 2). In the World Bank's view, the path to transformation calls for "upgrading a small number of existing universities that could have the potential of excelling (picking winners)" or creating new ones (7). After having justified the need for such universities, the World Bank observes that the approximate inception cost is about US$500 million per institution. But it adds that the bank stands ready to provide technical assistance and guidance, will help the new elite institutions to get exposure to relevant international experience through workshops and study tours during the start-years of the new institution, and will provide financial support for feasibility studies as well as investment costs for the actual establishment of the planned institutions (Salmi 2009, 11–12). And in countries that "have established a positive regulatory and incentive framework to promote the development of private tertiary education, International Finance Corporation loans and guarantees can be used to complement or replace World Bank support if the target universities are set up or transformed into public-private partnerships" (12). Clearly, the World Bank is not only pressing the need to create world-class universities but is also providing funds if such initiatives involve the private sector, thereby contributing substantially to both the diffusion and the implementation of a new policyscape.

Additional promoters of the world-class university include major universities themselves. For instance, the University of California, Berkeley (UC Berkeley) now offers a one-week summer institute on "essential characteristics of major research universities," at a cost of slightly over US$1,000 per day, covering such issues as strategic planning, faculty participation in governance, tenure, academic planning, university-industry interactions, and technology transfer. Again, these types of venues contribute to the dissemination of policyscapes.

Unlike the World Bank, which links its financial ideology to loan provision, the OECD and the European Union (EU) work more through what is called "soft power," or the ubiquitous and persistent dissemination of ideas of what are considered to be "best practices" or standards to follow in higher education. The OECD engages in "soft agenda setting" by promoting awareness of certain subjects through publications and reports distributed among member countries, particularly its thematic reviews and discussions of student outcomes measured by its Programme for International Student Assessment. Case studies of policy directives in Finland and the United Kingdom show congruence with OECD recommendations that universities should respond to the needs of their country's economy and its "competitiveness" (Kallo 2009).

Studies focusing on the EU find that this institution, no less than the OECD, deploys soft power through networking, seminars, reviews, and the appointment of expert groups to pursue not only a homogeneous European identity but also one in which the knowledge society and competition among universities in academic excellence, and among individuals in terms of qualifications, is paramount (Lawn and Grek 2012). Kallo finds that the collaboration between the OECD and the World Bank has resulted in "shared knowledge in several policy areas" and the "adoption of increasingly similar policy terminologies" (2009, 103).

Technology by itself is having a major impact in developing countries, with "the interconnectivity between sites made unavoidable by the globalization of experiences" (Carney 2009, 66). Castells, one of the most assiduous scholars of the impact of ICTs, points to the importance of Internet networks, which comprise people from "many cultures, many values, many projects that cross through the minds and inform the strategies of the various participants" (1996, 199). As time goes by, developing regions are gaining more access to electronic connectivity. Africa, a particularly disadvantaged region in terms of ICTs, is rapidly expanding its Internet capabilities, including major improvements from 2006 to 2009 in the telecommunications infrastructure in Southern Africa (Kotecha 2011).

SIMILARITIES AMONG INSTITUTIONS

As stated earlier, this chapter centres on the concept of policyscapes to signal emerging and yet stable similarities across four dimensions dealing with financial aspects: management and governance matters, professional identity, and internationalization issues.

Resource competition

Faced with declining state support, public universities now engage in a constant search for new sources of revenues. And private universities, alert to the competition from each other and from public universities, reinvent themselves by offering new programs and degrees to attract new students.[5] These efforts are combined with more and larger research contracts and grants, and partnerships with well-endowed universities at home and abroad. To facilitate the implementation of these objectives, several universities are establishing offices abroad; selected countries often target China (multiple cities), Korea, and Brazil. Given the decreased state support to public universities in the US, public universities are becoming increasingly similar to private institutions in their search for resources.

Research projects in engineering, medicine, and the physical sciences are especially desirable: their products are tangible and more marketable than those in the social sciences. The possibility of profits derived from inventions through patents, royalties, and licences is paramount. But the funding of certain research topics and not others has negative consequences. Brown, a professor at UC Berkeley, argues that at his university – world-famous for the student free-speech movement in the 1960s and renowned for its prestigious faculty – there is a climate that constrains research topics to those funded by sponsors and simultaneously "silences faculty who are seen as standing in the way of getting corporate funding" (Brown 2009). Policies that reduce state support and at the same time bring universities into global competition regardless of national or regional needs are a clear example of a policyscape that fosters action in decontextualized ways.

Linked to the competition for resources is the universities' competition for high academic rankings. Institutions such as the American Council on Education (ACE) and the World Bank hold that knowledge is not a zero-sum game,[6] but institutional rankings clearly identify winners and losers as these rankings generate readily interpretable indicators of quality and reputation. Moreover, reputation not only generates differential rankings, but the rankings themselves influence reputation (Bowman and Bastedo 2011).[7]

The several ranking systems in existence vary in what they consider "quality" and thus do not coincide in their classifications. Universities tend to cite the ranking system that most favours them. Expressing an international perspective, Hazelkorn notes that rankings are introducing substantial distortion into the university systems of many countries, albeit more in research than non-research universities. She asserts that "governments are making profound structural changes to their national systems in order to push a few elite universities into the top 20, 50, or 100 of global rankings" (Hazelkorn 2011, 5). This is quite evident in large countries such as China, Russia, and India; in middle-sized countries such as Korea; and in small countries such as Malaysia and Singapore (Ma 2007; Smolentseva 2007; for a comprehensive account of national efforts in search of world-class universities, see Liu et al. 2011). In this regard, although Canada gives much autonomy to its universities, it is also a fact that federal support has greatly favoured university research, which "has skewed the work of institutions away from teaching functions, and toward a greater concentration of research profiles of faculty and institutions" (CCL 2011, 16).

For some time, rankings were more important to US universities than to others in different parts of the world. This is changing. An instance in point concerns statements by several top French university administrators, who have noted that having a Nobel recipient provides "about 20 or 30 points" in the Shanghai rankings (or Shanghai Jiao Tong Institute of Higher Education, now called the Academic Ranking of World Universities), and they observe with sarcasm that just by announcing such a hire, a university's rankings would change immediately; indeed, "our research quality would radically improve all of a sudden" (Floc'h 2011). They deplore that universities with internationally recognized professors in the social sciences "don't bring a single point in the Shanghai rankings" (Jacqué 2011). But French scholars also realize that rankings seem to make a difference for the recruitment of international students, particularly now that some emergent economies (such as Brazil) are funding large numbers of students for study abroad (Jacqué 2011). Accreditation is another means by which to achieve recognition. By 2005, institutions and programs in over 100 countries had adopted this standard to receive recognition as being legitimate and a provider of high-quality programs.

A significant source of revenue derives from the creation of new programs, both degree- and non-degree–granting. In many US universities, the creation of executive doctoral degrees enables recipients to obtain very desirable credentials while providing the universities with much needed income. There is little research on these executive degrees, but important features are their short duration, easy access, and elevated costs compared to regular programs. A large, private US university now provides a "global education" EdD degree, a two-year, part-time program targeted to "senior educational leaders and policy makers" (i.e., persons with acquisitive power). The courses are delivered mostly online, with several in-person meetings; students pay about US$250,000 per person to participate in this doctoral program. Who can pay this rather high tuition? It is expected that most will be Chinese entrepreneurs moving into the provision of higher education through the multitude of private colleges springing up in their country.

The same university offers a very successful online master's degree in teaching. In operation since 2009, this program now has an enrolment of 1,600 students. The program costs US$50,000 for about a year and a half of coursework, generating gross annual revenues of approximately US$60 million, which has dramatically increased the wealth of the college of education. Faculty members who have been teaching in this program note that while its provision involves the latest technology, aspects related to course content and teaching are weak, and many students engage in little academic effort, knowing that it will be most difficult for them to "fail." As anticipated, the program draws a large number of students.

In the US university system, once proud of its land-grant system, major tensions are developing. Land-grant universities were created by individual states for the purpose of providing advanced knowledge to their state communities and serving the needs of their residents. One reading of this is that a state would not only give a practical orientation to the university (e.g., provide engineering and agricultural degrees) but also encourage admission of its own state students. But today, land-grant universities are increasingly soliciting international and out-of-state students (both of whom pay a higher tuition than state residents) while at the same time seeking to increase their reputations, for which selectivity in student admissions becomes a high priority. There can be a contradiction, however, between student selectivity and addressing the needs of local students. States with large numbers of African American and Mexican American minorities face the dilemma of whether to emphasize admitting students with high Graduate Record Examination scores or admitting minority students (who for a variety of historical and cultural reasons do not do as well in standardized tests).

The knowledge economy connection

The knowledge society has catapulted the value of advanced skills and knowledge into highly remunerated jobs. Firms turn to universities for support, and the latter in turn favour disciplines and fields more likely to yield returns from innovation, entrepreneurship, and marketing. US universities have long insisted on knowledge that results in products for a competitive economy, an effort that has recently intensified considerably. In other parts of the world, the link between knowledge and work is also taking hold (for Europe, see EHEA 2011). Writing of the European context, Conceição and Heitor (2001) note that the boundaries that have separated universities and companies are becoming blurred and that there is a clear trend toward institutional convergence. An interesting development is the recent emergence of the Russell Group, a coalition of 24 leading UK universities that have come together to provide high-calibre research, outstanding teaching and learning experiences, and "unrivalled links with business and the public sector" (Russell Group 2013).

As will be seen under "Management and governance" below, there are increasingly dense connections between the corporate world and universities in the US, not only in the form of agreements but also through the presence of influential business magnates on university boards of governors. Two significant manifestations of the connection between the university and the commercial world are i) an agreement by the University of Maryland to install on its own campus an international business incubator with China (Loh 2011), the first such arrangement for a US university, and ii) the investment of some of the University of Michigan's (UOM) endowment funds in start-up companies developed through university research to bring ideas to the market. In the latter case, up to US$500,000 will be given to each new company, with the university assigning a total of US$25 million in venture capital funding. UOM will also provide US$50 million in interdisciplinary research to support study abroad, undergraduate research, and entrepreneurial activities (Kiley 2011b). Explaining this initiative, the UOM director of investment risk management stated, "We [the universities] live in a different world" (Kiley 2011b).

University students, influenced by a persistent discourse that underscores the importance of science and technology, increasingly distance themselves from the humanities. Not surprisingly, the most common field of study at the bachelor's level in the US today is business administration, which comprises 20 percent of the students at that level (Menand 2010).

The discourse on research and knowledge production often invokes the need for interdisciplinary research. However, this takes place only among cognate or highly complementary sciences and mostly in disciplines that will produce marketable products. It might not be so easy to find intellectual endeavours that combine sociology and engineering or philosophy and medicine. But increasingly frequent are joint efforts in engineering, computer science, biochemistry, physics, and medicine. Some advances through this kind of collaboration offer enormous practical applications. However, much remains to be done to strengthen the physical sciences with perspectives from the humanities and the social sciences.

Some see the emergence of the research university as inevitable (Mohrman, Ma, and Baker 2007). This model, essentially American in nature, is considered to be the last stage of sophistication and efficiency in the process of knowledge production and its link to economic

development. The research university is costly, as research is its defining feature, but it is also highly desirable given its potential for helping
to boost national levels of technological and scientific development.
Research universities have existed on the basis of competitive research
grants, with priority given to science and technology over the social sciences and humanities. Many universities throughout the world struggle
to imitate this model. While research universities are making substantial
contributions to their respective nations, it is also the case that they are
becoming lopsided institutions with very instrumental objectives. In the
search for resources, it is clear that similar strategies are being followed.
The importance of research and serving the economic needs of society
permeate many higher education environments and are a salient dimension of policyscapes characterizing contemporary higher education.

Management and governance

University emphasis on managerialism has been observed in numerous
previous works on higher education, which I will not summarize at this
point.[8] Universities are becoming more complex and require more and
different types of management personnel. My purpose here is not to show
how widespread managerialism has become, but to link its existence to
authoritarian forms of academic governance. Beno Schmidt, who was
president of Yale University for six years, remarks, "The faculty is far too
compartmentalized, too divided, and too distracted to control strategic
planning. Any change of significance will affect the interest of some
faculty, and very small numbers of faculty can block any faculty action
that threatens them. Strategy must be the purview of the trustees" (Kiley
2011e). This assertion, fairly typical among administrators, clearly dis-
misses faculty engagement in institutional strategic thinking and, at the
same time, establishes administrators as the exclusive decision-makers.
Another sign of increasingly limited faculty influence is the common
absence of faculty participation in the selection of university provosts
and presidents in the US context (Kiley 2011a).
　This managerial view of top-down decision-making, characteristic
of many businesses, has become coupled with administrative salaries
that mirror the corporate world. As of 2009, 23 presidents in private US
universities earned salaries greater than US$1 million (de Vise 2009).
Also mirroring structural arrangements in the corporate environment,
universities are creating units with specialized divisions of labour. Since
the ability to convert assets into cash has become a major institutional
concern, many research universities have set up an office of finance
responsible for supporting cash management. Of course, now financial
officers play significant policy roles (Kiley 2011c).
　A key instrument for the implementation of managerial governance
is the strategic plan. Every major university in the US has one, and 70

percent of them now have an office charged with its implementation (IAU 2003). Internationally, these plans can be found from Korea to Peru. The strategic plans usually identify mid- and long-term strategies and action routes. Compliance is tightly monitored by the increasingly powerful office of the provost through frequent required reports by deans and heads of non-academic units and by linking salary bonuses and increases to prompt and efficient execution of strategic plan objectives (Stromquist 2012). Unquestionably, strategic plans – whose content is quite predictable as their references to "vision," "mission," and "opportunities" embody similar objectives and analyses – can be considered a solid example of the policyscapes that cut across domestic and international frontiers and that have become a symbol of institutional legitimacy.

Supported by technological developments that make it easy to design monitoring instruments and distribute them flawlessly and with great speed to the selected recipients, managerialism has also introduced the requirement of frequent reporting procedures by faculty members, all in the name of greater accountability. In addition to detailed annual performance forms, faculty members must fill out forms assessing undergraduate performance and even "graduate outcomes assessments." On this last instance, monitoring graduates requires identifying their placement upon graduation and whether such placement is in the academy or not. Implicitly, there is little regard for PhD graduates engaging in work with governments and non-governmental organizations. A conversation with a senior administrator in one of the universities now requiring graduate outcomes assessments indicated that the practice was being installed because "all other universities are doing it. You have to keep improving your department; otherwise, you will go down to the bottom." The same administrator characterized those professors who put up individual resistance to administrative fiats as "the most painful, most difficult persons to work with on campus" (Anonymous administrator, February 2010).

Since a number of managerial practices are imitated from other institutions, there is at times little understanding of the consequences of adopting them. A requirement in the strategic plan of one public research university is moving into a full-time, fully funded model of doctoral student. This model is expected to create students who concentrate totally on their studies so that they can then graduate within five years at most. Yet, the stipend that is being proposed for such students precludes students with families and those who are presently working in pertinent institutions. The model as designed will negatively affect PhD programs in professional schools (Stromquist 2011). There has been little response by administrators to modify this PhD model. The questions then become: Are they unaware of those implications of the model? Or worse yet, do they not care? Universities do not have systems to monitor the behaviour of senior administrators (Ginsberg 2011). Although faculty members are regularly asked to review the performance of department chairs and deans, reviews of the office of the provost and his or her associates, and that of the president, do not involve general faculty participation.

Increasing number of administrators

Several intense operations by universities today require the presence of persons with much more than academic expertise. In the US, for instance, close to 60 federal agencies have regulatory authority over institutions of higher education (Berrett 2011b). Fundraising from philanthropic donors and business firms – a major means of support for programs and institutional expansion – proceeds on the basis of close contact with such sources; social skills and command of the law are necessary for securing contracts. Research contracts with businesses as well as federal and state governments require the involvement of university lawyers to determine what is best for the institution and how it can be protected in cases of conflict. Student services, which range from understanding international visa requirements to housing and providing referral for medical health attention, involve a rather large number of individuals for whom academic credentials are not necessary but an understanding of the university as an organization is.

The denser the functions of the university, the more it relies on top- and mid-level administrators. And this, in turn, reshapes the university in many ways. There tends to be a replacement of shared governance with business management principles and, inexorably, a greater involvement of non-academics in academic matters (Brown 2009; Stromquist 2012). Based on his findings, Ginsberg (2011) charges administrators with having transformed the university from an instrument of social good and contribution to human knowledge to one centred on knowledge as an institutional revenue stream. Administrators are making themselves important by increasingly building up their own ranks with persons with no academic background (which, as I have stated above, is not always necessary for the task). Ginsberg's main evidence is that in the US between 1975 and 2005, administrative positions in universities grew by 85 percent, those in associated professional staff positions grew by 240 percent, while faculty grew by 51 percent (see also AAUP 2011).

It is argued here that with the prevalence of personnel in administrative positions, an instrumental rationality and technocratic logic is being introduced into the contemporary university. The new ethos values efficiency but at the same time displays a high inclination to cut costs with little reflection on what that might mean for the functioning of academic programs and even their very existence. Cost-cutting often involves school and program mergers and eliminations (reported in such diverse countries as Denmark [Colatrella 2007] and South Africa [Mabokela 2007]), a preference for part-time and non-tenure-track professors, increases in the size of students per course, and mandatory minimum class sizes. The concept of efficiency is widely applied within and across countries; it seems to be applied with limited reflection on its unintended consequences.

Redefined governance

Very different traditions of governance have operated in US universities and those in other countries. In the European and Latin American traditions, universities have had a great amount of autonomy, a situation that has meant that professors elected their institutional leaders, who then functioned as the final authority. The US model of governance, instead, has had a top-down hierarchy represented by a board of trustees, individuals with legal responsibility for the university, who, while not entering into micromanagement, have had substantial influence in guiding their institutions in particular growth directions.

As the US model becomes more widespread, more boards are being set up. The European Higher Education Area (EHEA) makes reference to the increasing participation of a wide range of actors, now including employers, unions, and professional organizations, in shaping educational programs (2011). But businesses are certainly the most influential. Danish universities, long a bastion of institutional autonomy, now have governing bodies with a majority of members appointed from outside (usually public sector and business executives), chancellors and/or rectors who report directly to these boards, and appointed institute leaders who report directly to the rector and not their colleagues (Carney 2009). As the practice of having elected officials disappears, new forms of governance emerge: university leaders have signed personal performance contracts with their boards; provosts or rectors do likewise with their presidents. As Carney notes in the case of Denmark, each Danish university has signed a detailed development contract, promising to deliver intellectual goods and services within the three-year contract period.

The university as a knowledge industry, with managers and boards of trustees representing people from the business world, is replacing faculty governance with administrative expertise. It is an essentially American model that is widely circulated and adopted throughout many institutions of higher education today, irrespective of their mission, their geographical location, or the particular constituency they are supposed to serve.

Professional identity

Normative and de facto practices are reconfiguring the academic profession. On the one hand, there is a growing perception that full-time professors with long-term affiliation to their institution are no longer needed. This feeling has been registered at individual levels, but only recently have there been manifestations of a collective position. In 2011, the AUCC, which includes most Canadian university presidents, issued a statement on academic freedom. Notably, while the statement declared support for the right of professors to follow their ideas in teaching and research, it made no reference to tenure (Jaschick 2011).

The proportion of full-time academicians with tenure in US universities is going down, and, simultaneously, the number of part-time professors working on short-term contracts is increasing. Adjunct professors are usually paid by the course, and this results in considerable cost savings for the university. But this reduction comes with several serious consequences. One of these is the weakened institutional identification of academicians; another is their concomitant reduced participation in decisions affecting themselves and the university. Professors at UC Berkeley, one of the most prestigious universities in the US, report a diminished sense of shared purpose and an increased difference among departments (Brown 2009). Baran (1961) was one of the first scholars to use the term "intellectual worker," by which he referred to those who work with their minds and who were not greatly dissimilar to those who labour with their muscles. The meaning today would refer to those who, while continuing to work with their minds, have undergone a declining status and identity with their place of work. Perhaps, as Ibarra Colado observes (2001, 361), the current working conditions of many professors may lead to "reinventing their identity along the lines of discipline and obedience."

Homogenization in degrees and programs of study

The US university operates with a widely accepted degree model and even degree program content. Homogenization of academic programs and degrees has been in effect for a long time. The situation in Europe has been quite different; the Bologna Accord therefore represents a recent step toward academic convergence in that part of the world (Nilsson and Nilsson 2004; Keeling 2006). Because of post-colonial ties, the accord is also having an impact on African universities (Shabani 2012).

The Bologna Accord is officially justified as an effort to strengthen supranational identity by allowing free mobility across countries and increasing the competitiveness of European vis-à-vis other countries. But the parameters of the new degrees (three cycles of shorter duration) conform closely to the US model – a model that has been at great variance with those of Europe, especially those of Eastern Europe, which have been heavily influenced by the Russian model of higher education (Smolentseva 2007). Further strengthening the Bologna Accord is the creation of the EHEA, launched in March 2010, the 10th anniversary of the Bologna Accord. EHEA recognizes "three pillars" of higher education: research, teaching, and student affairs and services. It sees the third pillar as a social responsibility that will facilitate retention and speedy completion. Again, this bears close resemblance to the provision of student services in US universities. Another related development pertains to the British universities' decision to adopt the US grade point average model instead of the three-level honours classification (Baker 2011). While adopted because it is more sensitive to student performance, the fact is that, again, it is the US model that prevails.

The homogenization of European universities in terms of degrees, processing, and services represents a policyscape dimension that covers countries that are quite diverse in history and socio-economic context with the same prescriptions. In this regard, the diffusion of the Bologna Accord and the British initiative may be interpreted as a convergence toward the largest and most powerful model – the US research university.

Internationalization

This institutional response has become very popular for several reasons: it promotes the enrolment of international students (a significant source of revenue), it enables universities to gain visibility abroad, it facilitates research in other physical settings, and, of course, it makes it possible to become acquainted with realities in other countries, particularly those of emergent economies and developing countries. Several US universities have a vice-president for global issues, while others have a vice-provost for the position.

The global patterns reveal that a major consideration in internationalization is the search for countries that can financially support the study abroad of their citizens or that have the knowledge and skills that would make them productive partners. Therefore, internationalization assumes, generally, a search for students as well as business and academic partnerships with China, India, and the oil-rich countries. China has become such a strong interest for US universities that several university presidents in the US do not hesitate to call it the "new centre of gravity" of the 21st-century world.

Although internationalization was meant to integrate an international and multicultural dimension into most aspects of university work (Knight and de Wit 1995), in reality this has given way to more economic rationales, such as developing joint research projects with foreign institutions of equal or higher reputation (the so-called peer institutions), recruiting more international students (fee-paying, mostly), and expanding the study abroad programs. Curiously, internationalization may be prominent in the discourse of US universities, but such an objective is not supported by the US government. Evidence of this is the reduction by 47 percent of the budgets for the US National Resource Centers for Foreign Language, Area and International Studies (Redden 2011). The number of US students going abroad is small, less than 5 percent (IIE 2011); this reflects the fact that internationalization is more frequent among students from other countries going to US universities rather than vice versa. Still, due to increased competition from other countries, the share of international students going to the US has been decreasing, from 23 percent of all students going abroad in 2000 to 18 percent in 2009 (OECD 2011).

Although US universities have not been interested in developing connections with African countries given the latter's limited financial resources, Africa has fortunately attracted institutions from the EU, Canada, China, India, and Brazil as well as some in the US (Teferra 2012). These forms of internationalization have involved university-development support and capacity-building.

The policyscape dimension embodied in internationalization functions at two levels: it heightens the visibility of US universities and thus facilitates their recruitment of international students; and, at the same time, it is favoured by universities in less developed parts of the world because contacts with desirable university models in Northern countries enhance the reputation of the sending university. This highlights one feature of successful policyscapes – their association with proven and prestigious models.

DIFFERENCES AMONG INSTITUTIONS

Is the process of institutional change identical across institutions? Of course not. Variations arise due to particular historical contexts, specific political conditions, and individual geographical characteristics. I explain this below.

While there is a universal tendency among universities to seek global recognition, their nation-states respond differently. In parts of Asia, governments provide strong state support for their universities, with the objective of moving many of them into "world-class" status. In the Asia-Pacific region, where as many as one-third of the world's top universities are presently located, China, Korea, and Taiwan are making substantial investments in their universities (Ilon 2010), seeking to further increase their numbers of world-class universities. Russia is also making investments in several universities to bring them up to world-class status (Smolentseva 2007; Stromquist and Smolentseva 2011). At this moment, Asia produces nearly twice the number of engineers as Europe and also surpasses Europe in the number of those in the natural sciences (Ilon 2010). The continuous commitment to succeed in science and technology is leading governments in many parts of Asia to take an active role in the financial support of their universities. This contrasts with the response by the state in mature capitalist countries in North America and Europe (except Germany).

China, a country in transition from communism to capitalism, evinces a hybrid structure in some parts of its administration. Its student affairs units are expanding their work to attend to student needs such as stress, health problems, violence, housing, and financial and career advice. At the same time, such units continue to provide ideological training. The provision of ideological, political, and moral guidance remains organized by the university division of the Chinese Community Party (Arnold and Zhu 2011).

The impetus of neo-liberal reforms includes a reliance on user fees, whether in private or public universities. An exception to this pattern is the Scandinavian countries and, more recently, Ecuador, where a new president came to power under the slogan of a "citizen's revolution" inspired by the "socialism of the 21st century." This led to the passing of a constitution in 2008 that removed all student fees, so public universities are now free and depend almost exclusively on state funding. However, the creation in 2010 of the position of national secretary of higher education, science, technology, and innovation is expected to make universities less autonomous (Estrella 2011).

A third source of difference can be linked to particular geographic conditions. In the case of a large private university located in Los Angeles, donors from the Hollywood film industry are interested in maintaining the region's comparative advantage. Thus, this university has been the recipient of multi-million-dollar grants to support the arts and the humanities. It must also be observed that occasionally, enlightened donors support the humanities in other universities – but those grants seldom reach the same monetary level as those bestowed to the natural sciences and certain other fields, such as medicine.

Small liberal colleges, unlike major research universities, seem to have been able to maintain a social justice emphasis by either keeping their original mission of serving their community or having career path programs to facilitate the success of minority students. This differential behaviour is possible because, not being research institutions, they are not on the same competition circuit.

The literature also refers to some universities where the priority given to local needs is leading to social rather than purely commercial investments. Such seems to be the case in Finland and Korea (Pillay 2011), where universities and polytechnics are collaborating with each other and with local government and business to ensure greater equity in regional development.

Resistance

There is some intellectual debate associated with the trends I have described above when discussing similarities. To these trends, some resistance – i.e., oppositional behaviour – can be observed; some universities deal with resistance to the increasing role of administrators in policymaking, but such resistance is weak and rare.

The most widespread manifestation of resistance has occurred in Denmark, where academic staff have fought successfully against new policies perceived to function as constraints on professional autonomy. The strategy followed was to organize into lobbying groups, which, while endorsing the government's agenda to make Danish institutions among the top in the world, introduced a twist to that objective by arguing that to undertake world-class research, faculty needed state funding and autonomy to determine their academic programs (Carney 2009).

In the US, the strongest expression of such resistance came in the form of a no-confidence vote in 2013 against the president of New York University for making a number of strategic decisions with little or no input from its faculty. This vote, reflecting the growing distance between faculty members and administrators, protested the enormous local and global physical expansion of the university (Kiley 2013). Another indicator of resistance was produced by the resignation of the dean of Columbia College of Columbia University in 2011 because, from her perspective, changes by central administrators would "transform the administrative structure" of the Faculty of Arts and Sciences, compromising her authority over "crucial policy, fund-raising and budgetary matters" (Hu 2011). A third instance of resistance took place at Idaho State University, also in 2011, but there the faculty lost. In response to a complaint by the Faculty Senate that a proposed manual of administrative policies and procedures would infringe on the faculty's responsibility for academic and faculty personnel decision-making, the Idaho State Board of Education suspended the operations and bylaws of the Faculty Senate and allowed the president to appoint instead an interim faculty advisory structure. The president was quoted as saying that the faculty governance system was "a cumbersome ... system that is often unproductive and inefficient" (AAUP 2011, 7).

Resistance at the institutional level also exists. An example comes from a failed attempt to merge two state universities proposed by state politicians in Maryland. The merger would have fused two institutions with very different cultures into a new university; combining their research funding would have propelled the new university's ranking into the top 10 US universities. The initiative was strongly resisted by the smaller institution, with the result that instead of a merger, the decision was made to enter into "a strategic alliance" that would centre on possible joint research projects between the two universities.

Opposition to tuition increases has been noticed among universities in the UK, where substantially higher rates have been instituted, and in the US, in the California University system, which has proposed tuition increases of 30 percent. The Berkeley campus registered the most concrete resistance actions. But there – a university well known for its political ethos – the resistance attracted a mere 200 professors (out of some 1,600 full-time faculty members), even when the faculty recognized that they had not been consulted regarding the tuition increase or the various budget cuts (Reich 2009). Students far and wide have been protesting tuition increases, which they attribute to the growth in the number of administrators and their high salaries (Kiley 2011d). Compounding increases in tuition is a reduction in program funding, which in May 2011 led to a campaign initiated by university professors in 21 US states to fight against cuts to their institutions' budgets and to make higher education more widely accessible (Berrett 2011a). This effort is currently in progress, and its impact remains to be felt.

In the area of education, teachers' unions and other collective actors have blocked negotiations on the General Agreement on Trade in Services (GATS) in several developing countries (Mundy 2009).[9] This resistance applies to primary and secondary schooling; it is not known to what extent there are similar manifestations of organized resistance in higher education.

CONCLUSIONS

The overall conclusion that can be drawn from the preceding examination is that the world of higher education is increasingly moving toward convergence. Universities are being reconfigured by multiple forces that not only affect their functioning but also, in doing so, reshape their nature. What a university is today is in a state of flux, and its new identity might not be what many of us wish.

A key theoretical concept that this chapter applied was "policyscapes." This concept is helpful in recognizing how the compression of time and space has disseminated a particular set of solutions and thus led to similar patterns of response throughout the US and the world. From one perspective, we may be witnessing the rebirth of the university – an institution to fit 21st-century requirements, more agile, and more linked to society and its material needs. From another perspective, we may argue that what is at work is the "deterritorialization" of the university since ideas about its proper functioning are widely spread throughout the world, irrespective of particular economic and social conditions. Globalization creates structural changes, including a greater reliance on market forces and fast developments in ICTs that increase global interdependence among organizations. It also creates strategic changes that push actors toward conformance in their actions, even in different contexts (Jessop 2002).

Policyscapes are not only cutting across countries but also producing an integrated space (Carney 2009). Applied to education, policyscapes are adopted because they often match expanding conceptions of what the university is about and because they provide easy, ready-made solutions. Globalization of education accelerates the diffusion of ideas and facilitates the emergence of similar approaches to problems. However, in these policyscapes, the overwhelming effort is toward improving the efficiency of the university and its relevance to the economy. A trend in US, UK, and Australian universities toward the principle of *efficiency*, defined as "the application of business principles and norms to education," introduced the rhetoric of "institutional autonomy." What it brought instead were indirect controls on the university through the imposition of market norms and processes (Welch 1998). Such trends have only intensified in subsequent decades. Key observations raised by DiMaggio and Powell (1983) concern the question of whose interests are being served through these institutional changes.

Policyscapes are producing elements that propel universities toward similar actions irrespective of differences in national contexts and needs. Certainly, not every institution is acting along the same lines. Speaking from a world-polity-theory perspective, Meyer (2012) holds that variation is inevitable in a world society where there is no central authority codifying the rules (see also Appadurai 2000). Similarly, Tsing (2005) finds that even similar patterns of funding across institutions do not lead to inevitable trajectories.

As we observe a movement toward greater convergence than divergence among higher education institutions, it has to be recognized that the various innovative ideas about a university undergo some modification as they travel from emitter to adopter. But the central point to be raised is that the increasing penetration of a global discourse, whether by imitation (as seems to be the case among industrialized countries) or by coercion (as seems to be unfolding in developing countries) signals a reconfiguration of the university. The procedures being deployed are aligning the university with commercial production and businesslike modes of organization. This will inevitably alter the university as a source of knowledge as well as redefine what knowledge should be.

In most countries, the substantial increase in university enrolments has not been matched by increases in state funding. Pleading economic difficulties, national and regional governments have not increased their budgets for higher education and in many instances have even reduced them. The persistent search for alternative sources of support has led to considerable change in the mission and functioning of universities. Higher tuition fees have resulted in the emergence of many private universities. But both private and public universities engage in strategies for revenue-raising that are very similar – both types of institutions vie for reputation, research funds, increased numbers of fee-paying students, and cost reductions that increasingly involve hiring part-time professors on limited-term contracts.

Similarities in university objectives and strategies cut across countries despite substantial national variation in historic, economic, and political conditions. A major source of change is said to be the response to "market needs," or the advent of science as the broad authority in social life, and thus the growing importance of higher education (Schofer and Meyer 2005). But if the market is still very small in several countries, the question becomes, why are higher educational policies not more different? If science has become so important, does this not mean that more scientific careers are being chosen? Yet this is not the case. It could be argued that rather than moving toward a more scientific and rational society, we are moving toward what Ramirez (2011, 260) calls a "certificational society" – again, the manifestation of a policyscape reflecting global ideas in circulation.

Can a transnational set of ideas be entirely centreless? The existence of centre-periphery circles has been detected when examining the distribution of goods and services (Pries 2007). Similar dynamics apply to the diffusion of policies in higher education. This chapter has presented evidence that ideas proposed by Northern institutions carry far more weight than those from the Global South. Policyscapes circulate from North to South and North to North, rarely South to North. In other words, although policyscapes can be described as flowing constellations of actions and processes perceived to be beneficial to education, they also have emitters that champion their dissemination, both unconsciously and with a strong conviction of what models are best suited for adoption by others.

Universities throughout the world are becoming alike. The greatest similarities are visible in the areas of administration and management. As this chapter shows, decision-making in administration and management gradually impinges on academic decisions. One clear manifestation of this is in the expansion of both degree and non-degree programs, which often takes place with limited faculty input.

The increasingly integrated global space propels the university toward industrial-scale and more businesslike modes of operation. The dynamics of the new knowledge production, by relying so much on problem-solving research leading to specific saleable products, generate a bifurcation of the academic profession. Those who are funded to do research commit themselves to intense engagement with data-gathering and analysis; the bulk of the professors do teaching and gradually find themselves with fewer labour protections and alienated from institutional identity.

My attempt to map key changes in the university shows that some local responses do demonstrate diversity. This may encourage some scholars to assert that local responses can be autonomous or can move toward different forms of organization and functioning. But the evidence toward convergence is overwhelming, and local responses manifest themselves essentially as exceptions to prevailing patterns. As we observe the ongoing process of transformation in higher education, we must ask, where is the university as an institution going? Is it moving along the path of progress? Or is it abandoning values and missions that have highlighted the common good? To what extent will the role of the university as a critical voice be maintained? And, perhaps even more importantly, to what extent will it remain a space where utopian ideas can germinate? Our knowledge of both the multiple transformations of the university and how the professoriate perceives them is still limited. It does seem, however, that resistance to ongoing changes is minor. Perhaps it is time to listen to Mzawi's admonition.

Academics need to turn their research tools inward, by critically unpacking the foundation of the higher education structures in which they work and by critically reflecting on their implication with state power. Such a critical engagement would help reclaim not only the centrality of academic work in development but would also connect the academic workplace with community engagement and social transformation. (2011, 13)

NOTES

1. Those who endorse the knowledge society notion argue that in a globalizing world, *all* countries need to have access to the tools required to succeed in the competitive labour market. Pillay (2011) argues, for instance, that African countries need to base their economies not solely on the production of primary commodities and manufactured goods – which require skills adequately provided by primary and secondary education – but also on the production of value-added goods and services, which require skills provided by higher education.

2. Carney acknowledges that his notion of policyscape builds upon the notion of ideoscape first proposed by Appadurai (1996, 2000). Appadurai writes of five global cultural flows, one of which is ideoscapes. These "scapes," a term he coins to mean fluid and irregular spaces, are the building blocks of our "imagined worlds." According to Appadurai (1990), scapes provide large and complex inventories of images and narratives, usually linked to progressive notions that flourished during the Enlightenment, such as freedom, welfare, rights, representation, and the master-term, democracy.

3. Neo-liberalism is a political and economic perspective that promotes an expanded role for market forces and a restrained function for the state in the attainment of objectives of efficiency and quality of goods and services (Colclough 1996; Jolly 2003). Neo-liberalism favours deregulation and thus the privatization of education, decentralization of public schooling, and school choice and cost-sharing by parents and students. For Hayek (1960), the original conceptualizer of neo-liberalism, competition is the core principle of social organization.

4. Some states have experienced considerable reductions in state support in recent years: 40 percent in Arizona; 50 percent in Pennsylvania; 35 percent in Louisiana; 15 percent in North Carolina; and 30 percent in California, Washington, and Minnesota (Kirwan 2011).

5. The global market in educational services, which includes some 3 million students in higher education institutions abroad, generated US$111 billion in 2008, thus becoming a major import for recipient countries (Tilak 2011).

6. See, for instance, ACE (2011) and the Task Force on Higher Education and Society (2000).

7. This was determined in a three-year study of world university rankings, which found that initial rankings shape perceptions of subsequent institutional reputation.

8.   Some authors consider that US universities have been managerial since the early 1900s. See, for instance, Ibarra Colado (2004).
9.   GATS is a major mechanism for the international trade of educational services, particularly higher education. It has been observed that negotiations are usually carried out by national arbitrators who know little about education and much more about trade and finance. In fact, these negotiators tend to use education as a mere pawn in their dealings for more favourable commercial conditions (Verger 2009).

REFERENCES

AAUP. 2011. *College and University Governance: Idaho State University*. Washington, DC: American Association of University Professors.

ACE. 2011. *Strength through Global Leadership and Engagement: U.S. Higher Education in the 21st Century*. Washington, DC: American Council on Education.

Anderson-Levitt, K., ed. 2012. *Anthropologies of Education: A Global Guide to Ethnographic Studies of Learning and Schooling*. New York: Berghahm Books.

Anh, D.T.K., and S. Marginson. 2010. "Vygotskian Socio-cultural Theory and Globalization: Implications for Educational Research." Paper presented at the annual conference of the Australian Association for Research in Education, Melbourne, Australia, 1 December.

Appadurai, A. 1990. "Disjuncture and Difference in the Global Cultural Economy." *Public Culture* 2 (2):1–24.

—. 1996. *Modernity at Large: Cultural Dimensions of Globalization*. Minneapolis: University of Minnesota Press.

—. 2000. "Grassroots Globalization and the Research Imagination." *Public Culture* 12 (1):1–19.

Arnold, K., and H. Zhu. 2011. "Student Affairs in China." *International Higher Education* 65:25–27.

Baker, S. 2011. "Going to GPA?" *Inside Higher Ed*, News section, 23 June.

Baran, P. 1961. "The Commitment of the Intellectual." *Monthly Review* 13 (1):1–8.

Berrett, D. 2011a. "Reframing the Debate." *Inside Higher Ed*, News section, 30 May.

—. 2011b. "The Fall of Faculty." *Inside Higher Ed*, News section, 14 July.

Bowman, N., and M. Bastedo. 2011. "'Anchoring' the World University Rankings." *International Higher Education* 65:2–3.

Brown, W. 2009. "Privatization Is about More Than Who Pays." Speech at "Save the University" teach-in at UC Berkeley, 23 September.

Carney, S. 2009. "Negotiating Policy in an Age of Globalization: Exploring Educational 'Policyscapes' in Denmark, Nepal, and China." *Comparative Education Review* 53 (1):63–88.

Castells, M. 1996. *The Rise of the Network Society*. Vol. 1 of *The Information Age; Economy, Society and Culture*. Cambridge, MA: Blackwell.

CCL. 2011. *What Is the Future of Learning in Canada?* Ottawa: Canadian Council on Learning.

Colatrella, C. 2007. "The Professoriate in Denmark in the Age of Globalization." In *The Professoriate in the Age of Globalization*, ed. N.P. Stromquist, 121–151. Rotterdam: Sense Publishers.

Colclough, C. 1996. "Education and the Market: Which Parts of the Neoliberal Solution Are Correct?" *World Development* 24 (4):589–610.

Conceição, P., and M. Heitor. 2001. "Universities in the Learning Economy: Balancing Institutional Integrity with Organizational Diversity." In *The Globalizing Learning Economy*, ed. D. Archibugi and B.A. Lundvall, 83–96. Oxford: Oxford University Press.

de Vise, D. 2009. "Ex-President of GWU Leads in Survey of Pay in 2007–08." *Washington Post*, 2 November.

DiMaggio, P.J., and W.W. Powell. 1983. "The Iron Cage Revisited: Institutional Isomorphism and Collective Rationality in Organizational Fields." *American Sociological Review* 48 (2):147–160.

EHEA. 2010. Home page. At http://www.ehea.info (accessed 30 June 2013).

—. 2011. July 13. Berlin Declaration on the Social Dimension: Recommendations for Strong Student Affairs and Services in Europe. At http://www.ehea.info/news-details.aspx?ArticleId=254 (accessed 30 June 2013).

Estrella, M. 2011. "'Free' Public Universities in Ecuador: Too Much of a Good Thing?" *International Higher Education* 65:22–24.

Fisher, D., and K. Rubenson. 1998. "The Changing Political Economy: The Private and Public Lives of Canadian Universities." In *Universities and Globalization: Critical Perspective*, ed. J. Currie and J. Newson, 77–98. London: Sage Publications.

Floc'h, B. 2011. "Les classements sont devenus incontournables." *Le Monde*, 6 October, p. 14.

Ginsberg, B. 2011. *The Fall of the Faculty: The Rise of the All-Administrative University and Why It Matters*. Oxford: Oxford University Press.

Hayek, F.A. 1960. *The Constitution of Liberty*. New York: Routledge.

Hazelkorn, E. 2011. "Rankings: Does What Gets Counted Get Done?" *International Higher Education* 65:3–5.

Hu, W. 2011. "Dean of Columbia College Resigns After Two Years." *New York Times*, 22 August. At http://www.nytimes.com/2011/08/23/education/23columbia.html?_r=0 (accessed 30 June 2013).

IAU. 2003. "Internationalisation of Higher Education: Trends and Developments since 1998." Background paper prepared by the International Association of Universities. Paris: UNESCO.

Ibarra Colado, E. 2001. *La universidad en México hoy: Gubernamentalidad y modernización*. Mexico: DGEP-UNAM/UAM/ANUIS.

—. 2004. "Origen de la *empresarialización* de la universidad: El pasado de la gestión de los negocios en el presente manejo de la universidad." In *Políticas globales y educación*, ed. R.M. Romo Beltrán. Guadalajara, Mexico: Centro Universitario de Ciencias Sociales y Humanidades, Universidad de Guadalajara.

IIE. 2011. *Open Doors 2011*. Washington, DC: Institute of International Education.

Ilon, L. 2010. "Higher Education Responds to Global Economic Dynamics." In *Higher Education, Policy and the Global Competition Phenomenon*, ed. V. Rust, L. Portnoi, and S. Bagley, 15–28. New York: Palgrave Macmillan.

Jacqué, P. 2011. "On a autre chose à faire que de se regarder tout le temps dans des miroirs." *Le Monde*, 6 October.

Jaschick, S. 2011. "Academic Freedom, Revised." *Inside Higher Ed*, 2 November. At http://www.insidehighered.com.

Jessop, B. 2002. *The Future of the Capitalist State*. Cambridge: Polity Press.

Jolly, R. 2003. "Human development and neo-liberalism: Paradigms compared." In *Readings in Human Development*, ed. S. Fukuda Parr and A.K. Shiva Kumar, 82–92. New York: Oxford University Press.

Kallo, J. 2009. OECD Education Policy: A Comparative and Historical Study Focusing on the Thematic Reviews of Tertiary Education. Helsinki: Finnish Educational Research Association.

Kaneko, M. 2012. "Incorporation of National Universities in Japan: Evaluation after Six Years." In *University Governance and Reform: Policy, Fads, and Experience in an International Perspective*, ed. H. Schuetze, W. Bruneau, and G. Grossjean. Houndmills, UK: Palgrave Macmillan.

Keeling, R. 2006. "The Bologna Process and the Lisbon Research Agenda: The European Commission's expanding role in higher education discourse." *European Journal of Education* 41 (2):203–223.

Kiley, K. 2011a. "A Faculty (Led) Search." *Inside Higher Ed*, News section, 25 August. At http://www.insidehighered.com/news/2011/08/25/faculty_constitute _majority_of_wisconsin_chancellor_search_committees (accessed 30 June 2013).

—. 2011b. "A Good Investment." *Inside Higher Ed*, News section, 6 October. At http://www.insidehighered.com/news/2011/10/06/university_of_michigan _to_invest_endowment_money_in_university_start_ups (accessed 30 June 2013).

—. 2011c. "Letting Numbers Tell the Story." *Inside Higher Ed*, News section, 15 November. At http://www.insidehighered.com/news/2011/11/15/colleges-place-more-emphasis-liquidity-and-tracking-it (accessed 30 June 2013).

—. 2011d. "Occupy Someone Else." *Inside Higher Ed*, News section, 9 December. At http://www.insidehighered.com/news/2011/12/09/public-universities-question-why-they-not-lawmakers-are-protesters-target (accessed 30 June 2013).

—. 2011e. "Trustees Take a Pass." *Inside Higher Ed*, News section, 15 December. At http://www.insidehighered.com/news/2011/12/15/report-finds-trustees-unwilling-push-institutional-change (accessed 30 June 2013).

—. 2013. "'No Confidence' in the System." *Inside Higher Ed*, News section, 18 March. At http://www.insidehighered.com/news/2013/03/18/new-york-university-vote-no-confidence-raises-debate-about-ambitions-and-governance (accessed 30 June 2013).

Kirwan, W. 2011. "Kirwan Says!" *The Faculty Voice* (University of Maryland) 24 (4):1, 7.

Klees, S.J., J. Samoff, and N.P. Stromquist, eds. 2012. *The World Bank and Education: Critiques and Alternatives*. Rotterdam: Sense Publishers.

Knight, J., and H. de Wit. 1995. "Strategies for Internationalization of Higher Education: Historical and Conceptual Perspectives." In *Strategies for the Internationalization of Higher Education*, ed. H. de Wit. Amsterdam: European Association for International Education.

Kotecha, P. 2011. "The Value of Research Networks in Africa." *International Higher Education* 65:17–19.

Lawn, M., and S. Grek. 2012. *Europeanizing Education: Governing a New Policy Space*. Oxford: Symposium Books.

Liu, N.C., Q. Wang, and Y. Chen, eds. 2011. *Paths to a World-Class University: Lessons from Practices and Experiences*. Rotterdam: Sense Publishers.

Loh, W. 2011. "Building the Global University." *Baltimore Sun*, 4 July.

Ma, W. 2007. "The Flagship University and China's Economic Reform." In *World Class Worldwide: Transforming Research Universities in Asia and Latin America*, ed. P.G. Altbach and J. Balán, 31–53. Baltimore: Johns Hopkins University Press.

Mabokela, R.O. 2007. "The Impact of Globalization on the Academic Profession in South Africa: A Case Study of the Merger of New University." In *The Professoriate in the Age of Globalization*, ed. N.P. Stromquist, 181–209. Rotterdam: Sense Publishers.

Menand, L. 2010. *The Marketplace of Ideas: Reform and Resistance in the American University*. New York: W.W. Norton.

Meyer, J.W. 2012. "Effects of the Global Expansion of Education." George F. Kneller Lecture, presented at the annual meeting of the Comparative and International Education Society, San Juan, Puerto Rico, April.

Meyer, J.W., F.O. Ramirez, D.J. Frank, and E. Schofer. 2006. "Higher Education as an Institution." Working Paper No. 57. Stanford, CA: Center on Democracy, Development, and the Rule of Law, Freeman Spogli Institute for International Studies, Stanford University.

Mohrman, K., W. Ma, and D. Baker. 2007. "The Emerging Global Model of the Research University." In Higher Education in the New Century: Global Challenges and Innovative Ideas, ed. P. Altbach and P. Peterson, 145–177. Rotterdam: Sense Publishers.

Mundy, K. 2009. "International and Transnational Policy Actor in Education: A Review of the Research." With M. Ghali. In *Handbook of Education Policy Research*, ed. G. Sykes, B. Schneider, and D.N. Plank, 717–734. New York: Routledge.

Mzawi, A. 2011. "The Arab Spring: The Higher Education Revolution That Is Yet to Happen." *International Higher Education* 65:12–13.

Nilsson, J., and K. Nilsson. 2004. *Old Universities in New Environments: New Technology and International Processes in Higher Education*. Lund Studies in Sociology 5. Lund: Lund University.

OECD. 2011. *Education at a Glance 2011*. Paris: Organisation for Economic Cooperation and Development.

Pillay, P. 2011. "International Lessons for Africa's Higher Education and Economy." *International Higher Education* 65:19–20.

Pries, L. 2007. "Transnationalism: Trendy Catch-All or Specific Research Programme; A Proposal for Transnational Organisation Studies as a Micro-Macro-Link." Working Paper 34. Bielefeld, Germany: Center for Interdisciplinary Research.

Ramirez, F. 2011. "Eyes Wide Shut: University, State and Society." *European Educational Research Journal* 1 (2):256–272.

Redden, E. 2011. "Confucius Says ...." *Inside Higher Ed*, News section, 4 January. At http://www.insidehighered.com/news/2012/01/04/debate-over-chinese-funded-institutes-american-universities (accessed 30 June 2013).

Reich, R. 2009. "What Is Public about a Public University." Speech at "Save the University" teach-in at UC Berkeley, 23 September.

Rizvi, F., and B. Lingard. 2006. "Globalization and the Changing Nature of the OECD's Educational Work." In *Education, Globalization and Social Change*, ed. H. Lauder, P. Brown, J.A. Dillabough, and A.H. Halsey, 247–260. Oxford: Oxford University Press.

Russell Group. 2013. The Russell Group, Home page. At http://russellgroup.ac.uk (accessed 30 June 2013).

Salmi, J. 2009. *The Challenge of Establishing World-Class Universities*. Washington, DC: World Bank.

Schofer, E., and Meyer, J.W. 2005. "The World-Wide Expansion of Higher Education in the Twentieth Century." Working Paper No. 32. Stanford, CA: Center
on Democracy, Development, and the Rule of Law, Stanford University.

Shabani, J. 2012. "West African Higher Education Reforms." *International Higher
Education* 66:17–19.

Smolentseva, A. 2007. "Emerging Inequality in the Academic Profession in Russia." In *The Professoriate in the Age of Globalization*, ed. N.P. Stromquist, 153–179.
Rotterdam: Sense Publishers.

Soudien, C. 2012. "'Quality's' Horizons: The Politics of Monitory Educational
Quality." In *The World Bank and Education: Critiques and Alternatives*, ed. S.J.
Klees, J. Samoff, and N.P. Stromquist. Rotterdam: Sense Publishers.

Stromquist, N.P. 2002. *Education in a Globalized World: The Connectivity of Economic
Power, Technology, and Knowledge*. Boulder, CO: Rowman and Littlefield.

—. 2011. "One Size Fits All? In Pursuit of … the Perfect Scholar." *The Faculty
Voice* 25 (1–2):5.

—. 2012. "The Provost's Office as Key Decision-Maker in the Contemporary U.S.
University: Toward a Theory of Institutional Change." In *University Governance
and Reform: Policy, Fads, and Experience in an International Perspective*, ed. H.
Schuetze, W. Bruneau, and G. Grossjean. Houndmills, UK: Palgrave Macmillan.

Stromquist, N.P., and A. Smolentseva. 2011. "The University in Turbulent Times: A
Comparative Study of the United States and Russia." In *Universities and Global
Diversity: Preparing Educators for Tomorrow*, ed. B. Lindsay and W. Blanchett,
29–43. New York and London: Routledge.

Task Force on Higher Education and Society. 2000. *Higher Education in Developing
Countries: Peril and Promise*. Washington, DC: World Bank.

Teferra, D. 2012. Partnerships in Africa in the New Era of Internationalization.
International Higher Education 65:15–17.

Tilak, J. 2011. "Trade in Higher Education: The Role of the General Agreement
on Trade in Services (GATS)." Fundamentals of Education Planning 95. Paris:
International Institute for Education Planning.

Tsing, A. 2005. *Frictions: An Ethnography of Global Connection*. Princeton, NJ: Princeton University Press.

Verger, A. 2009. "The Merchants of Education: Global Politics and the Uneven
Educational Liberalization Process within the WTO." *Comparative Education
Review* 53 (3):379–401.

Welch, A. 1998. "The Cult of Efficiency in Education: Comparative Reflections on
the Reality and the Rhetoric." *Comparative Education* 34 (2):157–175.

CHAPTER 11

TRANSLATING GLOBALIZATION INTO PRACTICE: UNIVERSITY NETWORKS – TOWARD A NEW STRATIFICATION OF HIGHER EDUCATION?

BJØRN STENSAKER[1]

INTRODUCTION

The internationalization and globalization of higher education have become increasingly important components of policy agendas throughout the world in recent decades. In the wake of this political interest, there is a growing literature on internationalization and globalization issues that attempts to provide better definitions and more conceptual understandings of this phenomenon (de Wit 2002; Marginson and Rhoades 2002; Kehm 2003; Vaira 2004). Still, much diversity and fragmentation can be said to characterize the research efforts so far (Beerkens 2004; Marginson and van der Wende 2007; Maringe and Foskett 2010). Examples of the wide research focus are an analysis of the interrelationship and differences between internationalization and globalization of higher education (Knight and de Wit 1995; Knight 2004; Altbach and Knight 2007; van Vught, van der Wende, and Westerheijden 2002), studies of geographically more defined processes (Teichler 1999; Horie 2002; Gornitzka and Langfeldt 2008; Marginson, Kaur, and Sawir 2011), for-profit higher education and academic capitalism (Morey 2004; Slaughter and Cantwell 2011), international student and staff mobility (Santiago et al. 2008; Wildavsky 2010), global university rankings (Kehm and Stensaker 2009; Hazelkorn 2007,

Making Policy in Turbulent Times: Challenges and Prospects for Higher Education, ed. P. Axelrod, R.D. Trilokekar, T. Shanahan, and R. Wellen. Kingston: School of Policy Studies, Queen's University.

2011), and university alliances and network establishments (Beerkens 2003, 2004; Beerkens and van der Wende 2007; Olds 2009).

These studies point to a changing higher education landscape where the key institution – the university – is itself allegedly being transformed (Marginson 2002; Bartell 2003; Currie et al. 2003; Ramirez 2010; Wildavsky 2010; Hazelkorn 2011). Some researchers also assert that globalization has led to a growing convergence of organizational forms and functions through which Western university models of organization are being emulated throughout the world (Wildavsky 2010; Ramirez 2010).

A detailed analysis of the convergence thesis is interesting for several reasons. First, while studies of national systems emphasize communalities and converging trends in policy-making, case studies of higher educational institutions can provide empirical tests of the implications of such internationalization and globalization policies (Enders 2004, 372). Since higher educational institutions are organizations with deeply embedded values, cultures, and traditions, an institutional focus can also provide evidence of possible transformation of the cultural foundations of the sector induced by globalization. In addition, by focusing upon higher educational institutions, one can create a more coherent picture of the changes related to globalization. While student and staff mobility, changes in funding schemes, and various policy initiatives regarding joint degrees or collaborative research all contribute to change along several dimensions, a focus on the institutional level provides a more overarching perspective on the changes in higher education (Taylor 2004, 169–170).

A focus on the institutional level must still consider national and international policy developments with respect to internationalization and globalization, especially given the impact of global ranking (Hazelkorn 2007). Such ranking often leads to emphasizing the importance of "elite" or "excellent" universities, seen as necessary for stimulating economic development and technological innovations. Hence, there are a number of countries in which policies are targeted toward the creation of such elite institutions (Hazelkorn 2011). With this starting point, one could anticipate that further global convergence would take place in higher education as more countries are trying to create "world class" higher educational institutions (Salmi 2009).

The higher educational institutions themselves are also active participants in such national policy initiatives. Fostering excellence is a key issue for a number of national elite university networks that are emerging. Some of the most well known of these networks are the Russell Group in the United Kingdom, the Group of Eight in Australia, and SKY in South Korea.

Numerous university networks or consortia have also been established internationally during the last decades (Chan 2004). Although their purposes, activities, and profiles are very different (Beerkens 2004; Olds 2009), there are some that emphasize excellence as a key motivation for their establishment. This is an interesting development since such networks can be interpreted in different ways. On the one hand, they can be seen as a logical consequence of global rankings, forcing institutions to act according to the ranking logic. On the other hand, they can also be seen as a form of counterforce to development, indicating an institutional interest in influencing their own destiny.

In this chapter, some of these elite networks are analyzed in more detail, with a particular focus on their potential impact on the new, globalized higher educational landscape. Elite university networks can be interpreted as a means for both collaboration and competition in various forms – for example, with internal competition and external collaboration, with collaboration also extended beyond the network members, or even with competition among the member institutions.

One aim of this chapter is to develop theoretical assumptions as to the different functioning of such networks. Another aim is to inform the debate on whether such network establishments can be seen as an example of increasing convergence of organizational forms and functions in higher education toward the ideal of world-class universities or whether elite networks are an indication of a growing stratification of higher education, pointing to several "layers" of institutions in the future global market for higher education. Since university networks could be seen as a mediating mechanism between macro- and micro-level change in the sector, more in-depth studies are needed to shed light on this phenomenon.

UNIVERSITY NETWORKS AS IDENTITY SYMBOLS

The establishment of university networks is often explained with reference to resource-based views of organizations (see, e.g., Chan 2004). Hence, university networks are established because organizations believe that they serve their economic interests in various ways (Beerkens 2004). In this chapter, the cultural, symbolic, and political aspects of elite university networks are explored in more detail. This implies not that economic arguments concerning university networks should be downplayed, but rather that cultural and symbolic explanations for understanding such network establishments should also be accounted for in understanding the complexity of the processes we are witnessing (Robertson 1992; Middlehurst 2002).

In general, neo-institutional theory has often been used as a point of departure for studying the increased internationalization and globalization in a number of industries and sectors of society, including higher education (Djelic and Sahlin-Andersson 2006; Drori, Meyer, and Hwang 2006; Ramirez 2010). The promises of neo-institutional theory in this respect are found in postulates that in situations characterized by uncertainty, organizations imitate other organizations that are perceived to be successful, that this imitation is triggered by environmental pressures for legitimacy, and that such pressures can often be defined as structures that force organizations to behave in "rationalized" ways. As a result, organizational change becomes a process leading to convergence and increasing conformity by triggering reproduction and reinforcement of existing modes of thought and organizations (Scott 2001).

While research can indeed be found supporting the convergence thesis of neo-institutional theory, one can also find several attempts to develop more dynamic models of change within the neo-institutional theory tradition (see, e.g., Greenwood and Hinings 1996; see also Greenwood et al. 2008). Stensaker (2004) has proposed that organizational identity is a concept that can be fruitful in developing explanations that explain not only convergence but also heterogeneity. To allow for such varied insights, both "new" and "old" forms of institutional theory must be combined.

The concept of organizational identity within the new institutionalism is a product of externally inspired, passive, and imitative adaptation, a symbol of environmental aspirations embodied by the organization (Scott 2001). Thus, organizational identities are produced externally as typifications, scripts, or archetypes (Greenwood and Hinings 1996; Ramirez 2010). For our purpose, typical examples of such scripts are images of what a world-class university should look like. Since external trends are exposed to rapid change, a consequence is that images of organizational identities may be exposed to such changes, with the effect that organizational identities can be more fluent, exchangeable, and adaptable.

In the old institutionalism, organizational identity has traditionally been perceived as the result of different forces, actors, and groups inside the organization that, over time, create unique ways of interacting, leading to organizational coherence (Selznick 1957). "Despite their diversity, these forces have a unified effect. In their operation we see the way group values are formed, for together they define the commitments of the organization and give it a distinct identity" (Selznick 1957, 16). Hence, in this version of institutional theory, organizational identity develops over time from within. As an example, world-class universities are thus to be found as historical evidence of proven excellence, often associated with institutions such as Oxford, Cambridge, Harvard, and Stanford. It follows from this that shifts in organizational identities are not easy since the organizational identity is deeply embedded within the organization. When identity change takes place, it takes time, is often incremental in character, and builds on key historical characteristics of the given organization.

By drawing on insights from both the old and the new institutional theory, organizational identity can be perceived as a concept that in principle can lead to convergence (new institutionalism) or divergence (old institutional theory).

However, organizational identity can also be very useful for analyzing university networks in particular since it allows for a different understanding of the imitation processes that are triggered by the external environment. In philosophy, identity is given a rather ambiguous definition. Stemming from the word "identical," *identity* actually refers to similarity or sameness, a fact that discloses two dimensions of the concept (see also Hall and du Gay 1996). In this way, organizational identity will not only be a matter of similarity; it is also a matter of difference. There will always be organizations or organizational identities that a given organization does not want to be associated with. Thus, imitation may include both adaptation and differentiation processes. In some instances, adaptation and differentiation may also occur in an integrated process, as when organizations imitate a specific aspect of another organization – e.g., when a university copies the computer science program of another institution, but perceives other central characteristics of that institution to be undesirable (Labianca et al. 2001, 314).

But the concept of organizational identity also allows for further nuances of imitation and differentiation processes. The argument launched to support this statement is that imitation should not be seen as only a "passive" process, as proposed by the new institutionalism. Imitation should rather be perceived as an active process (Czarniawska-Joerges and Sevón 1996; Sahlin-Andersson 1996; Sevón 1996). Thus, *imitation* is perhaps not the best term to use when trying to describe adaptation processes in more realistic terms. Czarniawska-Joerges and Sevón (1996) have suggested that *translation* is a better term, proposing that imitation is not necessarily the opposite of innovation. Imitation could be viewed as a process in which something new is also created (Sevón 1996, 51), especially as "perfect imitation" is difficult to accomplish. Related to the elite university networks, this could imply attempts to further develop the characteristics of elite universities beyond their current organizational identities.

Hence, the role of more elite university networks can, according to the assumptions outlined above, be interpreted in different ways. First, they can be seen as collective attempts to strengthen and reproduce the characteristics that are associated with the elite universities by which further, internal convergence related to such characteristics is the key objective. Second, they can be seen as collective attempts by elite universities to further differentiate themselves from those that are trying to catch up. Third, they can be seen as an attempt to further develop and explore the role of elite universities by exploiting new options and niches in the globalized higher education market.

DATA AND METHODOLOGY

Beerkens (2004, 50) has suggested a simple typology for describing and characterizing various forms of university consortia, networks, and alliances. His typology consists of eight dimensions: the number of members, membership (open/closed), interests, time span (limited/open ended), activities, level of integration, relations, and intensity. When combining these dimensions, a number of very different networks appear. In general, many of the dimensions identified by Beerkens (2004, 45) are focusing on economic and/or instrumental reasons to join a network (economies of scale, risk reduction, technology exchanges, etc.).

As mentioned earlier, this chapter seeks to analyze particular kinds of university networks, those that are established by universities that either have or want to have elite university status. Such networks would in principle emphasize some of the criteria outlined in the Beerkens typology: an assumption would be that they would have relatively few members and that membership would not be open to everyone. Hence, university interest organizations and associations would not be included as relevant networks for the current analysis. With respect to other criteria, the activities, the integration of the network, how the network institutions relate to each other, and the intensity of the network are some of the issues to be explored in this chapter.

Based on the selection criteria, a relatively high number of international university networks can be identified. However, since one of the aims of the current study has been to investigate assumptions about growing convergence among elite university networks, networks that have a somewhat different membership profile, age, number of members, and international outreach have been prioritized. In this way, potential findings supporting the convergence claim will have a stronger empirical basis. Thus, three networks have been chosen for closer analysis: the League of European Research Universities (LERU), the International Alliance of Research Universities (IARU), and Universitas 21. All three are international networks, although LERU has a particularly European focus. Data for analysis in this chapter has mostly been drawn from the networks' own websites and from the websites of individual members. The three networks are presented and discussed in more detail below.

LERU, IARU, AND UNIVERSITAS 21: CHARACTERISTICS AND ACTIVITIES

The League of European Research Universities (LERU)

There are 21 European research universities in the LERU network. This network was formed in 2002, and it includes universities such as Oxford and Cambridge in the UK; Helsinki and Lund in the Scandinavian countries; Barcelona and Milan in southern Europe; and Strasbourg, Utrecht, and Geneva in continental Europe. (For a full list of members, see the Appendix.) Together, the members can be said to be among the leading European research universities, although some institutions that are frequently listed in various university rankings from the European region are absent. However, elite European institutions that are not LERU members are often mono-disciplinary institutions and, in this respect, do not fulfill a key membership criterion of LERU – being a research-intensive, multi-faculty university.

LERU describes itself as "an association of twenty-one leading research-intensive universities that share the values of high-quality teaching in an environment of internationally competitive research."[2] The purpose of LERU is clearly stated: it is focused on a commitment to education, on the creation of new knowledge through basic research, and on promoting research. However, a key objective of LERU is also to influence policy in Europe and to develop best practices through the mutual exchange of experience. Interestingly, LERU, with the University of Leiden playing a central role, has also been active in trying to develop alternative university ranking systems (Deem, Lucas, and Mok 2009, 123; see also Boulton 2010).

In giving examples of the significance of the network, LERU states that member institutions have more than 550,000 students, of whom about 50,000 are PhD students, and that member institutions have a research budget that exceeds €5 billion, more than €1 billion of which is granted by research councils and more than €1.25 billion of which comes from contract research of various kinds. Furthermore, LERU states that research grants from the European Union (EU) account for approximately €300 million and that more than 20 percent of the European Research Council grants given out so far have been awarded to LERU member institutions.

The top decision-making body of LERU is the rectors' assembly. This body meets twice a year at different member universities. To take care of business in between these meetings, the assembly appoints three of its members to serve as the board of directors. However, LERU also has its own office, currently hosted by the Catholic University of Leuven. This office is run by the secretary-general, who is responsible for the daily management of the organization, external relations, and international co-operation.

While LERU has a number of activities related to ongoing research, one of the few committees that is promoted on its website is the Research Policy Committee, and policy initiatives, often in the form of policy papers or seminars, have focused on issues such as the organization of doctoral studies, research careers, research assessment, and EU research policy. In addition, a number of papers have also been produced related to issues strongly backed by the EU: environment, energy, food, nanotechnology, and student and researcher mobility within the EU.

The International Alliance of Research Universities (IARU)

The IARU network consists of ten elite research universities from different regions of the world. Member institutions include the Australian National University; University of California, Berkeley; University of Cambridge; and University of Tokyo. (See the full list of members in the Appendix.) The network was established as late as 2005. It stresses that the goal in forming the network was mainly strategic; it was not intended to develop into a representative network of members from every region of the world. The network also emphasizes that each member institution will determine the extent of its involvement in each activity decided upon to suit its own particular objectives and profile. Furthermore, membership in IARU is not meant to limit activities with partners outside the network.

IARU describes itself as "an alliance of ten of the world's leading research-intensive universities."[3] Its purpose is to meet the grand challenges facing humanity. The network places a special focus on identifying sustainable solutions to climate change. In addition, the network states that educating the future leaders of the world is a top priority, emphasizing education and enriching student life.

The governance of IARU is taken care of by the annual senior officers' meeting. This meeting assembles top-ranked officials, mostly from the international affairs, international strategy, and international relations offices within the member institutions. In this meeting, decisions are taken as to which activities will be branded with the IARU logo in the forthcoming year. However, the IARU network also has a chair, who is selected from among the rectors of the member institutions. The chair also hosts the secretariat of IARU during the period served.

In line with the stated purpose of the network, there are a number of initiatives that address environmental issues, including projects on campus sustainability, measuring the environmental impacts of the activities of the universities, sustainability fellowships, and a global summer program for students, but recent activities have also focused on issues such as human resources benchmarking, women and men in globalizing universities, and the creation of leadership best-practices programs for PhD students. A recent initiative also looked into more detailed undergraduate education programs at the member institutions, exploring the possibilities of developing joint courses and electronic resources for mutual sharing.

Universitas 21

Universitas 21 is a network of now 27 research-intensive universities in 15 countries around the world. Its members include the University of Melbourne, National University of Singapore, Lund University, University of Amsterdam, University of Nottingham, and University of Virginia. (See the Appendix for the full list of members.) The network was founded in 1997 and is the oldest of the three networks selected for this study.

Universitas 21 describes itself as "the leading global network of research universities for the 21st century."[4] Hence, the purpose of the network includes co-operating to stimulate and challenge thinking in relation to international higher education; providing a forum for university leaders to identify, adopt, and shape approaches to internationalization; and striving to be a globally recognized leader in internationalization. Another aim of the network is to scan the horizon for new challenges and opportunities in higher education and research that can be more effectively addressed within the network than by any individual university. Hence, the name Universitas 21 relates to the challenges universities have to face in the 21st century. Issues that are mentioned in this respect are management challenges in universities, the need to establish joint or dual degrees and other forms of educational co-operation, the promotion of research-inspired teaching, and the development of communities of learners through the use of new technology. Other researchers have also noted that Universitas 21 was a global front-runner in offering online education through the launch of its MBA course in 2003, targeting markets in Southeast Asia and China (Chan 2004, 36).

The network stresses its importance by highlighting the fact that collectively, it enrols over 830,000 students, employs over 145,000 staff, and has an alumni body consisting of more than 2.5 million graduates. Network members have a collective annual budget of over US$25 billion, with a research income of more than $US4 billion per year.

The Universitas 21 network does have a central secretariat, but in general, the structure of its activities are quite decentralized, encompassing separate networks within the network for deans and directors of graduate studies, deans of education, heads of administration, and international directors. But Universitas 21 also has several academically oriented networks in areas such as health sciences, water management, and teaching and learning.

A COMPARISON OF THE NETWORKS

Based on their governance structures, presentation, and activities, a number of similarities and differences among the networks can be identified. With respect to similarities, all networks present themselves as "world leading," with reference to the research profiles of their members. All networks want to identify and share best practices among their members – although what such best practices actually refer to differs among the networks. The only exception to be found, the only place where all three networks seem to share some common practices, is related to the goal of exposing their PhD candidates to an international environment. This is an activity that can also lead to greater convergence within the networks. Such convergence might take place as a product of greater knowledge of practices and experiences from the partner institutions; it might also be a process that stimulates, to a greater extent, the exchange of personnel among the network's institutions after PhD candidates have completed their degrees and are looking for employment.

However, a closer look at the networks reveals a number of quite striking differences. First, the profile and purpose of the networks seem very different. LERU is the network with the most visible policy-influencing profile targeted at the EU and with clear ambitions to influence the development of the European Research Area. LERU is the only network with a standing research policy committee; it regularly publishes advice and position papers commenting upon issues on the policy agenda within EU research policy, and it also takes the initiative to develop papers on topics that LERU thinks should be part of the EU policy agenda. Through a very top-heavy governance structure (consisting of the rectors of the member universities, who meet twice a year, as well as a secretary-general, who secures the organizational capacity to act), LERU is also well positioned to undertake a more strategic role in trying to influence the European policy agenda. While it could be argued that the geographical focus on Europe makes it easier for LERU to develop and articulate this policy interest, one could imagine that other global networks could also take on a stronger policy profile – for example, related to influencing the policy agenda in the home countries of their members.

In Europe, several other university networks and associations already exist that also have a clearly articulated policy role. Some are university interest organizations with an open membership and consequently with a far less-articulated elite profile. Among these is the European University Association (EUA), which, through the Bologna Process, has managed to acquire a central position within European policy-making. For example, it is a member of the so-called E4 group, which, in addition to the EUA, consists of the European Network of Quality Assurance Agencies, the European Association of Institutions of Higher Education, and the European Students' Union. Being an interest organization and measured by the number of members, the EUA is considerably larger than LERU, and it is tempting to argue that the emphasis on the success of LERU members in attracting research funding from the EU system is one way to compensate for this and to profile the network as something different than a "mass" interest organization.

IARU, compared to LERU, is a very different type of network. While in LERU the rectors are the central decision-making group, decision-making in IARU is taken care of by senior officials. While these officials are certainly positioned to make important decisions, the total profile of this group indicates that they would need to confer with their home institutions before taking any binding decisions on more strategic issues. A closer look at the activity profile of IARU signals that the aim of the network is about "saving the world." The emphasis related to taking on the grand challenges to humanity, and how initiatives taken should be branded as being sanctioned by IARU, indicate that external profiling and marketing are key objectives of the network. It follows from this that IARU has a number of activities that are directed at students, such as summer exchange programs, fellowships, etc. Hence, while IARU consists of research-intensive universities, it still seems that most initiatives are related to educational activities.

Compared to the other two networks, Universitas 21 stands out with a particular profile. While LERU has a very strong emphasis on influencing policy-making in the EU and IARU seems to put more effort into external profiling and marketing, Universitas 21 distinguishes itself by its highly decentralized structure, targeted at developing its member institutions as more competitive global players. Hence, in Universitas 21, developing innovative educational offerings and structures, and stimulating more efficient and more effective provision of administrative services internally, are key objectives. In this way, Universitas 21 distinguishes itself from the others by having a more introverted profile.

If we relate the role of the three networks to the analytical framework, LERU is the one that fits best with an assumption based on increasing convergence among the networked universities. The goal of this network of trying to influence EU research policy through various policy and position papers often has the result that the member institutions speak with one voice and that they are encouraged to develop some common measures as to how they should follow up their own suggestions (for example, concerning the designing of research careers, PhD education, how to respond to rankings, etc.). In this way, it can be assumed that the members of the LERU network over time will further develop elite characteristics that will lead to a converging reproduction of their organizational identities. LERU also applies quite strict criteria for membership (multi-faculty, high research output, high national standing, etc.), which can also lead to further convergence within the group.

While IARU can be characterized as being an elite university network, it can be argued that this network, through its profile, can be associated with another assumption sketched out in the analytical framework, that of trying to distinguish itself from other institutions. In this network, it is quite clearly stated that the member institutions have considerable discretion as to what membership activities they want to engage in and what other networks and strategic partnerships they want to be part of or want to pursue. While this network has no ambition of trying to speak to the outside world with one voice, it seems that external profiling is still highly emphasized. Through its goal of dealing with the global challenges of our time, this network signals that it wants to take global responsibility and that in this way, it goes beyond the traditional issues associated with internationalization and globalization – namely, how universities need to adjust their operations in light of these processes. Such global responsibility also indicates that these universities are in a position in which more altruistic rather than economic purposes guide their actions and orientations. This is a position that will distinguish these institutions from the many others that focus on the more instrumental aspects of internationalization and globalization.

It is tempting to argue that Universitas 21 is a network that strives to position itself in the more internationalized and globalized higher education market. However, while a number of its activities are related to improved educational and administrative efficiency and effectiveness, there is an attempt to frame these activities in a more innovative way, taking on the challenges of delivering a very future-oriented higher education provision. Here, exploring the options and possibilities of a more global higher education market seems to be the first and foremost goal. Hence, it can be argued that these universities are trying to create their own niche in this market, where innovation and more isomorphic processes are closely intertwined.

IMPLICATIONS OF INTERNATIONAL AND GLOBAL UNIVERSITY NETWORKS IN THE HIGHER EDUCATION LANDSCAPE

Although the empirical coverage of university networks in this chapter is too limited to come to decisive conclusions about the role that networks are playing with regard to the development of the global higher education landscape, there are a number of issues that deserve more reflection.

A question to be asked is whether the establishment of university networks is just an effect of global university rankings, where the networks established are simply reinforcing the difference between the elite institutions and the "rest," as implied through the rankings. Since the great majority of the members of the three analyzed networks also appear frequently in dominant global rankings, one could argue that university rankings and university networks are two measures with similar converging effects on the elite university landscape. Certainly, these networks link universities beyond national borders and create an image of a limited group of universities that can be perceived as global players. One should also not rule out the possibility that the corresponding positioning of the universities in the global rankings has been a key mechanism for them to join together in the new networks (see also Hazelkorn 2011).

Of particular interest here is the fact that some universities are members of several university networks. In the three networks analyzed, Lund and Amsterdam are members of both LERU and Universitas 21, Singapore is a member of both IARU and Universitas 21, while Oxford and Cambridge are members of both LERU and IARU. A large number of other universities in LERU, IARU, and Universitas 21 are members of other university networks not included in this study. Being a member of more than one network can indeed be seen as a way for these universities to emphasize their symbolic importance, with potential converging implications in the global higher educational landscape.

However, there are a number of arguments that can also be made against the hypothesis that rankings and networks are causally interrelated phenomena. One argument is that the purposes of the networks analyzed seem very different, a finding also supported by other studies (Beerkens and van der Wende 2007; Olds 2009). In the case of the IARU network, the goal of joining forces to face the great challenges to humanity seems, at least on the surface, to be very different from the more competitive agenda promoted by the global rankings.

Another argument is that some of the networks have tried to launch alternatives to the established global rankings. In 2012, for example, Universitas 21 published the first version of the *U21 Ranking of National Higher Education Systems* (Williams et al. 2012), in which the result of the ranking can be read as an alternative to institutionally focused rankings and offering a different perception of where high-quality education can be found. Also, LERU has taken the initiative to stimulate the development of alternative ranking systems, actively criticizing existing ranking systems (Boulton 2010) and downplaying the role of institutions in favour of a more disciplinary approach (Deem, Lucas, and Mok 2009). In the latter case, the network establishment is used as a means of counteracting the influence of the most popular global rankings.

A third argument is that networks such as LERU have a regional focus that, at least in principle, might stimulate some European distinctiveness among its members. In this case, regionalization could be viewed both as a response to globalization and as a possible alternative to globalization. A fourth argument against increasing convergence is related to the many difficulties facing university networks when going from the phase of signing formal documents of co-operation to launching specific activities on the shop floor (Chan 2004). Issues relating to different institutional cultures; reliance on adequate funding; internal alignment of strategies, purposes, and people – these are only some of the challenges facing those responsible for the networks' activities, indicating that university networks in principle can be much more dynamic and unpredictable than suggested by their formal aims, objectives, and plans.

Another interesting phenomenon in the networks analyzed is the relatively low visibility of higher education institutions in the United States. While US institutions are, for obvious reasons, not part of the LERU network, they are not in the majority in the IARU or the Universitas 21 networks, although US higher education institutions tend to dominate the top positions in global university rankings. One possible explanation for this is that US universities do not perceive global networks as adding special benefits and that they enjoy high reputational status elsewhere.

This does not imply that US institutions are not part of the globalization race. As pointed out by Wildavsky (2010), a number of elite US universities are extremely active in international co-operation and collaboration schemes. Still, these schemes are often characterized by a high level of decentralization not directly involving the institutional leadership, and these schemes are more concrete and bilateral, having a focus on specific activities and projects (see also Slaughter and Cantwell 2011). As Tilghman and Eisgruber (2007, n.p.) emphasized in a report about Princeton University in the world, "internationalization should be nimble and flexible," avoiding bureaucracy and heavily regulated institutions. In light of such a statement, university networks may not be seen as a relevant type of internationalization activity.

There seems to be a worry among at least some US institutions that university networks may be meeting places where managerial rather than academic agendas are pursued. The question then is whether the networks analyzed can be seen to be attempts by elite institutions in the rest of the world to provide a symbolic and political alternative to the US institutions or whether networks can be interpreted as a special form of internationalization and globalization where more managerial and strategic agendas are emphasized.

Summing up, this chapter has tried to launch a more multi-faceted view of university networks, one that goes beyond the convergence theses that are often mentioned as an effect of a more globalized higher education sector (Enders and Fulton 2002; Wildavsky 2010). In addition to showing that the assumption related to convergence can be challenged more theoretically even within an institutional framework, the chapter has also provided some evidence for the diversity among university networks, even more elite networks. The geographical focus of the networks, their purpose, their internal participation, and their activities are only some of the factors that can be seen as counteracting convergence.

The long-term implication of this development hints at a global higher education landscape that may become more stratified than today, indicating that the interesting area to investigate in the future is the placing of universities between the extreme positions of either convergence or divergence (see also Teichler 2009). It suggests that even for elite universities, there is a need for co-operation so that they become more visible and strengthen their influence in political arenas, as exemplified by the LERU network. With globalization, universities are also increasingly exposed to market failure (Slaughter and Cantwell 2011), and strengthened university networks and alliances that started out as more symbolic and political tools may also be transformed into stronger organizational actors to reduce the economic risks associated with the global marketplace.

Thus, one could also anticipate more dynamic developments among the networks. Just as mergers between institutions are a way to domestically strengthen a university economically and strategically, future mergers between university networks is a likely possibility if their growth continues at today's pace. The latter is a likely possibility in the networks dominated by university presidents and rectors, such as the LERU network. (This also opens up the possibility of increasing the number of members in the years to come.) Networks in which presidents and rectors are active participants may also have a stronger influence on the structures and processes of member universities and might be a driver toward greater organizational convergence.

The LERU network is also interesting with respect to its geographical scope and political ambition, and this may point to the development of more "policy oriented" networks in the future. Here, one could imagine that such political ambitions not only could be directed at certain regions such as Europe but also could be a way for elite higher education institutions to influence political authorities domestically. With respect to the discussion about the relation between university rankings and university networks, more politically oriented networks may be seen as a way for universities to take a more direct political role in the globalization race. While university rankings often force both governments (Deem, Lucas, and Mok 2009) and institutions (Hazelkorn 2011) into a more reactive role, it does seem that university networks also can be a way for institutions to take on a more proactive role.

Such a development still rests on the assumptions that the many promises of university networks are realized in practice and that the networks find ways and means to benefit from this co-operation. Hence, an issue worthy of more detailed investigation is then to study more closely how university networks are organized and managed, how their strategies are developed, and how member universities might change as a result. The fact that the three networks selected for the current analysis all have unique internal organizations and decision-making structures is also an interesting dimension to pursue further.

NOTES

1. The author is grateful to participants at the workshop "Policy Formation in Post-secondary Education: Issues and Prospects in Turbulent Times," held at York University in Toronto on 15–17 March 2012, for their comments on an earlier version of this chapter. Special thanks go also to Professor Peter Maassen for input and discussions and to two anonymous reviewers for valuable suggestions in developing the chapter further.
2. See http://www.leru.org/index.php/public/home, accessed 3 July 2013.
3. See http://www.iaruni.org./about-us/iaru, accessed 3 July 2013.
4. See http://www.universitas21.com/about, accessed 3 July 2013.

REFERENCES

Altbach, P.G., and J. Knight. 2007. "The Internationalization of Higher Education: Motivations and Realities." *Journal of Studies in International Education* 11:290–305.

Bartell, M. 2003. "Internationalization of Universities: A University Culture-Based Framework." *Higher Education* 45:43–70.

Beerkens, E. 2003. "Globalisation and Higher Education Research." *Journal of Studies in International Education* 7:128–148.

—. 2004. "Global Opportunities and Institutional Embeddedness: Higher Education Consortia in Europe and Southeast Asia." PhD diss., University of Twente, Enschede.

Beerkens, E., and M.C. van der Wende. 2007. "The Paradox in International Cooperation: Institutionally Embedded Universities in a Global Environment." *Higher Education* 53:61–79.

Boulton, G. 2010. "University Rankings: Diversity, Excellence and the European Initiative." LERU Advice Paper Nr. 3, Edinburgh: Edinburgh University.

Chan, W.Y. 2004. "International Cooperation in Higher Education: Theory and Practice." *Journal of Studies in International Education* 8:32–55.

Currie, J., R. DeAngelis, H. de Boer, J. Huisman, and C. Lacotte. 2003. *Globalizing Practices and University Responses: European and Anglo-American Differences.* Westport, CT: Praeger Publishers.

Czarniawska-Joerges, B., and G. Sevón. 1996. *Translating Organizational Change.* New York: Walter de Gruyter.

Deem, R., L. Lucas, and K.H. Mok. 2009. "The 'World-Class' University in Europe and East Asia: Dynamics and Consequences of Global Higher Education Reform." In *University Rankings, Diversity, and the New Landscape of Higher Education,* ed. B.M. Kehm and B. Stensaker. Rotterdam: Sense Publishers.

de Wit, H. 2002. *Internationalization of Higher Education in the United States of America and Europe: A Historical, Comparative and Conceptual Analysis.* Connecticut: Greenwood Press.

Djelic, M.-L., and K. Sahlin-Andersson, eds. 2006. *Transnational Governance: Institutional Dynamics of Regulation.* Cambridge: Cambridge University Press.

Drori, G.S., J.W. Meyer, and H. Hwang, eds. 2006. *Globalization and Organization: World Society and Organizational Change.* Oxford: Oxford University Press.

Enders, J. 2004. "Higher Education, Internationalization, and the Nation-State: Recent Developments and Challenges to Governance Theory." *Higher Education* 47:361–382.

Enders, J., and O. Fulton, eds. 2002. *Higher Education in the Globalising World.* Dordrecht: Kluwer Academic Press.

Gornitzka, Å., and L. Langfeldt, eds. 2008. *Borderless Knowledge: Understanding the "New" Internationalization of Research and Higher Education in Norway.* Dordrecht: Springer.

Greenwood, R., and C.R. Hinings. 1996. "Understanding Radical Organizational Change: Bringing Together the Old and the New Institutionalism." *Academy of Management Review* 21:1022–1054.

Greenwood, R., C. Oliver, K. Sahlin, and R. Suddaby, eds. 2008. *The Sage Handbook of Organizational Institutionalism.* London: Sage Publications.

Hall, S., and P. du Gay, eds. 1996. *Questions of Cultural Identity.* London: Sage Publications.

Hazelkorn, E. 2007. "The Impact of League Tables and Ranking Systems on Higher Education Decision Making." *Higher Education Management and Policy* 19 (2):87–110.

—. 2011. *Rankings and the Reshaping of Higher Education: The Battle for World-Class Excellence.* New York: Palgrave Macmillan.

Horie, M. 2002. "The Internationalization of Higher Education in Japan in the 1990s: A Reconsideration." *Higher Education* 43:65–84.

Kehm, B.M. 2003. "Internationalisation in Higher Education: From Regional to Global." In *The Dialogue between Higher Education Research and Practice*, ed. R. Begg. Dordrecht: Kluwer Academic Press.

Kehm, B.M., and B. Stensaker, eds. 2009. *University Rankings, Diversity, and the New Landscape of Higher Education.* Rotterdam: Sense Publishers.

Knight, J. 2004. "Internationalization Remodelled: Definition, Approaches and Rationales." *Journal of Studies in International Education* 8:5–31.

Knight, J., and H. de Wit. 1995. *Strategies for Internationalization of Higher Education: A Comparative Study of Austria, Canada, Europe and the United States of America.* Amsterdam: European Association for International Education.

Labianca, G., J.F. Fairbank, J.B. Thomas, and D. Gioia. 2001. "Emulation in Academia: Balancing Structure and Identity." *Organization Science* 12:312–330.

Marginson, S. 2002. Nation-Building Universities in a Global Environment: The Case of Australia." *Higher Education* 43:409–428.

Marginson, S., S. Kaur, and E. Sawir, eds. 2011. *Higher Education in the Asia-Pacific: Strategic Responses to Globalization.* Dordrecht: Springer.

Marginson, S., and G. Rhoades. 2002. "Beyond National States, Markets, and Systems of Higher Education: A Glonacal Agency Heuristic." *Higher Education* 43:281–309.

Marginson, S., and M. van der Wende. 2007. *Globalisation and Higher Education.* OECD Education Working Papers. No. 8. Paris: OECD Publishing.

Maringe, F., and N. Foskett, eds. 2010. *Globalization and Internationalization in Higher Education: Theoretical, Strategic, and Management Perspectives.* London: Continuum.

Middlehurst, R. 2002. "Variations on a Theme: Complexity and Choice in a World of Borderless Education." *Journal of Studies in International Education* 6:134–155.

Morey, A. 2004. "Globalization and the Emergence of for-Profit Higher Education." *Higher Education* 48:131–150.

Olds, K. 2009. "Associations, Networks, Alliances, Etc.: Making Sense of the Emerging Global Higher Education Landscape." Discussion paper. Paris: International Association of Universities.

Ramirez, F. 2010. "Accounting for Excellence: Transforming Universities into Organizational Actors." In *Higher Education, Policy, and the Global Competition Phenomenon*, ed. V. Rust, L. Portnoi, and S. Bagely. New York: Palgrave Macmillan.

Robertson, R. 1992. *Globalization: Social Theory and Global Culture.* London: Sage Publications.

Sahlin-Andersson, K. 1996. "Imitating by Editing Success: The Construction of Organizational Fields." In *Translating Organizational Change*, ed. B. Czarniawska and G. Sevón. New York: Walter de Gruyter.

Salmi, J. 2009. *The Challenge of Establishing World-Class Universities.* Washington, DC: World Bank.

Santiago, P., K. Tremblay, E. Basri, and E. Arnal. 2008. *Special Features: Equity, Innovation, Labour Market, Internationalisation.* Vol. 2 of *Tertiary Education for the Knowledge Society.* Paris: OECD.

Scott, W.R. 2001. *Institutions and Organizations.* 2nd ed. Thousand Oaks, CA: Sage Publications.

Selznick, P. 1957. *Leadership in Administration: A Sociological Interpretation.* New York: Harper & Row.

Sevón, G. 1996. "Organizational Imitation as Identity Transformation." In *Translating Organizational Change*, ed. B. Czarniawska and G. Sevón. New York: Walter de Gruyter.

Slaughter, S., and B. Cantwell. 2011. "Transatlantic Moves to the Market: The United States and the European Union." *Higher Education*, 10 July. DOI 10.1007/s10734-011-9460-9.

Stensaker, B. 2004. *The Transformation of Organizational Identities*. Enschede: Center for Higher Education Policy Studies, University of Twente.

Taylor, J. 2004. "Toward a Strategy for Internationalisation: Lessons and Practice from Four Universities." *Journal of Studies in International Education* 8:149–171.

Teichler, U. 1999. "Internationalization as a Challenge for Higher Education in Europe." *Tertiary Education and Management* 5:5–23.

—. 2009. "Between Over-Diversification and Over-Homogenization: Five Decades of Search for a Creative Fabric of Higher Education." In *University Rankings, Diversity, and the New Landscape of Higher Education*, ed. B.M. Kehm and B. Stensaker. Rotterdam: Sense Publishers.

Tilghman, S.M., and C.L. Eisgruber. 2007. Princeton in the World. At http://www.princeton.edu/reports/globalization-2007 (accessed 3 July 2013).

Vaira, M. 2004. "Globalization and Higher Education Organizational Change: A Framework for Analysis." *Higher Education* 48:483–510.

van Vught, F.A., M. van der Wende, and D. Westerheijden. 2002. "Globalization and Internationalization: Policy Agendas Compared." In *Higher Education in a Globalising World: International Trends and Mutual Observation; A Festschrift in Honour of Ulrich Teichler*, ed. J. Enders and O. Fulton. Dordrecht: Kluwer Academic Publishers.

Wildavsky, B. 2010. *The Great Brain Race: How Global Universities Are Reshaping the World*. Princeton, NJ: Princeton University Press.

Williams, R., G. de Rassenfosse, P. Jensen, and S. Marginson. 2012. *U21 Ranking of National Higher Education Systems: A Project Sponsored by Universitas 21*. Melbourne: University of Melbourne.

APPENDIX

Full member lists of LERU, IARU, and Universitas 21

LERU

Catholic University of Leuven
Imperial College London
Ludwig-Maximilian University Munich
Lund University
Paris-Sud University
Pierre and Marie Curie University
University College London
University of Amsterdam
University of Barcelona
University of Cambridge
University of Edinburgh
University of Freiburg/Albert-Ludwigs University
University of Geneva
University of Heidelberg
University of Helsinki
University of Leiden
University of Milan
University of Oxford
University of Strasbourg
University of Zurich
Utrecht University

IARU

The Australian National University
ETH Zurich
National University of Singapore
Peking University
University of California, Berkeley
University of Cambridge
University of Copenhagen
University of Oxford
University of Tokyo
Yale University

Universitas 21

Australia	University of Melbourne University of New South Wales University of Queensland
Canada	McGill University University of British Colombia
Chile	Pontificia Universidad Católica de Chile
China	Fudan University Shanghai Jiao Tong University
Hong Kong	University of Hong Kong
India	University of Delhi
Ireland	University College Dublin
Japan	Waseda University
Mexico	Technológico de Monterrey
New Zealand	University of Auckland
Singapore	National University of Singapore
South Africa	University of Johannesburg
South Korea	Korea University
Sweden	Lund University
The Netherlands	University of Amsterdam
United Kingdom	University of Birmingham University of Edinburgh University of Glasgow University of Nottingham
United States	The Ohio State University University of Connecticut University of Maryland University of Virginia

CHAPTER 12

CROSS-NATIONAL EDUCATION POLICY
CHANGE IN QUALITY ASSURANCE:
CONVERGENCE OR DIVERGENCE?

CHUO-CHUN HSIEH AND JEROEN HUISMAN

INTRODUCTION

In policy studies, increasing attention is being paid to issues of policy convergence and divergence (Knill 2005). An interesting debate has emerged regarding whether there is an omnipresent trend – particularly under the influence of globalization – toward policy convergence across countries and regions. The belief in, and support for, convergence is contested by those who have argued that "all globalization is local" (Douglass 2005) – that is, the impact of globalization cannot be denied, but the effects vary. Some of the literature on policy change (policy-borrowing, transfer, and diffusion) relates to (higher) education (Phillips and Ochs 2003), and recently, the topic has gained renewed interest among educational and policy science researchers in the light of the Bologna Process.

The Bologna Process is a European higher education (HE) change project encompassing 46 countries and arising out of the 1999 Bologna Declaration. In Bologna, European ministers responsible for higher education agreed on a change agenda across signatory countries (Bologna Declaration 1999). The ultimate outcome of the process would be the creation of a European Higher Education Area (EHEA). The process invited signatory countries to work toward more compatible and comparable HE systems.

Making Policy in Turbulent Times: Challenges and Prospects for Higher Education, ed. P. Axelrod, R.D. Trilokekar, T. Shanahan, and R. Wellen. Kingston: School of Policy Studies, Queen's University.

The Bologna Process has led many researchers to investigate to what extent harmonization or convergence has taken place over time (Witte, van der Wende, and Huisman 2008; Westerheijden et al. 2010; Voegtle, Knill, and Dobbins 2011). Although the research carried out so far seems to suggest (some) convergence, it is striking that there are big differences in the foci of the study, with quite different conceptualizations of policy change and measurement(s) of convergence and divergence. In particular, studies on policy development regarding quality assurance (QA) in HE – the focus of this chapter – have also yielded contradictory findings. Some argue that it was a convergent process for the Bologna signatory countries (Voegtle, Knill, and Dobbins 2011) or that there would be a general QA model across different regions (van Vught and Westerheijden 1993). On the other hand, a considerable amount of variation in terms of QA approaches and methods has been found (Huisman and Kaiser 2002; Westerheijden, Hulpiau, and Waeytens 2007). Apparently, behind the general theoretical debate on trends and factors, there is an equally important conceptual-methodological debate on how to measure policy change.

Our contribution aims to shine a light on policy change using a theoretical framework building on institutional theory, particularly the work of Campbell (2004) and Ostrom (2005, 2007). We focus on patterns of divergence and convergence of QA systems (for education) in three European countries: England, the Netherlands, and Denmark, all early adopters in the 1980s of QA policies and mechanisms. These countries have been qualified as pioneers and trend-setters in QA.

Two decades later, the Bologna Process urges co-operation in QA, and in many Bologna countries, increasing attention is being paid to internal and external QA, and, arguably, lessons learned and practices adopted by early implementers have influenced the recently innovating countries. Also at the supranational level, noteworthy developments have taken place, including the setting up of various QA networks (such as the European Network for Quality Assurance, or ENQA), the development of European Standards and Guidelines (ESG) for QA, and the launch of the European Quality Assurance Register (EQAR). Theoretically, it could be argued that the policy context created very favourable conditions for policy transfer and policy-borrowing through international co-operation and communication and that it is likely that policy convergence took place.

STUDIES ON CROSS-NATIONAL POLICY SIMILARITY AND THE MEASUREMENT OF THE CHANGE

Comparative-policy scholars, who focus their attention particularly on policy change and adoption, have contributed to a large body of literature concerned with how domestic policies are affected by the forces emitted from the global and/or other international contexts. Most of their discussions revolve around notions such as policy transfer (Dolowitz and Marsh 2000), borrowing (Phillips and Ochs 2003), learning (Bennett and Howlett 1992), diffusion (Mooney 2001), and policy convergence (Holzinger and Knill 2005). Knill (2005) distinguishes among these concepts regarding cross-national policy similarity over time using two analytical foci: process patterns and effects/outcomes. This chapter concentrates on the latter in particular.

The measurement of increasing policy similarity across nations concerns several aspects: the policy dimensions, the time frame, the direction, the degree, and the scope of the change (Heichel, Pape, and Sommerer 2005; Holzinger and Knill 2005). With respect to the first issue, the conceptualization of the policy investigated remains controversial. In a review of empirical studies on policy convergence, Heichel, Pape, and Sommerer (2005) determined that most of the studies considered policy to be an aggregate concept. Some scholars, such as Hall (1993) and Cashore and Howlett (2007), have looked at policy in a more sophisticated way.

We adhere to the latter approach and argue that it is crucial to apply a conceptual-theoretical framework in light of both the complexity and the comparability involved in the process of policy change. With respect to the complexity, we postulate that policy is multi-dimensional and that policy change is perceived as a dynamic, complex, multi-tiered, nested phenomenon (Howlett 2009; Sabatier 2007). In addition, it is vital that the policy aspects chosen to be compared can convey salient meanings. This approach aims to address interactive relationships among various policy actors and policy dimensions. With regard to the comparability, it is essential to set comparative reference points for policy analyses in order to ensure cross-national equivalence. In other words, it is fundamental to develop a set of conceptual categories that fits all policies across nations.

RESEARCH QUESTIONS, CONCEPTUAL APPROACH, AND METHODS

In light of the remarkable inconsistency in the results of the studies, this chapter tracks policy change in national QA systems, particularly in European HE systems. We focus on i) the amount of change in this policy area and ii) the pattern of change. An analytical framework for conceptualizing QA policy change is devised to address these two questions. First, given that multi-level analysis would help to improve the understanding of the complexity of policy change, we followed Campbell's recommendation (2004) for specifying critical institutional dimensions in question. In particular, we focused on the formal part of QA rules. Second, we applied the Institutional Analysis and Development framework (Ostrom 2005, 2007) to analyze the regulative pillar of QA systems. It provides solid support for the relationships and meanings among the selected key policy aspects of the QA rules, which would also constitute cross-national reference points for comparative policy analysis.

More specifically, the regulations of the formal QA schemes were defined as being "laid down by an authority" (Ostrom 2005, 16) and were further divided into three types: i) position and boundary rules, which relate to the membership of managing agencies responsible for a QA system and also to those who are eligible to determine quality standards and procedure guidelines; ii) information rules, which are concerned with characteristics of data, data collection, and reporting; and iii) payoff and scope rules, which assign benefits and costs to participants in light of the outcomes achieved, as well as follow-up activities. Apart from these policy aspects, the QA approach was included as another policy dimension in terms of a cognitive idea of the policy instrument.

The measurement of the policy similarity across nations focused on the pattern of the policy change. As Holzinger and Knill (2005) suggest, two indicators (namely, the direction and degree of change) were included in the present study. By policy change, we meant the difference between the existing policy element and the new one. The characters of the four policy elements – i.e., the QA approach and the three types of QA rules – were classified under the intrinsic, mixed, or extrinsic orientation. Extrinsic QA elements are derived from those purposes targeting accountability and reflect the viewpoints of external stakeholders, while intrinsic QA elements are connected to the value placed on improvement as the predominant function as well as the important role of the expectations of internal stakeholders.

Instances of these QA elements are listed in Table 1, which provides the conceptual lens through which we can analyze whether the policy aspects have become more similar over time. As explained in the introduction, we focus on developments in three countries: England, the Netherlands, and Denmark.

POLICY CHANGE IN ENGLISH QA ELEMENTS

The development of QA systems in England is divided into three stages, primarily based on the variation in QA approaches.

Period 1: 1990–1991

In the English university community, HE quality fell into an internal control model under which the government had no direct power to interfere in teaching matters (van Bruggen et al. 1999). Discretionary trust was placed in the academics and intellectuals who guaranteed and monitored the quality of HE provision. Also, the universities enjoyed comprehensive autonomy over curricula, finances, and even the election of self-governing authorities (Westerheijden 2005; Westerheijden,

TABLE 1
Extrinsic- and intrinsic-oriented QA elements

Element of QA schemes	Extrinsic orientation	Intrinsic orientation
1. QA approaches	Accreditation of programs	Evaluation of programs; audit of universities
2. Position and boundary rules	An external quality agency, collectively owned by the government and the university community, claimed ownership of the national QA system	A coordinator independent of the government claimed ownership; or membership was collectively owned by the universities
3. Information rules	Information for judgments was merely collected by outside actors, e.g., employers and alumni; final reports of peer reviews were published	Subjective and descriptive information was valued or acceptable; data judgments such as results of peer reviews were conducted mainly by academics
4. Payoff and scope rules	Follow-ups were included in light of accountability to external stakeholders such as government and industry	QA outcomes were either not directly or only indirectly linked with certain governmental decisions, such as funding allocation and program registration

Source: Authors' compilation.

Stensaker, and Rosa 2007). The predominant perception of the so-called professional quality would be: "quality is best protected by institutions' own quality arrangements, which reflect and reinforce the values and professionalism of staff" (Brown 2004, 151).

Due to significant freedom in how provision delivered in the sector was evaluated, university teaching and learning was seldom subject to an external quality control system, nor was it affected by any national agency independent of the institutions. Therefore, even after governmental concern about the absence of an external quality regime was raised and the sector was under pressure to address the issue, the inclination to retain as much academic autonomy as possible remained unchanged. The Academic Audit was eventually introduced by the Committee of Vice-Chancellors and Principals (CVCP) after the universities had created their own quality agency, the Academic Audit Unit (AAU), in October 1990 to externally scrutinize quality arrangements in individual universities (Brown 2004).

The QA system was concerned with the quality of the institutional methods of maintaining or improving quality rather than the quality of HE provision. That is, the Academic Audit evaluated how institutional standards were determined and maintained and how quality procedures were arranged. By providing evaluation accounts of individual universities and sharing good practices, the Academic Audit was expected to stimulate internal change in the universities, which would ultimately improve the quality of teaching and learning. In general, the universities claimed ownership of the QA system, and theoretically, the AAU had no right to enter any institution without receiving an invitation; universities, to a large extent, took the initiative (Williams 1992).

The three types of regulative rules were all intrinsic-oriented. With respect to the position and boundary rules, the AAU as a unit of the CVCP was devised to scrutinize institutional quality arrangements. The majority of its management board, setting up the methods of the Academic Audit, consisted of university vice-chancellors. Auditors were selected from a list of nominations by vice-chancellors, and all came from the academic community (Williams 1992). With regard to information rules, an audit report would be drafted for the university as a whole, drawing on the institutional self-evaluation document along with the information that the audit team had gathered during the on-site visit (HEQC 1993).

There was no overall, adversarial commentary or absolute judgments about quality offered in the report for the scheme; it merely attempted to provide an account of a university's quality mechanisms and arrangements (Williams 2009). Furthermore, the audit reports were perceived to be the property of the corresponding university, and the CVCP did not formally publish the QA results (HEQC 1996). On the whole, the audit process can be conceived of as an intrinsic QA approach, with quality control undertaken under the control of universities.

Period 2: 1992–2001

The passing of the *Further and Higher Education Act* in 1992 represents a watershed in British university development. In accordance with the act, polytechnics and colleges were incorporated into the sector where universities had predominated. For the new HE system, a consequence of upgrading the polytechnics to university status, the government envisaged the quality regime to be common to both types of institutions, even though they had initially been devised to be responsive to different societal demands and to fall under correspondingly different quality arrangements. In order to abolish the binary line between the two sectors, the government proposed a dual QA system that encompassed audits and assessments, which to a considerable extent were the two sets of quality procedures that have existed in the universities and polytechnics, respectively, since then.

The policy initiative that encompassed the Quality Audit and the Teaching Quality Assessment (TQA) adhered to an intrinsic orientation. This is, first, accounted for by an intensive involvement of academics in the process of policy implementation. The amalgamation was made on the premise that the primary responsibility for maintaining and enhancing quality should rest with the individual institutions, and the external QA arrangements would work in partnership with the internal audit procedures of individual institutions. Drawing on these, self-assessment and academic peer review were included in the QA approach as two fundamental components. Second, the institutions were allowed to develop their own internal audit arrangements.

At the outset of the amalgamation, the traditional universities managed to retain their internal quality control model, which was to work in conjunction with a system of professional examiners who were appointed by the institutions on behalf of specific subjects and disciplines (Barnett 1996). However, due to an increasing involvement of external demands and policy actors, the idea of HE quality gradually changed from an intrinsic orientation to a mix of intrinsic and extrinsic orientations.

In relation to the position and boundary rules, the orientation leaned toward the extrinsic side since the two managing agencies, the Higher Education Quality Council (HEQC) and the Quality Assessment Committee (QAC), engaged in the quality process during 1992 and 1997. The majority of the HEQC board were academics (Brown 2004). Therefore, the board can be categorized as an intrinsic quality agency exerting collective control over HE quality on behalf of the academic community. On the other hand, the QAC would have oversight of the course of quality assessment on behalf of the Higher Education Funding Council for England, or HEFCE (Kogan and Hanney 2000; Salter and Tapper 2000).

The activities of the HEFCE and QAC were subject to guidance from the secretaries of state (DES 1991); therefore, ownership of the QAC did not fully rest with the universities. After 1997, the Quality Assurance Agency (QAA) was established to administer British QA implementation, and the extrinsic feature became more obvious, for the QAA recruited academics from the HEQC and the QAC, and its board consisted of the heads of representative bodies of both institutions as well as the funding councils (JPG 1996). The ownership of the QAA was, to a considerable extent, controlled by people from outside the university community.

With respect to information rules, there was no significant change in relation to data collection. The vast majority of the auditors and assessors involved in the QA implementation were drawn from academic staff and managers of the institutions (HEQC and HEFCE 1994). The information appended to the self-assessment reports submitted by an institution aimed to provide an initial understanding of the provision before the auditors and assessors visited. Also, the information collected and reviewed in the process of performing a quality audit included commendation and formative descriptions. Although statistical indicators were required to be compiled in the process, universities were allowed to provide commentaries on the indicators from which they made their own choices (HEFCE 1994; HEQC and HEFCE 1994; QAA 2003).

Regarding data judgments and reporting, the orientation moved to a mixture of intrinsic and extrinsic orientation after the TQA was conducted in 1995. Initially, evaluation judgments made in the course of peer review would refer to a program provider's aims in relation to teaching and learning so as to reflect sensitivity to institutional variation (HEQC and HEFCE 1994). However, in order to differentiate among providers, a four-point scale was incorporated into the TQA (HEFCE 1994). The new, quantifiable scale would facilitate the production of a summative judgment of each assessment unit, along with a threshold judgment. In addition, there were some extrinsic characteristics identified in relation to the delivery of QA results.

In 1992, the HEQC board resolved to publish audit reports in order to disseminate the necessary information on a wide scale (HEQC 1993). Likewise, the HEFCE published an overview of the outcomes of all assessment visits within each subject area, compiled from the institutions' statements regarding self-assessment and the assessors' judgments and recommendations. The reporting would be based on an aggregate scale and published to facilitate public understanding of the quality of the programs (HEFCE 1993, 1994).

With respect to payoff and scope rules, the English case represents an intrinsic orientation throughout the whole time period under investigation. In the course of the TQA, the HEFCE linked the outcomes of its assessment processes with governmental decisions about the allocation of public funding to teaching and learning activities (HEFCE 1993, 1994). However, given the low level of HEFCE funding to do this, the exercise had only a marginal impact. In addition, quality judgments were only one of several factors considered when the HEFCE made funding decisions (van Vught and Westerheijden 1993). As with the TQA, there were no direct rewards or sanctions dedicated to quality audit or any legitimate link between audit results and funding allocation.

Period 3: 2002–2010

Influenced by new public management ideas, governance strategies and regulations in the English HE system were increasingly associated with market mechanisms (Shattock 2008). As a result, the government favoured performance indicators as reference points against which the quality of HE provision was to be judged (NCIHE 1997). Accordingly, the new QA scheme carried out by the QAA was devised as a quality framework consisting of the threshold standards and benchmarks that were to be developed and collectively agreed to by the academics. Moreover, the creation of a national qualification framework and the provision of an approved list from which to select external examiners were perceived as a necessary approach to the quality standards. In relation to these proposals, the university community argued that the academic standards should be viewed as an institution's business and function as a means for it to analyze and benchmark its provision (Brown 2004).

Gradually, consensus was reached. It was agreed not only that institutions' self-regulation and national quality framework could coexist, but also that a balance between national standards and local diversity of provision could be achieved. Based on these two points, individual institutions would be allowed to develop and operate their own set of internal QA arrangements, but they had to conform to the national standards. In addition, the national reference points relating to standards and qualifications were considered to be common characteristics that could be expected in any qualification, subject, and program (HEFCE et al. 2001).

A QA alternative was proposed by the chief executive of the QAA and was collectively endorsed by the HEFCE, Universities UK, and the Standing Conference of Principals in July 2001 (Brown 2004). Details of the QA scheme were contained in the Operational Description in March 2002, and the required methods were set out in the Handbook for Institutional Audit, published in August of the same year (HEFCE et al. 2001; QAA 2002a; QAA 2002b).

The whole set of QA procedures was composed of i) the periodic internal reviews of institutions, which were to be carried out by independent external reviewers and which aimed to identify weaknesses and ensure that prompt action was taken to address them; ii) external audits, which would be conducted by audit teams; and iii) subject reviews, as follow-ups, which only a small number of providers who had been identified as having failings or seriously weak quality would be required to undertake (HEFCE et al. 2001).

This 2002 QA scheme differed from all of its predecessors, going back to 1992, in a number of ways. First, it was a unified approach. Unlike previous schemes, this system employed subject review not as a fundamental activity but as a subsequent one. The implementation of subject review would be on a highly selective basis, only for those areas that the audit team judged to have negative aspects or that had to meet certain requirements in relation to accreditation (HEFCE et al. 2001). Second, the new scheme relied more heavily on an institution's own internal audit, and it focused on quality management processes rather than directly on teaching and learning experiences. Moreover, the 2002 Institutional Audit and the 1991 Academic Audit were different in relation to data judgments. According to Williams (2009), the 1991 Academic Audit made no recommendations, only points for further consideration. In other words, while there was no tendency to extrapolate general judgments in the earlier system, it *was* the case in the later version. Also, the audit reports, in accordance with the 1991 rules, merely offered conclusions rather than making summative judgments.

With respect to position and boundary rules, an extrinsic orientation emerged after the QAA was put in charge of the QA implementation. There was a stance in favour of fulfilling the expectations of employers and students. The viewpoints of the external stakeholders, rather than diverse objectives suiting the respective institutions, prevailed (QAA 1998). Apart from these differences, the 2002 Institutional Audit, to some extent, paralleled the QA scheme conducted during the previous time period in terms of orientation. Mixed and intrinsic features remained in the information rules and the payoff and scope rules, respectively.

POLICY CHANGE IN DUTCH QA ELEMENTS

In the Netherlands, the policy development of QA during the years under investigation occurred in two stages.

Period 1: 1988–2001

The fulfilment of detailed regulations, coming under the notion of *ex ante* approval, as well as academic peer review, were part and parcel of the traditional Dutch quality control mechanisms (van Vught and Westerheijden 1993). At the beginning of the 1980s, the government aimed to respond effectively to societal demands and be more efficient in relation to HE matters, and as a result, part of the sovereignty over the system was transferred to the universities. Co-operation between the government and the university community, in conjunction with *ex post* evaluation, has become the new model of safeguarding quality in the system (Teichler 1989; Westerheijden, de Boer, and Enders 2009).

In particular, the 1985 white paper entitled *Higher Education: Autonomy and Quality (HOAK)* is widely perceived as being a watershed in Dutch governance because it moved HE from being steered by the state to the institutional autonomy model (Gornitzka and Maassen 2000). Consequently, the responsibility for assuring HE quality shifted toward the universities and the Inspectorate for Higher Education, under the "boundary conditions" set by the government (Vroeijenstijn and Acherman 1990, 82). QA, against the backdrop of decentralization, was thought of as a vehicle to compensate for any potential damage to quality that could be caused by deregulation. Also, academic professionals were perceived as being more capable of determining evaluation criteria and measuring the quality of HE provision than stakeholders external to the university community.

As a result of the collective decision-making, which involved the umbrella organizations of HE institutions, the Inspectorate for Higher Education, and the government, the institutions assumed primary responsibility for the quality of provision. The Association of Cooperating Universities in the Netherlands (VSNU) was to be responsible for the establishment of an external system of QA as well as its implementation in the university sector. With respect to the Inspectorate for Higher Education, its role was defined to be the meta-evaluator on behalf of the government, overseeing the conduct of external quality assessments and follow-ups to assessment results (Acherman 1990; van Vught and Westerheijden 1993). In addition, the QA schemes would be conducted at the faculty or department level. All study programs in the given subject areas, instead of the university as a whole, had to implement self-evaluation and be assessed by the visitation committee every six years (Maassen and Weusthof 1989). The set of quality procedures, consisting of the self-evaluation implemented by the universities and the academic peer reviews conducted by external visitation committees, represented the internal feature of the QA approaches.

With respect to the orientation of the QA schemes, the analysis of the three rule categories revealed more intrinsic than extrinsic features. The position and boundary rules, first, were concerned with a mixture of intrinsic and extrinsic orientation due to the nature of the primary bodies involved in the process. The members of a visitation committee, according to the protocol provided by the VSNU, were to come merely from within professional fields (VSNU 1990). From the academic year 1991–92 on, each committee was required to have a student representative (van Vught and Westerheijden 1993). As far as the Inspectorate for Higher Education was concerned, its responsibilities included supervising the composition of the visitation committees, evaluating their performance, and determining whether their reports were made on the basis of valid information. In addition, the body would be required to provide information and advice to the government (Bresters and Kalkwijk 1990; Maassen 1998).

Regarding the information rules, a considerable number of internal stakeholders were involved in the process of data collection. In particular, the faculty of a program would produce a report of internal quality assessment (Acherman 1990). In addition, during the (normally) two-day visit, the visitation committee would hold discussions with representatives of a study program (Zijderveld 1997). Generally speaking, the data used for the quality process featured an intrinsic form with normative information. With respect to data judgment, the frame of reference against which the study program was to be evaluated would be determined by the visitation committee (Zijderveld 1997). Aligned with the intrinsic feature, the committee's report was required not to involve single, summary judgments, but was to cover various dimensions of the nature of quality (Maassen 1998).

After all visits in a particular discipline had been made, the committee would write a draft report and send it to all of the reviewed programs so as to collect responses from each program. Finally, a general statement, including the committee's recommendations, judgments, and comparative analysis of all of the visited faculties across all of the disciplines, would be published as a final report (Acherman 1990; VSNU 1990). Although the public final report of the visitation committee was geared toward contributing to accountability to society, the process of formulating the report functioned as a mixture of intrinsic and extrinsic orientations. Both internal and external stakeholders were involved.

Third, the payoff and scope rules showed the intrinsic quality. This is accounted for by the fact that there would be no direct financial consequences of the results of the external quality procedures (van Vught and Westerheijden 1993). In addition, there were no strict rules about follow-ups, and departments and faculties had much leeway in determining their response to the visitation committee findings (Acherman 1990; Zijderveld 1997).

Period 2: 2002–2010

From the middle of the 1990s on, quality was looked at from an international perspective. The establishment of the International Network for Quality Assurance Agencies in Higher Education, for sharing information among the bodies responsible for QA, was one instance of the attempt to enhance international co-operation (van der Wende 1999). Under the Bologna Process, there was an expectation that comparable criteria and methodologies would be developed (Bologna Declaration 1999). Accordingly, quality was thought of as something that should be judged against a common set of descriptors or comparable standards, with an international benchmark in the European HE area.

More specifically, the ENQA created in 1999 served the purpose of transparency, exchanging information and experiences by assembling QA agencies across European countries. Also, the ESG developed by the ENQA, and accepted by the European higher education ministers in 2005, contributed to achieving consensus on good practices regarding QA procedures. The EQAR, the register of QA agencies, was created later, in 2008, and the quality agencies would have to be peer-reviewed before being granted entry and given membership in the ENQA, which would rely on the fulfillment of the ESG (Eurydice 2010). In sum, it appears that there was significant European influence on the conception of the quality of provision and the QA system in the Netherlands.

To be in line with the common objectives in the European HE systems rooted in the Bologna Declaration, the Minister of Education, Culture and Science decided to take action. In 2000, after consulting with the major stakeholders in the sector, the government incorporated accreditation in the subsequent policy initiative sent to Parliament: "Accreditation in Dutch Higher Education" ("Keur aan Kwaliteit") (Ministry of Education, Culture and Science 2000). In the regional context, the Dutch government considered an accreditation system to be a promising policy initiative for achieving greater mobility, comparability, and transparency with the neighbouring Flemish-speaking Belgians, particularly in relation to the establishment of a bachelor's-master's degree structure, as well as for enhancing mutual international recognition.

In general, the accreditation system was established in conjunction with a set of assessment procedures, including the process of self-assessment, peer review by expert panels, and published reporting. These components, to some extent, were similar to those of the previous QA system, but were different in the conduct of peer review. More specifically, program deliverers would be allowed to choose those preferred quality agencies whose assessment formats and quality criteria could reflect their program's specific profile. Because one of a multitude of suppliers of accreditation could be selected, the QA system was considered multiple-accreditation (Westerheijden 2001) and could accommodate a variety of evaluation processes.

Moreover, the QA scheme formulated on the basis of program accreditation was virtually linked with an extrinsic orientation. With respect to the position and boundary rules, the Netherlands Accreditation Organisation, established in 2002, was responsible for verifying and validating external assessment as well as granting accreditation for existing programs and licensing new programs. The national accreditation body was transformed into a binational organization named the Dutch-Flemish Accrediting Organisation (NVAO), which commenced work in 2004. The members of the executive board and the general board would be appointed by both governments after consultation with the academic communities. The task of overseeing the external assessments, which had been held by the Inspectorate for Higher Education as a meta-evaluation, was also transferred to the NVAO (Eurydice 2005).

With respect to the other two types of QA rules, extrinsic features were reflected in general. In accordance with the national QA body's quality assessment protocol, the committee would judge whether a program fulfilled the minimum requirements and would then score program performance on a four-point assessment scale, drawing upon the program's self-assessment report and site visits. The committee's report would then be sent back to the institution that wanted to submit a request for accreditation to the NVAO. After receiving the request, the national QA body would verify and validate the report, then make its decision within three months. This decision would be binary (either pass or fail), published, valid within one year (Dittrich, Frederiks, and Luwel 2004; NVAO 2003), and valid for six years. In sum, it was deemed that the accreditation framework and criteria for judgments should have explicit, objective definitions, and accordingly, the yes-or-no decisions made by the NVAO could have financial consequences.

POLICY CHANGE IN DANISH QA ELEMENTS

The policy development of QA in Denmark during the years under investigation occurred in two stages.

Period 1: 1992–2007

The Danish HE system has featured strong state regulation and sovereignty over most activities, such as budgets, as well as educational inputs and processes. In particular, the Ministry of Education vested quality control on a body of external examiners who had participated in university examinations for over 200 years. The extrinsic authority was geared toward ensuring student performance and the comparability of academic standards among HE institutions (Stensaker, Brandt, and Solum 2008). Current students, recent graduates, and employers also engaged in the process of policy-making in the system (Thune 2001). As a result, stakeholders extrinsic to the universities carried weight in relation to quality control, influencing the definitions of HE quality and reflecting contemporary governmental goals and societal demands.

Moving into the 1990s, the government proposed to incorporate a national QA approach along with certain other initiatives (e.g., the introduction of a new degree structure) into the system. These proposals for educational reform were endorsed by a majority of the parties in Parliament in 1992, who aimed to instill greater autonomy into the universities and more flexibility into the centralized sector (Maassen 1997). However, the establishment of QA in the early 1990s tended to be perceived as a "symbolic action" (Stensaker 2010, 186).

The initial QA scheme was implemented through program assessment, which featured an intrinsic orientation. At the outset of the quality process, self-assessment was conducted on a seven-year rotation, and all study programs in the HE system were subject to it. Drawing upon the assessment reports generated by an institution as well as the results of a user survey, steering committees (i.e., visiting teams) would make judgments about the quality of programs in both the university and the non-university sectors. The assessment procedures were completed by the publication of a final report submitted by the visiting team (Thune 1997).

In relation to the features of the QA scheme in general, there was a mixture of intrinsic and extrinsic orientation. More specifically, the position and boundary rules revealed an extrinsic feature, primarily due to the characteristic of the quality agency, the Centre for Evaluation and Quality Assurance of Higher Education (EVC). The QA body was established in 1992 and funded by the Ministry of Education, and its board was composed of the chairs of the national education councils. This agency would determine not only the members of the steering committees but also a detailed protocol for self-assessments, which included assessment procedures along with a frame of reference (Thune 1997; Thune 2001).

After the initial period of QA implementation was completed, the EVC was evaluated by a consultancy firm commissioned by the Ministry of Education in 1998 (Thune 2001). The next year, the national QA body was incorporated into the Danish Evaluation Institute (EVA), which controlled evaluations in the whole education system. Moreover, with the mandate from Parliament, the scope of the EVA's role was extended. In accordance with the *EVA Act* and two ministerial regulations, the new QA body was regulated and answerable to the Ministry of Education and Ministry of Science, Technology and Innovation. Appointment of the members of the board, nominations of the chairs, and approvals for initiatives and budgets all had to be made by the government (Sursock 2011). Generally speaking, there was no guarantee that representatives of the universities would be represented on the board of the EVC or in the EVA. Although government would allegedly not intervene in the formulation of QA procedures and evaluation methods, state ownership of the QA scheme is evident.

With respect to the information rules, some intrinsic features were involved, and these led to a mixed orientation. In particular, the self-assessment reports were generated by the universities, which made judgments of strengths and weaknesses against the program's objectives and proposed corresponding internal QA initiatives. In addition, the quality process stressed dialogue among institutions, and performance indicators that represented an objective method of assessment were thus not integrated into the QA scheme. Generally speaking, the mixture of intrinsic and extrinsic orientations was primarily reflected in the characteristic of the information gathered in the visiting phase. Program evaluation reports that would be completed by the steering committees were based on the information gathered by the self-assessment report, user survey results, and observations of external examiners.

In addition to the involvement of internal stakeholders, external ones were involved. Each visiting panel included three to four academic representatives independent of the program being evaluated and one or two external members who reflected the interests of employers. Also, the private consultancies contracted by the EVC would conduct surveys of highly relevant program users (i.e., students, graduates, and employers). Drawing upon such documentation, the steering committee would complete its program evaluation report after a final conference at which the stakeholders internal to the program (e.g., senior management, teaching staff, and students), the visiting committee, and the QA body had gathered to have a discussion. The final report would be delivered to those relating to further assignments (e.g., the educational council concerned, the ministry, and HE institutions), and all evaluation reports would be made publicly available (Thune 1997).

The last part of the QA scheme referred to the payoff and scope rules, which are concerned with an intrinsic orientation. Initially, the QA scheme was devised as a policy instrument for dealing with the difficult situation combining HE expansion and a decrease in public funding (Thune 1997). Under the circumstances, the function of the quality system was directed to accountability by providing more information about the performance of program provision in light of societal demands (Stensaker 2010). On the other hand, the diversity of institutions was taken into consideration due to the importance of intrinsic functions such as improvement.

As a result, the universities were encouraged to prioritize their tasks and activities based on the objectives they had set themselves. The evaluation judgments had to be made in light of the extent to which an institution achieved its own institutional objectives. Therefore, no ranking or funding allocation would be linked to the published evaluation results (Thune 1997). Also, the QA purpose of improvement caused the universities to assume more autonomy and responsibility for the quality of their provision, particularly in relation to follow-ups. The universities would be required to provide action plans addressing the recommendations in their final evaluation reports and implement the corresponding follow-ups (Sursock 2011).

Period 2: 2007–2010

Although accreditation has been included in the Danish QA framework since the period of the EVA, the government used this approach for ministerial approval of student grants in private teaching programs (Hämäläinen et al. 2001). In the university sector, accreditation had yet to be fully accepted as a core QA approach as emphasis on quality improvement and accountability was still equally central to governmental expectations of QA (Thune 2001). However, the balance gradually shifted in the 2000s.

In 1999, university performance contracts were introduced as part of the reform of the Danish *University Act*. Public sentiment about the quality of HE provision, as a result, appeared to prefer the inclusion of customer specifications in the QA process. This new ability of universities to engage in performance contracts also implied that HE governance in the form of governmental control was to be replaced by dialogue or negotiation among relevant stakeholders (Thune 2001). Moreover, the commencement of the Bologna Process led to more extrinsic policy frames. It was deemed important that Danish universities would have competitive strengths in the European or global HE market (Sursock 2011).

Against the development of international and transnational HE, market value and principles grew significantly in the university sector. On the one hand, the diversity of the universities in terms of institutional goals and action plans was valued in terms of the local context of individual institutions. On the other, the traditional involvement of a wide range of external stakeholders in the Danish HE system deepened in the international and transnational context. With the subsequent development of the EHEA, the emphasis on extrinsic purposes such as accountability seemed to gradually outweigh that on intrinsic ones (e.g., improvement) as Danish HE policy-makers considered the policy alternatives to the current QA scheme.

Under the circumstances, preferable strategies toward QA took a more transparent, comparable, and compatible approach in a regional and global sense, yet they were more flexible in the local sense because institutions along with different missions would be able to fit into the QA scheme. Accreditation, as a QA approach that included a predefined framework of quality standards and procedures as well as a corresponding yes-or-no decision, was perceived as a compelling policy alternative. The new scheme deviated from standardized procedures, whereby study programs in different subject areas would follow different evaluation principles of data judgments (Thune 2001).

In 2007, the *University Act* ushered in program accreditation as the new QA approach, which was paralleled with the QA system conducted in the non-university sector. In accordance with this development, ACE Denmark was established as a new QA body in charge of the accreditation of long-cycle study programs in the university sector. With respect to the Danish short- and medium-cycle programs in the college sector, the conduct of their accreditation procedures was part of EVA's role (Stensaker 2010). In practice, the Danish universities were allowed to choose a QA agency to implement the external QA process after the announcement of the *University Act* in 2003 (Vinther-Jørgensen and Hansen 2006). Generally speaking, changes in the position and boundary rules that occurred during this period were minor and did not affect the extrinsic orientation.

Likewise, although there were some differences between the QA schemes conducted before and after 2007, their information rules remained unchanged, being categorized as the mixed orientation in general. For example, on the one hand, the data collected after 2007 in the process of carrying out accreditations showed more intrinsic features than the previous evaluation procedures in that reflective information was required in the protocol for self-assessment. On the other hand, the feature of data judgments became more extrinsic insofar as yes-or-no QA results would be generated. In contrast, the orientation of the payoff and scope rules switched from the intrinsic to the extrinsic orientation. In relation to this, the Accreditation Council would make the determination of accreditation based on final reports generated by the quality agencies. Inspired by the Dutch QA system commencing in 2002, the Danish accreditation procedures conducted after 2007 linked negative results to program closure. The inclusion of the governmental sanctions, having a connection with institutions' follow-ups, represented an extrinsic feature (Stensaker 2010; Sursock 2011).

COMPARISONS

Table 2 compiles the data regarding the policy orientation of the five dimensions of the QA systems in the three case countries. Most QA elements in the 1990s were geared toward the intrinsic orientation (and to some extent the mixed orientation). In the 2000s, these countries moved

TABLE 2

Policy change in the QA elements of the three case countries

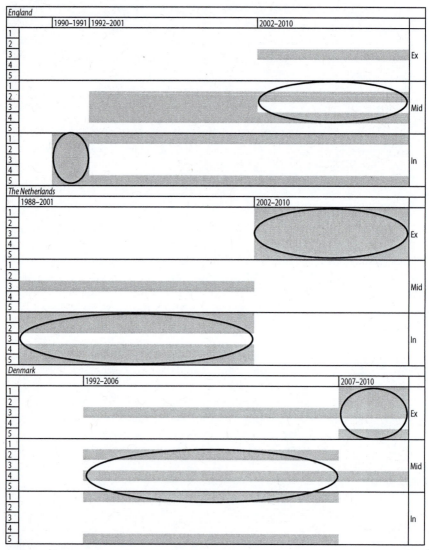

Legend:

1 – QA approaches

2 – QA schemes

3 – Position and boundary rules

4 – Information rules

5 – Payoff and scope rules

Ex – Extrinsic orientation

Mid – Mixed orientation

In – Intrinsic orientation

Source: Authors' compilation.

toward the extrinsic and mixed orientations. At the same time, again as an overall assessment, we do not detect a strict pattern of convergence. That is, the situation in 2010 is as diverse as in the middle of the 1990s. In addition, the degrees of change in England and Denmark are more evolutionary than they are in the Netherlands, where most QA elements switched from the intrinsic orientation to the extrinsic. If considering the time frames, the pace of policy change of QA elements in England are on aggregate the slowest of all case countries.

However, looking in more depth at the QA elements, it is interesting to note that there is an increasing diversity with respect to QA approaches and payoff and scope rules (Table 3). Whereas throughout the 1990s, all QA approaches were of an intrinsic orientation (program evaluations, audits), we see differences in the new millennium (with England clinging to an intrinsic orientation and Denmark and the Netherlands moving toward an extrinsic orientation: accreditation). This also applies to the payoff and scope rules. Whereas there were, generally speaking, "no strings attached" in the 1990s, Denmark and the Netherlands have implemented stronger accountability rules, including taking measures if quality is not up to the standards.

TABLE 3
Policy change in QA approaches and in payoff and scope rules

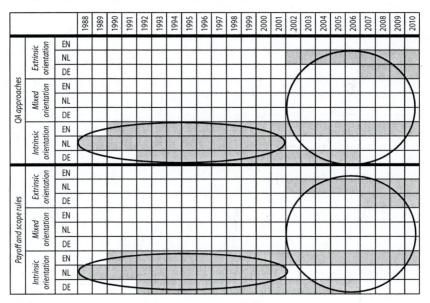

Legend:
EN – England
NL – The Netherlands
DE – Denmark

Source: Authors' compilation.

Taking the position and boundary rules into account (Table 4), we see a small decrease in diversity. This means that we found policy convergence in the QA schemes regarding the actors who decide on QA mechanisms and/or who conduct quality assessments.

TABLE 4
Policy change in position and boundary rules

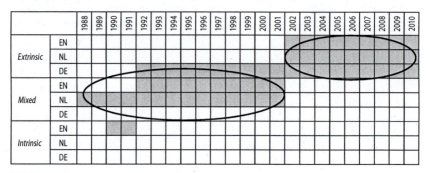

Legend:
EN – England
NL – The Netherlands
DE – Denmark
Source: Authors' compilation.

With respect to information rules (Table 5), there is no obvious difference in degree of diversity between the 1990s and 2000s; policy alternatives range either from intrinsic to mixed orientation or from extrinsic to mixed. This also applies to QA schemes.

In sum, we detected no strong policy convergence in the development of the five QA elements in general. We see some patterns of convergence, but also countertrends and situations being stable over time.

Generally speaking, we find that similarity in the position and boundary rules of QA schemes increased and the degree of the change was incremental. Conversely, the QA approach and the payoff and scope rules became less similar over time and revealed relatively revolutionary changes. The development of the information rules in the three countries was rather stable over time. Furthermore, the payoff and scope rules and QA approaches that emerged in the Netherlands and Denmark changed more frequently than they did in England, whereas the position and boundary rules and QA functions in England showed higher frequency of change than those in the other two countries.

TABLE 5
Policy change in QA schemes and information rules

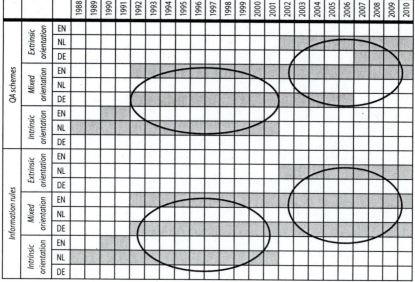

Legend:
EN – England
NL – The Netherlands
DE – Denmark

Source: Authors' compilation.

CONCLUSIONS AND REFLECTIONS

This chapter highlights policy change in QA schemes against the EHEA context and shows the change patterns in three case countries. Two of our pioneers, Denmark and the Netherlands, have set European standards and as such have paved the way for a particular European QA model, a model that has been taken up as an example by many other European countries. This has led to convergence over time. England may be a (relative) outlier in the European pattern given its continuous focus on the intrinsic orientation with respect to the QA approaches and the payoff and scope rules.

Drawing upon our comparisons, we find, first, that the degree and the direction of change in different policy elements differed from country to country. Also, our findings reveal that different QA aspects led to different patterns of policy change. Generally speaking, we do not support the idea of there being a strong policy convergence among the European QA schemes in the three countries, although there was a common deviation from the intrinsic to the extrinsic side.

Our conclusion based on three case countries is different from some other comparative research projects. They have observed a considerable policy convergence among the Bologna signatory states, but it appears that there is a trade-off between a small set of in-depth case studies versus a larger set of cases, with less focus on detail. Except for that, there are two other explanations for the discrepancy. We use the study of Voegtle, Knill, and Dobbins (2011) as an example. They mainly looked at – in our terminology – the information rules. Not discounting the importance of these rules, we argue that we have taken a broader (and thus more valid) approach to the operationalization of the QA schemes. In addition to the difference in policy dimensions chosen for analysis, our approach in assessing the growing similarity is distinctive. Voegtle, Knill, and Dobbins (2011) focused on whether there was convergence toward an ideal-typical model (one that emerged from the ESG). In contrast, our conclusions were based on an analysis using a framework of intrinsic and extrinsic dimensions of QA mechanisms, analyzing whether the variations among the national QA schemes decreased or increased.

Our findings suggest that although policy convergence might be increasingly evident in European QA systems, there is obvious variation in policy change for the selected QA elements. Our conclusion is that even in a favourable policy context (the Bologna Process, which aims at convergence), it is not a given that national HE policies become increasingly similar across countries and over time.

REFERENCES

Acherman, H.A. 1990. "Quality Assessment by Peer Review: A New Area for University Cooperation." *Higher Education Management* 2:179–192.

Barnett, R. 1996. "The Evaluation of the Higher Education System in the United Kingdom." In *The Evaluation of Higher Education Systems*, ed. R. Cowen. London: Kogan Page.

Bennett, C.J., and M. Howlett. 1992. "The Lessons of Learning: Reconciling Theories of Policy Learning and Policy Change." *Policy Sciences* 25:275–294.

Bologna Declaration. 1999. "Joint Declaration of the European Ministers of Education Convened in Bologna on the 19th of June 1999." Bologna.

Bresters, D.W., and J.P.T. Kalkwijk. 1990. "The Role of the Inspectorate of Higher Education." In *Peer Review and Performance Indicators: Quality Assessment in British and Dutch Higher Education*, ed. L.C.J. Goedegebuure, P.A.M. Maassen, and D.F. Westerheijden. Utrecht: Lemma.

Brown, R. 2004. *Quality Assurance in Higher Education: The UK Experience since 1992.* London: RoutledgeFalmer.

Campbell, J.L. 2004. *Institutional Change and Globalization.* Princeton, NJ: Princeton University Press.

Cashore, B., and M. Howlett. 2007. "Punctuating Which Equilibrium? Understanding Thermostatic Policy Dynamics in Pacific Northwest Forestry." *American Journal of Political Science* 51:532–551.

DES. 1991. *Higher Education: A New Framework.* Cm. 1541. London: HMSO.

Dittrich, K., M. Frederiks, and M. Luwel. 2004. "The Implementation of 'Bologna' in Flanders and the Netherlands." *European Journal of Education* 39:299–316.

Dolowitz, D., and D. Marsh. 2000. "Learning from Abroad: The Role of Policy Transfer in Contemporary Policy-Making." *Governance* 13:5–23.

Douglass, J.A. 2005. "How All Globalization Is Local: Countervailing Forces and Their Influence on Higher Education Markets." *Higher Education Policy* 18:445–473.

Eurydice. 2005. *Focus on the Structure of Higher Education in Europe 2004/5: National Trends in the Bologna Process.* Brussels: Eurydice.

—. 2010. *Focus on Higher Education in Europe 2010: The Impact of the Bologna Process.* Brussels: Eurydice.

Gornitzka, Å., and P. Maassen. 2000. "Hybrid Steering Approaches with Respect to European Higher Education." *Higher Education Policy* 13:267–285.

Hall, P.A. 1993. "Policy Paradigms, Social Learning, and the State: The Case of Economic Policymaking in Britain." *Comparative Politics* 25:275–296.

Hämäläinen, K., J. Haakstad, J. Kangasniemi, T. Lindeberg, and M. Sjölund. 2001. *Quality Assurance in the Nordic Higher Education: Accreditation-Like Practices.* Helsinki: ENQA.

HEFCE. 1993. *Assessment of the Quality of Education.* Circular 3/93. Bristol: HEFCE.

—. 1994. *The Quality Assessment Method from April 1995.* Circular 39/94. Bristol: HEFCE.

HEFCE, QAA, UUK, and SCOP. 2001. *Quality Assurance in Higher Education: Proposals for Consultation.* Consultation 01/45. Bristol: HEFCE.

Heichel, S., J. Pape, and T. Sommerer. 2005. "Is There Convergence in Convergence Research? An Overview of Empirical Studies on Policy Convergence." *Journal of European Public Policy* 12:817–840.

HEQC. 1993. *Review of Quality Audit: Coopers & Lybrand Report.* London: HEQC.

—. 1996. *Learning from Audit 2.* London: HEQC.

HEQC and HEFCE. 1994. *Joint Statement on Quality Assurance.* M1/94. Bristol: HEFCE.

Holzinger, K., and C. Knill. 2005. "Causes and Conditions of Cross-National Policy Convergence." *Journal of European Public Policy* 12:775–797.

Howlett, M. 2009. "Governance Modes, Policy Regimes and Operational Plans: A Multi-Level Nested Model of Policy Instrument Choice and Policy Design." *Policy Sciences* 42 (1):73–89.

Huisman, J., and Kaiser, F. 2002. "A Comparative View on Policy Trends in Western European Higher Education." *German Policy Studies* 2 (3):1–23.

JPG. 1996. *Assuring the Quality of Higher Education.* Final Report. London: CVCP.

Knill, C. 2005. "Introduction: Cross-National Policy Convergence: Concepts, Approaches and Explanatory Factors." *Journal of European Public Policy* 12:764–774.

Kogan, M., and S. Hanney. 2000. *Reforming Higher Education.* London: Philadelphia.

Maassen, P.A.M. 1997. "Quality in European Higher Education: Recent Trends and Their Historical Roots." *European Journal of Education* 32:111–127.

—. 1998. "Quality Assurance in the Netherlands." *New Directions for Institutional Research* 99:19–28.

Maassen, P.A.M., and P.J.M. Weusthof. 1989. "Quality Assessment in Dutch Higher Education: A Big Leap Forward or a Trojan Horse." In *Dutch Higher Education in Transition: Policy Issues in Higher Education in the Netherlands*, ed. P.A.M. Maassen and F.A. van Vught. Culemborg, The Netherlands: Lemma.

Ministry of Education, Culture and Science. 2000. "Keur aan kwaliteit." Zoetermeer, The Netherlands: Ministry of Education, Culture and Science.

Mooney, C.Z. 2001. "Modeling Regional Effects on State Policy Diffusion." *Political Research Quarterly* 54:103–124.

NCIHE. 1997. *Higher Education in the Learning Society.* Main Report. (The Dearing Report.) London: HMSO.

NVAO. 2003. *Accreditation Framework: The Netherlands.* The Hague: NVAO.

Ostrom, E. 2005. *Understanding Institutional Diversity.* Princeton, NJ, and Oxford: Princeton University Press.

—. 2007. "Institutional Rational Choice: An Assessment of the Institutional Analysis and Development Framework." In *Theories of the Policy Process,* ed. P.A. Sabatier. Boulder, CO: Westview Press.

Phillips, D., and K. Ochs. 2003. "Processes of Policy Borrowing in Education: Some Explanatory and Analytical Devices." *Comparative Education* 39:451–461.

QAA. 1998. "The Way Ahead." *Higher Quality* 4.

—. 2002a. *Handbook for Institutional Audit: England, 2002–2005.* Gloucester: QAA.

—. 2002b. *QAA External Review Process for Higher Education in England: Operational Description.* Gloucester: QAA.

—. 2003. *Learning from Subject Review 1993–2001.* Gloucester: QAA.

Sabatier, P.A. 2007. "The Need for Better Theories." In *Theories of the Policy Process,* ed. P.A. Sabatier. Boulder, CO: Westview Press.

Salter, B., and T. Tapper. 2000. "The Politics of Governance in Higher Education: The Case of Quality Assurance." *Political Studies* 48:66–87.

Shattock, M. 2008. "The Change from Private to Public Governance of British Higher Education: Its Consequences for Higher Education Policy Making 1980–2006." *Higher Education Quarterly* 62:181–203.

Stensaker, B. 2010. "Subject Assessments for Academic Quality in Denmark." In *Public Policy for Academic Quality: Analyses of Innovative Policy Instruments,* ed. D.D. Dill and M. Beerkens. Dordrecht: Springer.

Stensaker, B., E. Brandt, and N.H. Solum. 2008. "Changing Systems of External Examination." *Quality Assurance in Education* 16:211–223.

Sursock, A. 2011. "Accountability in Western Europe: Shifting Quality Assurance Paradigms." In *Accountability in Higher Education: Global Perspectives on Trust and Power,* ed. B. Stensaker and L. Harvey. New York: Routledge.

Teichler, U. 1989. "Government and Curriculum Innovation in the Netherlands." In *Governmental Strategies and Innovation in Higher Education,* ed. F.A. van Vught. London: Jessica Kingsley.

Thune, C. 1997. "The Balance between Accountability and Improvement." In *Standards and Quality in Higher Education,* ed. J. Brennan. London: Jessica Kingsley.

—. 2001. "Quality Assurance of Higher Education in Denmark." In *Global Perspectives on Quality in Higher Education,* ed. D. Dunkerly and S.W. Wong. Aldershot: Ashgate Publishers.

van Bruggen, J.C., J.P. Scheele, J.P. Westerheijden, and D.F. Westerheijden. 1999. "To Be Continued … Syntheses and Trends in Follow-Up of Quality Assurance in West European Higher Education." *European Journal for Education Law and Policy* 2:155–163.

van der Wende, M.C. 1999. "Quality Assurance of Internationalisation and Internationalisation of Quality Assurance." In *Quality and Internationalisation in*

Higher Education, ed. H. de Wit and J.A. Knight. Paris: Organization for Economic Co-operation and Development.

van Vught, F.A., and D.F. Westerheijden. 1993. *Quality Management and Quality Assurance in European Higher Education: Methods and Mechanisms.* Luxembourg: Office for Official Publications of the Commission of the European Communities.

Vinther-Jørgensen, T., and S.P. Hansen. 2006. *European Standards and Guidelines in a Nordic Perspective.* Helsinki: ENQA.

Voegtle, E.M., C. Knill, and M. Dobbins. 2011. "To What Extent Does Transnational Communication Drive Cross-National Policy Convergence? The Impact of the Bologna-Process on Domestic Higher Education Policies." *Higher Education* 61:77–94.

Vroeijenstijn, T.I., and H. Acherman. 1990. "Control Oriented Versus Improvement Oriented Quality Assessment." In *Peer Review and Performance Indicators: Quality Assessment in British and Dutch Higher Education,* ed. L.C.J. Goedegebuure, P.A.M. Maassen, and D.F. Westerheijden. Utrecht: Lemma.

VSNU. 1990. *Guide for External Program Review.* Utrecht: Association of Universities in the Netherlands.

Westerheijden, D.F. 2001. "Ex oriente lux? National and Multiple Accreditation in Europe after the Fall of the Wall and after Bologna." *Quality in Higher Education* 7:65–75.

—. 2005. Walking Towards a Moving Target: Quality Assurance in European Higher Education." *The Quality of Higher Education/Aukstojo Mokslo Kokybe* 1:52–71.

Westerheijden, D.F., E. Beerkens, L. Cremonini, J. Huisman, B. Kehm, A. Kovac, P. Lazetic, A. McCoshan, N. Mozuraityte, M. Souto-Otero, E. de Weert, J. Witte, and Y. Yagci. 2010. *Bologna Process Independent Assessment: The First Decade of Working on the European Higher Education Area.* Brussels: European Commission.

Westerheijden, D.F., H.F. de Boer, and J. Enders. 2009. "Netherlands: An 'Echternach' Procession in Different Directions: Oscillating Steps Towards Reform. In *University Governance: Western European Comparative Perspectives,* ed. C. Paradeise, E. Reale, I. Bleiklie, and E. Ferlie. Dordrecht: Springer.

Westerheijden, D.F., V. Hulpiau, and K. Waeytens. 2007. "From Design and Implementation to Impact of Quality Assurance: An Overview of Some Studies into What Impacts Improvement." *Tertiary Education and Management* 13 (4):295–312.

Westerheijden, D.F., B. Stensaker, and M.J. Rosa. 2007. Introduction to *Quality Assurance in Higher Education: Trends in Regulation, Translation and Transformation,* ed. D.F. Westerheijden, B. Stensaker, and M.J. Rosa. Dordrecht: Springer.

Williams, P. 1992. *Annual Report of the Director 1990/91.* Birmingham: CVCP, AAU.

—. 2009. "The Result of Intelligent Effort? Two Decades in the Quality Assurance of Higher Education." Lecture delivered at the Institute of Education, University of London.

Witte, J., M. van der Wende, and J. Huisman. 2008. "Blurring Boundaries: How the Bologna Process Changes the Relationship between University and Non-University Higher Education in Germany, the Netherlands, and France." *Studies in Higher Education* 33 (3):31–42.

Zijderveld, D.C. 1997. "External Quality Assessment in Dutch Higher Education: Consultancy and Watchdog Roles." *Higher Education Management* 9:31–42.

CHAPTER 13

DESIGNING HIGHER EDUCATION POLICY IN THE AGE OF GLOBALIZATION: IMPERFECT INFORMATION AND THE PURSUIT OF THE PUBLIC GOOD[1]

DAVID D. DILL

INTRODUCTION

There have been remarkable changes in the higher education policies of the developed countries over the last quarter century. "World class" universities are now believed to be a primary contributor to comparative advantage among the advanced nations – a critical source of needed human capital, of industrial technology, and of economic innovation (Dill and van Vught 2010). Because universities are still primarily funded or subsidized by national governments, higher education policy is perceived to be one of the more influential instruments that policy-makers in the leading nations can employ to sustain economic development in the new, more competitive global economy. Therefore, national governments are pursuing substantial reforms in the governance and management of the university sector.

But questions have been raised by a number of scholars (Calhoun 2006; Marginson 2007; Brown 2010; Molesworth, Scullion, and Nixon 2010) about whether these policy changes, which have introduced greater "privatization" and market competition into higher education systems (i.e., so-called neo-liberal reforms), are negatively affecting academic behaviour and diminishing universities' ability to contribute to the "public

Making Policy in Turbulent Times: Challenges and Prospects for Higher Education, ed. P. Axelrod, R.D. Trilokekar, T. Shanahan, and R. Wellen. Kingston: School of Policy Studies, Queen's University.

good." However, as our German colleague, Professor Ulrich Teichler, once so wonderfully put it, the main difference between research on mad cow disease and research on higher education policy is that when the mad cow researchers present their findings, the mad cows are not in the room!

While the effects on those actively engaged in the production of higher education should certainly be included in any calculation of the public good and/or the social benefits derived from higher education, focusing primarily on the impacts upon producers may not provide a totally objective assessment of the public good. Therefore, in a volume devoted to higher education policy in which the contributors are primarily academics, it is important to ask the traditional questions posed to policy analysts: which public? and for whose good? (Powell and Clemens 1998).

For example, in the introduction to a report on Canadian higher education policy, the academic researchers noted, "Granting council policies that do not fully cover overheads and indirect costs ... require user universities to short-change undergraduate training in order to ease up funds for prestige research projects" (Beach, Boadway, and McInnis 2005, 5). One can certainly argue that current reforms in research policy may negatively affect the incentives for university teaching, but the implication that universities are therefore "required" to short-change undergraduate training may reinforce the view among some policy-makers and members of the public that academics are using their granted autonomy to pursue professional preferences by cross-subsidizing research expenditures with funds intended for instruction.

I will argue that there are demonstrable weaknesses in a number of the current reforms of higher education. But the goal of my analysis is to determine how best to regulate universities to assure the provision of education (with a particular focus on academic quality), research, and public service that maximizes, in as efficient and equitable a manner as possible, the total social benefits of higher education.

Many recent national policies have been significantly influenced by the theories of the "new institutional economics" (Barzelay 2001; Scott, Ball, and Dale 1997), which attempt to make the assumptions about the nature and distribution of information in human behaviour much more explicit (Weimer and Vining 1996). For example, in higher education policy, there is a much greater emphasis now on providing public information about academic quality as a means of helping students choose the most effective university, on linking the award of university funds for research to measures of scholarly performance, and on the reallocation of intellectual property rights within universities as a means of motivating increased technology transfer. But are the assumptions about information in human behaviour that are currently guiding higher education reforms valid?

With the assistance of a number of distinguished international colleagues, I have recently completed two comparative studies of the influence of national policies on higher education (Dill and Beerkens 2010; Dill and van Vught 2010). The first is a study of the new regulatory instruments for assuring academic quality in universities, while the second is a study of the impact of national policies on the academic research enterprise among the leading nations of the Organisation for Economic Co-operation and Development (OECD). Drawing upon these studies, I would like to explore what we are learning about the role of information in the design of more effective higher education policy.

ACADEMIC QUALITY

Let me begin with the policies regarding academic quality. In many countries around the globe, the design of university quality assurance policies has become a "contested field" between universities and the state (Dill and Beerkens 2010). For example, does academic quality refer to the overall academic reputation of a university, to the quality of research by members of the academic staff, to objective indicators of the ability of admitted students, to the effectiveness of the processes by which university teaching and learning occur, and so on? From the standpoint of the public good, I would argue that the concept of academic quality is best defined by the concept of academic standards, by which I mean the level of knowledge, skills, and attitudes attained by university graduates as a result of their academic program or degree – what is increasingly referred to as the "value added" by a university education. This definition of academic quality is similar to the economists' conception of general "human capital" (Becker 1994; McMahon 2009), which over students' lifetimes provides both private and public economic benefits as well as valued social benefits in the form of improved parenting, healthier lifestyles, greater civic participation, and increased social cohesion.

One assumption of the new institutional economics, reflected in the statements of policy-makers in both the United Kingdom and the United States, is that if student consumers have sufficient information about the quality of universities, their subsequent enrolment choices will provide a powerful incentive for the institutions to improve the quality of academic programs, thereby increasing the human capital that benefits society.

However, the research evidence on the impact of the commercial university league tables that have proliferated rapidly around the world suggests that they do not effectively assure or improve the academic standards of universities (Dill and Soo 2005; Hazelkorn 2011). The challenge and cost of developing genuinely valid measures of academic program quality to inform student choice are significant. Furthermore, commercial publications have already achieved significant sales as well as influence among opinion leaders, higher-achieving students, and even university personnel by publishing *institutional* rankings using indicators of academic prestige, although they have dubious validity as predictors of student learning outcomes (Pascarella and Terenzini 2005).

More troublesome, the global focus on university prestige, which these commercial rankings have helped to foster, has distorted the expected constructive link between information on academic quality and university efforts to improve academic standards. Motivated by commercial institutional rankings based upon prestige, many universities have responded to market competition, not by improving the quality of student learning in academic programs, but by investing greater amounts of time and resources in marketing student admissions as well as developing attractive student facilities, "cream skimming" students by selecting the highest-achieving applicants, and engaging in other activities designed to enhance university prestige (Dill and Beerkens 2010).

The failure of the market to effectively provide consumer information about academic quality has inspired several non-profit efforts to provide more valid and socially beneficial academic rankings. These include the carefully designed academic program rankings developed by the Center for Higher Education in Germany (Beerkens and Dill 2010) and now being implemented in Canada. These league tables provide rankings of academic subjects rather than whole institutions, information genuinely useful to student choice, and these rankings were systematically developed by professionals based upon relevant research as well as current studies of student needs.

But while these rankings are genuinely superior to commercial league tables, they also have weaknesses for informing student choice (Beerkens and Dill 2010). For example, the program-level student surveys used to construct these rankings have limited reliability because of the low and/ or highly variable response rates in different academic fields. Also, an association has been discovered between rankings scores and institutional size. Finally, the stated differences among subjects or institutions are insignificant and stable over time, providing limited guidance to student decision-making.

Furthermore, the international research to date on student choice suggests that many university applicants are "naïve consumers" whose education choices are influenced by a wide variety of educational, social, and personal factors, including the immediate consumption benefits of education. In mass higher education systems, quality rankings influence the educational decisions of a relatively small but growing segment of university applicants, primarily those of high ambition and achievement (Dill and Soo 2005). This suggests that the choices of even better-informed university applicants may not effectively represent the interests or values of the larger public good. Rather, as suggested below, information on the quality and performance of academic programs is most likely to benefit the public good if we focus on its application to the collective actions of the primary producers of higher education – that is, the academic staff.

While the empirical evidence to date suggests that even better-informed student choices are unlikely to provide strong incentives for the assurance and improvement of academic standards within universities, there is some evidence – particularly in the US (Romer 2000) and some other countries – of a poor fit between student selection of subjects and needed human capital. Students appear to be choosing in societally insufficient numbers demanding academic fields such as the sciences and engineering, which clearly provide substantial private as well as public benefits. Therefore, countries such as China and the UK have recently proposed policies limiting enrolments and/or abolishing state subsidies for academic fields deemed less vital to society. A constructive first alternative to such restrictive regulation would be a national policy, similar to that adopted in Australia, requiring the provision of more useful performance information on academic fields to help guide student choice of university subject. Such a policy would require publication of data on student retention, student progression, and graduate outcomes (e.g., the nature of graduates' employment, their average salaries, and their further education) *by subject field* for all institutions of higher education (Santiago et al. 2008).[2]

Finally, in contrast to the market for first-degree-level education, where student preferences may not effectively reflect the public good, the international market for research doctoral students appears more consistent with classic economic assumptions (Dill 2009; Hazelkorn 2011). Many universities now provide full financial support to the best doctoral applicants in an effort to compete aggressively for the most able international students. Doctoral applicants are an older, more educationally experienced set of consumers than first-degree applicants, and they are pursuing advanced degrees primarily for vocational reasons. Doctoral applicants, therefore, are less likely to be swayed by consumption benefits, social factors, geographical considerations, or institutional reputation in their choice of academic programs and more likely to be influenced by valid information on doctoral program quality.

In this more perfectly competitive market, there is evidence that the well-designed National Research Council rankings of research doctoral programs in the US, which are subsidized by the federal government, are not only highly influential on student choice, but have also motivated demonstrable improvements in US PhD programs in a number of leading universities (Dill 2009). Given the acknowledged positive influence of research doctoral graduates on economic growth in the OECD countries (Aghion 2006) and the current efforts in many countries to improve the quality of research doctoral programs (Kottmann 2011), government support for doctoral-quality rankings appears to be a particularly well-justified policy for assuring the public good.

Much of the critical analysis of current reforms in higher education also warns of a possible decline in academic standards, arguing that "neo-liberal" policies may "privatize" academic life, thereby altering in a negative manner the constructive educational relationship between students and academic staff (Calhoun 2006; Barnett 2011). For example, the greater policy emphasis on competition for university research resources in many countries increases incentives for individual professors to devote more time and effort during their careers to academic specialization and research activity as well as for their universities to invest a greater proportion of available resources in an academic "arms race" for research prestige (Dill and van Vught 2010).

As a consequence, academic staff may have less motivation and time to commit to the collective actions necessary to assure and improve academic standards in subject programs, and their universities may be even less inclined to require them to do so. Furthermore, the academic policies that often seem to accompany the "massification" of higher education, including modular teaching, continuous assessment, student surveys of instruction, program funding based upon enrolment, and university funding based upon student graduation rates, may actually encourage the inflation of grades or marks as well as the relaxation of academic standards. Indeed, a recent and much discussed study of a national sample of US college and university students suggests that academic standards in the world's most expensive as well as most market-driven system of higher education may be declining (Arum and Roksa 2011). The studied US college students reported minimal classwork expectations and spent less time on academic work than comparable European Union (EU) university students. Over a third of those who graduated failed to demonstrate significant improvement in learning over their four years of college.

Consequently, in addition to the discussed instrument of quality information for student choice, recent government reforms have emphasized the development of external quality assurance (QA) instruments intended to maintain and improve academic standards in all university programs. Our analyses of these national QA mechanisms suggest some principles to guide the design of more effective policies (Dill and Beerkens 2010).

First, our analyses made clear that developing a stronger culture of quality in teaching and student learning, and creating conditions for the continual assurance and improvement of academic standards within universities, will require actively engaging *both* the collegial leadership of an institution as well as the academic staff in departments and subject fields. The positive impacts of the subject assessments, accreditations, and academic audits we studied in a number of countries (Dill and Beerkens 2010) were most clearly visible in the increased discussions about academic quality[3] as well as measurable changes in curricula organization, student assessment, and modes of instruction that took place within academic programs. It is, after all, at the subject level that academic standards are most clearly assured and improved.

However, the external reviews or accreditations of all subjects recently implemented in some EU countries are costly to sustain for an entire system, their benefits tend to decline over time, they fail to assess the effectiveness of the university's own collegial mechanisms for assuring quality, and these external processes appear to conflict with the global trend toward increased university autonomy. A more effective and efficient external quality assurance instrument would create incentives for the collective university to assume ongoing responsibility for maintaining academic standards and implementing rigorous and valid collegial processes for assuring and improving academic quality in all of the institution's academic programs. For this to occur, the university's core academic processes for assuring academic standards must be externally evaluated or audited by competent peer reviewers, and the efficacy of these processes must be confirmed by assessing their influence and impact on the quality of teaching and student learning in a representative sample of study programs within each institution – what in the UK are termed "audit trails."[4]

A second design principle that can be deduced from the studied instruments relates to the core academic processes that must be externally evaluated. As in the Hong Kong Academic Audit process (Massy 2010), this requires a laser-like focus on the essential processes that universities themselves employ for assuring academic standards. Therefore, primary attention should be paid to the institutional processes for designing and approving new course modules and programs of study, reviewing academic programs, maintaining the equivalence of grading and marking standards within and among subject fields, evaluating teaching, assuring the effectiveness of student assessments, and identifying and sharing best practices for sustaining and improving academic standards among all academic programs. It is worth noting that these same collegial processes are likely relevant for assuring academic standards in all types of universities, whether public or private, traditional or distance-based.

A third design consideration is the appropriate methodology for these external reviews. The most effective and legitimate instruments in the views of academic staff possess characteristics similar to those exhibited by the Teacher Education Accreditation Council in the US (El-Khawas 2010), the accreditation and quality processes of the General Medical Council in the UK (Harvey 2010), and the ABET international accreditation process in applied science, computing, engineering, and technology (Prados, Peterson, and Lattuca 2005; Volkwein et al. 2007). These external subject reviews all strongly emphasize a culture of evidence-based decision-making within institutions that would be directly applied to the improvement of academic programs. Accordingly, they place much weight on assessing the validity and reliability of institutional measures and mechanisms for assuring the quality of teaching and student learning.[5] In several of these assessments, the external peer reviewers are carefully trained, supported during the review process by professional staff, and employ systematic, standardized procedures and protocols.

A final issue in the design of academic quality assurance regulation is the predictable problem of "regulatory capture" (Laffont and Tirole 1991), whereby those whose interests are affected by the relevant regulation gain influence over the regulatory agency and promote their private interests over those of the public. Simply stated, who guards the guardians? The typical policy response to this question is to require a public evaluation of the academic quality agency itself as a means of protecting the public interest by effective regulation (Dill 2011).

However, the evaluations of national academic quality assurance agencies have, to date, often been controlled by the agencies themselves in co-operation with associations of agency professionals and/or selected representatives of the regulated universities. This type of evaluation may lack independence, often fails to employ a suitably relevant and/ or robust method of validation, and generally ignores the critical issue of the efficiency of external quality assurance regulations (Blackmur 2008). Since QA agencies are essentially regulatory bodies, the public good would, therefore, likely be better served if the effectiveness and efficiency of external academic quality assurance agencies were evaluated by established, respected, and truly independent national evaluation or audit agencies similar to the Government Accountability Office in the US, the National Audit Office in the UK, and the Auditor General of Canada.

In sum, better information on the quality and performance of academic programs could make a valuable contribution to protecting the public good if public policies provided incentives for their valid measurement and effective use by academic staff in the core collegial processes for improving and assuring academic standards within universities. As Pascarella and Terenzini concluded in their exhaustive review of the available empirical research on teaching and learning in higher education:

> Assessment of department-specific learning outcomes can be a useful vehicle for change. *Assessment plans and activities developed and approved by faculty* can provide an empirical foundation of systematic and ongoing rethinking, redesigning, and restructuring programs and curricula. For faculty members, trained to be skeptical about claims, evidence is the gold standard in the academy, and they are unlikely to adopt new ways of thinking or behaving without first being convinced that the new pedagogies and organizational structures are better than the old. In addition, *the findings of assessment studies specific to faculty members' academic units will generate more interest and action than general or institution-wide evidence.* (2005, 648; emphasis added)

RESEARCH

A second area of higher education policy that reflects the assumptions of the new institutional economics is performance-based funding, or contracting for research. Performance-based funding of university research, based upon output indicators such as publications and citations, has been implemented in a number of OECD countries. The most prominent example of this approach is the Research Assessment Exercise (RAE) in the UK. Evidence suggests that performance-based funding of research has increased the productivity as well as the quality of UK academic research, stimulating latent capacities for research that previously were not efficiently organized (Henkel and Kogan 2010; Hicks 2008). In the OECD nations that have adopted performance-based funding, many universities are now reporting a more strategic approach to their research efforts, with marked improvements in the internal organization and management of research programs and activities (Dill and van Vught 2010).

It is likely that this improvement in university research programs is due not only to recently implemented research policies, but also to the general reductions in funding for publicly supported universities that have occurred in conjunction with the massification and expansion of higher education in many countries. As a consequence, universities in some of our case study countries (Dill and van Vught 2010) have become highly motivated to pursue alternative sources of revenue for their research programs and therefore have been required to develop the research centres and internal research management processes necessary to survive in this more competitive market.

However, performance-based funding has other reported impacts on university research (Hicks 2008). There is concern that the focus on peer-reviewed publications may suppress excellence, inducing a certain homogenization of research at the upper levels. Furthermore, the emphasis on publication counts encourages some researchers to become more calculating in their publication patterns, slicing their research into smaller topics and more numerous articles. The benefits of performance-based funding in Australia and the UK also appear to have been discontinuous, creating a one-time shock to the overall system; this initially motivates increased research productivity in all universities eligible for the funding, but appears to dissipate over time (Beerkens 2009; Crespi and Geuna 2004).

Performance-based funding also contributes to an observed stratification of universities, concentrating research in those institutions with richer resources, larger numbers of internationally recognized academic staff, and well-established reputations (Dill and van Vught 2010). There are also particular challenges involved in designing effective performance-based funding policies for university research. These include the need to continually adjust the output indicators in order to address the complexities of academic research, the high costs of monitoring university research performance externally, and the already noted difficulties of controlling cross-subsidies of research by teaching in a complex organization like the university, which produces the multiple outputs of teaching, research, and public service.

In addition, the global attention awarded to the RAE has distracted policy-makers and analysts from attending to alternative research assessment approaches. For example, the Netherlands has also implemented a system of peer-based research assessments for its universities. But unlike the RAE, it is not based primarily on research publications – it included from the beginning international peers – and it is not tied to university research funding. Instead, every six years, each university conducts an external peer review of its research programs involving internationally respected researchers (Jongbloed 2009, 2010). These reviews follow a Standard Evaluation Protocol (SEP) designed by the universities themselves in concert with national research organizations. The SEP evaluates the academic quality, scientific productivity, and long-term vitality of each research program, with implications for the management of research and the training of doctoral students. The research assessments use a variety of information sources, including on-site interviews, university self-reports, and bibliometric evidence. The evaluations are made public, but do not inform government funding.

Research suggests that these evaluations have had positive impacts on research productivity and research citations, as well as on improvements in each university's practices for managing research, that are similar to the much more highly publicized performance-funding system in the UK (Jongbloed 2009, 2010). And the more qualitative and collegial process implemented in the Netherlands has not produced the same degree of acrimony and divisiveness in the Dutch academic profession, nor has it contributed to a similar degree of research stratification among universities, as in the UK.[6] In addition, and in direct contrast to the RAE, the system in the Netherlands has experienced fewer changes in design, is likely less costly to run, and arguably provides more nuanced and useful information to each university as a means of improving its research activities. As such, the Dutch research evaluations will likely continue to make, over time, an effective contribution to improving the academic research enterprise.

In addition, the nature of information on academic research may be relevant to achieving the allocative efficiencies expected of policies promoting greater competition among universities. For example, recent econometric studies in the US suggest that university research funds allocated through competitive peer review by the National Science Foundation are associated with research publications and patents, but increases in university research support by industry are positively associated with research output only when competitively awarded federal research funds remained dominant (Adams and Clemmons 2009; Foltz et al. 2005). In sum, US corporate support for university research may not be efficiently allocated.

Similarly, our research (Dill and van Vught 2010) suggests that in the more globally competitive economy, many sub-national governments in federal systems such as Australia, Canada, Germany, and the US are increasingly investing in research at their local universities as a means of stimulating regional economic development. But analyses of state funding of university research in the US states of California and Pennsylvania (Geiger 2010; Zumeta 2010) suggest that local governments frequently lack the "honest broker" institutions with strong norms for scientifically based selection of both university research priorities and projects. Instead, they "scatter" their funds in response to the demands of local stakeholders for immediate job creation in business and/or permit users to be too closely involved in defining the nature of the research.

Finally, both of the US state cases suggest that the more political orientation of sub-national governments may lessen incentives to conduct truly objective and independent evaluations of the effectiveness of regional knowledge transfer policies and university research investments. Therefore, as countries seek to encourage more diverse sources of financial support for publicly funded universities, national policies that clearly identify, through rigorous peer review, centres of excellence in research may provide valuable information (a market signal, if you will) that could help lead to more socially beneficial investments in academic research by sub-national governments, corporations, and other research patrons.

A final example of national higher education policies being influenced by the new institutional economics is the attempt to create innovative marketable goods by the reallocation of intellectual property rights. The much mimicked Bayh-Dole legislation in the US was motivated by a desire to speed knowledge to market. Therefore, the rights to patent and license government-funded academic research were reallocated to universities through new laws intended to increase university incentives for technology transfer. This policy was never expected to create a major new source of funding for higher education, but the adoption of similar policies in other countries has motivated many universities around the world to create technology transfer offices as a means of "cashing in" on their research outcomes.

Our analysis suggests that the majority of universities in the OECD countries (Dill and van Vught 2010) are at best breaking even, and many are suffering net losses, from their investments in technology transfer offices and affiliated activities. While many universities hope that their technology transfer investments will produce significant revenues over time, the institutions that substantially benefit from patenting and licensing are the established, world-class research universities. Even in these institutions, there tends to be a natural limit to the amount of revenue earned from technology transfer because patents and licences are influential on innovation and profits in a relatively small number of industries and technical fields, biotechnology being the best-known example (Cohen, Nelson, and Walsh 2002).

One unintended impact of public policies emphasizing intellectual property rights as a means of stimulating technology transfer is their possible negative influence upon the core processes of academic science (Geiger and Sá 2009). By increasing incentives for universities to patent and license their discoveries as a means of raising revenue, some theoretical results and research tools that have been publicly available to other scholars and researchers are now being restricted. This constriction of open science, what has been termed the "tragedy of the anticommons" (Heller and Eisenberg 1998), may in fact lessen the economically beneficial "spillovers" for society that have been a primary rationale for public support of basic academic research.

PUBLIC SERVICE

While the education and research missions have long been two expected roles of the university, the third, or public service, mission is now receiving greater emphasis in national higher education policies because of the assumed connection among university research, technical innovation, and economic development (Dill and van Vught 2010; Zomer and Benneworth 2011). The link between the university and economic development did not clearly emerge until the second half of the 19th century, when the insights of academic research were applied to the improvement of agriculture in a number of countries (Lundvall and Borrás 2004). Denmark's development of the Agricultural University in Copenhagen in 1856 and the Agricultural Research Station in 1883 disseminated effective farming practices throughout the country and facilitated the development of the successful Danish dairy industry. The *Morrill Act*, signed into law by President Abraham Lincoln in 1862, initiated the US federal policy supporting land-grant universities and agricultural extension stations and is frequently credited with the economic successes of US agriculture. The earliest science-based industry developed in late 19th-century Germany from university-based research (Murmann 2003). The increased financial support for organic chemistry at German universities by the federal and state governments, and the adoption of new laws protecting the patent rights of private businesses, were principal reasons why German industry led the world in the production of synthetic dyestuffs and organic chemical products until World War II.

A strong case can be made that "knowledge transfer" through university adult and continuing education, public access to the expertise of academic staff, and university cultural events in all subject fields including the humanities and social sciences provides measurable cultural, democratic, and economic benefits for society (Benneworth and Jongbloed 2010). But contemporary higher education policies have tended to place a "one size fits all" emphasis on technology transfer – the commercialization of university scientific knowledge by business. However, even if one focuses on the economic benefits of university research in the natural sciences and engineering, policies that emphasize the "hard" outputs of academic research may undercut effective economic development. Comparative research involving Finland, Japan, the UK, and the US (Lester 2007) suggests that the technology transfer processes favoured by many national higher education policies – i.e., patenting, licensing, and new business formation – were not the most significant university influence on economic development. While some "global" universities produce scientific artifacts that are transferable worldwide, effective technology transfer for most universities is a more local process and depends upon the nature of industrial development occurring in the regional economy.

Universities do contribute to the creation of new businesses, but much more commonly, they help to upgrade mature industries, support the diversification of existing businesses into new fields, and assist in the transplantation of industries. In these roles, traditional publications, the provision of skilled science and technology graduates for the regional economy, and technical problem-solving with local business and industry through consulting and contract research are much more significant channels for influencing technical innovation than patents and licences (Cohen, Nelson, and Walsh 2002; Agarwal and Henderson 2002). Universities also play a crucial role by providing a "public space" (Lester 2007) in which, through meetings, research conferences, and industrial liaison programs, local business practitioners can discuss in a non-collusive fashion the future direction of technologies, markets, and regional industrial development.

This contribution to regional development is potentially a role that all comprehensive and technical universities, not just world-class institutions, can perform. Again, a critical factor in designing effective national policies for regional development is a more nuanced understanding of the role that information plays in technology transfer. Most influential in local innovation are the "softer" knowledge-transfer processes such as publications, meetings, consultants, and the hiring of new PhD graduates, whose added expertise is a primary means of transferring academic knowledge to industry (Cohen, Nelson, and Walsh 2002).

Policies encouraging this type of local and regional focus would provide incentives for universities to focus less on their possibly wasteful investments in conventional technology transfer and more on developing a strategy for encouraging innovation in their region, as illustrated by policies adopted in the Canadian province of Ontario (Wolfe 2007) and by the national government in Finland (Nilsson 2006). Such policies would encourage universities to better understand the development and circumstances of local industry, their own research strengths, and the most appropriate channels for aligning their capabilities with the needs of the local economy (Lester 2007). The Finnish Centre of Expertise Programme offers one well-regarded national example of developing universities as nodal points in regional networks of innovation by helping them better integrate their research expertise with local industry and business along the lines suggested here (OECD 2007).

CONCLUSION

Over 40 years ago, when I successfully completed my doctoral degree, the president of the University of Michigan personally awarded me my doctoral hood. In the US, the folds of that hood contain a vestigial "pocket" symbolizing the role of market forces in the medieval university because that is where scholars were paid directly by their peripatetic students. Today, in contrast, despite the increasing marketization of contemporary higher education, there is little evidence that the public good would be better served by encouraging each student to assemble an academic program through individual choice of modules or courses in the way that she or he might shop for the best meat and vegetables for dinner. Instead, given the necessary uncertainty and complexity of academic knowledge, the most beneficial university education for students as well as for society consists of academic programs that have been designed by, and whose academic standards are assured through, the collective actions of knowledgeable university professors. In sum, the most effective institutional framework for assuring the public good in higher education still appears to be the collegial mechanisms by which members of the academic profession themselves monitor, socialize, and reinforce the values essential to effective university teaching, research, and public service.

In her Nobel Prize lecture, the collective action theorist Elinor Ostrom (2010) similarly argued that market forces and the rules of the state are not the most effective institutional arrangements for governing, managing, and providing complex public goods. Instead, she has attempted to identify design principles that permit individuals to voluntarily address collective action dilemmas. These basic principles include the self-organization of governance arrangements, the importance of face-to-face communication among peers for increasing trust, and the active collective monitoring of valid measures of performance. In my preceding analyses, I have tried to suggest – through contemporary examples such as the research doctoral rankings in the US, the academic audit process in Hong Kong, the research assessment process in the Netherlands, and the regional development initiative in Finland – how comparable principles might inform the design of public policies that will assist universities in improving the collegial processes necessary for assuring the public good in the new age of academic globalization.

NOTES

1. Revised version of a paper presented at the workshop "Policy Formation in Post-secondary Education: Issues and Prospects in Turbulent Times," Toronto, Canada, 16 March 2012.

2. There are a number of important methodological issues that would need to be addressed in such a policy (Dill and Soo 2005) – for example, assuring the validity and reliability of student performance information reported by institutions as well as the graduate outcomes reported in alumni surveys, addressing the limitations of the identified differential response rates by academic fields in student surveys, the fact that graduate salaries may reflect regional differences more than university differences, etc.

3. Policy-makers may understandably question whether external assessments that promote greater collegial discussion among academic staff about improving academic standards are of significant public benefit. But both laboratory and field research suggests that face-to-face communication in social dilemmas is the most effective means of producing substantial increases in needed co-operation and coordination over time (Ostrom and Walker 1997). Similarly, research on universities (Braxton and Bayer 1999) suggests that effective deterrence and detection of proscribed academic behaviour is more likely to occur in departments with frequent social contact. Departmental meetings about assuring program quality, information exchanges with respected peers from other departments about ways of improving educational activities, and face-to-face collegial performance reviews regarding the quality of teaching and student learning in an academic program appear to promote the social ties necessary for the more effective observation, communication, and enforcement of academic standards (Dill and Beerkens 2010).

4. The issue of evaluating academic subjects as part of university academic audits has been a particularly contentious issue in the UK, but the failure to do so undermines the effectiveness of the external audits. Logically, the only valid means of assessing the effectiveness of teaching or instruction is to evaluate its impact upon student learning. Similarly, the only valid means of evaluating the effectiveness of a university's processes for assuring academic standards is to investigate their impact upon and the responses by academic subjects or programs. This is the approach taken in the academic audit process in Hong Kong.

5. Note that for an individual member of the academic staff to invest time and effort in collective actions to improve student learning, he or she needs to make a rational calculation of the benefits of such a decision. However, in many universities, information on the summative learning produced by academic programs is of questionable validity and reliability or is not available. This "second order" collective action dilemma makes improving the collegial processes for assuring academic standards within universities especially challenging (Dill 2007). Therefore, external evaluations of the validity and reliability of university assessments of student learning, as well as of the active use of this information in the collegial processes governing the quality of academic programs, could provide a valuable incentive for institutional assurance and improvement of academic standards.

6. However, an important difference between the Netherlands and the UK is that the former has also retained a binary system of higher education featuring polytechnic institutions, which do not receive funding for basic research or research doctoral education. This polytechnic system has absorbed a substantial amount of the recent growth in higher education enrolments in the Netherlands. The maintenance of this binary line has arguably also helped sustain institutional differentiation in the overall Dutch system, providing incentives for the polytechnics to be more efficient and more fully focused on their educational mission and having less need for research stratification in the university sector. In contrast, the elimination of the binary line in the UK and Australia has increased incentives for the above-noted costly academic "arms race" for research prestige among all of the existing and newly named universities, and this has likely contributed to cost inflation and less emphasis on effective teaching and learning in the university sector. This issue of the appropriate design of a higher education system and its implications for university efficiency has also been raised in Canada (Skolnik 2005).

REFERENCES

Adams, J.D., and J.R. Clemmons. 2009. "The Growing Allocative Inefficiency of the U.S. Higher Education Sector." In *Science and Engineering Careers in the United States: An Analysis of Markets and Employment*, ed. R.B. Freeman and D.L. Goroff, 349–382. Chicago: University of Chicago Press.

Agarwal, A., and R. Henderson. 2002. "Putting Patents in Context: Exploring Knowledge Transfer from MIT." *Management Science* 48 (1):44–60.

Aghion, P. 2006. "A Primer on Innovation and Growth." *Bruegel Policy Brief* 6:1–8.

Arum, R., and J. Roksa. 2011. *Academically Adrift: Limited Learning on College Campuses*. Chicago: University of Chicago Press.

Barnett, R. 2011. "The Marketised University: Defending the Indefensible." In *The Marketisation of Higher Education and the Student as Consumer*, ed. M. Molesworth, R. Scullion, and E. Nixon, 39–51. London: Routledge.

Barzelay, M. 2001. *The New Public Management: Improving Research and Policy Dialogue*. Berkeley: University of California Press.

Beach, C.M., R.W. Boadway, and R.M. McInnis. 2005. *Higher Education in Canada*. Queen's Policy Studies Series. Montreal & Kingston: McGill-Queen's University Press / John Deutsch Institute for the Study of Economic Policy.

Becker, Gary. 1994. *Human Capital: A Theoretical and Empirical Analysis with Special Reference to Education*. Chicago: University of Chicago Press.

Beerkens, M. 2009. "Policy Environment and Research Concentration: Evidence from Australia." In *The Research Mission of the University: Policy Reforms and Institutional Response*, ed. P. Clancy and D.D. Dill, 79–94. Rotterdam: Sense Publishers.

Beerkens, M., and D.D. Dill. 2010. "The CHE University Ranking in Germany." In *Public Policy for Academic Quality: Analyses of Innovative Policy Instruments*, ed. D.D. Dill and M. Beerkens, 65–86. Dordrecht, The Netherlands: Springer.

Benneworth, P., and B.W. Jongbloed. 2010. "Who Matters to Universities? A Stakeholder Perspective on Humanities, Arts and Social Sciences Valorization." *Higher Education* 59 (5):567–588.

Blackmur, D. 2008. "Quis custodiet ipsos custodes? The Review of the Australian Universities Quality Agency." *Quality in Higher Education* 14 (3):249–264.

Braxton, J.M., and A.E. Bayer. 1999. *Faculty Misconduct in Collegiate Teaching.* Baltimore: Johns Hopkins University Press.

Brown, R. 2010. *Higher Education and the Market.* London: Routledge.

Calhoun, C. 2006. "The University and the Public Good." *Thesis Eleven* 84 (1):7–43.

Cohen, W.M., R.R. Nelson, and J.P. Walsh. 2002. "Links and Impacts: The Influence of Public Research on Industrial R&D." *Management Science* 48 (1):1–23.

Crespi, G., and A. Geuna. 2004. *The Productivity of Science.* Report prepared for the Office of Science and Technology, Department of Trade and Industry. Science and Technology Policy Research Unit, University of Sussex. At http://akgul.bilkent.edu.tr/inovasyon/crespiost2.pdf (accessed 4 July 2013).

Dill, D.D. 2007. "Are Public Research Universities Effective Communities of Learning? The Collective Action Dilemma of Assuring Academic Standards." In *Future of the American Public Research University*, ed. R.L. Geiger, C.L. Colbeck, R.L. Williams, and C.K. Anderson, 187–203. Rotterdam: Sense Publishers.

—. 2009. "Convergence and Diversity: The Role and Influence of University Rankings." In *University Rankings, Diversity, and the New Landscape of Higher Education*, ed. B.M. Kehm and B. Stensaker, 99–118. Rotterdam: Sense Publishers.

—. 2011. "Governing Quality." In *A Handbook on Globalization and Higher Education*, ed. R. King, S. Marginson, and R. Naidoo, 438–453. Cheltenham, UK: Edward Elgar.

Dill, D.D., and M. Beerkens. 2010. *Public Policy for Academic Quality: Analyses of Innovative Policy Instruments.* Dordrecht, The Netherlands: Springer.

Dill, D.D., and M. Soo. 2005. "Academic Quality, League Tables, and Public Policy: A Cross-National Analysis of University Ranking Systems." *Higher Education* 49 (4):495–533.

Dill, D.D., and F.A. van Vught. 2010. *National Innovation and the Academic Research Enterprise: Public Policy in Global Perspective.* Baltimore: Johns Hopkins University Press.

El-Khawas, E. 2010. "The Teacher Education Accreditation Council (TEAC) in the USA." In *Public Policy for Academic Quality: Analyses of Innovative Policy Instruments*, ed. D.D. Dill and M. Beerkens, 37–54. Dordrecht, The Netherlands: Springer.

Foltz, J.D., B.L. Barham, J.-P. Chavas, and K. Kim. 2005. "Efficiency and Technological Change at U.S. Research Universities." Agricultural and Applied Economics Staff Paper Series No. 486. Madison, WI: University of Wisconsin–Madison, Department of Agricultural and Applied Economics.

Geiger, R.L. 2010. "State Policies for Science and Technology: The Commonwealth of Pennsylvania." In *National Innovation and the Academic Research Enterprise: Public Policy in International Perspective*, ed. D.D. Dill and F.A. van Vught, 438–479. Baltimore: Johns Hopkins University Press.

Geiger, R.L., and C.M. Sá. 2009. "Technology Transfer Offices and the Commercialization of University Research in the United States." In *The Research Mission of the University: Policy Reforms and Institutional Response*, ed. P. Clancy and D.D. Dill, 177–196. Rotterdam: Sense Publishers.

Harvey, L. 2010. "The Accreditation and Quality Processes of the General Medical Council in the UK." In *Public Policy for Academic Quality: Analyses of Innovative Policy Instruments*, ed. D.D. Dill and M. Beerkens, 249–274. Dordrecht, The Netherlands: Springer.

Hazelkorn, E. 2011. *Rankings and the Reshaping of Higher Education: The Battle for World-Class Excellence.* New York: Palgrave Macmillan.

Heller, M.A., and R.S. Eisenberg. 1998. "Can Patents Deter Innovation? The Anticommons in Biomedical Research." *Science* 280 (5364):698–701.

Henkel, M., and M. Kogan. 2010. "National Innovation & the Academic Research Enterprise: The UK Case." In *National Innovation and the Academic Research Enterprise: Public Policy in International Perspective,* ed. D.D. Dill and F.A. van Vught, 337–386. Baltimore: Johns Hopkins University Press.

Hicks, D. 2008. "Evolving Regimes of Multi-university Research Evaluation." School of Public Policy Working Papers #27. Georgia Institute of Technology. At http://smartech.gatech.edu/bitstream/handle/1853/23496/wp27.pdf?sequence=1 (accessed 4 July 2013).

Jongbloed, B. 2009. "Steering the Dutch Academic Research Enterprise: Universities' Responses to Project Funding and Performance Monitoring." In *The Research Mission of the University: Policy Reforms and Institutional Response,* ed. P. Clancy and D.D. Dill, 95–131. Rotterdam: Sense Publishers.

—. 2010. "The Netherlands." In *National Innovation and the Academic Research Enterprise: Public Policy in Global Perspective,* ed. D.D. Dill and F.A. van Vught, 286–336. Baltimore: Johns Hopkins University Press.

Kottmann, A. 2011. "Reform of Doctoral Training in Europe: A Silent Revolution?" In *Reform of Higher Education in Europe,* ed. J. Enders, H.F. de Boer, and D.F. Westerheijden, 29–43. Rotterdam: Sense Publishers.

Laffont, J., and J. Tirole. 1991. "The Politics of Government Decision Making: A Theory of Regulatory Capture." *Quarterly Journal of Economics* 106 (4):1089–1127.

Lester, R.K. 2007. "Universities, Innovation, and the Competitiveness of Local Economies: An Overview." In *Innovation, Universities, and the Competitiveness of Regions,* ed. R.K. Lester and M. Sotarauta, 9–30. Helsinki: Tekes.

Lundvall, B.-Å., and S. Borrás. 2004. "Science, Technology, and Innovation Policy." In *Oxford Handbook of Innovation,* ed. J. Fagerberg, D.C. Mowery, and R.R. Nelson, 599–631. Oxford: Oxford University Press.

Marginson, S. 2007. *Prospects of Higher Education: Globalization, Market Competition, Public Goods and the Future of the University.* Rotterdam: Sense Publishers.

Massy, W.F. 2010. "Academic Quality Audit as Applied in Hong Kong." In *Public Policy for Academic Quality: Analyses of Innovative Policy Instruments,* ed. D.D. Dill and M. Beerkens, 203–225. Dordrecht, The Netherlands: Springer.

McMahon, W.W. 2009. *Higher Learning, Greater Good: The Private and Social Benefits of Higher Education.* Baltimore: Johns Hopkins University Press.

Molesworth, M., R. Scullion, and E. Nixon. 2010. *The Marketisation of Higher Education and the Student as Consumer.* London: Routledge.

Murmann, P. 2003. *Knowledge and Competitive Advantage: The Coevolution of Firms, Technologies, and National Institutions.* Cambridge: Cambridge University Press.

Nilsson, J.-E. 2006. *The Role of Universities in Regional Innovation Systems: A Nordic Perspective.* Copenhagen: Copenhagen Business School.

OECD. 2007. *Higher Education and Regions: Globally Competitive, Locally Engaged.* Paris: OECD.

Ostrom, E. 2010. "Beyond Markets and States: Polycentric Governance of Complex Economic Systems." *American Economic Review* 100 (3):641–672.

Ostrom, E., and J. Walker. 1997. "Neither Markets nor States: Linking Transformation Processes in Collective Action Arenas." In *Perspectives on Public Choice: A Handbook,* ed. D.C. Mueller, 35–72. Cambridge: Cambridge University Press.

Pascarella, E.T., and P.T. Terenzeni. 2005. *A Third Decade of Research*. Vol. 2 of *How College Affects Students*. San Francisco: Jossey-Bass.

Powell, W.W., and E.S. Clemens. 1998. Introduction to *Private Action and the Public Good*, ed. W.W. Powell and E.S. Clemens. New Haven, CT: Yale University Press.

Prados, J.W., G.D. Peterson, and L.R. Lattuca. 2005. "Quality Assurance of Engineering Education through Accreditation: The Impact of Engineering Criteria 2000 and Its Global Influence." *Journal of Engineering Education* 94 (1):165–184.

Romer, P.M. 2000. "Should the Government Subsidize Supply or Demand in the Market for Scientists and Engineers?" In *Innovation Policy and the Economy*, ed. A.B. Jaffe, J. Lerner, and S. Stern. Chicago: University of Chicago Press.

Santiago, P., K. Tremblay, E. Basri, and E. Arnal. 2008. *Special Features: Governance, Funding, Quality*. Vol. 1 of *Tertiary Education for the Knowledge Society*. Paris: OECD.

Scott, G., I. Ball, and T. Dale. 1997. "New Zealand's Public Sector Management Reform: Implications for the United States." *Journal of Public Policy Analysis and Management* 16 (3):357–381.

Skolnik, M.L. 2005. "The Case for Giving Greater Attention to Structure in Higher Education Policy-Making." In *Higher Education in Canada*, ed. C.M. Beach, R.W. Boadway, and R.M. McInnis, 53–75. Queen's Policy Studies Series. Montreal & Kingston: McGill-Queen's University Press / John Deutsch Institute for the Study of Economic Policy.

Volkwein, J., L.R. Lattuca, B.J. Harper, and R.J. Domingo. 2007. "Professional Accreditation on Student Experiences and Learning Outcomes." *Research in Higher Education* 48 (2):251–282.

Weimer, D.L., and A.R. Vining. 1996. "Economics." In *The State of Public Management*, ed. D.F. Kettl and H.B. Milward, 92–117. Baltimore: Johns Hopkins University Press.

Wolfe, D.A. 2007. "The Role of Higher Education and New Forms of Governance in Economic Development: The Case of Ontario." In *How Universities Promote Economic Growth*, ed. S. Yusuf and K. Nabeshima, 119–138. Washington: World Bank.

Zomer, A., and P. Benneworth. 2011. "Rise of the University's Third Mission." In *Reform of Higher Education in Europe*, ed. J. Enders, H.F. de Boer, and D.F. Westerheijden, 81–101. Rotterdam: Sense Publishers.

Zumeta, W. 2010. "The Public Interest and State Policies Affecting Academic Research in California." In *National Innovation and the Academic Research Enterprise: Public Policy in International Perspective*, ed. D.D. Dill and F.A. van Vught, 480–526. Baltimore: Johns Hopkins University Press.

V

PUBLIC POLICY
AND HIGHER
EDUCATION:
INTERNATIONAL
PERSPECTIVES

CHAPTER 14

OSCILLATIONS AND PERSISTENCE IN CHINESE HIGHER EDUCATION POLICY: A PATH DEPENDENCE ANALYSIS

QIANG ZHA AND FENGQIAO YAN

INTRODUCTION

It is widely anticipated that China will catch up to the United States around 2040 in the aggregate size of its gross domestic product, if other things stay on their present track. Such a goal will naturally require a strong educational system – in particular, a strong higher education system – given today's increasingly knowledge-based economy. Partly for this reason, China has managed to expand its higher education system into the world's largest in the past decade, and it is determined to push for world-class standing in the next decade. This ambition is clearly indicated in the *National Outline for Medium- and Long-Term Educational Reform and Development (2010–2020)* (State Council of China 2010), or the 2020 Blueprint, which was officially unveiled on 29 July 2010. With respect to higher education, a top priority in the document is summarized as increasing "the global competitiveness of higher education" by nurturing "world-leading innovative talents" and creating "internationally renowned flagship disciplines" and "world-class universities" (State Council of China 2010, Ch. 7, n.p.).

On the other hand, Chinese higher education appears to be facing a variety of constraints – if not crises – such as deterioration in both quality and equity, academic corruption, and cynicism among scholars. All of these culminate in the famous question asked by Qian Xuesen,[1] why have Chinese universities failed to nurture innovative minds? If a higher

Making Policy in Turbulent Times: Challenges and Prospects for Higher Education, ed. P. Axelrod, R.D. Trilokekar, T. Shanahan, and R. Wellen. Kingston: School of Policy Studies, Queen's University.

education system fails to do this, it can hardly claim success on any count. How can we understand the huge gulf between China's ambition to create a university system of world-class standing and this complicated reality? This chapter employs path dependence and social embeddedness frameworks as theoretical lenses through which to scrutinize how the 2020 Blueprint was formed and analyze its linkage to other major strategic plans since the late 1970s. The chapter will attempt to shed light on how Chinese higher education has evolved into its current form and how it is going to grow over the next decade.

OVERVIEW OF CHINESE HIGHER EDUCATION EVOLUTION AND POLICIES SINCE THE LATE 1970s

A sketch of Chinese higher education evolution and policy changes since the late 1970s shows the trajectory of a pendulum, swinging between a focus on growth on the one hand and on the improvement of the system on the other, while throughout this process, Chinese higher education has been steadily expanding. This oscillating trajectory is clearly depicted in Figure 1 by the roughly symmetrical variations in the line, which capture the cumulative changes in Chinese higher education enrolment from 1977 to 2010.

FIGURE 1
Cumulative changes in Chinese higher education enrolment, 1977–2010*

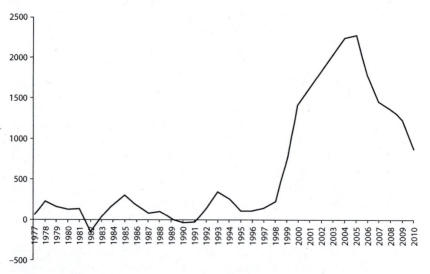

*The figure for each year represents the change in enrolment from the previous year (per 1,000 students).

Source: Authors' compilation from data collected from the *China Education Statistics Yearbook*.

With China's adoption of an economic reform policy in the late 1970s, human capital became vital. The Chinese higher education system, which had been shaped by rigid macro planning in the 1950s and 1960s, failed to prepare the kind of labour force that could support a rapidly growing socialist market economy. In the higher education sector, brisk growth took place soon after China's shift toward a market economy. The number of institutions jumped from 404 in 1977 to 1,016 in 1985, and enrolments from 0.63 million to 1.70 million, both almost tripling over this period.

The *Decision on the Reform of the Education System* (Central Committee of the CCP 1985), or 1985 Decision, aimed to infuse dynamism into the system, optimize its capacity, and grant institutions some independent decision-making power – in particular, with respect to their plans for re-cruiting new students. It also aimed to improve the relevance of curricular offerings to the needs of an emerging market economy. The document thus reflected the policy guideline for higher education development over this period. The main rationale for reforming the Chinese system was

> to change the management system of excessive government control of the institutions of higher education; expand decision-making in the institutions under the guidance of unified education policies and plans of the state; strengthen the connection of the institutions of higher education with production organizations, scientific research organizations, and other social establishments; and enable the institutions of higher education to take the initiative and ability to meet the needs of economic and social development. (Central Committee of the CCP 1985, n.p.)

In short, the goal was to expand Chinese higher education by con-necting the system to the market and relaxing government control. Expansion in the 1980s increased the aggregate size of Chinese higher education, resulting in an annual increase of 9.2 percent in the student population and 6.1 percent in the number of institutions between 1978 and 1988.

After 1986, enrolments continued to grow, from 1.70 million in 1985 to 2.54 million in 1993, but between 1986 and 1995, the number of insti-tutions remained stable because the emphasis shifted from setting up new institutions to adjusting the structure of existing institutions and improving them. Growth in enrolments was now achieved by tapping into existing resources and extending existing institutions. As a result, higher education enrolments saw a steady growth from the mid-1980s to the early 1990s and, at some point, seemed to exceed actual needs (Li 1999).

During the period of rapid expansion up to 1985, serious tensions had arisen – between growth and quality control and between expansion and cost-effectiveness – placing a heavy financial burden on the Chinese government. Thus, after 1992, system expansion was replaced by system adjustment and consolidation. The reform of China's higher education system in the 1990s was prompted by the *Outline for Educational Reform and Development in China* (Central Committee of the CCP and State Council 1993), or 1993 Outline, which emphasized economies of scale and structural rationalization of the system: "In the 1990s, higher education must ... actively explore a new path of development, in order to achieve bigger growth in size, better rationalization in structure, and a visible improvement in quality and efficiency" (n.p.). With structural rationalization and quality and efficiency consolidation as the focus of concern, the major schemes and measures for the system and its institutions were set out as joint construction, jurisdiction transference, institutional co-operation, and institutional amalgamation (Yan 2000; Zha 2006).

"Joint construction" refers to a central-local collaboration in running institutions that had previously been managed solely by the central government, while "jurisdiction transference" signifies a complete change from central to provincial government ownership. By 2002, out of the original total of 367 regular higher education institutions administered by ministries of the central government, nearly 250 had been transferred to local jurisdiction (Zha 2006). If "joint construction" and "jurisdiction transference" were meant to mobilize local resources and ease the financial burden on the central government, "institutional co-operation" and "institutional amalgamation" aimed to optimize resource use at the institutional level for the purpose of improving the quality of education provided.

"Institutional co-operation" helps coordinate the advantages that each institution can offer and allows intersecting disciplines to improve educational quality. Mergers among higher education institutions were intended to consolidate small institutions and achieve economies of scale. Mergers were also seen as a shortcut to producing large, comprehensive, and academically prestigious universities. By 2002, for example, 597 higher education institutions had been involved in mergers, resulting in 267 new institutions (Zha 2006) that were larger in size and more comprehensive in their program offerings. Thus, most of the 1990s witnessed a modest enrolment growth, at a reasonable pace of 5.6 percent per annum, while between 1989 and 1998, the number of institutions actually declined, from 1,075 to 1,022, because the focus was placed on absorbing the rapid expansion since the late 1970s and on consolidating the system.

A notable outcome of the strengthening effort was the launch in the 1990s of two elite university schemes – Project 21/1 and Project 98/5. Project 21/1 was initiated by the 1993 Outline, which expressed the state's intention to identify and give special financial support to 100 top universities and elevate them to "world standards" in the 21st century. Following this initiative, top Chinese leaders further announced in May 1998, at the centennial celebration of the prestigious Peking University, that our nation needs to have a few first-class universities at the world's advanced level, for the sake of China's modernization campaign. Such universities should be the cradle of nurturing and bringing about creative talent of high quality; should be the frontier of exploring the unknown world, pursuing the truth of objectivity, and generating scientific evidence for resolving the critical issues confronting our humankind; should be an important force for advancing knowledge, driving and turning scientific research results into real productive forces. (Jiang 1998, n.p.)

Shortly after this announcement, the *Program of Educational Revitalization for the 21st Century* (Ministry of Education of China 1998), or 1998 Action Plan, was released, documenting China's ambition of creating world-class universities. This is commonly regarded as the elitist part of Project 21/1, although it was otherwise coded by the date of the initial announcement as Project 98/5.

In the late 1990s, following the period of consolidation described above, the Chinese government pushed for another, much greater, expansion of higher education. This was primarily based on economic considerations (Zha 2011a). The 1998 Action Plan indicated this new goal by stating its intention to raise China's higher education participation rate considerably, to 11 percent by 2000 from approximately 9 percent in 1998. One year later, the 1999 *Decision on Deepening Educational Reform and Pressing Ahead with Quality Education in an All-Round Way* (State Council of China 1999), or 1999 Decision, set a further goal of 15 percent for 2010.

With these goals in place, the year 1999 saw an abrupt jump in new enrolments, with 1.59 million new students being registered – up from 1.08 million in 1998 – representing an annual increase of 47.2 percent. As the expansion picked up speed, the 15 percent goal was reset for 2005 in the *Tenth Five-Year Plan for Educational Development* (Ministry of Education of China 2002), and it was actually met in 2002. This round of rapid expansion continued until 2005, when higher education enrolment of all kinds reached 23 million. This was more than six times the total enrolment of 3.6 million in 1998. After 2005, enrolments continued to rise, to 31 million in 2010, but at a relatively slower pace.

There is no doubt that this round of expansion is unprecedented. The regular enrolment in Chinese higher education (not including enrolment in adult and further education programs or institutions) grew at an annual rate of 24.3 percent between 1998 and 2005 and 7.4 percent from 2005 to 2010. When the dust of such a significant expansion settled, the Chinese higher education system had become incredibly massive and steeply hierarchical, with Project 98/5 universities sitting on the pinnacle, followed by Project 21/1 universities, local universities, higher vocational colleges, and private institutions. This was the context in which the issues of quality and equity came to the fore.

It is against this backdrop that the 2020 Blueprint was unveiled. This document announced China's ambition to transform itself into a nation possessing "globally competitive human resources" from its status at the time, which was defined as merely "abundant human resources" (State Council of China 2010, n.p.). Driven by this ambition, the document's section on higher education emphasizes that "higher education performs the important task of cultivating high-calibre professionals, developing science, technology and culture.... Raising quality is at the heart of this task, and a basic requirement of the effort of building the nation into a power to be reckoned with in the global higher education landscape (Ch. 7, Clause 18)." It paints a brilliant picture for 2020, when "quite a few world-famous universities with original features shall come to the fore; some of them shall have reached or approached the level of world-class universities" (Ch. 7, Clause 18).

While continuing this expansion plan, which aims to absorb 40 percent of the appropriate age cohort by 2020 from the current figure of some 25 percent, this policy document features an explicit effort to nurture innovative minds among students. It calls for further reforms, with new aspects that stress and meet individual needs in learning. Along parallel lines, the promotion of educational equity is now one of the guiding principles for China's educational development. This notion had never appeared in the important policy papers analyzed above – namely, the 1993 Outline, the 1998 Action Plan, and the 1999 Decision. This suggests that equity issues have emerged, amid the massification and diversification of the Chinese system, over the past decade so that they now must be more fully addressed. In general, the 2020 Blueprint seems to be tilting to the side of consolidation again, this time stressing both quality and equity issues in the system.

It appears that the trajectory of policy changes in Chinese higher education over the past three decades follows regular oscillations between emphasizing speed of growth and consolidation of the extended system, between the efficiency and effectiveness of the system, and, more recently, between efficiency and equity. In this context, Qian Xuesen's question highlights the mounting tension between pursuing efficiency and fulfilling human potential in Chinese higher education. On this theme, Gidley et al. (2010, 124) suggest that accessibility is only the first step in fulfilling social inclusion in higher education, and they propose that "access, participation and success are ordered according to a spectrum of ideologies – neoliberalism, social justice and human potential, respectively – by way of a nested structure with human potential ideology offering the most embracing perspective."

The authors' notion is better illustrated by Figure 2, which clarifies how these different ideologies frame the issues surrounding access, participation, and success in higher education. Such a perspective advocates maximizing the potential of each human being and supporting them to "go well beyond their role in the political economy of a nation" (Gidley et al. 2010, 136). They argue that, first and foremost, the notion of success in higher education should be "uncoupled from its default neoliberal connections with global competitiveness, and reconsidered in the light of more collaborative and normative ideologies such as those grounded in social justice and human potential" (142).

FIGURE 2
Spectrum of ideologies underlying access, participation, and success in higher education

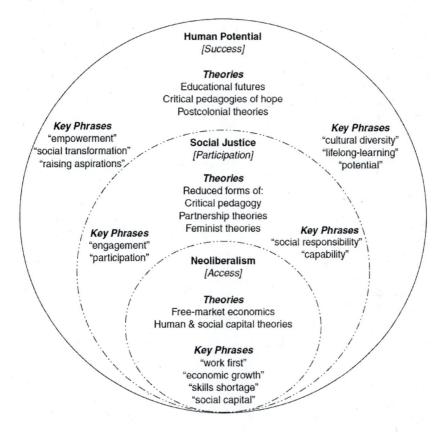

Source: Gidley et al. (2010, 131). Used with permission.

In light of this framework, we might claim that China's shift to mass higher education is now moving between the inner and the intermediate circles in the diagram, or moving from a demand for access to higher education to quality of, and then to equality in, the higher education experience. Should China's higher education move to the outer circle, it seems that Qian Xuesen's question would be resolved. Is such a move expected?

In the remainder of this chapter, we will argue that the policy oscillations between speed and consolidation, or between efficiency and improvement, can be easily observed and captured on the surface. There is a deeper layer of the story, however, and that is the policy oscillations between exercising and relaxing political control over the higher education system and its institutions, and between stressing the political agenda and the educational function of the system. This deeper layer could play a bigger role in determining the path that Chinese higher education follows in the next decade and whether or not the system will truly assist in optimizing human potential.

THE ANALYTICAL FRAMEWORK

We believe that the perspective of path dependence can provide a needed analytical lens for this analysis. Path dependence means that "what happened at an earlier point in time will affect the possible outcomes of a sequence of events occurring at a later point in time" (Sewell 1996, 262–263) or, to put it in the form of a loose assertion, that "history matters." The central claim of this perspective is that "we cannot understand the significance of a particular social variable without understanding 'how it got there' – the path it took" (Pierson 2000, 252). The concept of path dependence spans four related causes: increasing returns, self-reinforcement, positive feedback, and lock-in. They are all linked but typify different forms of path dependence (Page 2006).

Increasing returns have the effect that "the more a choice is made or an action is taken, the greater its benefits" (Page 2006, 88). In the increasing returns process, "the probability of further steps along the same path increases with each move down the path" (Pierson 2000, 252). Self-reinforcement means that a choice or an action brings with it the forces or complementary institutions that tend to sustain that move. Positive feedback, on an action or a choice, produces positive externalities when the same choice or action is followed by more people. Some treat the processes of increasing returns, self-reinforcement, and positive feedback as more or less the same. Finally, lock-in signals that one particular choice or action becomes better than any other when it is favoured by a sufficient number of people who have made that choice or action (Page 2006).

In general, the concept of path dependence is relevant and applicable to policy analysis in Chinese higher education, given the fact that the entire process of China's reform (certainly including reform in the higher education realm) is guided by the wisdom of "crossing the river by touching the stones." Decision-making under uncertainty often leads to path dependence, as Page (2006) notes.

Departing from the four types of path dependence outlined above, Page argues further for the notion of path-dependent equilibrium. He asserts that the "future is not deterministic, but stochastic and biased toward early decisions" (Page 2006, 91). "History dependence need not imply deterministic dependence. It need only imply a shift in the probabilities of outcomes as a function of the past" (92). His framework enables us to identify two ways of denoting that "history matters": outcome-dependence vs. equilibrium-dependence. The former maintains that history matters in determining the outcome at a later time, and the latter holds that history matters for the sake of limiting the long-run distribution over outcomes – i.e., the "convergence of the long-run distribution of outcomes" or a kind of balancing process (92). Arthur (1994) notes that "any major changes will be offset by the very reactions they generate" and that "equilibrium marks the 'best' outcome possible under the circumstance" (1). By the same token, Page (2006) claims "equilibrium dependence implies outcome dependence" (92) and elaborates his points more fully in the following words:

> If this period's outcome depends on the past, that does not imply that the long-run equilibrium does. When scholars refer to history mattering, they typically do not mean that it matters only for singular events. They mean that the course of the future has changed. And yet, evidence that what happened in one period depended on what happened earlier is not sufficient to make such claims. A system can exhibit outcome path dependence yet still have a unique equilibrium, as I show in the Balancing Process. (91)

Path dependence perspective treats history as creating externalities that would influence how people make decisions later or in the future (Page 2006; Bednar and Page 2007). Similarly, social embeddedness, a related sociological concept, sees any system or organization as intertwined and interacting with its broader environment. Therefore, it cannot behave freely because it is constrained by the environment. Drawing on the social embeddedness perspective, some higher education theorists interpret higher education as a subsystem, consisting of individual higher education organizations, embedded in a supra-system or an environment that contains the social, political, and economic conditions. The subsystem of higher education as well as higher education organizations operate in such an environment and are inevitably limited by those conditions.

This has the following implications: first, the goal of higher education is often not determined by itself, but is conditioned as part of the national strategy; second, higher education organizations receive inputs from and produce outputs for their environment, in the form of resources, graduates, research, etc. and thus depend for survival on taking account of their environment in order to secure favourable conditions for their own operations (van Vught 1996).

In this sense, the social embeddedness perspective is complementary to the path dependence view in the way that it takes account of
present externalities. Again, this is pertinent to the Chinese context,
where governmental factors dominate the operating environment for
higher education and are the principal driver of changes in the sector.
Notably, all of the major reform programs in Chinese higher education
have been triggered by state policies. For the most part, those major
reform programs embody the attempts to make adjustments internally,
within the Chinese system, and improve its adaptability to the external
environment, and it is often the tension between these two aspects of
reform that is responsible for the pendulum-like movement of Chinese
higher education policy.

DISCUSSION AND ANALYSIS

Growth, quality, and equity: the shifting stress driving a spiral development of Chinese higher education

The Chinese higher education policy changes since the late 1970s seem
to show a trajectory of constant oscillations among growth, speed, and
systemic consolidation and improvement. In a way, these oscillations
reflect the ideological struggle behind the scenes between various views
associated with elitism on the one hand and the massification of higher
education on the other. Employing the equilibrium-dependent perspective, this phenomenon could be conveniently interpreted as a convergence
in the distribution of policy changes over a long term. Put another way,
this phenomenon manifests a balancing process among policy choices.
On the one hand, the rapid expansion of Chinese higher education is required and driven by the human resource needs of an ever faster-growing
Chinese economy; on the other, it has often come at the expense of higher
education quality and, in a related sense, equality.

Expansion occurred mostly in the low-echelon institutions, while the
elite universities tended to be protected. However, this dramatic expansion did not see a proportionate increase in higher education funding.
Many institutions suffered a severe deficiency in teaching and learning
conditions, with the teacher-student ratio in many universities and colleges exceeding 1:20. These institutions, especially those located in the
less-developed regions, where alternative revenue sources are few, had
to borrow huge amounts from the banks in order to extend their facilities
and capacities and therefore went heavily into debt. They have subsequently struggled to repay these amounts.[2]

Both institutional stratification and regional disparities have affected
higher education equity and equality in China. As a result, the focus of
Chinese higher education policy moved from rapid growth to systemic
improvement to absorb the pressures of and repair the issues brought

on by the expansion, then back to fast growth to meet economic and social needs. This is evident in the succession of central themes for higher education revealed in the major policy papers reviewed earlier. The 1985 Decision demanded freeing up the dynamism within the higher education sector to optimize its capacities and achieve fast growth. By contrast, the 1993 Outline and the 1998 Action Plan stressed structural and quality consolidation in higher education and creating centres of excellence (i.e., such elite university schemes as projects 21/1 and 98/5). At the same time, they encouraged tapping into the existing resources and extending the existing institutions in a modest expansion. This new focus stayed firm until 1999, when the 1999 Decision called for another round and much faster expansion of higher education enrolment.

As a result of these policy changes, the Chinese higher education system has become very large in size and steeply stratified in structure. There is a widening gap among institutions at different tiers in the hierarchy and a concomitant difference in students' learning experience. Table 1 sets out the average difference in 2006 institutional revenue received by the various institutional clusters – namely, the Core Project 98/5 universities, the Other Project 98/5 universities, the Project 21/1 universities, the local universities, and the higher vocational colleges – in order of prestige and status.[3] These differences are highlighted in the striking ratio of 45:26:10:4:1. Notably, the research revenues of the combined Project 98/5 universities (37 on the 2006 list, now 39) were roughly four times as high as those of the 68 Project 21/1 universities (a prestigious group in itself) and the 588 local universities.

Arguably, the Chinese system now presents a steep pyramid, and this, in turn, brings equity concerns to the fore. Indeed, the Chinese approach has started to show its inner constraints – in particular, the downsides for social equity in terms of participation and consequently in students' lifetime opportunities. Research confirms that students from upper-socio-economic-status families tend to be favoured for access to more selective universities (Xie and Wang 2006). Given the enormously differentiated study experience, resulting from a widening gap in faculty qualifications, research facilities, and per-student spending between the selective and less selective intuitions, those students in the lower-echelon institutions will suffer from very limited mobility opportunity in the system and later in society at large. Such inequity may accompany them throughout their lifetimes. It is claimed that social mobility facilitated by higher education started to be increasingly difficult in the 1990s, and it has been particularly problematic since the late 1990s (Ding 2008).

In this context, the 2020 Blueprint ranks the promotion of educational equity as a top priority for China's educational development, even ahead of improving quality in education. It asserts that educational equity upholds social equity and that the government should take the major responsibility for advancing educational equity, while other societal sectors

TABLE 1
Differentiation in institutional revenue by source and cluster, 2006 (in millions of renminbi*)

Revenue source	Core Project 98/5 universities (n = 9)		Other Project 98/5 universities (n = 28)		Project 21/1 universities (n = 68)		Local universities (n = 588)		Higher vocational colleges (n = 712)	
	Amount	%	Amount	%	Amount	%	Amount	%	Amount	%
1. Appropriated revenue	9,017.20	49.4	16,289.60	50.5	15,292.00	49.2	47,614.90	43.1	12,341.60	38.3
1.1 Fiscal appropriations	8,370.90	45.9	15,087.80	46.7	13,513.30	43.5	43,516.40	39.4	11,009.50	34.1
1.1.1 Operating	4,776.60	26.2	10,620.50	32.9	10,769.40	34.7	38,031.30	34.4	9,771.40	30.3
1.1.2 Research	2,720.60	14.9	3,523.20	10.9	1,640.00	5.3	1,529.00	1.4	41.80	0.1
1.1.3 Special purposes	873.70	4.8	944.10	2.9	1,104.00	3.6	3,956.10	3.6	1,196.30	3.7
1.2 Infrastructure	590.20	3.2	1,201.80	3.7	1,758.70	5.7	3,535.70	3.2	958.40	3.0
1.3 Tax transfer	56.10	0.3	0.00	0.0	20.00	0.1	562.80	0.5	373.70	1.2
2. Unappropriated revenue	9,240.50	50.6	15,995.00	49.5	15,768.60	50.8	62,959.30	56.9	19,869.30	61.7
2.1 Operating income	6,690.00	36.6	12,936.30	40.1	12,540.00	40.4	53,939.60	48.8	18,300.10	56.8
2.1.1 Tuition and fees	2,610.30	14.3	6,819.00	21.1	8,393.00	27.0	41,850.10	37.9	16,151.50	50.1
2.1.2 Other operating income	4,079.60	22.3	6,117.30	19.0	4,147.00	13.4	12,089.50	10.9	2,148.70	6.7
2.2 Sales of products and services	186.00	1.0	413.10	1.3	560.20	1.8	11,843.40	1.1	100.90	0.3
2.3 Donations	649.20	3.6	268.10	0.8	177.00	0.6	794.40	0.7	126.70	0.4
2.4 Other sources	1,715.30	9.0	2,377.50	7.4	2,491.40	8.0	7,041.00	6.4	1,341.50	4.2
Total	18,257.70	100.0	32,284.60	100.0	31,060.60	100.0	110,574.20	100.0	32,210.90	100.0
Mean	2,028.6		1,153.0		456.8		188.1		45.2	

*In 2006, the nominal exchange rate between the US dollar and the Chinese renminbi was approximately 1:7.8 (http://en.wikipedia.org/wiki/List_of_Renminbi_exchange_rates).

Source: Zha (2011b, 758).

should put forth effort as well. As part of the goal of attaining equity in higher education, this policy document proposes giving greater resources to the universities and colleges located in China's less-developed central and western regions. This move, to a large extent, addresses the reality of Chinese higher education: 90 percent of institutions are now supported by local governments, and those located in the central and western regions suffer a severe deficiency of resources, in contrast with their counterparts in the affluent eastern region.

In addition, private higher education will be better supported than before. When conditions permit, private institutions will be allowed to offer advanced degree programs at the master's and doctoral levels and obtain government education and training contracts. Nevertheless, systemic differentiation is still seen in a positive light. Instead of flattening the existing hierarchy, the 2020 Blueprint exhorts higher education institutions to identify and strengthen their own niches. Eventually, they will be compelled to compete at different levels and in different areas. Strategically, the current policy seems to stress quality (or excellence) in the top tiers of the system and employability in the bottom tiers.

Judging from a policy perspective, Chinese higher education appears to be following a kind of spiral development, steered by the oscillating policies that have been described earlier. Now the 2020 Blueprint adjusts the focus again by calling for "upgrading the concepts of talent cultivation" and "innovating in the mode of talent cultivation" (State Council of China 2010, Ch. 11, Clause 31). Specifically, this policy document sketches scenes such as the following in Chinese education over the next decade: "We will foster the sense of diversity of talents, so that individuals' personal choices can be respected, individualized development encouraged, and talents groomed in more than one way" (Ch. 11, Clause 31). "We will advocate teaching to be heuristic, exploratory, discussion-based, and participatory and help students learn how to study. We will stimulate students' curiosity, develop their interest and pursuits, and foster a fine environment for independent thinking, exploration, and innovation" (Ch. 11, Clause 32).

The 2020 Blueprint states that for China to reach these goals, there must be reform of and improvement in the evaluation mechanisms for teaching and learning in an effort to explore the "diverse evaluation approaches that help promote student development, and encourage students to be optimistic, independent thinking and to pursue their interest rigorously" (State Council of China 2010, Ch. 11, Clause 33). For this reason alone, China would ultimately need to bring its higher education model and patterns up to contemporary standards. The document also calls for the separation of government power from school affairs and of school governance from school operations: to "build a modern school system in which schools are run according to law, under autonomous governance and democratic supervision, and with public participation, and to foster a new relationship among government, schools, and society" (Ch. 13, Clause 38).

In the higher education sphere, the document advocates implementing and expanding institutional autonomy and exploring effective ways of practising professorial rule in teaching, research, and university governance (State Council of China 2010, Ch. 13, Clauses 39, 40). With these goals and these statements in place, can we envision that Chinese higher education is now set on a course that will eventually lead to a real fulfillment of human potential? If so, it would be fortunate, but such an assumption may be a too easy answer to Qian Xuesen's question.

The enduring tension between political control and university autonomy and its impact on the future of Chinese higher education

The question of whether or not Chinese higher education is truly set on the right course is, to a large extent, dependent on the outcome of another policy oscillation, happening at a much deeper level, between tightening and relaxing political control over the Chinese system. There have always been two ideologies that have tended to steer higher education development in China: a political argument and a human capital one. Hayhoe (1989) argues that China has a tradition of regimenting knowledge for political order. She claims that "regimentation of curricular knowledge and its use for purposes of political control" took place in each of China's modern regimes (27–28).

Indeed, political control over higher education predominated throughout the 1950s and into the early 1980s, penetrating into and interfering with all aspects, from appointment of university leaders to curricular content and pedagogical methods, and even to evaluation and assessment of academic research methods and outcome (Chen 2011; Li 2011). When the 1985 Decision called for reducing "excessive government control of the institutions of higher education" (Central Committee of the CCP 1985, n.p.), it was observed that the Chinese leadership "remains ambivalent about the implications of this transformation for the political power structure" (Hayhoe 1989, 57). Rather, the Chinese leadership appeared to be "searching for curricular reforms that will serve economic modernization without pressing the issue of political democratization" (29).

Prompted by China's modernization drive, the human capital ideology has since the 1980s been a major force behind the expansion of Chinese higher education. Political control appears to be loosening, yet it is never gone, only appearing under different guises and forms or sometimes becoming more relaxed.[4] Typically, political and ideological programming has a firm position in the curriculum, and students have to devote a considerable amount of time to these courses. Ideologically, Chinese higher education is mandated to accomplish two things: to produce both the "successors for the socialist cause" and the "builders" of China's modernization drive (Ministry of Education of China 1999, Art. 4). Thus, the Chinese leadership simply cannot afford to completely loosen political control over higher education. The *Higher Education Law of China*, which took effect on 1 January 1999 and granted legal-person status to higher education institutions, legitimized such control.

> In developing socialist higher education, the State adheres to Marxism-Leninism, Mao Zedong Thought and Deng Xiaoping Theory as its guide. (Ministry of Education of China 1999, Art. 3)

> In higher education institutions run by the State, the system shall be applied under which the presidents take overall responsibility under the leadership of the primary committees of the Communist Party of China in higher education institutions. Such committees shall, in accordance with the Constitution of the Chinese Communist Party and relevant regulations, exercise unified leadership over the work of the institutions and support the presidents in exercising their functions and powers independently and responsibly. In exercising leadership, the committees shall chiefly perform the following duties: to adhere to the lines, principles and policies of the Chinese Communist Party, to keep to the socialist orientation in running the schools, to provide guidance to ideological and political work and moral education in the institutions, to discuss and decide on the internal structure and heads of departments of the institutions, reform, development and basic management systems of the institutions and other important matters, and to ensure fulfillment of all the tasks centring on the training of students. (Ministry of Education of China 1999, Art. 39)

Despite the fact that this law legally sanctions the kind of autonomy to which the higher education institutions are entitled in seven major domains,[5] it (and other education laws, regulations, and policy papers) never explicitly limits the capacity of the government – or the Chinese Communist Party (CCP) – to interfere in university affairs. Consequently, there is a friction or a paradox here: on the one hand, Chinese higher education institutions have been obtaining an increasing amount of decision-making power over the years for their own affairs; on the other hand, the Chinese government can tighten its control over the institutions whenever it believes it necessary. Now the 2020 Blueprint sends a message of building a modern university system in China, which centres on granting and indeed securing academic freedom and institutional autonomy for Chinese universities. Yet, at the same time, the Central Committee of the CCP amended and re-promulgated the *Mandate of CCP Primary Organizations in Regular Higher Education Institutions* (Central Committee of the CCP 2010) only two weeks after the proclamation of the 2020 Blueprint.

Compared with the earlier version of the Mandate (which was introduced in 1996), the new version features a tighter grip on personnel appointments and talent management (the latter term manifesting a new focus of the task) and such tasks as setting up a student work division at the university level, which oversees student affairs university-wide, and extending CCP organizations to the grassroots units and among students on campus. With respect to the guidelines for Chinese higher education, this document highlights nurturing "qualified builders and reliable successors for the socialist cause that carries Chinese characteristics" (Central Committee of the CCP 2010, Art. 2). Notably, the words "qualified" and "reliable" are new and create an interesting contrast with the relevant content in the 2020 Blueprint.

It seems that the timing of this revised Mandate was not entirely coincidental. Arguably, this phenomenon of perpetual political or governmental control constitutes the core element that restrains the emergence of truly independent modern universities and is responsible for academic corruption and cynicism on Chinese soil. Ironically, the government now often plays the role of watchdog over academic corruption and misconduct.

When related to the milestone reform policies outlined above, the evolutionary course of Chinese education is sometimes romanticized as covering three major phases that characterize different dominant ideologies – namely, political, economic, and human development (Cheng and Li 2011).

In the phase dominated by political ideology (ever since the CCP established its bases with schools in the revolutionary era up to the late 1970s or early 1980s), Chinese education and schools were treated as instruments for serving proletariat politics, stressing ideological cultivation of the young generation, who would carry the torch of the socialist cause. In short, they were driven by political needs. The Chinese education system in this phase featured a high level of centralization of governance and administration, with schools having absolutely no decision-making power and being closely affiliated to the government.

In the 1980s, China entered the educational phase steered by an economic ideology, when the economic function of education predominated and schools (in particular, higher education institutions) were required to directly serve socialist economic growth, as highlighted in the 1985 Decision. Universities were given some flexibility and freedom to bring market forces into play in the educational arena. Consequently, there emerged a tendency to overemphasize market factors and overstress efficiency in using resources, and this, in turn, has resulted in certain issues and problems – e.g., industrializing (or even commercializing) educational services and educational inequities.

Most recently, the 2020 Blueprint is meant to steer Chinese education toward moulding students' innovative minds and nurturing a healthy character. It demands that this task be placed above everything else and as the bottom line for education. As such, it signals a move to a new phase that upholds the ideology of developing human potential.

Employing the path dependence perspective, we speculate that this move, if it is happening at all, is not without challenges. The previous jump, from a politicized education model to one featuring economism, could take advantage of some common attributes shared by the two models – for instance, the doctrines of pragmatism and utilitarianism – while the current shift signals a fundamental step away from the historical path. This shift thus bears much greater difficulties and risks. In the face of likely uncertainties arising from this process, the Chinese government is also likely to be constrained by historical inertia and may easily slide back into the familiar approach of interfering in internal university affairs in order to bring things under control as quickly as possible. In fact, this appears to be happening right now. Furthermore, the mounting pressure to maintain and secure China's social stability might well create the kind of externalities that are in favour of tightening control over the higher education sector.[6]

CONCLUSIONS

Higher education as a system in China is essentially located within a supra-system consisting of social, political, and economic environments. This system is open in the sense that there is always an interaction with the environment, through which universities come to accept certain values and adapt to structures and processes judged to be important by the environment. While agents of change can arise from within, especially in the case of universities, which are commonly regarded as the home of knowledge workers – the intellectuals – change would still depend, to a large extent, on equilibrium and often a kind of gaming outcome of the relevant forces or factors in the environment where higher education institutions operate. The state of equilibrium is often a dynamic process comprising the balancing of policy options that are conditioned by not only present but also past externalities. Over the years, this social embeddedness in the nature of higher education could create a path dependence, or in some cases an inertia, with the decisions for change deferred down the road. For Chinese higher education, perpetual political and state control might be a notable manifestation of path dependence or an enduring dilemma. In many ways, higher education in China has always carried a strong sense of "state instrumentalism" and has been fundamentally embedded in state policy and strategy for national development.

In some ways, the Chinese model could demonstrate appealing aspects and even attractions. For instance, the Chinese government could launch the two elite university schemes (i.e., projects 21/1 and 98/5) with a single hand, and it could pour in public resources in such a large amount and with such incredible efficiency that it could raise those selected universities to world-class standing quickly; this is something not even thinkable in many other systems. Essentially, such a bold move as launching projects 21/1 and 98/5 has triggered a worldwide competition to create world-class universities.

Also, China has embraced mass higher education at an unprecedented speed. In the process, most Chinese universities have borrowed to expand their facilities and, in many cases, built new campuses to accommodate their fast-growing enrolments. Consequently, many of them are heavily indebted and suffering enormous pressure to pay back bank loans. Not surprisingly, again, the Chinese government has stepped in to bail them out with public funds in a very short time (Zha 2011c). This situation might be seen as a sign of increasing returns and positive feedback from the Chinese model and serve to reinforce the path dependence, if not result in a lock-in.

Nevertheless, the Chinese model reveals serious constraints with respect to maintaining social equity and fulfilling human potential. The 2020 Blueprint sends a strong message for change, yet still features a state-driven momentum. This policy document signals the kind of managerialism and technical rationale that expect a number of state-engineered projects (for example, those aiming to produce high-achieving and innovative learners and to launch a modern university model on Chinese soil, etc.) to bring about fundamental change. We argue that, unless the dynamism comes truly from the bottom, with universities and colleges enjoying full academic freedom and institutional autonomy, it is hard to anticipate those fundamental changes. Essentially, "an open society would better accommodate academic freedom, and, in turn, better facilitate creativity and innovation in pursuing knowledge" (Zha 2012, 221).

NOTES

1. Qian Xuesen (11 December 1911 to 31 October 2009) is better known to the West as Hsue-Shen Tsien. Educated at the Massachusetts Institute of Technology and the California Institute of Technology (Caltech) in the 1930s, he established a reputation as one of the leading rocket scientists in the US, and he became one of the founders of the Jet Propulsion Laboratory at Caltech. After his return to China in 1955, he made important contributions to the missile and space programs of the country. This question was posed in "Qian Xuesen de zuihou yici xitong tanhua – tan keji chuangxin rencai de peiyang wenti [H.T. Tsien's last systematic talk on nurturing creative talent of sciences and technology]," *People's Daily*, 5 November 2009, 11.
2. These debts have accumulated to hundreds of billions renminbi, exceeding the yearly state appropriations for higher education as a whole.
3. The "Core Project 98/5 universities" are the first nine universities included in the project in 1999 and 2000. More universities joined this project up until 2009, and they are labelled "Other Project 98/5 universities" in this study. All universities selected for Project 98/5 are national and are included in

Project 21/1 as well. The "Project 21/1 universities" include those selected for this project only (i.e., excluding those with both projects 21/1 and 98/5 status). The remaining universities are sorted into "Local universities" and all of the colleges into "Higher vocational colleges."

4. Political control was considerably relaxed in the 1980s, a period that is now viewed as the new enlightenment era in modern Chinese history. It experienced a backlash in the late 1980s and the early 1990s resulting from the Tiananmen Square tragedy in 1989. Most recently, control appears to have been tightened through various government-led evaluation exercises, whereby central, provincial, and local governments send out inspection teams to evaluate and scrutinize all kinds of work in the higher education institutions within their jurisdictions. The scope of such exercises ranges from undergraduate-program teaching evaluation to anti-corruption appraisal, from tuition fee audits to campus safety checks. The higher education institutions seem to become drained of energy and resources in the process of satisfying these evaluations and examinations. A recent survey of a group of Chinese university leaders (NAEA 2012) reveals that interference by the Chinese government is common and constant and that such behaviours are exercising direct control over the university's personnel management, resources supply, and curriculum and program development. The development targets and strategies as well as the performance indicators being imposed are viewed as having the greatest impacts on the daily operation and development direction of Chinese universities.

5. These seven domains are student admission, new program development, teaching, research and service, international exchange and co-operation, arrangement of internal structure and personnel management, and property management. They were first initiated with the 1985 Decision.

6. Two examples help elaborate the externalities that might work to create political constraints on Chinese higher education. Addressing the rivalry between the US and China at a presidential candidates' debate on foreign policy and national security, held on 13 November 2011 in Spartanburg, South Carolina, Jon Huntsman, the former US ambassador to China, said, "We should be reaching out to our allies and constituencies within China. They're called the young people. They're called the internet generation. There are 500 million internet users in China.... And 80 million bloggers. And they are bringing about change, the likes of which is gonna take China down" ("CBS News/NJ Debate Transcript, Part 1," at http://www.cbsnews.com/2102-505103_162-57323734.html?tag=contentMain, accessed 15 November 2011). Huntsman is obviously placing his hopes on Chinese university students.

As a sort of reaction, Hu Jintao, China's party and state leader, warned on 1 January 2012, "Hostile international powers are strengthening their efforts to Westernize and divide us" (quoted in the CCP's theoretical journal *Qiu Shi* [Seeking truth], "Jian ding bu yi zou zhongguo tece shehuizhuyi wenhua fazhan daolu, nuli jianshe shehuizhuyi wenhua qiang guo" [Follow unshakably the path of developing socialist culture with Chinese characteristics and stride to build a culturally strong socialist nation], at http://www.qstheory.cn/zxdk/2012/201201/201112/t20111228_132538.htm, accessed 24 March 2012).

REFERENCES

Arthur, W.B. 1994. *Increasing Returns and Path Dependence in the Economy*. Ann Arbor: University of Michigan Press.

Bednar, J., and S. Page. 2007. "Can Game(s) Theory Explain Culture? The Emergence of Cultural Behavior within Multiple Games." *Rationality and Society* 19:65–97.

Central Committee of the CCP (Chinese Communist Party). 1985. *Guanyu jiaoyu tizhi gaike de jueding* [Decision on the reform of the education system]. At http://www.edu.cn/special/showarticle.php?id=301 (accessed 16 September 2001).

—. 2010. *Zhongguo gongchandang putong gaodeng xuexiao jiceng zuzhi gongzuo tiaoli* [Mandate of CCP primary organizations in regular higher education institutions]. Beijing: Chinese Communist Party.

Central Committee of the CCP and State Council. 1993. *Zhongguo jiaoyu gaige he fazhan gangyao* [Outline for educational reform and development in China]. At http://www.edu.cn/special/showarticle.php?id=298 (accessed 16 September 2001).

Chen, Y. 2011. "Zhongguo gongchandang lingdao gaodeng xuexiao de jiben tezheng yu zou xiang" [The characteristics and trend of CCP's leadership on higher education institutions]. *Fudan Education Forum* 9 (3):13–18.

Cheng, S., and Z. Li. 2011. "Cong zhengzhi jiaoyu xue dao min sheng jiaoyu xue" [From political pedagogy to humanistic pedagogy]. *Fudan Education Forum* 9 (4):5–14.

Ding, X. 2008. "Dazhong ziben zhuyi: zhongguo de chulu" [Mass capitalism: China's opportunity]. *Financial Times Chinese*, 19 December. At http://www.ftchinese.com/story/001023770 (accessed 3 January 2012).

Gidley, J., G. Hampson, L. Wheelera, and E. Bereded-Samuel. 2010. "From Access to Success: An Integrated Approach to Quality Higher Education Informed by Social Inclusion Theory and Practice." *Higher Education Policy* 23:123–147.

Hayhoe, R. 1989. *China's Universities and the Open Door*. Armonk and London: M.E. Sharpe.

Jiang, Z. 1998. "Zai qingzhu beijing daxue jian xiao yibai zhounian dahui shang de jianghua" [A speech marking the centennial celebration of the founding of Peking University], 4 May. At http://www.moe.edu.cn/edoas/website18/info3311.htm (accessed 18 November 2005).

Li, J. 2011. "Zhongguo gongchandang lingdao jiaoyu shiye de lishi zhuanbian he shidai mingti" [The Communist Party's leading role in China's educational development: historical transformation and theme of the times]. *Fudan Education Forum* 9 (4):15–18.

Li, R. 1999. "Wushi nian zhongguo gaodeng jiaoyu fazhan hui mo" [A look back at Chinese higher education in the past 50 years]. *Jiaoyu kexue yanjiu* [Educational science research] 4:3–9.

Ministry of Education of China. 1998. Mianxiang 21 shiji jiaoyu zhengxing xingdong jihua [Program of educational revitalization for the 21st century]. At http://www.moe.edu.cn/publicfiles/business/htmlfiles/moe/moe_177/200407/2487.html (accessed 11 July 2013).

—. 1999. *Higher Education Law of China*. In *The Laws on Education of the People's Republic of China*, 86–116. Beijing: Foreign Languages Press.

—. 2002. *Quan guo jiaoyu shiye di shi ge wu nian jihua* [Tenth five-year plan for educational development]. At http://www.edu.cn/20020807/3063570.shtml (accessed 8 January 2012).

—. n.d. *China Education Statistics Yearbook.* At http://www.moe.edu.cn/public files/business/htmlfiles/moe/s7382/list.html (accessed 16 March 2012).

NAEA of China. 2012. *Gaodeng xuexiao xingzheng hua wenti diaocha* [A survey on bureaucratization of Chinese universities]. At http://www.naea.edu.cn/news/detail.asp?newsid=2075&classid=176 (accessed 4 July 2012).

Page, S.E. 2006. "Path Dependence." *Quarterly Journal of Political Science* 1 (1):87–115.

Pierson, P. 2000. "Increasing Returns, Path Dependence, and the Study of Politics." *American Political Science Review* 94 (2):251–267.

Sewell, W.H. 1996. "Three Temporalities: Toward an Eventful Sociology." In *The Historic Turn in the Human Sciences*, ed. T.J. McDonald, 245–280. Ann Arbor: University of Michigan Press.

State Council of China. 1999. *Guanyu shenhua jiaoyu gaige, quanmian tuijin suzhi jiaoyu de jueding* [Decision on deepening educational reform and pressing ahead with quality education in an all-round way]. At http://www.moe.edu.cn/edoas/website18/level3.jsp?tablename=208&infoid=3314 (accessed 16 September 2001).

—. 2010. *Guojia zhong chang qi jiaoyu gaige he fazhan guihua gangyao (2010–2020)* [National outline for medium- and long-term educational reform and development (2010–2020)]. At http://www.gov.cn/jrzg/2010-07/29/content_1667143.htm (accessed 7 August 2011).

van Vught, F. 1996. "Isomorphism in Higher Education? Towards a Theory of Differentiation and Diversity in Higher Education Systems." In *The Mockers and Mocked: Comparative Perspectives on Differentiation, Convergence and Diversity in Higher Education*, ed. V.L. Meek, L. Goedegebuure, O. Kivinen, and R. Rinne, 42–58. Oxford: Pergamon / IAU Press.

Xie, Z., and W. Wang. 2006. "Gaodeng jiaoyu dazhonghua shiye xia woguo shehui ge jiecheng zinu gaodeng jiaoyu ruxue jihui chayi de yanjiu" [The difference in higher education access opportunity of the children in different strata in China in the context of mass higher education]. *Jiaoyu xuebao* [Journal of educational studies] 19 (2):65–74, 96.

Yan, F. 2000. "The Theory of Transaction Cost and Choosing Appropriate Reform Models for the Higher Education Administrative System in China." In *Current Issues in Chinese Higher Education*, 45–54. Paris: OECD.

Zha, Qiang. 2006. "Diversification or Homogenization: How Governments Shape the Chinese Higher Education System." PhD diss., University of Toronto, Toronto.

—. 2011a. "Understanding China's Move to Mass Higher Education from a Policy Perspective." In *Portraits of 21st Century Chinese Universities: In the Move to Mass Higher Education*, ed. R. Hayhoe, J. Li, J. Lin, and Q. Zha, 20–57. Hong Kong: Springer / Comparative Education Research Centre, Faculty of Education, University of Hong Kong.

—. 2011b. "China's Move to Mass Higher Education in a Comparative Perspective." *Compare: A Journal of Comparative and International Education* 41 (6):751–768.

——. 2011c. "China's Helping Hand to Indebted Universities: The Good, the Bad, and the Ugly." *WorldWise* (Chronicle of Higher Education blog), 5 December. At http://chronicle.com/blogs/worldwise/chinas-helping-hand-to-indebted-universities-the-good-the-bad-and-the-ugly/28930 (accessed 8 January 2012).

——. 2012. "Intellectuals, Academic Freedom and University Autonomy in China." In *University Governance and Reform: Policy, Fads, and Experience in International Perspective*, ed. H.G. Schuetze, W. Bruneau, and G. Grosjean, 209–224. New York: Palgrave Macmillan.

CHAPTER 15

THE EUROPE OF KNOWLEDGE: AN ANALYSIS OF THE EU'S INNOVATION STRATEGY

HARRY DE BOER AND FRANS VAN VUGHT

INTRODUCTION

The focus of the European Union (EU) on innovation has its own history. In response to the ongoing process of globalization, the EU has set an "innovation agenda," promulgated since the beginning of this century. On this agenda, knowledge is explicitly viewed as the new strategic production factor. *Innovation*, defined here as "the creation, transfer, and application of knowledge," is assumed to be of prime importance for the processes of economic and social reorientation and development in Europe. There is a strong belief in a Schumpeterian "renaissance": a belief in innovation as the essential source of competitive advantages, economic development, and societal transformation – i.e., innovation as a growth-propelling engine. Flowing from this policy belief, the EU has become more proactive and assertive in its efforts to influence the behaviour of knowledge providers, especially higher education and research organizations. Knowledge providers are viewed as vital players in the "innovation game" and therefore have become important objects of EU strategies and policies in the areas of higher education, research, and innovation.

Recently, European leaders have again stressed the importance of knowledge and innovation for Europe's future. According to the European Commission (EC), innovation is the best response to the current global

Making Policy in Turbulent Times: Challenges and Prospects for Higher Education, ed. P. Axelrod, R.D. Trilokekar, T. Shanahan, and R. Wellen. Kingston: School of Policy Studies, Queen's University.

economic crisis. Though the outcomes of the current economic and political processes, at both the EU level and that of the member states, are highly unpredictable, the EC, as a strong player in these processes, is clear in its intentions. Following a twin-track approach of stability and growth (the Stability and Growth Pact),[1] the EC argues that both short-term and long-term measures are required to secure a prosperous Europe. Several instruments, in accordance with existing treaties, have recently been developed: the Treaty Establishing the European Stability Mechanism; the Treaty on Stability, Coordination and Governance in the Economic and Monetary Union; the European Semester; and the Six Pack. These are described in the next section.

The EU's long-term goal is to invest in Europe's brains by increasing the levels of funding allocated to education, training, research, and innovation, which, as noted, are considered critically important for Europe's global competitiveness (EC 2011c). This message is clearly communicated in the recent multi-annual financial framework 2014–20, in which the EC proposes to allocate more funds to research, innovation, education, and development of small and medium-sized enterprises (SMEs).

In this chapter, we will discuss the EU's innovation strategy and its consequences for European higher education and research. We will describe, analyze, and evaluate the EU's innovation strategy in the period 2000–10 (the so-called Lisbon Strategy) and explore the ambitions of the new strategy for the period 2010–20 (the Europe 2020 Strategy). Based on this analysis, we will present an inventory of what may be assumed to be the major policy issues in European higher education and research in the years to come.

A CONTEXT OF UNCERTAINTY

Since the turn of the millennium, several significant events have occurred to shape the current context and functioning of the EU. For example, the number of countries increased significantly when the Eastern European countries joined. Of this writing, Croatia has just become the 28th member state of the EU (in 2013). In 2002, the euro was introduced, leading to the Eurozone, consisting of 17 member states. In 2009, the first president of the European Council was installed. The other major developments concern the EU constitution and the (global) financial and economic crisis. An EU constitution was drafted but rejected in referenda in France (2005), the Netherlands (2005), and Ireland (2008), leading to a period of uncertainty and confusion. Subsequently, the European political leaders reached an agreement: formally, there would no longer be a constitution but only an amendment of the existing treaties in a Treaty of Lisbon (which came into force on 1 December 2009).[2] The Lisbon Treaty establishes, *inter alia*, the EU's main political institutions, their composition, and their authorities for a number of policy areas.[3]

The financial crisis that began in the late 2000s has shown that the limited capacity for common fiscal coordination and the relatively weak political decision-making mechanisms of the Eurozone led to the occurrence of serious financial problems for both the Eurozone and the EU. In response to the economic and financial crisis, Europe has reached several agreements on a more integrated European fiscal policy in the last few years, such as the Treaty Establishing the European Stability Mechanism, which came into effect on 27 September 2012; the Treaty on Stability, Coordination and Governance in the Economic and Monetary Union (the Fiscal Compact), effective 1 January 2013; the European Semester (2010); and the Six Pack (December 2011).

The general aim of these new instruments is to replace the "soft" approach to structural economic reform that was part of the Stability and Growth Pact by much stricter (fiscal) rules. For example, the Six Pack[4] aims to achieve i) stronger preventive and corrective action to ensure fiscal sustainability and ii) a reduction of macro-economic imbalances. It states, among other things, that national budgets should not exceed 3 percent of a country's gross domestic product (GDP) and that national debt levels should not exceed 60 percent. If these conditions are not met, an excessive deficit procedure will be initiated that can include warnings, recommendations, and financial sanctions.

Despite these and other measures, doubts and uncertainty remain, and the challenges are real. The future of the EU is very much in flux. The current financial crisis appears to force the member states to reconsider their sovereignty levels in the broader European context. It may even generate the essential next step toward European integration. It is in this turbulent context that the EC argues that investing in knowledge to create smart, sustainable, and inclusive economic growth is the way out of the economic crisis. Fiscal discipline and austerity measures are perceived to be needed, but, as expressed in the Stability and Growth Pact, cutting back on Europe's knowledge production and utilization would be the worst possible scenario for its future.

THE LISBON STRATEGY: GRAND AMBITIONS AND HARSH REALITIES

The EU sees the need to modify its socio-economic system in response to the challenges presented by the process of globalization and the recent economic crisis. Particularly since the early 2000s, the political leaders of the EU have embarked upon an overall EU innovation strategy with the objective of boosting the EU's competitiveness and growth. When the European leaders met in 2000, they decided that they wanted to create a "Europe of Knowledge," which by 2010 should be "the most competitive and dynamic knowledge-based economy in the world, capable of sustainable economic growth with more and better jobs and greater social cohesion" (European Council 2000, n.p.). This so-called Lisbon Strategy includes a number of interrelated fields. Two major policy domains of this strategy are the fields of higher education and research, which we address below.

Higher education policy

Generally speaking, higher education has crept slowly onto the European innovation agenda. Although some educational activities were developed at the European level during the 1970s and intra-European mobility programs were launched in the 1980s, the higher education sector was for a long time "taboo" for European policy initiatives. However, in the context of the Lisbon Strategy, the EU's policy interest in higher education increased. Although legislative powers for education in general and higher education in particular remained firmly at the level of the member states, the notion that the EU could and should play a complementary role started to take root more seriously.

At the EU level, co-operation among member states could be encouraged through a range of actions, such as (further) promoting mobility and designing joint programs and networks. The first main tool for putting this goal into practice has been the two Socrates programs (1995–99 and 2000–06). The aim of Socrates was to promote a Europe of Knowledge and encourage lifelong education through learning foreign languages, encouraging mobility, promoting co-operation at the European level, opening up new methods of access to education and increasing the use of new technologies in the field of education.

The Socrates programs were followed by the Lifelong Learning program (2007–13). A crucial component of all of these programs was and is the Erasmus subprogram, aimed to enhance the quality and reinforce the European dimension of higher education by encouraging transnational co-operation among universities, boosting mobility, and improving the transparency and recognition of studies and qualifications. Erasmus is the EU's flagship education and training activity, enabling 200,000 students to study and work abroad each year.[5] In addition, it funds co-operation among higher education institutions across Europe. Erasmus supports not only students but also professors and business staff who want to teach abroad as well as helping university staff to receive training.

With this overall perspective, the EU linked its higher education policy closely to another, broader political process in European higher education: the Bologna Process. The Bologna Process started in 1999 as an intergovernmental political initiative, when 29 European ministers of education signed the Bologna Declaration. Its objectives were to create the European Higher Education Area, promote mobility and employability, and increase the compatibility and comparability of the European higher education system. In the span of a decade, Bologna has led to many changes in many European higher education systems (and beyond), such as the introduction of a three-cycle structure, development of the European Credit Transfer and Accumulation System, and adoption of European Standards and Guidelines for Quality Assurance.

The EC launched its Integrated Lifelong Learning Programme (2007–13) in line with the Bologna Process with the objectives of strengthening both the numbers and the quality of Europe's human resources and becoming globally competitive in higher education performance. The higher education institutions of the EU were reinforced to contribute more strongly to the European innovation agenda (ECom 2006).

Apart from these achievements, the EC is critical of European higher education. In 2003, the EC initiated a debate on the "place and role of European universities in society and in the knowledge economy" (EC 2003, 4). Since the European universities are at the heart of the European knowledge society, being responsible for 80 percent of Europe's fundamental research, the EC intended to explore the conditions under which Europe's universities would be better able to play their role in the knowledge society and economy. The EC's analysis was stern: "the European university world is not trouble-free, and the European universities are not at present globally competitive ..." (2). The universities need to realize that the traditional model of Wilhelm von Humboldt no longer fits the current international context and that the high degree of fragmentation of the European university landscape prevents Europe from responding to new global challenges. These challenges go beyond national frontiers and have to be addressed at a European level. "More specifically, they require a joint and coordinated endeavour by the Member States ..., backed up and supported by the European Union, in order to help to move towards a genuine Europe of knowledge" (10).

According to the EC, European universities have so far failed to unleash their full potential to stimulate economic growth, social cohesion, and improvement in the quality and quantity of jobs. In a policy paper in 2005, the EC identified several bottlenecks: a trend toward uniformity and egalitarianism in many national higher education systems, too much emphasis on mono-disciplinarity and traditional learning and learners, and too little world-class excellence (EC 2005). European higher education remains fragmented into medium or small clusters, with different regulations and languages; it is largely insulated from industry; graduates lack entrepreneurship skills; and there is a strong dependency on the state. European higher education is also over-regulated and therefore inefficient and inflexible. In addition, European universities are underfunded.

By the end of the Lisbon Strategy period, in 2010, the results of the various policies appeared to be disappointing. The grand ambitions expressed in the Lisbon Strategy were nowhere in sight. And various countries in the world appeared to outperform the EU countries in higher education. For example, relative to GDP, the United States invests more than twice as much in higher education as the EU (2.6 percent versus 1.2 percent of GDP), mainly due to much lower private spending in the EU (EC 2011a). As a result, education expenditure per graduate or PhD student in Europe is a fraction of what it is in the US. Furthermore, in the EU, 32.3 percent of the population aged 25–34 had a university degree in 2009, lower than the over 55 percent in Japan and the nearly 42 percent in the US. The higher education attainment level in the US is also substantially higher than in the EU (EC 2011a).

The conclusion has to be drawn that although the innovation agenda of the Lisbon Strategy identified higher education as a major force for the creation of the knowledge-based society, its ambitious political goals in the field of higher education appear to be difficult to reach. European higher education is not performing at a level that makes it globally competitive. According to the EC, the European higher education systems still need to be further "modernized." Both the structures and the cultures of these systems and their institutions need to be adapted to the global challenges that the EU is facing.

Research policy

Compared to the higher education policy domain, the field of research has been a focus of EU policy since the very beginning of the European integration process. In one of the 1950s treaties, an article was included that allowed European policy initiatives if they were deemed to be necessary for the joint European development process. However, a more comprehensive EU research policy has been developed only since the 1980s. The major policy program in this context was and is the so-called Framework Programme (FP). The various FPs that have been implemented over the decades have become *the* strategic documents describing the EU's broad research priorities, each to be implemented through specific operational programs and linked to specific budget categories.

However, while the financial and political strengths of the FPs are considerable, the proportion of their research investments on a Europe-wide scale is limited. In the sixth FP, this proportion was only 5 percent; the other 95 percent invested in European research came from the member states. The overall European research landscape suffers from fragmentation and unnecessary duplication of effort and resources. In the context of the EU's innovation agenda, the major challenge in the European research policy domain is to create critical mass and joint investment schemes. This is the challenge that is being addressed in the proposals that aim to develop a European Research Area (ERA).

The ERA was formally launched in 2000 (EC 2000), when the Lisbon summit of that year endorsed its creation as a key component of the Lisbon Strategy. However, it was only in 2002 that the ERA really took shape. The EC noted that European research represented a jigsaw of (then) 15 often very different national scientific and technological policies. The FPs appeared to be no more than "a sort of '16th' research policy, coming on top of national efforts, but not dynamic enough to have a truly integrating effect" (ECom 2002, 8).[6] The result was fragmentation and duplication of European research efforts as well as a failure to assemble the critical mass of human, technological, and financial resources that major contemporary scientific advances demand.

The EC also stated that the only way to reach the ambitious targets was to increase general investment in research to 3 percent of GDP and that a substantial part of this effort should come from business and industry. In March 2002, the 3 percent figure (of which two-thirds was expected to come from private funding) was accepted as the target to be reached by 2010. This appeared to be a difficult task, with European research and development (R&D) expenditure by business and industry lagging well behind that in the US. At mid-term, it became clear that the EU was far from reaching its target. It was concluded that "halfway to 2010 the overall picture is very mixed and much needs to be done in order to prevent Lisbon from becoming a synonym for missed objectives and failed promises" (ECom 2004, 10). There was a large gap between the political rhetoric about the knowledge society and the realities of budgetary and other priorities, and action was urgently needed. In particular, it was thought that the EU member states would have to contribute more effectively to the joint EU innovation strategy.

The current seventh FP (FP7), with a budget of €53.2 billion, is a major program for realizing the "re-launched" Lisbon agenda. It is the current chief instrument for funding research and innovation and, through the Technology Platforms and Joint Technology Initiatives, is creating a dialogue and co-operation with industry. In addition, it reaches out to the academic world through the creation of the European Research Council (ERC), which is designed to provide support for the best European "frontier research."

With FP7, the ERA's scope has broadened from a focus on how to improve the effectiveness and efficiency of the fragmented European research landscape to an awareness that more public and private investment in research is needed and that research policy should be related to other EU policies to achieve coherence and synergies in the context of the overall Lisbon Strategy. According to the EC, the expanded ERA must comprise six features: i) an adequate flow of competent researchers with high levels of mobility among institutions, disciplines, sectors, and countries; ii) a world-class research infrastructure, accessible to all; iii) excellent research institutions engaged in public-private co-operation, attracting human and financial resources; iv) effective knowledge-sharing between the public and private sectors and with the public at large; v) well-coordinated research programs and priorities; and vi) the opening of the ERA to the world, with special emphasis on neighbouring countries (EC 2007). A crucial aspect of the Lisbon Strategy is the desire to stimulate the transfer and application of research outcomes and hence to create stronger links between the research communities and business and industry.

In 2006, the EC published a policy paper to stimulate "putting knowledge into practice" and frame policy discussions on innovation at the national and EU levels. It outlines the most important planned and ongoing initiatives, identifies new areas of action, and, in particular, introduces a focused strategy to facilitate the creation and marketing of new, innovative products and services in promising areas – "the lead markets" (EC 2006, 3). According to the EC, there are major barriers to greater knowledge transfer in the EU, including cultural differences between the academic and business communities, legal barriers, fragmented markets, and lack of incentives. Some member states had set up initiatives to promote knowledge transfer, but these largely ignored its international dimensions (EC 2007). In this context, a number of measures were suggested, including creating a workforce of skilled knowledge transfer staff in universities (and a professional qualification and accreditation scheme), developing a more entrepreneurial mindset in universities, and providing for exchanges of staff between research organizations and industry. In addition, voluntary guidelines to help improve knowledge transfer cover issues such as intellectual property management, incentives for researchers to participate in knowledge transfer activities, and the development of knowledge transfer resources (EC 2007).

As in the policy field of higher education, the final results of the Lisbon Strategy in the field of research are certainly disappointing. The ambitious investment target of 3 percent of GDP appears not to have been reached. Despite a more than 20 percent real-term increase in research expenditure over the period 2000–09, the R&D intensity of the EU has stagnated to about 1.85 percent of GDP since 2000, with a slight increase to 2.01 percent of GDP in 2009. This is still substantially below the R&D intensity level of the US, which was already at 2.69 percent of GDP in 2000 and climbed to 2.76 percent of GDP in 2008. The stagnation of the R&D intensity in the EU (and the US) contrasts sharply with the strong increases observed in Japan, South Korea, and China, with Japan reaching 3.44 percent of GDP, South Korea 3.21 percent of GDP, and China 1.54 percent of GDP – all in 2008 (EC 2011b).

The EU's under-investment in R&D is most visible in the business sector, where Europe is falling further behind the US and the leading Asian countries. EU business expenditure on R&D stagnated at 1.25 percent of GDP in 2009, which is much lower than the 2.01 percent in the US in 2008, the 2.6 per cent in Japan in 2007, and the 2.45 percent in South Korea in 2007 (EC 2011b).

Nevertheless, the EU is the top producer of peer-reviewed scientific publications in the world, with 29 percent of total world production in

2009, ahead of the US at 22 percent, China at 17 percent, and Japan at 5 percent. But in spite of this, the US continues to perform better than the EU in terms of R&D excellence. The share of the total number of scientific publications in the top 10 percent most-cited publications for the EU is 11.6 percent, while for the US, the number is 15 percent (EC 2011b).

In terms of development of competitive technology, too, the EU is losing ground. In recent years, the rate of growth in the number of patent applications in Japan and South Korea is almost double that of the EU. If the current trend is extrapolated to 2020, the EU's share will be 18 percent, while the five leading Asian countries will have a share of 53 percent and the US 15 percent (EC 2011a).

A major problem regarding the EU's innovation capacity is its failure to create large, new companies investing in R&D. Although the European SMEs are innovative, they are generally less active in patent applications than their US counterparts. As a result, the growth of SMEs into larger companies remains limited in the EU. The share of companies created after 1975 is three times higher among the top US companies investing in R&D, at 54.4 percent, than among similar companies in the EU, at 17.8 percent (EC 2011b). The EU shows a consistently lower capacity to create and grow new knowledge-intensive companies and hence is confronted with an industrial structure that lacks sufficient innovative power to confront the global competitive economic challenges.

As in the field of higher education, the conclusion regarding the policy field of research (and knowledge transfer) can only be that the ambitions of the Lisbon Strategy have not been realized. The challenge of increasing research investment levels remains a key priority. But further steps will have to be taken to improve the excellence of European science, strengthen Europe's technological competitiveness, and stimulate the growth of the innovation sectors of European industry. According to the EC, these challenges show that European research systems and research institutions (including universities) need to be further adapted.

THE EUROPE 2020 STRATEGY: A RESTART?

By the end of 2010, the general EU policy context had changed substantially. The former Lisbon Strategy was superseded by a new, overall innovation strategy: the Europe 2020 Strategy. This new orientation of the EU's major ambitions to the year 2020 is currently dominating the European political agenda. Knowledge is put at the heart of the EU's efforts to achieve "smart, sustainable and inclusive growth" (EC 2010). The *Europe 2020* document provides a comprehensive vision for a range of EU policy programs, including those in higher education and research. For this, it distinguishes seven "flagship initiatives," among them the Innovation Union and the Agenda for New Skills and Jobs. In addition, five "headline targets" have been agreed upon, which will guide the various EU policy programs in the coming years (EC 2010, 5).

- employment: 75 percent of 20-to-64-year-olds to be employed
- R&D/innovation: 3 percent of the EU's GDP to be invested
- climate change/energy: 20 percent reduction of greenhouse gas emissions; 20 percent renewable energy; 20 percent increase in energy efficiency
- education: school drop-out rate below 10 percent; at least 40 percent of 30-to-34-year-olds completing third level
- poverty/social exclusion: at least 20 million fewer people at risk

The argument for a range of far-reaching programs is that the EU is not sufficiently setting the pace in the race for knowledge, excellence, and talent. For instance, while the forecasts show that 35 percent of all jobs in the EU will require high-level qualifications by 2020, only 26 percent of the workforce currently has a higher education qualification. Compared to its competitors, such as the US and Japan, the EU is also underperforming in the numbers of graduates and research jobs, scientific excellence, technological competiveness, and innovative companies. The new Europe 2020 Strategy wants to address these issues and intends to trigger policies that can increase the EU's overall innovation capacity.

In the context of this new innovation strategy, two crucial policy papers (each with its own substantial budget for the years 2014–20) are the new higher education policy *Supporting Growth and Jobs: An Agenda for the Modernisation of Europe's Higher Education Systems* (EC 2011c) and *Horizon 2020*, the new draft FP for research and innovation, 2014–20 (EC 2011d). The new higher education policy (often called the new Modernisation Agenda) makes it clear that students will have to be trained in new mixes of employment skills in higher education, that higher education institutions will have to develop their specific "excellence profiles," and that more transparency will be needed in profiles and performance in higher education. The delivery of Europe's 2020 strategy will require higher education institutions to improve their quality and performance. To realize these lofty ambitions, the EC argues that more higher education reforms in key areas are needed, aiming to:

- increase the number of higher education graduates at all levels
- enhance the quality and relevance of human capital development in higher education
- create effective governance and funding mechanisms in support of excellence
- strengthen the knowledge triangle among education, research, and business
- recognize the growing internationalization of higher education

The new research policy focuses on three overall priorities for the EU: establishing an excellent science base, developing industrial leadership, and tackling societal challenges (such as demographic change, food security, energy efficiency, climate action, and social inclusion).

The Europe 2020 Strategy appears to be a restart of the earlier Lisbon Strategy. The strategic ambitions reflect the earlier focus on building the European knowledge society, and they try to reinforce the view that knowledge is the EU's most valuable resource. Knowledge is seen as the indispensable asset for Europe's future. The processes of knowledge transfer and knowledge exchange must be improved, and, in these processes, higher education and research organizations are regarded as crucially important: "Better exploitation of the expertise and knowledge found in higher education institutions can strengthen innovation potential and, thus, economic performance at regional, national and European level" (EC 2011e, 10). Higher education should contribute to the 2020 Strategy by enhancing close, effective links among higher education, research, and business. In spite of all of the reform and change that have occurred in European higher education in the last two or three decades, further action is needed to achieve the goals of the EU 2020 strategy since "the capacity of higher education institutions to integrate research results and innovative practice into the educational offer, and to exploit the potential for marketable products and services, remains weak" (EC 2011c, 7).

Therefore, the EC considers it absolutely necessary to further modernize European higher education in such a way that it can be the engine of European economic growth, competitiveness, innovation, and social cohesion. While the EC acknowledges that the member states have primary responsibility for education as well as autonomy over their higher education institutions, it sees a clear role for itself in developing a Europe of Knowledge through setting an agenda, developing common goals and monitoring progress toward them, pushing particular initiatives, and funding. The EC monitors progress and supports the reform efforts of member states, including through country-specific recommendations and EU funding programs. It is also clear that as a consequence of the EU's ambitions and related initiatives, European higher education and research institutions will be confronted with a set of policy issues that will have a major impact on their existence in the years to come. This topic is discussed in the following section.

Consequences for higher education and research organizations: rethinking the balance among education, research, and community services

The strengthening of the knowledge triangle of education, research, and innovation should be the point of departure for future reform. Closer co-operation and intensified interaction among knowledge providers (higher education and research institutes); business and industry; and local, regional, and national governments are seen as the way forward. It means that higher education and research organizations should not screen off their activities from the outside world (in their "ivory towers"), but should actively, strategically, and commercially engage in interactions with external stakeholders. They should not only pass on knowledge (uni-directional) but also absorb knowledge from elsewhere into their curricula and future research.

The new EU innovation strategy indeed implies a Modernisation Agenda for European institutions of higher education and research. The EC's 2010 communication on this agenda (EC 2010) mentions two basic pillars for knowledge exchange improvements, the first related to teaching, the second one to research. With respect to both pillars, interactions and partnerships among knowledge providers such as higher education and research organizations and businesses are essential. This means placing a stronger emphasis on developing entrepreneurial, creative, and innovation skills; promoting interactive learning environments; and strengthening the knowledge transfer infrastructure. For example, higher education and research organizations should increase their capacity to engage in start-ups and spin-offs, partnerships and collaborations with business should be regarded as a core activity, and higher education and research organizations should be systematically involved in the creation of regional hubs of excellence and specialization.

In diversified higher education systems, knowledge exchange should be geared to a wider range of student needs, should better respond to labour market needs, and should have a stronger focus on innovation and entrepreneurial skills. Highly skilled human capital is Europe's competitive edge, and it must be provided through higher education. "Highly skilled, creative individuals with critical mindsets are needed to create the businesses of the future and more generally to help businesses and the public sector to innovate. Within this context, higher education staff play a crucial role in transmitting knowledge through well-designed and structured programmes of education and research. At the same time, programmes ... can benefit from insights from business and other organisations external to higher education" (EC 2011e, 10).

Delivering high-quality and labour-market-relevant education to an even larger proportion of the population requires adaption of curricula and mentality. It requires changes in the traditional approaches to designing and delivering educational programs. "For education to fulfil its role in the knowledge triangle, research and innovation objectives and outcomes need to feed back into education, with teaching and learning underpinned by a strong research base, and with teaching and learning environments developed and improved through greater incorporation of creative thinking and innovative attitudes and approaches" (Council of the European Union 2009, 4).

The member states should develop policies "which encourage partnership between professional institutions, research universities, business and high-tech centres" (EC 2011c, 7) in such a way that the relationship between basic and applied research improves and knowledge is transferred to the market more effectively. National policies and initiatives geared to a more innovative culture within institutions should take away barriers that prevent universities from making profits or from engaging in public-private partnerships. And connected knowledge providers can drive regional economic development through centres of knowledge that service regional and local economies and societies.

What the Modernisation Agenda basically asks from member states and particularly higher education institutions is a culture shift. "The traditional academic culture in universities needs to be complemented by an awareness that it also has a key role in delivering a more highly skilled, enterprising and flexible workforce which will form the foundation for economic growth and prosperity ..." (Council of the European Union 2009, 4). A positive attitude to innovative behaviour in both teaching and research that would make the knowledge triangle work is required and should be pursued. This means, among other things, bridging the gap between traditional academic values and those of commercial sectors. Traditional academic cultures in universities must be complemented with a focus on delivering a highly skilled, enterprising, and flexible workforce.

The challenge for higher education institutions is to develop a strategic agenda that strengthens knowledge exchange within existing university activities. This requires higher education institutions to enhance their strategic management capacities. The first step is to better understand what knowledge exchange is and how to use it and the strategic opportunities it offers. Institutions have to be selective in how they exchange knowledge and with whom. The EC argues that higher education institutions often seek to compete in too many areas. Selectivity – that is, making strategic choices – is necessary in the pursuit of excellence not only in basic research but in other areas as well and in order to avoid mission overload or unwanted mission stretch.

The Modernisation Agenda expects higher education systems to simultaneously improve their performance in various ways. With regard to teaching, the number of graduates should increase (productivity), dropout rates should decrease (efficiency), the qualifications and competences (e.g., creativity and entrepreneurial skills) of these graduates should better meet labour market demands (relevance), and the quality of teaching should improve. Knowledge should be shared with "non-traditional" audiences: more part-timers, lifelong learners, and international students. In terms of research, knowledge transfer and exchange should be strengthened (e.g., collaboration, staff sharing, licensing, patenting, start-ups, and spinoffs) but still underpinned by a strong (traditional) research base.

We believe that the key issues for European higher education and research organizations are selectivity, strategic decisions, and distinct profiles. The Modernisation Agenda gently pushes higher education and research organizations to enhance their strategic intelligence. In carefully reconsidering the range of potential activities, the sector should establish realistic profiles and strategies based on internal strengths and external opportunities. Those unable or unwilling to do so are likely to be marginalized, particularly when other actors such as governments, businesses, and students increasingly employ external benchmarks for rewarding or selecting a particular institution.

The need for institutional profiling

In succeeding the 2000 Lisbon Strategy, the Europe 2020 Strategy and its related communications, such as the flagship initiatives the 2011 Modernisation Agenda and *Horizon 2020,* continue to reflect Europe's ambition to become the world's most competitive knowledge economy and to include a wide range of recommended activities for, among other stakeholders, Europe's higher education and research organizations. These documents also put higher education and research organizations in a challenging position. These organizations need to fulfill many expectations across the full spectrum of activities to make a contribution to the EU's ambitions and to demonstrate their own (added) value to society and economy. And they must accomplish all of this in unfavourable financial environments ("doing more with less public money"). This means that higher education and research organizations, probably more than ever in their long histories, require clear and courageous institutional strategies. Profiling, in the sense of developing clear and selective portfolios of their activities based on internal strengths and external needs, is going to be their paramount challenge.

There are several reasons why it is unlikely that higher education and research organizations will escape this challenge. Generally speaking, increased levels of competition for scarce resources such as money, staff, and students will compel these organizations to proactively promote the kinds of services they deliver. What kinds of markets does an institution want to be active in? What kinds of services, and at what price, does it want to deliver? In a nutshell, increased competition calls for institutional strategies, which imply strategic profiling.

Resource dependence as well as unavoidable institutional pressures leave higher education and research organizations no choice but to critically examine their portfolios. The frameworks within which these organizations operate, the rules of the game, are changing in such a way that cunning strategies and smart organizational policies are necessary. Across the board, national governments in Europe are changing the way they regulate their education and research systems. New steering devices are being introduced. National governments increasingly introduce market-based instruments and incentives to pursue what used to be considered public goals (e.g., Jongbloed 2003). Market-based incentives are introduced to promote competition, which should contribute to better efficiency, higher quality, and increased responsiveness. Privatization, deregulation, establishment of quasi-markets, contracting out (competitive tendering), and the establishment of public-private partnerships are examples of market-based governance. The governments' new steering devices can be seen as an extension of more traditional notions of steering to which higher education and research institutions, still largely dependent on public budgets and subject to various regulations, have to adapt.

The increasing use of competitive and performance-oriented funding mechanisms, a trend embraced by the Modernisation Agenda and supported by many national governments, encourages higher education and research organizations to think strategically about their activities. As an example, the German Excellence Initiative has shaken up the German higher education and research system. Higher education and research organizations have begun to realize how important it is to explicitly reconsider (and advertise) their profiles. This trend has, to some extent, been further intensified by the use of target agreements in some German states as well as in several other European countries. Contracts, as another steering and funding trend, also ideally pay greater attention to differentiated institutional profiles. Institution-specific efforts, initiatives, and performance can be laid down in contractual agreements between governments and institutions. The Modernisation Agenda would like to see funding mechanisms targeted to the needs of different institutional profiles.

A second factor that leads higher education and research organizations to increasingly consider their institutional profiles concerns the growing number of accountability requirements for these organizations. New requirements, accompanying the shift in modes of governance aiming to enhance transparency, contribute to reconsidering the activities and services offered. Accountability measures, monitoring systems, and transparency tools ask for a clear view of what an institution stands for. These instruments not only force institutional leadership and management to think strategically but also provide information that can be used to determine an institution's strategic course.

A third factor enhancing the strategic importance of institutional profiles are the various EU and national policies, particularly in the areas of research and innovation, that adhere to notions of "focus" and "mass." At both the European and the national levels, research policies increasingly focus on the need to be selective in times of limited public resources, strong competition for public resources from various public sectors, and rapidly growing costs of "big science." The selection of a rather limited number of research priorities and research fields and a redistribution of funds are, of course, not without consequences for higher education and research organizations. Such focus strategies imply that higher education and research organizations must reconsider their research portfolios.

At the same time, we are witnessing "mass strategies." Mergers, strategic alliances, networks, and public-private partnerships are examples of a changing higher education landscape. Both concentration and scale enlargement are forcing higher education and research organizations to think strategically about their positions as well as those of others. In the processes of competition and co-operation, institutional profile development and analysis (what kinds of activity portfolios do we have and/or do we want to have?) are increasingly important.

Barriers to providing higher education and research organizations opportunities to develop institutional profiles and to encouraging their strategic management capacities should be removed. Effective governance mechanisms should be developed to provide sufficient space for these organizations to make strategic decisions about such tasks as managing income streams, selecting the best academic staff, setting admission policies, and developing teaching and research programs.

This is exactly what the EC is arguing for. It holds the view that over-regulation and micro-management from the member states should be avoided. With respect to many European higher education systems, institutional autonomy should be increased, and higher education and research organizations should accept full institutional responsibility to society at large for their performance. Institutional autonomy is a precondition for responding strategically to changes in the environments in which these organizations operate; it allows them to develop their service-delivery portfolios and to differentiate themselves from others.

Since the EU does not have legislative powers, the member states are encouraged to break down the barriers that prevent higher education and research organizations from taking full responsibility for their actions. Greater autonomy, accompanied by more accountability requirements (to various stakeholders), places new demands on institutional leadership and management, particularly in those European higher education systems that have a tradition of being "state controlled" (instead of being state supervised – see, for instance, Neave and van Vught 1991). Professionalization of strategic management of higher education and research organizations is needed both to develop and to implement strategic activity portfolios.

While there have been a significant number of governance reforms designed to enhance institutional autonomy, studies in higher education reveal that higher education and research organizations still face limitations in their managerial flexibility. As long as barriers exist that prevent these organizations from fully exploiting their strategic potential, it is likely that the EC will stress the need to further modernize their governance structures. Moreover, modern steering devices of the state (such as individual contracts), in combination with dependency from public budgets, may further limit the space for higher education and research organizations to manoeuvre the way they want. And of course internal resistance – for instance, from academics who, rightly or wrongly, fear a loss of academic freedom – could be another barrier to developing and implementing institution-wide strategic choices. Therefore, smart (legitimate) as well as effective (decisive) institutional leadership is crucially important for successful profiling.

SUMMARY

In this chapter, we have addressed the EU's innovation strategy, presented as the way forward to a Europe of Knowledge that can successfully meet competition from other parts of the world. Since the late 1990s especially, European political leadership has explicitly expressed the will to launch a European-wide innovation strategy to boost Europe's competitiveness and growth. In 2000, it was decided to create a Europe of Knowledge, which was expected to have the most dynamic knowledge-based economy in the world in ten years' time. Well before 2010, however, it became clear that Europe would not reach the ambitious goals of the Lisbon Strategy. Various policies linked to the Lisbon Strategy showed disappointing results in higher education, research, and innovation.

Nevertheless, the EU presented the Europe 2020 Strategy in 2010 as the successor of the Lisbon Strategy. Knowledge was again at the heart of the EU's efforts to achieve "smart, sustainable and inclusive growth." The EU also announced certain flagship initiatives, including the establishment of an Innovation Union and an Agenda for New Skills and Jobs, and related strategic programs, such as a renewed Modernisation Agenda and *Horizon 2020*. This range of far-reaching programs will affect higher education and research. Though the EU lacks the power to directly intervene in national higher education and research systems in various areas (due to the principle of subsidiarity), it is unrealistic to assume that higher education and research organizations will be able to ignore the EU's efforts to shape Europe's future.

The new EU initiatives offer two ways to change the knowledge exchange processes of higher education and research organizations. First, in terms of education, institutions should consider more fully adapting their curricula to labour market needs. They should place a stronger focus on innovative and entrepreneurial skills and be geared to a wider range of student needs. The number of graduates should increase, and the number of dropouts should be reduced. Second, with respect to research, while still being underpinned by an excellent research base, knowledge transfer and valorization should be strengthened. Intensified interaction with other actors such as businesses and "regions" is a must.

To cope with such an array of demands for a culture shift in higher education and research organizations, these institutions will have to focus on establishing clear and courageous institutional strategies. For several reasons, selectivity, strategic direction, and distinct profiles are likely to be the buzzwords in many European institutions in the coming years. Careful deliberations, based on internal strengths and external demands and leading to clear institutional profiles, should become routine among institutional leadership. To further facilitate such a development, barriers must be removed. Regulations that limit an institution's strategic decision-making (autonomy) should be looked at critically, and further professionalization of institutional leadership and management is to be considered seriously.

In its communications, the EU is rather clear about the role of higher education and research organizations in contributing to its 2020 Strategy. Although the Lisbon Strategy of 2000 failed in some respects, the plan to achieve Europe's grand ambitions will be continued. Given the EU's past integration experience, which shows both progress and stagnation, the current mixed political attitudes toward an integrated Europe, and the unfavourable financial situation, there is no certainty that the EU will meet these goals. Failure, however, will imperil the achievement of the Europe of Knowledge. And if the EU's policy framework is incorrect, this in turn will jeopardize Europe's future competitiveness and wealth.

NOTES

1. The first Stability and Growth Pact was established in the early to mid-1990s, followed by reforms in 2003–05 and 2010–11. For an overview, see Schuknecht et al. (2011).
2. See http://europa.eu/lisbon_treaty/full_text/index_en.htm.
3. The political institutions laid down in the Lisbon Treaty (Art. 13) are the European Parliament, European Council, Council of the European Union, European Commission, European Court of Justice, European Central Bank, and European Court of Auditors.
4. The Six Pack applies to all 28 member states, with some specific rules (financial sanctions) for the Eurozone countries. The Fiscal Compact is an intergovernmental agreement (not an EU law) signed by 26 member states (all but the UK and Czech Republic), but will be binding only on the Eurozone countries. See http://ec.europa.eu/economy_finance/articles/governance/2012-03-14_six_pack_en.htm, accessed 8 July 2013.
5. See http://ec.europa.eu/education/lifelong-learning-programme/doc80_en.htm, accessed 8 July 2013.
6. The "16" refers to the fact that at the time, there were 15 EU member states.

REFERENCES

Council of the European Union. 2009. "Conclusions of the Council and of the Representatives of the Governments of the Member States, Meeting within the Council, of 26 November 2009 on Developing the Role of Education in a Fully-Functioning Knowledge Triangle." *Official Journal of the European Union.* C 302. At http://eur-lex.europa.eu/LexUriServ/LexUriServ.do?uri=OJ:C:200 9:302:0003:0005:EN:PDF (accessed 8 July 2013).

EC (European Commission). 2000. *Towards a European Research Area.* Communication from the Commission to the Council, the European Parliament, the Economic and Social Committee and the Committee of the Regions. COM(2000) 6 final. Brussels: EC.

—. 2003. *The Role of the Universities in the Europe of Knowledge.* Communication from the Commission. COM(2003) 58 final. Brussels: EC.

—. 2005. *Mobilising the Brainpower of Europe: Enabling Universities to Make Their Full Contribution to the Lisbon Strategy.* Communication from the Commission. COM(2005) 152 final. Brussels: EC.

—. 2006. *Putting Knowledge into Practice: A Broad-Based Innovation Strategy for the EU.* Communication from the Commission to the Council, the European Parliament, the European Economic and Social Committee and the Committee of the Regions. COM(2006) 502 final. Brussels: EC.

—. 2007. *Commission Staff Working Document Accompanying the Green Paper "The European Research Area: New Perspectives."* SEC(2007) 412/2. Brussels: EC.

—. 2010. *Europe 2020: A Strategy for Smart, Sustainable and Inclusive Growth.* Communication from the Commission. COM(2010) 2020 final. Brussels: EC.

—. 2011a. *Innovation Union Competitiveness: Report 2011.* Brussels: EC/DG Research & Innovation.

—. 2011b. *Innovation Union Scoreboard 2010: The Innovation Union's Performance Scoreboard for Research and Innovation.* Brussels: EC/DG Enterprise & Industry.

—. 2011c. *Supporting Growth and Jobs: An Agenda for the Modernisation of Europe's Higher Education Systems.* Communication from the Commission to the European Parliament, the Council, the European Economic and Social Committee and the Committee of the Regions. COM(2011) 567 final. Brussels: EC.

—. 2011d. *Horizon 2020: The Framework Programme for Research and Innovation.* Communication from the Commission to the European Parliament, the Council, the European Economic and Social Committee and the Committee of the Regions. COM(2011) 808 final. Brussels: EC.

—. 2011e. *Commission Staff Working Document on Recent Developments in European Higher Education Systems.* Accompanying the document *Supporting Growth and Jobs: An Agenda for the Modernisation of Europe's Higher Education Systems* (Communication from the Commission to the European Parliament, the Council, the European Economic and Social Committee and the Committee of the Regions). SEC(2011) 1063 final. Brussels: EC/DG Education & Culture.

ECom (European Communities). 2002. *The European Research Area: An Internal Knowledge Market.* Luxembourg: Office for Official Publications of the European Communities.

—. 2004. *Facing the Challenge: The Lisbon Strategy for Growth and Employment.* Luxembourg: Office for Official Publications of the European Communities.

—. 2006. "Decision of the European Parliament and the Council Establishing an Integrated Action Programme in the Field of Lifelong Learning." *Official Journal of the European Union*. Brussels.

European Council. 2000. "Presidency Conclusions Lisbon European Council, 24 March." Nr. 100/1/00. Lisbon. At http://www.consilium.europa.eu/uedocs/cms_data/docs/pressdata/en/ec/00100-r1.en0.htm (accessed 8 July 2013).

Jongbloed, B. 2003. "Marketisation in Higher Education: Clark's Triangle and the Essential Ingredients of Markets." *Higher Education Quarterly* 57 (2):110–135.

Neave, G., and F. van Vught. 1991. *Prometheus Bound: The Changing Relationship between Government and Higher Education in Western Europe*. Oxford: Pergamon Press.

Schuknecht, L., P. Moutot, P. Rother, and J. Stark. 2011. *The Stability and Growth Pact: Crisis and Reform*. Occasional Paper Series No. 129. Frankfurt am Main: European Central Bank. At http://www.ecb.europa.eu/pub/pubbydate/2011/html/index.en.html (accessed 8 July 2013).

CHAPTER 16

INSTITUTIONAL ALLIANCES:
PASSING POLICY FAD OR
NEW ORGANIZATIONAL MODEL?

Maria Slowey

INTRODUCTION

The fostering of institutional alliances, regional clusters, strategic networks, and the like features high on policy agendas for higher education
in many European countries. The nature and the intensity of these arrangements, however, vary greatly. At one end of the scale, the alliance
may represent little more than a nominal "letterhead" indication of intent
by universities and/or other higher education institutions that they plan
to work collaboratively in specified areas. At the other extreme, it may
involve a detailed memorandum of agreement (MOA) as the first step
toward the full merger of two or more institutions.

Individual academics, and groups of academics, have, of course, always
engaged in regional, national, and international collaborative arrangements. This is a natural, organic aspect of the search for new knowledge
and cross-fertilization: transcending institutional and national boundaries, in pursuit of innovative ways of looking at, and understanding,
the world.

In recent years, however, there appears to have been something of a
qualitative shift in this aspect of the higher education landscape. Thus,
we find many examples of public policy-steering, with the objective
of fostering alliances, networks, and mergers of institutions of higher

Making Policy in Turbulent Times: Challenges and Prospects for Higher Education, ed. P. Axelrod, R.D. Trilokekar,
T. Shanahan, and R. Wellen. Kingston: School of Policy Studies, Queen's University.

education. Sometimes this steering is accompanied by incentives to establish and reinforce a variety of types of academic alliances, while sometimes institutions that are unwilling – or indeed, unable – to so engage find themselves at a disadvantage.

The complex interactions of economic, political, and organizational factors that underpin this trend are explored in this chapter in a comparative perspective. The focus is on the more flexible, "softer" end of the spectrum outlined above – that is, on collaborative arrangements that stop well short of merger, such as networks, in which participating institutions retain full autonomy while committing, to varying degrees, to work in collaboration with other autonomous universities and/or other institutions of higher education.

The case of Ireland is used to illustrate a number of more general developments at the European level. While a small country, Ireland is interesting for a number of reasons: it has a binary system of higher education that is well represented (that is, disproportionate to its size) in international rankings; it is part of the anglophone world, yet is also an active player in European higher education developments – in particular, the Bologna Process and the establishment of the European Higher Education Area (EHEA). In addition, by 2005, the economy of Ireland had been transformed to become one of the fastest-growing in Western Europe – epitomized by the term "Celtic Tiger," which quickly extended beyond its original political and economic meaning of an Irish, export-led economic boom to encompass dominant aspects of Irish culture and identity over this period (for example, Keohane and Kuhling 2004; Healy and Slowey 2006). A healthy surplus in the government coffers enabled a significant step change in levels of investment in higher education and, in particular, in the expensive research areas related to STEM (science, technology, engineering, and mathematics) subjects. This period of unsustainable boom was rapidly followed by an economic crisis with major implications for not only the funding of higher education but also, and even more importantly, its contribution to society at a time of significant economic and social turmoil.

As is discussed in detail below, in Ireland, as illustrative of what was also happening in many other European countries, the fostering of greater collaboration and alliances among universities (and other institutions of higher education) became quite a consistent topic on the higher education policy agenda. From a policy perspective, alliances and collaborative approaches have several potential advantages for helping states address the interconnected demands of globalization and national priorities. Governments look to them for assistance in i) delivering larger scale and critical mass, ii) generating synergies, iii) reducing duplication, and, perhaps most importantly, iv) improving cost-effectiveness. From this perspective also, steering higher education through collaborative arrangements and alliances may appear both bureaucratically neater and politically less challenging than dealing with a larger number of universities, all greatly protective of their autonomy.

In exploring these issues, the analytic perspective draws on Clark's (1998) concept of the "enhanced developmental periphery," derived from his classic qualitative case studies of a number of universities in England, Scotland, the Netherlands, Sweden, and Finland as they sought to develop in a context of constant external change. The enhanced developmental periphery represents both an approach and a body of expertise that supplements those of traditional disciplinary departments, exploring new interfaces with the external world – supporting institutions as they seek to engage proactively with a wide variety of external relationships and the increasing complexity of the (often competing) demands they face from the state, students, industry, employers, and civil society.

This chapter is divided into four parts. The first outlines key socio-economic factors contributing to a policy focus on fostering collaboration and alliances in higher education and the associated issue of the role of the "steering state." The second outlines a number of models of alliances. The third explores the general issues by examining the case of Ireland and the steering role of the state in "encouraging" institutions to form regional alliances and clusters. The final part locates the theme of alliances, collaborative networks, and the like within the context of Clark's analysis of the enhanced developmental periphery and the interesting question, raised by Peterson (2010, 154) in his overview of research on colleges and universities as organizations, as to whether these are simply manifestations of how institutions respond – at the margins or peripheries – to their changing environments or whether they, just possibly, signal a new "emerging organizational" model in higher education.

WHY THE POLICY FOCUS ON FOSTERING COLLABORATION AND ALLIANCES?

An international review of factors behind the increasing interest of governments in the use of mergers and other forms of collaboration to achieve systemic restructuring identified five important underlying drivers (Harman and Meek 2002, 1):

- to increase efficiency and effectiveness, especially in relation to dealing with increasing student numbers
- to deal with "non-viable" institutions and institutional fragmentation
- to widen access and implement wider-scale equity strategies
- to differentiate course offerings with a view to responding to diversity and enhancing quality
- to increase government control of the direction of higher education systems with a view to ensuring that higher education institutions serve "more directly national and regional economic social objectives"

A decade after this analysis, the force of these drivers has not diminished; if anything, following the economic crisis that hit Europe and the global economy in 2008, it has intensified. Inevitably, this has led governments to seek increased cost savings as public expenditure budgets have been drastically reduced. Many have also intensified their utilitarian perspective on higher education, prioritizing both research and teaching in areas that are perceived to be most associated with economic competitiveness. Despite the demonstrable failure of the neo-liberal market policies adopted by many countries, the classic neo-liberal contradiction remains: at the same time as many governments seek to reduce the extent of state investment in higher education (and to encourage students and employers to make more substantial contributions), they are equally intent on extending their influence, if not control, of the system.

The culture, traditions, structures, funding, and governance of higher education are, of course, different in each country. It is important to note that, in some countries (including Ireland and the United Kingdom), universities have always been legally autonomous institutions, while in many European countries, universities have been autonomous in terms of academic freedom, but legally subordinate to state administrations. While the Bologna Process and the associated establishment of the EHEA have allowed universities to retain their distinctive national traditions, a major outcome has been, for good or ill, to reduce some of these differences. As Scott points out in his comprehensive review of the impact of Bologna, there are many "examples of multiple readings of Bologna" (Scott 2012, 4). The Bologna Process was initiated in times of economic prosperity and optimism for the "European project," but the 2010–11 crisis of the Eurozone has changed the environment dramatically. "Paradoxically, the pressure on social expenditure has placed greater emphasis on 'market' solutions in higher education – at a time when 'market' solutions in the wider economy have been called into question by the catastrophic events since 2008" (Scott 2012, 6).

The UK, frequently regarded as leading the charge toward entrepreneurialism and marketization in higher education, has also been in the forefront of using targeted and strategic funding to "shape" the system. A 2010 report on alliances, clusters, and mergers commissioned by the Higher Education Funding Council for England (HEFCE) highlighted the following key contextual factors: the end of "old style growth" with reductions in public expenditure, unprecedented increases in recent demand for places, increased expectations regarding quality of provision, demand from employers with respect to the role of higher education in giving students "employability" skills and the alignment of provision with employer and employment market demand, and growing international competition (HEFCE 2010).

According to this report, universities and other institutions of higher education adopt a number of approaches to deal with these challenges, including seeking to establish a "distinctive" mission and profile, reviewing and realigning their academic portfolios, focusing on enhancement of the student experience, and carrying out a variety of cost-cutting exercises. The same challenges also provide "an impetus for the sector to examine the full spectrum of the different models and types of collaborative activity (ranging from informal collaboration, strategic alliances, consortia or joint ventures through to more formal federations and full mergers of institutions)" (HEFCE 2010, 3).

In 2002, Harman and Meek's analysis of the drivers for alliances and mergers drew attention to the desire of many governments to gain greater control over their higher education systems – seeking to steer them toward national and regional social and economic objectives. A decade later, as the national policy aim of creating a "knowledge economy" becomes almost ubiquitous across European and other states of the Organisation for Economic Co-operation and Development (OECD), the ideological underpinnings of this motivation have become even more explicit.

> The discourse over the role and future of national and supranational systems of higher education is tied increasingly to the perceived and real economic benefits of state sponsored tertiary education. Governments and policy makers ubiquitously frame science policy and the productivity and interrelationships of universities with industry and innovation as the essential means for maintaining or advancing economic competitiveness within a globalising economy. Even issues of access and degree production are increasingly discussed largely in terms of national or regional competitiveness. (Douglass 2007, 96)

In this context, as will be discussed further below, in many countries and at broader international or regional levels (such as Europe), one additional driver promoting collaboration and alliances needs to be added. This relates to the intertwined issues of research excellence and institutional differentiation – in effect, the reinforcing of institutional hierarchies. The focus on global rankings, coupled with the widely held view that there is a strong connection between university-based research and economic growth, has led to a significant step change in the emphasis on research. In modern times (in this context, since 1945), research, particularly in STEM subjects, has gained an increasingly central place in the mission of universities. The decade 2002–12 also saw, for European institutions, a major new emphasis on public accountability, quality assessment, "relevance," and dissemination of research.

Many areas of scientific and technological research necessitate levels of investment in expensive equipment and facilities beyond the reach of many individual institutions – or even some countries. As Altbach points out, it

> may not be possible for each country to have a research university, but many developing and middle-income countries can develop universities with research capacity and the ability to participate in the world knowledge system. Smaller countries can form regional academic alliances to build enough strength in selected fields to promote participation in global science. (Altbach 2007, 112–113)

So given the autonomous status of universities – and to varying degrees, other institutions of higher education – how can public policy stimulate desired responses? While governments may not be in a position to intervene directly in higher education, the growing importance of the sector to policy agendas connected with knowledge and skills, research and development, and innovation have led to the increasing use of "policy steering mechanisms" in the shaping of higher education (Neave 2004). Aspects of these developments are clearly associated with a dominant policy focus on the "reform" of higher education and international harmonization – both of which are criticized as fostering new managerialism and new governance structures and potentially paving the way for further marketization in higher education in Europe and elsewhere (UNESCO 2005; Enders and van Vught 2007; Hackl 2009).

To take the European Union (EU) as an example, policy is steered largely through engagement with stakeholders and networks of experts and the like – what has been termed the "open method of coordination" (Cort 2009, 170). It is, however, also accompanied by the increased use of earmarked funding. In this respect, it is important not to underestimate what Batory and Lindstrom (2011, 311) refer to as "the power of the purse" and the considerable steering impact of targeted funding provided by EU-supported higher education initiatives.

Models of alliances

In response to these pressures – whether direct or indirect, carrot or stick – a number of types of alliance structures can be identified, with both vertical and horizontal dimensions (Marginson 2011). Some contemporary models include:

- Groups of institutions at a national level with common definitional characteristics, which also distinguish them in terms of status – for example, the Russell Group of universities in the UK and the Australian Group of Eight.
- International institutional associations formed by institutions with similar characteristics – for example, Universitas 21, the Coimbra Group, and the Alliance of Innovative Universities.

- "Big science" collaborative groupings, such as those fostered by the EU's seventh Framework Programme for Research, with networks of up to 35 institutions across Europe.
- Networked developmental alliances, often led by regional development agencies, city councils, and the like, focused on civic engagement, innovative pedagogy, and curriculum development – for example, work on universities and regional engagement supported by the OECD, the Observatory PASCAL, Melbourne Knowledge Capital, Creative Dublin Alliance, and other organizations.

A number of potential advantages of such forms of alliance are evident: as voluntary associations of independent institutions, they are not exclusive, thereby allowing institutions the benefits of strengthened collaborative networks, while maintaining the autonomy to develop other partnerships as suits their interests (even to the point of merger if they so wish).

Such forms of alliances also possibly fit more closely with an emerging "network governance" approach, which has been described as a shift in the policy arena away from the new public management approach associated with neo-liberalism that dominated the first decade of the 21st century (Ferlie, Musselin, and Andresani 2007). While acknowledging that few countries currently display all of the features associated with this approach, these authors argue that particular elements can be discerned, including less emphasis on market-based reforms or hard budgetary constraints and more on the "development of higher education networks between higher education institutions and between higher education institutions and other social actors" (Ferlie, Musselin, and Andresani 2007, 68). These networks are not simply managed from above but, at their best, may have the capacity to become self-steering and with a focus on organizational learning, joint problem recognition, and problem-solving capacity, diffusing good practice through these networks – all with the overall aim of enhancing quality across the system.

This network approach may already be replacing a traditional linear model of technology transfer, with contract research and consultancy services engaging in more dynamic ways. "Reach-out units are established and financial incentives are introduced alongside reforms in governance and organizational structures in order to improve the links between public sector research and the business sector. These changes have made the traditional picture of higher education fuzzier around the edges" (Jongbloed, Enders, and Salerno 2007, 46).

The focus here is on collaborative work within strategic alliances. But what does this mean in practice at the institutional level, as institutions seek to maintain autonomy and independence while collaborating within such strategic alliances? What about the imbalances in status, resourcing, and scale of different partners? What about the relative commitment to alliances based primarily on research compared to those with broader educational objectives?

To help describe some of these general issues, I now consider recent developments in higher education in Ireland.

"STEERING" COLLABORATION AND ALLIANCES: THE CASE OF IRELAND

As mentioned in the introduction, Ireland provides an interesting case for a number of reasons. It is a small English-speaking country with a university system derived largely from the 19th-century ideas of John Henry Newman (1913). It has, in recent years, played an active role at the European level in the development of the Bologna Process and the EHEA and was, for example, among the first countries to fully sign up to the implementation of the Bologna approach to learning outcomes. Its university system is generally perceived to be efficient: a study by the economic and financial ministers of the European Commission (EC), for example, showed Ireland coming first both in terms of graduates per 1,000 inhabitants and in terms of how international employers rate Irish graduates (St. Aubyn et al. 2009).

Fostering research collaboration

In relation to research investment and output, Ireland's performance progressed significantly over the first decade of the 21st century – described, with forgivable hyperbole, by the minister of education and skills in a speech to the Royal Irish Academy as "meteoric" – to a point where it "ranked within the top 20 nations in the world across all research fields, and Irish research institutions feature within the top 1 per cent in the world in 18 key fields" (DES 2011, 3). While highlighting the limitations of international rankings, an analysis by Hazelkorn (2011) shows a relatively strong performance of the Irish system in such rankings. Eight Irish higher education institutions featured in the global top 500 out of more than 15,000 universities, and, measured on a per capita basis, Ireland had the eighth-highest number of high-ranking institutions. This was achieved despite relatively limited resource support for teaching – for example, investment per student in Trinity College Dublin (Ireland's internationally highest-ranked university) is estimated to be less than one-sixth that of universities in the United States with comparable research outputs (Hazelkorn 2011).

In terms of research investment, in Ireland, as in many other countries, a complex "steering" model was used to support work in areas defined as being of national strategic importance. From a historically low base, it is estimated that investment in Irish higher education–based research from all sources (public and private) quadrupled over the decade to 2009, raising Ireland to around the OECD and EU-25 average (Department of Enterprise, Trade and Employment 2009). This steep change in levels of investment was particularly concentrated in areas perceived to have the most direct potential economic impact, such as biotechnology and information and communications technologies (ICTs). Competitive proposals were subject to international peer scrutiny, with a strong emphasis on fostering collaboration among researchers across different institutions and engagement from relevant industrial partners.

The main channels through which this investment was delivered were Science Foundation Ireland, which supported leading-edge research in science and technology, with a particular focus on biotechnology and ICTs; the Programme for Research in Third-Level Institutions (PRTLI), under the Higher Education Authority (HEA), with a particular focus on supporting strategic research infrastructure development in universities and other institutions of higher education; and the Irish Research Council for Science, Engineering, and Technology and the Irish Research Council for Humanities and Social Sciences, with a particular focus on supporting high-quality academic research.

A common feature of these quite different initiatives was a focus on encouraging inter-institutional collaboration. To take the case of PRTLI, for example, from a policy perspective, the scheme succeeded in engendering "a culture of strategic collaboration in higher education institutions, so as to develop critical mass around research activity and education provision across all disciplines especially in the areas of science and technology but also including the Arts, Humanities and Social Sciences" (HEA 2012, 67).

The examples above focus on research. What about collaboration in other areas such as teaching and learning and regional engagement?

Collaboration in teaching and learning: the Dublin Region Higher Education Alliance

In 2004, an OECD review of the higher education system in Ireland commented that competition among institutions was

> generally regarded as a force for quality and institutional development but Irish HEIs [higher education institutions] need to recognise that they are relatively small and that the undoubted strength of the system will only be fully realised through institutional collaboration whether in research, postgraduate programmes, first degree work or lifelong learning. We believe that collaboration should be *incentivised* in funding mechanisms in order to break down the sectoral and other barriers that undoubtedly exist. (OECD 2004, 20; emphasis added)

In the context of both formal university autonomy and fiercely independent institutional cultures, how might such institutional collaboration be "incentivized"? The approach adopted could be viewed as a classic illustration of Neave's policy-steering mechanism. In 2006, the HEA initiated a Strategic Innovation Fund (SIF) aimed at stimulating innovation in areas of policy priority associated with educational innovation. A significant investment was announced to support innovative strategic approaches, aimed at enhancing the quality and effectiveness of various dimensions of higher education (HEA 2013). The mechanism required matched funding from institutions and an associated commitment from senior levels within universities and the other institutions of higher education that these should be strategic initiatives (as opposed to one-off projects) with a strong focus on not only inter-institutional, but also cross-sectoral collaboration.

In February 2008, the result of the competitive bidding round for the second cycle of the SIF was announced: 31 projects were approved, of which 30 were collaborative, including two "sectoral" submissions from the Irish Universities Association (the body representing the seven universities in Ireland) and Institutes of Technology Ireland (the representative body for the 14 institutes of technology). The press release issued by the minister of education and skills at the time drew attention to the development, through the SIF, of new strategic alliances, which would create

> new synergies and potential for the higher education system.... Through the range of initiatives being supported, SIF is providing new impetus to the development of system-wide quality. It is driving reform of structures and systems within and across institutions to cater for growing student numbers at all levels, improved teaching and learning quality, ensuring graduates are equipped for a lifetime of innovation and change in the workplace and enhancing our research and innovation capacity. (DES 2008)

One such alliance formed in response to the SIF competitive bidding process was the Dublin Region Higher Education Alliance (DRHEA). (An overview is provided in the Appendix.) This alliance was unusual in two respects. The first was in terms of scale, with its members representing more than half of the entire Irish higher education sector. The second was that it crossed the binary divide, being made up of four universities – Dublin City University (DCU), National University of Ireland, Maynooth (NUIM), University College Dublin (UCD), and Trinity College Dublin (TCD) – and four institutes of technology (Dublin Institute of Technology (DIT), Institute of Art, Design and Technology (IADT), Institute of Technology Blanchardstown (ITB), and Institute of Technology Tallaght (ITT).

The DRHEA secured SIF funding for a program of work around four major strands: i) Enhancement of Learning, ii) Graduate Education, iii) Widening Access, and iv) Internationalization. Different institutions took the lead on each of these four strands, their respective presidents signed an MOA, and the DRHEA was launched with appropriate fanfare. As the intention was to keep administrative overhead to a minimum, the DRHEA was not set up as a legal entity; instead, all the resourcing for the detailed work packages was channelled through individual institutions. A complex governance structure was thus necessitated to ensure appropriate leadership and lines of accountability for delivering the detailed program of work and financial reporting.

An external evaluation commissioned by the HEA two years into the operation of the SIF identified the DRHEA as a "flagship" initiative (Davies 2010, 47). The evaluator noted that expectations were high and that there were a number of successes, including the signing by the presidents of eight institutions of an MOA, the establishment of a governance structure allowing for a common approach to research students across all institutions, and the development of trust and mutual respect. However, the review also recommended that the HEA take a more active role in monitoring the DRHEA until a "comfortable level of collaboration" (47) was achieved and that the HEA should consider dealing only with the DRHEA on SIF projects rather than with individual institutions. The evaluation concluded that the DRHEA was a very significant development for Irish higher education at both national and international levels and that it should be actively supported.

The reality, however, was that the allocation of SIF funds had been from the beginning, as the external evaluator pointed out, highly erratic. This was partly because many of the projects had been slow to get off the ground. More importantly, just as the main activity was set to commence, the national economic situation deteriorated drastically. In the early 2000s, Irish government balances had sat comfortably above the gross domestic product, mainly based on unsustainable taxes derived from property building and transactions. When the bubble burst, there was no "soft landing," and public finances collapsed (EC 2011).

As a result, not only the institutions, but also the HEA itself was uncertain whether the funding earmarked and agreed to for SIF projects was to be delayed, reduced, or slashed drastically. Institutions had entered into contractual commitments for expenditure without knowing whether the agreed-upon funds would actually be made available. It was, as the evaluator pointed out, rather ironic "given the name of the fund, that fiscal uncertainty has made strategic innovation very difficult. As one senior person advised during a site visit, 'Don't let this drag on. If you can't support it, end it'" (Davies 2010, 47).

In the midst of this rather tumultuous situation for the DRHEA, the announcement of a new research-led Innovation Alliance by two Dublin universities (TCD and UCD) did not pass unremarked.

Later in 2010, an external review was commissioned by the chair of the DRHEA, with a view to informing future development in the light of changed economic and social circumstances. Based on interviews with key players from each of the eight member institutions, and the external chair of the board, this review made six recommendations (Morgan 2011, 4).

1. There should be a "rejuvenation" of the DRHEA involving an exam-
    ination of its purpose, the strands that it might encompass, as well
    as the process by which its funding occurs.
2. A particular focus in the revised program should be on the success-
    ful strands in the earlier phase, particularly Graduate Education and
    Teaching and Learning.
3. As far as possible, there should be a linkage with a Dublin identity
    and visions for the Dublin region.
4. Particular attention should be given to the public profile of the project.
5. A funding mechanism should be put in place through which funds
    will accrue to the activities in the program.
6. Any MOA should take into account interactions between the program
    and the other arrangements among the institutions involved.

These recommendations reflect the fact that although the DRHEA was an alliance that had been voluntarily established and shaped by the partner institutions – and was, to that extent, a "bottom up" creation – it had been formed as a response to an incentivized national policy initia-tive and was, therefore, also the product of a "top down" policy focus. Furthermore, the commitment of individual members (ranging from small institutes of technology to Ireland's highest-ranked university) to particular aspects of the collaborative work inevitably varied, depending on the extent of the fit with their strategic objectives and mission.

And, in all of this, a question that merits further investigation concerns the relative strengths and sustainability of different types of alliances – a comparison between, on the one hand, those that are primarily designed to support teaching and learning and regional development and, on the other, those that are primarily designed to promote research collabora-tion. When the economic crisis hit Ireland, every effort was made to protect investment in research, especially in scientific and technological areas. The external evaluator for SIF, in teasing out the response to the rhetorical question as to why, in times of fiscal difficulty, funding for teaching and learning projects tends to be hit first, while comparable strands of funding for research are more likely to remain intact, com-mented that the

standard answer, I would think, is that research projects are intended to produce tangible advancements in knowledge, while projects to strengthen the very institutions within which teaching and research are carried out are less specific and more problematic. But this answer reflects a bias, surely unintended, toward advancement of knowledge and against human development. Put somewhat crudely, there is a knee-jerk reaction against cutting research projects and an unspoken assumption that institutional improvement can always wait. (Davies 2010, 52)

Regional clusters and the emergence of a new national strategy

Four years after the establishment of the DRHEA – conceived in a time of economic boom and operational at a time of economic crisis – a *National Strategy for Higher Education to 2030* was published (DES 2011). A series of recommendations in the Strategy concerned the need to find new ways of promoting greater collaboration. These were subsequently developed further by the HEA, with the introduction of the concept of "regional clusters."

> The future landscape of Irish higher education will require a coherent framework comprised of a variety of institutions of different kinds, with distinct well-defined roles, responsibilities and inter-relationships. The building of regional collaborative clusters of such distinct institutions is key to the delivery of many of the most important objectives of the National Strategy and to the delivery of the overarching objective of achieving a more coherent, higher quality and more efficient higher education system. Clusters will allow programmes of teaching and learning to be better planned and co-ordinated, resources to be used more efficiently, more flexible student pathways and better progression opportunities to be put in place, and better and more coordinated services to enterprise and society to be provided at a regional level. (HEA 2012, 19)

The strategy specifies that regional clusters are expected to i) form an important mechanism to bridge the gap between further and higher education through better student pathways and recognition of learning outcomes, ii) include mission-based (in addition to geographical) clusters to guarantee the continuing provision of labour-market-oriented and practice-led specialist provision, iii) provide an "ideal platform" to ensure coherence and comprehensiveness of provision locally and regionally and eliminate unnecessary duplication, and iv) include international collaboration.

In addition, it is expected that smaller and specialist institutions (such as colleges of education) will be consolidated through incorporation into or merger with existing universities, institutes of technology, or technological universities.

The report drew attention to a number of existing groupings, including the DRHEA, as nascent clusters on which regional clusters might build.

It is important to note that, in a typical example of policy-steering, the report envisages that *all* higher education institutions will be expected to actively participate in regional clusters.

So from "bottom up," voluntary alliances among institutions, the case of Ireland shows a fairly typical firming up of the policy focus over the decade since the Harman and Meek analysis in 2002. This can be traced from a recommendation in a review of higher education (OECD 2004) through a range of incentivized policy initiatives (such as the SIF in 2007) to the publication of a national strategy for higher education (DES 2011).

ALLIANCES IN HIGHER EDUCATION: A NEW ORGANIZATIONAL MODEL OR A CASE OF "BUSINESS AS USUAL"?

The case of the establishment of the DRHEA highlights both the potential and some of the challenges for collaborative alliances among universities and/or other institutions of higher education. The factors underlying the popularity of this approach with European and other OECD governments and public policy agencies remain evident, including building scale and critical mass, generating synergies, cutting down on duplication, and, it is hoped, improving cost-effectiveness. Over and above these issues may lie a view that steering higher education through collaborative arrangements and alliances may be bureaucratically and politically less challenging than dealing directly in certain areas with autonomous universities.

Widespread policy confidence in this approach raises many interesting questions, just three of which are highlighted here. First, to what extent are institutional alliances almost inevitably likely to be transient, rather fragile entities? Second, how successful do research-based alliances appear to be compared to those primarily based on teaching and learning? And third, from an analytic perspective, to what extent does the formation of alliances among institutions of higher education constitute "business as usual" for universities in the 21st century or, potentially, point to the emergence of some form of new organizational model?

In relation to the general issue of the longevity or otherwise of alliances and networks, on the assumption that the participating institutions are relatively strong in their own right, perhaps it might be more appropriate to think of an alliance or network as serving a specific purpose for a particular period of time rather than becoming a semi-permanent arrangement. Not only will institutional priorities vary over time, but so also will institutional leadership and other key actors.

It may be interesting, perhaps, to draw on experience from the business sector. One investigation into why it is estimated that around half of alliances in business and industry end in failure points to the way they are "traditionally organized and managed" (Kaplan, Norton, and Rugelsjoen 2010, 114) as the prime culprit. The authors argue that most alliances are defined by service level agreements (SLAs) that identify what each side commits to delivering rather than what each hopes to gain – so that when the external environment changes, the managers responsible for the alliance do not know the extent to which they should remain faithful to the original objectives and conditions or seek to renegotiate, by which time

> the companies' leaders have returned to run their own organizations and haven't followed up to ensure that their vision for synergies is being realized. The middle managers coordinating the alliance, who have no clear way to translate their leaders' vision into action, simply focus on achieving the operational SLA targets instead of working across organizational boundaries to make the alliance a strategic success. And because the managers usually remain under the HR policies and follow the career development paths of their parent organization, they have little incentive to commit much energy to the project. (Kaplan, Norton, and Rugelsjoen 2010, 114)

For higher education, there is a second, related question concerning the relative weight – and hence sustainability – of research-led alliances over those mainly oriented to teaching and learning. The Irish examples discussed above clearly point to factors that explain why this may be the case – including the fact that it may be easier to identify the potential for complementary strengths in research among institutions and hence the associated "win win" necessary for lasting institutional commitment.

Finally, what about the analytic implications? As Ferlie, Musselin, and Andresani point out, there may well be advantages for institutions in the form of collaborations, consortia, and strategic alliances that can be "hybrid states between stand alone status for each higher education institution and mergers" (Ferlie, Musselin, and Andresani 2007, 70). But do they really constitute some type of new organizational form in higher education?

Here it is interesting to draw on the work of Peterson (2010), who traces the major strands in the emergence of analytic frameworks (often competing) for the study of universities and other institutions of higher education in the US over three broad periods: i) 1950–1972, "from traditional to mass higher education"; ii) 1972–1995, "the post-secondary era"; and iii) 1975–2005, "the emerging post-secondary knowledge industry." This analysis is summarized in Table 1.

Peterson discusses the emergence in the mid-2000s of strategic alliances, networks, joint ventures, and the like among higher education institutions. He proceeds to pose the question as to whether these ways that universities and other institutions of higher education work together may be of lasting significance – in effect, constituting an emerging new type of organizational model, one that does not yet have an underpinning academic literature and body of independent research. In this, Peterson points out that this phenomenon might simply be an illustration of one of the five dimensions proposed by Burton Clark (1998) as being important for contemporary universities if they wish to actively self-manage their environment.

The enhanced developmental periphery is both an outward-looking perspective and a body of expertise that supplements traditional disciplinary-based departments. It is a part of the university that helps the institution survive and develop by exploring and managing complex new interfaces with the external world, including relationships with other universities and institutions of higher education. Or, in contrast, we may be observing the emergence of a genuinely new form of "inter-organizational model" (Peterson 2010, 176).

TABLE 1
Overview of primary institutional challenges and some associated analytic frameworks applied to the study of higher education in the US (1950–2005)

Dominant environment pressures	Primary institutional challenges	Emerging analytic frameworks and organizational models
1950–1964 Growth and expansion	Direction and accountability	Community; rational or bureaucratic
1972–1995 "Disruption" and equity demands	Order, control, and access	Saga, political, conglomerate; loose coupling, organized anarchy
1972–1985 Declining demand, economic recession, and constraint	Market pressure, efficiency, and productivity	Market, institutional theory, resource dependence, techno-managerial, strategic
1985–1995 Quality, access, and equity	Effectiveness, complexity, restructuring, and re-engineering	Cultural, matrix, cybermetric
1995–2005 Rapid change, high expectations, unpredictable	Institutional redesign	Adaptive, contextual, entrepreneurial, virtual
Diversity, telematics, new learning "markets," quality, productivity, globalization, and resource constraint	Redefinition, redirection, reorganization, and renewal	Alliances, partnerships, joint ventures, networks, cross-national

Source: Author's compilation from Peterson (2010, 152–153, Table 6.1).

So alliances, clusters, and other more structured forms of collaboration (short of merger) could simply be a case of "business as usual" as higher education institutions seek creative ways to survive and develop in collaboration with other partners. Alternatively, might they now constitute more permanent features of the higher education landscape? Perhaps they are phenomena so widespread that they may ultimately require different governance models than those that apply to stand-alone institutions (Shattock 2006).

These are interesting analytic questions that would benefit from indepth empirical analysis. The practical challenges of fostering collaboration at regional levels also warrant detailed investigation. Watson, in his analysis of the ways in which universities might achieve greater levels of civic and community engagement in their regions, points out that among the myriad of external relationships that have to be managed, the most sensitive set of external relationships "is likely to be with other HEIs [higher education institutions] especially in the same city or the same region" (Watson 2007, 126).

The ebb and flow of many alliances over time may be inevitable. However, given the fact that, in many institutions, faculty and staff at all levels expend a great deal of time and energy in the formation and operation of strategic alliances, it is to be hoped that the outcomes are superior to what an individual institution might be able to achieve if working in isolation from other partners – whether in terms of widening access, enhancing the student experience, creating vibrant links with civic society, engaging with public and private sector employers, or engaging in greater research activity.

REFERENCES

Altbach, P. 2007. "Peripheries and Centres: Research Universities in Developing Countries." *Higher Education Management Policy* 19 (2):111–134.

Batory, A., and N. Lindstrom. 2011. "The Power of the Purse: Supranational Entrepreneurship, Financial Incentives, and European Higher Education Policy." *Governance: An International Journal of Policy, Administration, and Institutions* 24 (2):311–329.

Clark, B.R. 1998. *Creating Entrepreneurial Universities: Organizational Pathways of Transformations*. Oxford: Elsevier.

Cort, P. 2009. "The Open Method of Coordination in Vocational Education and Training: A Triangle of EU Governance." In *Research of vs Research for Educational Policy*, ed. D. Desjardins and K. Rubenson, 170–184. Saarbrücken: VDM.

Davies, G. 2010. *Interim Evaluation of SIF Cycle II: Report to the HEA*. Dublin: HEA.

Department of Enterprise, Trade and Employment. 2009. *Science, Technology and Innovation: Delivering the Smart Economy*. Dublin: Government Publications.

DES. 2008. "Minister Hanafin Announces Almost €100 Million for Higher Education Reform Process." Press release, 19 February. At http://www.education.ie/en/Press-Events/Press-Releases/2008-Press-Releases/PR08-02-19.html (accessed 12 August 2012).

—. 2011. *National Strategy for Higher Education to 2030.* Dublin: DES.

Douglass, J.A. 2007. "The Entrepreneurial State and Research Universities in the United States: Policy and New State-Based Initiatives." *Higher Education Management and Policy* 19 (1):95–132.

EC. 2011. *The Economic Adjustment Programme for Ireland.* Occasional papers 76. Brussels: EC.

Enders, J., and F. van Vught, eds. 2007. *Towards a Cartography of Higher Education Policy Change.* Twente: Centre for Higher Education Policy Studies.

Ferlie, E., C. Musselin, and G. Andresani. 2007. "The 'Steering' of Higher Education Systems: A Public Management Perspective." In *Higher Education Looking Forward: Relations between Higher Education and Society.* Brussels: European Science Foundation.

Hackl, E. 2009. "Reconceptualising Public Responsibility and Public Good in the European Higher Education Area." Paper presented at the 6th International Workshop on Higher Education Reforms, Mexico City, 9–11 November.

Harman, K., and L. Meek. 2002. Introduction to Special Issue: "Merger Revisited: International Perspectives on Mergers in Higher Education." *Higher Education* 44:1–4.

Hazelkorn, E. 2011. *Rankings and the Reshaping of Higher Education: The Battle for World-Class Excellence.* Basingstoke: Palgrave Macmillan.

HEA. 2012. *Towards a Future Higher Education Landscape.* Dublin: HEA.

—. 2013. Strategic Innovation Fund (SIF). At http://www.hea.ie/content/strategic-innovation-fund-0 (accessed 15 July 2013).

Healy, T., and Slowey, M. 2006. "Social Exclusion and Adult Engagement in Lifelong Learning: Some Comparative Implications for European States Based on Ireland's *Celtic Tiger* Experience." *Compare: A Journal of Comparative and International Education* 36v (3):359–378.

HEFCE. 2010. *Literature Review for the Higher Education Collaborations, Alliances and Mergers Project.* Manchester: Oakleigh Consulting.

Jongbloed, B., J. Enders, and C. Salerno. 2007. "Higher Education and Its Communities: Interconnections and Interdependencies." *Higher Education Looking Forward: Relations between Higher Education and Society.* Brussels: European Science Foundation.

Kaplan, R.S., D.P. Norton, and B. Rugelsjoen. 2010. "Managing Alliances with the Balanced Scorecard." *Harvard Business Review* January–February.

Keohane, K., and C. Kuhling. 2004. *Collision Culture: Transformations in Everyday Life in Ireland.* Dublin: Liffey Press.

Marginson, M. 2011. "Higher Education and Public Good." *Higher Education Quarterly* 65 (2):411–433.

Morgan, M. 2011. *An Investigation of the Process and Functioning of the DRHEA.* Dublin: Dublin City University.

Neave, G. 2004. "Higher Education Policy as Orthodoxy: Being One Tale of Doxological Drift, Political Intention and Changing Circumstances." In *Markets in Higher Education: Rhetoric or Reality?* ed. P. Teixeira, B. Jongbloed, D. Dill, and A. Amaral, 127–160. Dordrecht: Kluwer Academic Publishers.

Newman, J.H. 1913. *The Idea of a University Defined and Illustrated.* London: Longmans.

OECD. 2004. *Review of National Policies for Education: Review of Higher Education in Ireland.* EDU/EC(2004)14. Dublin: OECD.

Peterson, M.W. 2010. "The Study of Colleges and Universities as Organizations." In *The Sociology of Higher Education*, ed. P. Gumport. Baltimore: Johns Hopkins University Press.

Scott, P. 2012. "Going beyond Bologna: Issues and Themes." In *European Higher Education at the Crossroads: Between the Bologna Process and National Reforms*, ed. A. Curaj, P. Scott, L. Vlasceanu, and L. Wilson. Amsterdam: Springer.

Shattock, M. 2006. *Managing Good Governance in Higher Education*. Basingstoke: Society for Research in Higher Education / Open University Press.

St. Aubyn, M., A. Pina, F. Garcia, and J. Pais. 2009. *Study on the Efficiency and Effectiveness of Public Spending on Tertiary Education*. Economics Papers 390. Brussels: EC.

UNESCO. 2005. *Implications of WTO/GATS on Higher Education in Asia and the Pacific*. UNESCO Forum Occasional Series Paper No.8. Paris: UNESCO.

Watson, D. 2007. *Managing Civic and Community Engagement*. Maidenhead, UK: Open University Press / McGaw-Hill.

APPENDIX

Dublin Region Higher Education Alliance*

The Dublin Region Higher Education Alliance (DRHEA) is a strategic alliance of the Higher Education sector in the wider Dublin city-region. It includes four Universities and their linked Colleges (TCD, UCD, DCU and NUIM) and four Institutes of Technology (DIT, IADT, ITB and ITT Dublin), many with long established and internationally renowned reputations for excellence in teaching and research. The Dublin Region Higher Education Alliance (DRHEA) has been awarded funding under the Higher Education Authority's Strategic Innovation Fund Cycle II (SIF II).

The DRHEA has been created to strengthen the region's higher education sector as an important contribution to the growth of Dublin's competitive advantage in a European and broader international context. In recognising the continuing, pivotal role of the region in the broader context of national development, as affirmed by the Irish government's National Spatial Strategy (2002), the Dublin Region Higher Education Alliance will facilitate and catalyse the sector's contribution to achieving the high level goals set out in the National Development Plan 2007–2013, and other supporting strategies such as the Strategy for Science, Technology and Innovation 2006–2013 and Building Ireland's Smart Economy: A Framework for Sustainable Economic Renewal.

International trends identify that city-regions are becoming the focal points for knowledge creation and learning in the new age of global, knowledge-intensive economies. The Dublin city-region has been Ireland's most dynamic economic zone and a principal source of the innovation which has underpinned the country's development of a knowledge-intensive economy in recent times. The diverse higher education sector in the city-region has been a core element of the infrastructure that has supported the emergence of the fastest growing region in Europe, measured along axes such as population, number of students, and economic output.

The DRHEA seeks to combine the strengths of its constituent member institutions in key areas, driving economies of scale and efficiencies that will enable both forward planning and agile responses to national and international demands for high quality, accessible Higher Education that underpins sustainable socio-economic development.

---

*This overview is taken from the DRHEA website at http://www.drhea.ie/about_us.php, accessed 1 November 2012. For a visual representation of the DRHEA structure, see http://www.drhea.ie/governance.php.

Principal activities

The eight members of the Alliance have identified four strands of activity where collaborative action will lead to efficiencies and increased capacity for development:

1. Enhancement of Learning
2. Graduate Education
3. Internationalization
4. Widening access

Of these four areas, the two largest programs of work relate to Enhancement of Learning and Graduate Education.

The Enhancement of Learning (EOL) strand is transforming undergraduate education and teaching and learning approaches across the Dublin region. EOL brings together 8 diverse institutions, from the largest university (UCD) to the smallest institute of technology (IADT), the oldest university (TCD) to the newest institute of technology (ITB) with the added dimension of a cross sectoral, regional perspective. Catering for over 75,000 students in the most densely populated region in Ireland but with a view to the growing global and international climate of Irish higher education, the EOL partner institutions know that perhaps their greatest strength lies in their diversity.

The Enhancement of Learning (EOL) strand is convened by Dublin City University (DCU) and involves all 8 of the collaborating institutions and it comprises a number of projects organised into four major areas:

• The Dublin Centre for Academic Development
• Transforming the Curriculum/Learning Outcomes
• Teaching for Engagement and Retention
• Enabling E- and Blended learning

The DRHEA Graduate Education strand aims to reposition the Dublin region as an International Centre for Graduate and in particular, Doctoral Education, by combining the strengths of the participating institutions. The DRHEA Graduate Education strand has established an inter-institutional network in the disciplines of Biomedical Science; Chemistry; Economics; Engineering; Physics and Politics/Sociology and Public Policy. Disciplinary Leaders have been working together and have already provided some advanced discipline specific taught modules and master classes available to all doctoral students in the alliance. A memorandum of understanding (MOU) for inter-institutional collaborative agreement on module delivery, graduate student mobility and credit exchange across the DRHEA has been signed and is currently being implemented.

CHAPTER 17

THE BUILDING OF INTERNATIONAL ALLIANCES: A CASE STUDY OF CANADA-INDIA COLLABORATIONS IN POST-SECONDARY EDUCATION

Sheila Embleton

INTRODUCTION

This chapter explores the development of international academic alliances using Canada-India collaborations in post-secondary education as a case study. After a slow start with few players (e.g., the Shastri Indo-Canadian Institute), there has been a flurry of recent activity in response to India's rapid rise to world prominence. This includes the parade of government and university delegations, the memorandum of understanding (MOU) signed between the Association of Universities and Colleges of Canada (AUCC) and the Association of Indian Universities (AIU), the Ontario-Maharashtra-Goa (OMG) exchange program, the India campus of the Schulich School of Business, a variety of university and college activities, International Science and Technology Partnerships Canada (ISTPCanada), Mitacs Globalink, and the Canada-India Research Centre of Excellence (CIRCE). In India, it includes the role of the Federation of Indian Chambers of Commerce and Industry (FICCI) and the Indian Council for Cultural Relations (ICCR). The chapter describes these alliances, then concludes with an assessment of current issues and challenges, and their potential impact on future collaborations.

Making Policy in Turbulent Times: Challenges and Prospects for Higher Education, ed. P. Axelrod, R.D. Trilokekar, T. Shanahan, and R. Wellen. Kingston: School of Policy Studies, Queen's University.

CANADA-INDIA ACADEMIC RELATIONS: THE PAST

The history of Canada-India academic collaborations is short; many aspects are similar to that of any "Western," especially anglophone, country. India shares a British colonial history with Canada (even if it might be radically different in some crucial ways), and the outward markers of that colonial history are evident even to a superficial traveller in India: the style of many historic buildings, the names of streets and buildings (despite post-Independence renaming attempts), the presence of historical monuments and plaques with familiar names (Dufferin, Lansdowne, Minto, Dalhousie, Elgin, etc. all spent time in both countries), the legal system, government and bureaucratic terminology, the structure of the school and university systems, cultural legacies (like cricket), etc. After Indian Independence in 1947, the pattern of bright young men travelling to England for university education continued, just as it did for other countries in the British Empire. Gradually, some of that traffic in higher education shifted to the United States. In total, though, very few undergraduates went overseas, from either Canada or India to either Britain or the US.

There was very little other academic mobility between India and Canada, and it was mainly at an individual level emanating from the specific research interests of individual academics – Canadian academics with interests in some aspect of India (e.g., Sanskrit; mythology; religion; anthropology; sociology; British colonial history in India; Indian art, dance, music; etc.) and, in the other direction, Indian scholars with an interest in Canadian literature or Canada's political or legal systems. These two groups seldom shared mutual academic interests, minimizing the prospects of direct interaction or longer-term relationships. Governments funded some of this mobility – for example, the Colombo Plan, the Canadian Studies Program, the Commonwealth Scholarship Program, and the Shastri Indo-Canadian Institute fellowships.

There was a steady stream of post-doctoral fellows coming from India to Canada under the Colombo Plan (Canada was a member from its founding in 1950 until 1992). However, as a development aid program, it was a one-way stream. In general, few Canadian academics found any reason to study or research in India, unless working in a field that required it. Canada has never committed to any large-scale international academic exchange program such as the US Fulbright program or Germany's DAAD (German Academic Exchange Service) programs – never committing, in other words, to a "soft power" approach (Trilokekar 2010). The Indian government also did not commit funding to international academic collaborations and relied solely on the funding it received as part of international collaborations with developed countries, generally earmarked as "development aid" – e.g., from Canada through the Canadian International Development Agency (CIDA).

The general view in Canada of India as an underdeveloped, poverty-stricken, inefficient, Third World country in the Soviet sphere, coupled with the specific political issues in the wake of India's nuclear test in 1974 (allegedly using material from a Canadian-supplied research reactor), meant that few Canadians had the urge to travel there. Thus, Canada-India academic relations were rather ad hoc and minimal, with little if any significance to either country. (For more information on institutional linkages between India and Canada, see Seethapathy and Johnston 2004). The one exception, running regular programs stimulating mobility between Canada and India, was the Shastri Indo-Canadian Institute, founded in 1968, now headquartered in Calgary and with an office in Delhi. Shastri's funding at that time came almost entirely from CIDA, the Department of External Affairs (predecessor of the Department of Foreign Affairs and International Trade, or DFAIT, now changed yet again to Department of Foreign Affairs, Trade, and Development), and Canadian university membership fees.

CANADA-INDIA ACADEMIC RELATIONS: CHANGING CONTEXTS

Since the late 1990s, relationships began to broaden, slowly at first and then more rapidly. This happened first via the field of development studies, which became more widely construed, going beyond strict development work into other areas such as women's issues, environmental concerns, children's rights, literacy education, health and nutrition, and related legal aspects. Much of this (including the crucial visits of faculty members and students) was funded by the federal government (CIDA) as India was (and remains for some themes) one of CIDA's priority countries.

As it had been earlier – e.g., under the Colombo Plan, the relationship was still "us" transferring "knowledge" or "expertise" to "them" – whether that transfer took place in India (mostly) or Canada (occasionally). This broadening of fields was less a matter of policy than of pressure from researchers themselves, as with experience they individually matured beyond their own practice of development work to looking at broader implications and wider systemic issues, often with a view to societal change through empowerment of disadvantaged groups.

The Shastri Indo-Canadian Institute was still the only organization operating with any consistency in this arena. Although always lagging slightly, its programs kept up well with changes such as the broadening of academic areas. This lag is indicative of the changes being driven from below by researchers rather than top down by government policy. Also, at this point, very little could be termed an "institutional alliance" (just individual post-doctoral fellowships or research projects), and there was no policy designed to build institutional alliances. Again, the one exception was Shastri, with its ongoing granting programs and with a network of institutional connections in India as well as its Canadian membership.

Since about 2004, interest in India has increased exponentially. Part of this is the sudden emergence of and interest in Brazil, Russia, India, and China – the BRIC countries (largely China and India, with Brazil rapidly catching up), both by governments at all three levels (federal, provincial, municipal, as rapidly growing economies offer many trade opportunities) and by universities and colleges (senior academic administrators but also researchers seeing new possibilities). Expanded international trade requires graduates with knowledge of these countries (not just their economies, but also language, culture, and way of life).

Financially strapped governments and post-secondary institutions are increasingly seeing the possibilities for education to generate revenue, both directly through tuition fees and less directly in the broader economic impact from living costs (the term "hidden export" is often used). Some governments also predict labour shortages and see international students educated in Canada as a potential source of highly skilled immigrants. Although policy has not yet crystallized in this area, it is expected that this trend will continue, stretching beyond the BRIC countries to other countries with high-growth economies and with large youth populations.

Although government investments in marketing Canadian education internationally have so far been minimal, there had been an expectation that this would increase after the August 2012 report of the Advisory Panel on Canada's International Education Strategy (2012), chaired by Dr. Amit Chakma, but the March 2013 federal budget was disappointing in this regard. At the undergraduate level, increased recruiting does not normally lead to educational alliances; at the graduate level, it can, as research teams come to know each other and feel comfortable working together.

Of all the possible countries for expansion, India is of particular interest to Canada, as there are relatively few language barriers since English is an official language in India, widely spoken, and the language of almost all higher education. Shared history, Commonwealth membership, the "rule of law," and a stable if slow-moving democracy also reduce barriers and create familiarity and comfort. Over a million Canadians of Indian origin in a diaspora that remains highly connected to India will also continue to facilitate the building of academic linkages.

THE DEVELOPMENT OF INSTITUTIONAL ALLIANCES:
THE CASE OF YORK UNIVERSITY

One of the first Canadian institutions to explore significant relationships in India was the Schulich School of Business at York University in Toronto. Today, we are used to business schools frequently referring to a "global" economic context, but Schulich (previously called the Faculty of Administrative Studies) set out in the late 1980s to give its students a global outlook before it was fashionable to do so. This is part of the visionary yet practical leadership of its long-time dean, Dr. Dezső Horváth, who advocated the necessity for global engagement of Canadian business at a time when Canadian business elites viewed MBA education primarily as a training ground for future managers in the financial and resource sectors, which have always played a central role in the Canadian economy. Horváth created relationships and exchanges with India, specifically with IIM-A (Indian Institute of Management, Ahmedabad), IIM-B (Indian Institute of Management, Bangalore), and ISB (Indian School of Business, Hyderabad). This was part of his global approach, giving students an opportunity to spend some time in India, first formally as part of the International MBA (IMBA), which he created, then later with the International BBA, which included a similar compulsory overseas stint.

Later, in the early 2000s, conscious of India's impending emergence as a large market that Westerners needed to understand and of that country's undersupply of highly qualified MBAs, Schulich decided to establish a permanent physical presence there. It chose to locate in Mumbai, India's financial hub, and in January 2010, the first cohort of MBA students in the India program began their studies. Students did the first year of the two-year MBA (the year with core curriculum rather than electives or streams) in India, taught by Schulich instructors who fly over to deliver their courses in two- or three-week modules, using the premises of the SP Jain Institute of Management and Research, and then they did the second year of the MBA (the year with all the electives and streams) on the Schulich-York campus in Toronto.

There is much demand for business education in India, particularly "world class" business education, but this is also part of the global positioning of the Schulich School. The Indian situation is complicated by the fact that there is a bill currently stalled in the Indian Parliament, Bill 57 ("The Foreign Educational Institutions [Regulation of Entry and Operations] Bill", originally drafted in 2004), which would allow foreign education providers meeting certain detailed provisions to deliver degrees in India. Schulich technically does not deliver the degree in India as the second year is spent in Toronto, with the degree earned and conferred in Toronto. If and when Bill 57 passes, Schulich intends to provide both years in India, on a purpose-built campus in Hyderabad, currently awaiting construction in a twinning arrangement with the GMR Varalakshmi Foundation. The current arrangement will move from Mumbai to Hyderabad, with the next intake in September 2013. (There was no intake in January 2013.)

However, even before the Mumbai campus opened, Schulich had been delivering a number of services in India from a Mumbai office, which it used as a base for executive education (a profit centre – Schulich does executive education for major Indian companies and non-Indian multinationals operating in India), for interviewing prospective MBA students (who come to Canada for both years of the MBA or IMBA in the "traditional" way as international students), and for career placement services for those who graduate with a Schulich MBA or IMBA and wish to go or return to India.

My own explorations in India began in 2004, in my role as vice-president academic at York, as we needed to construct York's India strategy in this rapidly emerging market. At the time, I was certain that other universities must be developing India strategies and that we were lagging in our planning. My first trip, later than I had hoped, took place in January 2006. I had done much reading and talking to people, both in general and about specific institutions, before going (and could draw on the huge expertise of Dr. Roopa Desai Trilokekar, who at the time was senior staff at York International). I travelled to several dozen institutions all over India in approximately two weeks. Since this was an exploratory trip, and I needed to think comprehensively of all faculties at York, all regions of India, and institutions that could be a good fit, it meant that I saw many more institutions than we eventually signed agreements with.

To reinforce the point about how relationships were now starting to move from personal or individual-project-based to institutional, I cite one example of an association with the University of Madras, begun earlier simply because one York faculty member, Dr. Martin Bunch in Environmental Studies, had a long-term research project along the coast south of Chennai that had evolved into a signed agreement between the University of Madras and York's Faculty of Environmental Studies. As a result of my visit, we expanded this into an institution-wide agreement. Approximately half a dozen other relationships for York resulted from this particular visit: with Jadavpur University (Kolkata); Jawaharlal Nehru University (JNU) (Delhi); the Indian Institute of Technology Bombay (IITB); BITS-Pilani (Birla Institute of Technology and Science, with its campuses in Pilani, Goa, Hyderabad, and Dubai); and St. Xavier's College (Mumbai). Other institutions have been added since then, including one private and two national law schools, the University of Calcutta, IITM (Indian Institute of Technology Madras), and more to come.[1]

THE GROWTH IN INSTITUTIONAL ALLIANCES: OTHER ONTARIO UNIVERSITIES AND COLLEGES

The number of individual institutional relationships between Canadian and Indian academic institutions has increased rapidly, from very few just several years ago to dozens today. Each of these relationships has taken a different form depending on the individual strengths of the institutions, any previous relationship with India, and any in-house expertise or networks, often involving their own Indian-diaspora scholars.

For example, in contrast to York's Schulich School of Business, the Richard Ivey School of Business at Western University in London, Ontario, has taken the approach of writing up and then incorporating in its instruction (and making available to others) many Indian case studies. Ivey is currently expanding its footprint in India through partnerships in areas of case study preparation, research, and executive education. In February 2012, Ivey signed an MOU with the Management Development Institute (MDI), Gurgaon (near Delhi), to develop and distribute India-focused business case studies worldwide. This is astute global positioning. Ivey will also develop an executive program for a large Indian telecom company. These types of relationship often lead to long-term linkages both between institutions and between Canadian institutions and Indian businesses.

Carleton University in Ottawa began a relationship a number of years ago with Koh-i-Noor Business School in Navi Mumbai (a new area east of Mumbai) to deliver the Carleton BBA. Several cohorts graduated, but this program is no longer offered. In February 2010, Carleton's president, Dr. Roseann O'Reilly Runte, made the first of several trips in quick succession, leading to a number of agreements and the establishment of the Canada-India Centre for Excellence in Science, Technology, Trade and Policy, with considerable community support (including significant fundraising within the Indian diaspora). This centre has hosted a number of delegations, but its most visible activity to date was in June 2011, when it hosted the Canada-India Education Summit (with AUCC, the Shastri Indo-Canadian Institute, DFAIT, and the Government of India), followed immediately by the Canada-India Innovation Summit (with ISTPCanada).

The University of Toronto unveiled its India Innovation Institute, a joint initiative of the Munk School of Global Affairs and the Rotman School of Management, in October 2011. It is explicitly about forming connections and recognizes that innovation can be found in any field, not just science, technology, engineering, and mathematics (STEM) disciplines. President Naylor, quoted in *India Abroad* on 9 March 2012, stated that the University of Toronto's

> ties with South Asia have never been stronger. Over the past five years, our professors have co-authored over 330 publications with researchers from South Asia. Many of our faculty members are developing new and exciting partnerships and joint programs that encourage student mobility, training and research. Our joint initiative with IITB, which allows engineering students to study energy futures of both Canada and India is just one example. In the years to come, I am confident that the University of Toronto will continue to strengthen its relationships with all levels of government, academia and industry in South Asia.

What is striking about this statement is the way it typifies the total change in orientation of Canada-India academic relations compared to quite recent history. Today, these relationships are intended to be long

term, across all disciplines, and well-funded, with both partners contributing equally and valued equally – quite a contrast to a decade ago, when
the relationships were still about one-off projects or individual scholars,
when they were unequal and poorly funded and in which industry and
government were not involved.

To summarize, international academic relationships between Canada
and India have recently grown rapidly, often driven by the interest and
commitment of senior academic administrators at individual institutions.
Beginning with individual faculty interests, today these collaborations are
more institutional in nature, formalized with the signing of agreements
and promising much more academic activity than the simple exchange
of individual scholars or students. Some agreements or programs (such
as OMG and Globalink, described below) network beyond single institutions. The fields have broadened beyond the social sciences, humanities,
and fine arts to include business, law, science, technology, and health.
These international activities are somewhat better funded (although much
remains to be improved), with funding deriving from the higher education community, all levels of government, the private sector, and some
donors from the diaspora. The diversity of funding sources goes hand
in hand with broader mandates around research, commercialization,
innovation, training, and trade, along with the more traditional forms
of academic collaboration.

THE ROLE OF GOVERNMENTS IN SUPPORTING
INTERNATIONAL ACADEMIC ALLIANCES

As mentioned above, the increasing interest of governments in international academic activity has helped support some growth and development of Canada-India academic relationships. In Canada, there has been
federal support (e.g., DFAIT's Science and Technology Agreement with
India) as well as a more recent role played by the provincial governments
(see, for example, then premier McGuinty's comments in the Speech from
the Throne [Onley 2010]). Due to Canada's constitutional peculiarities,
which allocate different responsibilities to the federal government (research, foreign policy, international trade) and the provincial and territorial governments (education), the overall strategy is less coordinated than
that of our competitors (Shubert, Jones, and Trilokekar 2009; Trilokekar
2010) – a fact also frequently remarked upon by Indian government officials and university administrators. Beginning with a description of the
role of the Ontario government in furthering Canada-India exchanges,
I detail some recent initiatives.

Ontario provincial government

Recognizing the increasing global importance of India, and of trade
relationships for Ontario, then premier Dalton McGuinty led his first

trade mission to India in January 2007. The mission (to Delhi, Bangalore, Mumbai, and Chandigarh) was focused on increasing trade as well as a recognition of the importance of the Indo-Canadian diaspora in Ontario, but it was very much an exploratory mission. I was one of the few non-Indo-Canadians on the mission who had been to India, and that was enough for me to be considered "the expert" on academic matters (which shows the lack of depth of knowledge of India at that time), advising officials in the Ministry of Training, Colleges and Universities before and during the trip. This first mission was considered a great success, with the signing of several MOUs between Ontario and Indian academic institutions and the establishment of Ontario's first student exchange program with India, described in detail below.

McGuinty understood that relationships, particularly in India, require nurturing and repeat trips, so he made a second trip, focused on clean energy, in December 2009. It was on this visit that, during the reception on the terrace of the Taj Palace Hotel in Mumbai (still not fully open again after the terrorist attacks of a year earlier, itself symbolic), he announced that the IIFA (India International Film Awards) would come to Toronto in June 2011. Given the role of Bollywood in contemporary India (and beyond), this visibility gave a large boost to interest in Canada, particularly Toronto. This trade mission was much smaller than the first, and only a few universities were invited (University of Toronto, Queen's University in Kingston, University of Waterloo; I was there but representing the Shastri Indo-Canadian Institute). Just before the provincial election in October 2011, McGuinty stated at an Indo-Canadian event that if re-elected, he would make a third trip to India. Complicated by his subsequent minority government status, and then his resignation as premier, that trip never happened.

Ontario-Maharashtra-Goa exchange program

One of the announcements made during McGuinty's first mission to India was the establishment of the Ontario-Maharashtra-Goa (OMG) exchange program. I provide some background below.

At that time, two provincial exchange programs had already been in existence for almost 20 years: Ontario-Rhône-Alpes (ORA) and Ontario-Baden-Württemberg (OBW). These had originated as part of a project to set up educational and broader cultural exchanges with regions of other countries that shared similarities with Ontario (e.g., a key automotive industry, a major financial centre, a similar-sized population or similar population proportion compared to the nations of which they were a part, etc.).[2] Just before McGuinty's first trip to India, the then German consul general in Toronto, Dr. Klaus Rupprecht, and I (as chair of the Ontario Council of Academic Vice-Presidents, or OCAV) were successful in having provincial funding restored to OBW and ORA.

My associate vice-president international at York, Dr. Adrian Shubert, and I had already mused about how wonderful it would be if some of the previously envisioned "Four Motors" exchanges could now be enabled or, even better, if they could be expanded to non-European parts of the world, including India, China, Brazil, and possibly elsewhere. (Remember the context, which was that "BRIC" was only just becoming a household word.) We had gone so far in our musings as to identify particular regions of some of these countries, and for India we had settled on Maharashtra, but in order to attract some other good-quality universities, we thought to add adjacent Goa. But there was no funding, so we did not pursue it, and nothing more happened.

Then, in the autumn of 2006, the then minister of Training, Colleges and Universities, Chris Bentley, came to York to give a short speech at an internationalization conference, and York's then president, Dr. Lorna Marsden, was absent; protocol dictated that as acting president, I would meet Bentley, escort him to the lecture hall, and, at the end of his speech, accompany him back to his car. In both my speech and his, OBW and ORA were mentioned (favourably, given the recently restored funding). As I was escorting him to his car, he mentioned McGuinty's upcoming trip to India and how his ministry needed an "announceable," but there was no money. I immediately pitched the idea of the OMG exchange and its approximate annual cost. He instantly took to the idea and got into his car. (Fundraisers would call this a classic "elevator pitch.") By the time I had walked back to my office seven minutes later, my assistant had already received phone calls from various staffers in the minister's office, urgently wanting the program details by 9 a.m. the next morning. I spent the night writing it up as a proper proposal, with budget, and thus OMG was born. McGuinty signed the agreement in Mumbai in January 2007.

The OMG agreement provides funding for 25 students to go in each direction each year, with a subsidy of $2,000 (one term) or $2,500 (two terms); the subsidy is designed to support airfare plus some additional costs. This exchange is unique among the Ontario consortial exchanges in that Ontario also pays a subsidy for Indian students to come here; the reality is that without that, most Indian students would not be able to afford to come, and then it would not be an exchange.[3]

There are 28 member universities of OMG. York University serves as the Ontario hub (16 member universities), as it does for all of what is now called OUI (Ontario Universities International, which includes ORA, OBW, OMG, Ontario-Jiangsu (OJS), and any others launched in the future; the University of Pune serves as the hub in India, with 12 member universities. The first and so far only academic director is Dr. Lalu Mansinha, professor emeritus of geoscience at Western University. While the first two years of the program saw a number of excellent applicants from India, there were comparatively low numbers participating from

Ontario. However, as word has spread, and as alumni of the program have talked about their experiences, the numbers have rapidly increased, and now there are more students participating than there are funded spots (well over 40, so roughly 20 students in each direction are not funded in each year).

Other provinces and territories

So far, this chapter has been Ontario-centric – partly because, of course, of my own history and knowledge, but also because Ontario has clearly been a leader in the formation of institutional linkages. I turn now to other provinces.

In British Columbia (BC), Simon Fraser University (SFU) was probably the most visible first with increased activity in India, with former president Michael Stevenson (also a former vice-president academic at York) constructing a strategy, including some dedicated fundraising around India, in the mid-2000s. The SFU strategy was far more closely linked with the Indo-Canadian community than many others. So, for example, there was an annual Diwali dinner, which was one of many excellent connections to the community, and there was a President's Advisory Council on India, co-chaired by the SFU president and a prominent member of the Indo-Canadian community. (The first was Dr. Arun Garg, a leading physician and prominent community member in the Lower Mainland.) Stevenson travelled several times to India (including on former premier Gordon Campbell's missions to India, during which academic connections played a prominent role), and several active exchange agreements were established.

SFU was closely followed by the University of British Columbia (UBC), currently very active in India, under the leadership of President Stephen Toope, who led the AUCC presidential mission to India in April 2011. In November 2011, when Toope again visited India (speaking at FICCI, the Federation of Indian Chambers of Commerce and Industry) as a member of Premier Christy Clark's delegation, he announced the opening of a UBC office in Delhi (joint with the University of Toronto and run by Faisal Beg, formerly a locally engaged trade commissioner at the Canadian High Commission in Delhi) and in Bangalore (joint with UBC's Sauder School of Business).

The Canada-India Research Centre of Excellence at UBC has now opened, with an investment of $15 million. Known as the India-Canada Centre for Innovative Multidisciplinary Partnerships to Accelerate Community Transformation and Sustainability, or IC-IMPACTS, it is part of a broad science and technology (S&T) agreement recently signed between Canada and India. The areas of research include improving drinking water quality, developing infrastructure, minimizing environmental pollution from economic activities, developing alternative energy sources, and conducting medical research to contain infectious diseases caused by viral outbreaks and parasitic infections.

The Indian Institutes of Technology (IITs) in Roorkee, Hyderabad, Delhi, and Bombay will work with UBC, the University of Toronto, and the University of Alberta. The project has identified Reliance Industries and Stewols Industry from Nagpur as industrial partners. The main surprise here is the choice of Nagpur, a smaller, "lower tier" city, not at all easy to get to, but this can also be seen as a further and more pervasive stage in the historical development of linkages, with penetration to much smaller cities.

At approximately the same time, in February 2012, UBC's School of Nursing renewed its partnership with the Canada India Education Society (CIES) to support the development of nursing education in Punjab. The CIES and the School of Nursing began their partnership in 1999, with the goal of supporting the nursing education program at Guru Nanak College of Nursing in Banga, Nawanshahr District, Punjab. Through visits, exchanges, and advocacy for nursing, the partnership has increased the profile and status of nursing as a profession in India, thus improving the health of citizens in more than 60 nearby villages in Punjab, and helping many women and poorer families improve their lives through employment in a growing field. Both of those announcements were part of the buildup to the CIRCE competition (see below).

The University of the Fraser Valley, or UFV (beginning when it was the University College of the Fraser Valley), influenced by the large Punjabi diasporic community in Abbotsford and elsewhere in the Fraser Valley, offers a BBA at an affiliated college of Panjab University in Chandigarh. In Canada, UFV offers an India-Canada Studies certificate and, since 2007, houses a BC Regional Innovation Chair in Canada-India Business and Economic Development as well as a Centre for Indo-Canadian Studies. In late February 2012, UFV announced an MOU with Punjabi University in Patiala to work together to develop diaspora studies programs and courses, research, and student exchange opportunities.

The University of Victoria has a close relationship with Participatory Research in Asia (PRIA), headquartered in Delhi, using this to send significant numbers of students to various parts of India for a full academic year. The umbrella MOU covers other types of faculty and student linkage as well. The University of Victoria also offers courses in partnership with PRIA.[4]

BC in particular is ramping up its recruitment, especially of undergraduate students in India, and in November 2011, Premier Christy Clark made her first trip to India, accompanied by delegations from most of the province's universities and colleges, for many of whom recruitment was a prime goal.

The University of Alberta, led by its president, Dr. Indira Samarasekera, has been extremely active, particularly in trying to forge meaningful connections and alliances. The University of Alberta and IITB currently have a five-year agreement in nanotechnology, with $1 million per year to facilitate mobility around research projects. The University of Alberta, along with the University of Toronto, is one of UBC's partners in IC-IMPACTS.

In Saskatchewan, there are many Indian students at the University of Regina (whose president, Dr. Vianne Timmons, has been a leader on the India file, partly because much of her own research has involved India) and at the University of Saskatchewan. One of the little known facts about Saskatchewan is that it drives well over a third of Canada's exports to India – primarily potash and pulses. This trade in commodities is starting to be followed up by services (e.g., in agricultural technology), and this is creating academic and research linkages. Saskatchewan provides particularly favourable conditions for recruiting international students by refunding the differential fee that they pay if they live and work (i.e., file income tax returns) in Saskatchewan for a few years after graduation.

In Manitoba, President Lloyd Axworthy at the University of Winnipeg, a former minister of External Affairs, has been pushing India connections, including a recent visit to inaugurate a development-oriented project in Punjab.[5]

In predominantly French-speaking Quebec, academic linkages are somewhat complicated by language issues, although there are English-speaking universities (including two large universities, McGill and Concordia), and much activity in fields of interest to many Indian institutions and students takes place in English regardless of institutional language. For example, ETS (École de technologie supérieure), a component of the Université du Québec system focused on engineering and technology, recruits graduate students from India, with the clear intent to work in English. So does the Université de Sherbrooke. One small niche in all this is a Quebec Studies program at JNU, which has led to good institutional linkages in this one small corner of that vast institution. In February 2010, while in Delhi, former premier Jean Charest signed a tuition fee agreement, administered on behalf of the Quebec government by the Shastri Indo-Canadian Institute, allowing a total of 29 Indian graduate students to study in Quebec while paying only in-province tuition.

There is surprisingly little activity in Atlantic Canada in relation to India. A few institutions are members of the Shastri Indo-Canadian Institute, but that seems to be the extent of any significant institutional linkages. There is no activity involving the territories.

Thus, India has now become a destination of choice for Canadian international academic collaborations. It would not be a stretch to suggest that it is now a virtual rite of passage for new presidents and other senior academic administrators from Canadian universities (and colleges) to make a first trip to India early in their tenure. Given the past weak relationships with India, coupled with general inattention to the international dimensions of higher education, many people reaching these positions have little or no experience with India.

This lack of India experience does put Canada at a disadvantage internationally, where other countries seem to have both more presence and more continuity. In India, one continually crosses paths with delegations from Ireland, Scotland, the United Kingdom, Australia, the US, Germany, France, etc. In November 2011, BC and Alberta representatives were criss-crossing each other as well as delegations from Scotland and the US, as well as the Australians, who seem to be permanently everywhere. The Canadian government is far behind when it comes to supporting international academic relationships, especially compared to these competitor countries (Shubert, Jones, and Trilokekar 2009; Trilokekar 2010). The lack of committed funding and support, institutionally and governmentally, and the frequent lack of follow-through by senior university administrators, has resulted in damage to Canada's reputation among both Indian government officials and senior academic administrators. This harms us both institutionally and as a country in our efforts to compete and to move forward with a consistent message about the importance to Canada of academic relationships with India.[6]

Colleges

Right across the country, colleges are starting to recruit very intensively in India (at the undergraduate level, obviously, although also for college diplomas, particularly for students who already have bachelor's degrees). Colleges receive support for recruitment in India from the federal government through the SPP (Student Partnership Program), which Citizenship and Immigration Canada introduced as a way to increase the number of student visas from India to Canada. The program has been extremely successful, seeing a sharp rise in visas issued to Indian students coming to Canadian colleges. (There is no parallel program for Canadian universities.)

A number of potential issues are starting to surface – that many students regard this purely as a way to get a work visa for Canada, that many take offers from colleges not in major cities because it is easier to get in, but then either try to go directly or transfer very quickly to colleges in major cities.[7]

Pan-Canadian activity

AUCC has responded to its members' interest in India. It and the AIU signed a five-year MOU in November 2008 in Delhi, which spoke to furthering agreements, information-sharing, collaboration on policy dialogue and advocacy, and other types of support for mutual benefit. The MOU was symbolic rather than anything else, but it helped raise

Canada's profile in the Indian university community, at a point where the importance of India still needed to be signalled to some Canadian universities. Ever since, AUCC has had a regular presence at the annual AIU meeting as well as some further India-related activity – for example, at least three significant workshops in Ottawa (which included a number of participants from India), an event on graduate education in Delhi in December 2009 (in co-operation with the Shastri Indo-Canadian Institute), and a mission of 15 university presidents and vice-presidents academic in April 2011.

Along with other organizations, such as the Canada India Education Council (CIEC), described below, and provincial governments, AUCC has started an ongoing relationship with FICCI, which has a large forum every November in Delhi, always with some emphasis on education, and which is now a regular stop on the tours of Canadian academic administrators to India. The first and largest AUCC-led delegation of presidents attended FICCI in November 2008. In November 2011, several Canadian university presidents, vice-presidents, and deans again attended FICCI. A different group, CII (Confederation of Indian Industry), is also trying to play this role of academic connector, and in November 2011, it held a forum, also in Delhi, right after the FICCI forum, which was attended by some of the same Canadian delegates who had attended FICCI.

Subsequently (in April 2012), there was a delegation of presidents to Brazil even larger than the one to India. There are clear signals that the federal government is interested in Brazil, especially in the STEM areas, and Brazilian federal and state governments have shown very clear interest in Canada, again mostly in the STEM areas (e.g., the Science without Borders program). The interest in Brazil is excellent and, in my view, long overdue, but not if it comes at the expense of proper follow-through with India. We need strong relationships with both, and we are not yet finished building sufficiently robust linkages with India.

AUCC administers and CIDA funds the Students for Development program, in existence since 2005 and originally known as Canada Corps; it was cut in the 2012 federal budget, but projects in progress will run their course. It has had various incarnations; India has always been one of the countries allowed and where, in every round, significant projects have been awarded. The projects must all contribute to one or more of several specified development goals articulated by CIDA (e.g., maternal and child health, sustainability of the food supply). The program was recently revised to allow interns to travel in both directions – from the developing country to Canada as well as from Canada abroad – and also to allow longer-term partnerships, not just one-off projects. Several universities have successfully used this program to develop longer-term partnerships with Indian institutions or non-governmental organizations (NGOs). It is to be hoped that these will be self-sustaining now that the original funding has been cut.

The Canadian Commonwealth Scholarship Program (funded by DFAIT, administered by the Canadian Bureau for International Education, or CBIE) used to allow students from both India and Canada to study for a full graduate degree in the other; it used to bring a number of Indian graduate students to Canada who often graduated and remained in Canada, often as professors themselves. In more recent years, these programs have been altered to provide only shorter-term stays (generally four to six months) in Canada, with the degree still being earned in the home country so as to alleviate some of the "brain drain" issues perceived to be problematic in the earlier version of the program. The effect of this program in its current form is not to create or sustain institutional linkages, but to have the same type of outcome as exchange programs in building connections at the level of the individual.

The Canada India Education Council (CIEC), an offshoot of the Canada-India Business Council, was founded in 2010. Its mandate is to further academic relations between Canada and India at both universities and colleges. It is self-funded from membership fees and private or corporate donations (rather than being government-funded). These latter two features distinguish it from the Shastri Indo-Canadian Institute. It organizes an annual Synergy event, so far only in Toronto, but with a plan to hold a second event annually that will rotate around locations outside Ontario. Synergy has attracted 200 participants in each of the last few years, who come together to hear (and share) the latest on developments in the Canada-India academic corridor. It has also provided support and intelligence for institutions, particularly so far for colleges, that are making their first forays into and strategic plans for India, including but not limited to recruitment (Embleton and Neemuchwala 2011).

There is also the important bilateral S&T agreement to encourage, develop, and facilitate co-operative activities in S&T for peaceful purposes in fields of common interest and on the basis of equality and mutual benefit. Funding mechanisms have been identified through which industry, universities and colleges, and research organizations may seek support for joint bilateral research and development (R&D) projects and other activities intended to generate new or expanded international research and technology-based partnerships (known as Partnership Development Activities). For Canada, funding and other services are provided through ISTPCanada,[8] an NGO selected by the federal government for this purpose. For India, the Global Innovation & Technology Alliance (GITA), also an NGO, has been engaged by the Department of Science and Technology (DST), and the Department of Biotechnology (DBT) provides funding and a Partnership Development Activities program.

Four years ago, MITACS (Mathematics of Information Technology and Complex Systems, at the time part of the Networks of Centres of Excellence program funded by the Natural Sciences and Engineering

Research Council of Canada), launched a pilot program, Globalink, in BC involving UBC, SFU, and the University of Victoria. It proved to be extremely successful. It brought 20 IIT students to BC to work in university research labs for three months in the summer between their third and fourth years. The students were also introduced to industry and entrepreneurship and developed skill sets (e.g., networking, business planning, and presentation skills).

Globalink was a huge success, also attracting significant media and government attention, and since then it has grown, first in the number of students from India and participating provinces, then in the range of Indian institutions and disciplines, and finally to other countries (China and Brazil and a pilot with Mexico). Funding comes from federal and provincial sources. It has been a wonderful advertisement for both Canada and its universities in some of the best institutions in India and has greatly increased graduate applications from India. (Acceptances have not increased as much yet because many of these students go to top US schools instead, but at least we are now starting to build our profile.)

The federal budget of March 2011 announced a competition for CIRCE, with $15 million over five years; the competition was run by the tri-council secretariat in Ottawa, the same agency that runs the Canada Research Chairs program. The aim is to build research relationships between Canada and India, networking multiple universities and industry in both countries. There were 20 responses to the notice of intent, several of which subsequently dropped out or amalgamated with other proposals. After the letter of intent stage, four (the original intent had been three) were chosen to go on to the full proposal stage, with the proposals due in August 2012. This competition accounted for much of the flurry of announcements of India centres and other India-related activity in 2011 and 2012. The winner of the competition was announced in Delhi during Prime Minister Harper's visit in November 2012 – the UBC, University of Alberta, University of Toronto consortium.

Parallel to the Canadian developments described above is that there is also an increasing interest in India in sponsoring academic collaborations. The Indian Council for Cultural Relations (ICCR), sponsored by the Government of India, has started to fund visiting chairs in Canada. Currently there are three – at Toronto, York, and Carleton – with other universities also submitting requests.[9] These continue, so help build relationships, even if the individual incumbent and precise disciplinary area may change from year to year. The funding comes partly from ICCR and partly from the host university. The ICCR also maintains several Indian Cultural Centres abroad, and a centre for Toronto is in the early planning stages. Such a centre is important in building the infrastructure needed to support academic and cultural linkages and could provide a major boost to post-secondary collaborations, especially in Toronto and environs.

CANADA-INDIA ACADEMIC RELATIONSHIPS: THE FUTURE

The last few years have seen a compounding of factors creating a flurry of activity between Canada and India. Although many of these factors are likely to be long term (globalization, dependence on tuition revenue from international students, India's position politically and economically on the world stage), it is not clear how sustainable the current level of activity is or whether there will be follow-through to solidify the current network of relationships. I conclude with an assessment of some current issues and challenges, and their potential impact on Canada-India academic relations.

One of the lingering problems in the Canada-India academic relationship has been the difficulty in shifting negative attitudes toward India. A relic of this but also of lack of knowledge of the Indian educational system is the treatment of the Indian three-year degree when its holder applies to a Canadian graduate school. (Many engineering schools – in particular, the IITs – have four-year degrees, so the issue does not arise in those cases.) Normally, such degree holders are asked to do one more year, equivalent to fourth year or an honours or qualifying year, as a form of make-up before they can be admitted to a master's program. Indian students greatly resent this, not just because of the greater cost, time away from home, and delay in eventual completion of their graduate program, but primarily because they believe that this year is truly wasted, only covering material already studied in their undergraduate degrees.

In examining this problem, which also came to the fore at the same time that York needed to formulate a policy around applicants with a three-year "Bologna" degree from Europe, Dr. Adrian Shubert, former associate vice-president international at York University, decided to examine the actual content of the various degrees. (I will refer here only to India, but it was the same for the Bologna degrees.) He found that in every case, Indian students had covered at least as much as and, in most cases, more of the subject matter in their major in three years than our students had covered in four. Our students had far more general education and elective courses, of which Indian students had almost none. Our students also had more opportunity to do double majors or major/minor combinations.

Thus, the Indian students were fully qualified from the point of view of disciplinary knowledge to enter directly our master's programs with their three-year degrees. What they were lacking was breadth, but nobody ever asked them to make that up – and one might argue that by then, it is inappropriate to do so. There was a related problem – namely, that students with an Indian master's degree who applied to a doctoral program in North America were generally required to do a second master's; this has now also changed for the same reason (namely, by examining content rather than number of years elapsed).

In light of our limited knowledge and persistent view of India as underdeveloped, those first-time visits of presidents and other senior academic administrators remain worthwhile. They need to see the quality, dynamism, and ingenuity of the scientific and medical research, the innovation in health care and delivery, and the perspectives in the social sciences, humanities, and fine arts. Clearly, for law and business, some knowledge of India is required to gain a global perspective and many direct practical applications.

It is equally important for government delegations (prime ministers and premiers, and their senior staff) to continue to travel to India, to show interest but also gain knowledge themselves, and keep the relationship thriving and visible because India has many wealthier and more globally important suitors than Canada. All of these delegates need to see exactly who else is visiting India; to realize the huge prominence that US and UK education have; to see how the Australians are everywhere; to realize that various European countries are very present, particularly Germany but also smaller countries that are nevertheless very productive in, particularly, S&T research, such as Finland; and to observe that unexpected players such as the Japanese are starting to recruit undergraduates in India (perhaps an imperative because of Japan's weakening demographic in the relevant age group). Those visits by university administrators and premiers need to be followed up by truly working visits by many others, to actually operationalize all the lofty words and articulated goals.

Besides increasing our knowledge and consistency, the problem has been not lack of ideas or willingness, but lack of commitment to invest significant sums of money, especially in comparison to other countries and, in particular, our major competitors. This is true whether the topic is student fellowships, branding, money for student recruiting, or research partnerships. Some recent announcements (from universities, but also of CIRCE, and programs like Mitacs[10] Globalink and ISTPCanada, which have significant government funding behind them) are starting to change this.

One problem that many universities have, or will soon have, is that the sheer number of agreements signed is unsustainable, given distance, costs (despite optimistic talk about Skype teleconferences and other electronic means), and just the general difficulty of being away for long periods of time (both from the university and also from personal obligations). This is exacerbated by the fact that there is simultaneously heightened activity in China and Brazil. The approach to India has been scattershot so far, and what is needed now is a deepening and broadening of relationships, not more relationships. (Nevertheless, relationships should always be re-examined, and one should not shut the door on new ones – especially as new players are continually emerging in India, including some new and reputable private universities) (Touhey 2009).

India is still very much a priority for the federal government, and academic relationships are an integral part of this. At the end of the G20 summit in Toronto in June 2010, there was a bilateral summit between Canada and India, culminating in prime ministers Stephen Harper and Manmohan Singh signing an MOU of co-operation concerning higher education. Also, both countries are moving ahead as quickly as possible with a Comprehensive Economic Partnership Agreement (CEPA, a type of free trade agreement), and education and mobility will be very much part of that.

Finally, the international education community is pleased with, although not surprised at, the report of the Chakma Advisory Panel, which recommended increased recruitment of international students to Canada as well as an increase in the number of Canadian students studying and/or interning abroad (Advisory Panel on Canada's International Education Strategy 2012). Both, particularly in combination, would augur well for strengthening academic linkages between Canada and India throughout the post-secondary sector. The report should also help sharpen federal government strategic policy in this area; it is to be hoped that there are no federal vs. provincial/territorial jurisdiction entanglements in the implementation.

It would lengthen this chapter unduly to write about another major topic, educational reform and growth of the academic system in India. For excellent backgrounds on these topics, see Agarwal (2009), Thorat (2006), and Altbach (2010). However, there are some potential impacts on and opportunities for Canadian institutions, their linkages, and other relationships.

As is widely known, the proportion of the relevant age group studying in higher education institutions in India (the GER, gross enrolment ratio) is extremely low on a worldwide scale, and the Government of India has an ambitious plan to raise it considerably within the decade (from about 12 to 14 percent in 2009 to 30 percent in 2020). There are huge challenges in implementing this vision, beginning with problems in the K–12 system, including a shortage of teachers. The capacity of the post-secondary system is nowhere near large enough. There is a great need for vocational education and training, akin to what many of our colleges do, which can provide opportunities for our colleges, for partnerships and revenue-generating opportunities, through activity in both Canada and India. There are also possible impacts on our universities. An expansion of this magnitude will require hundreds of thousands of new professors, and the system is already considerably short now.

Where will these new professors come from? Clearly, there are opportunities for Canadian universities in educating this new cohort of professors. Those professors, if Canadian-educated, will easily enter (or continue) research collaborations with Canada, thus enabling both countries to profit over the longer term. They may also be more inclined to recommend Canada as a destination for graduate or professional education to the students they themselves will teach in India.

India has announced the establishment of a large number of new universities, IITs, etc. (although news from March 2012 indicates that this number may be reduced slightly for budgetary reasons). Some of these have already been established – e.g., IIT-Patna in Bihar – and they offer many opportunities for mentoring relationships, new research relationships, etc. There is also an excellent opportunity for sharing expertise in the delivery of distance education (especially to remote areas with less technological access and in the context of massification). It is important to note that the Indian strategy or policy is designed to increase the number of graduates, thus to be focused on teaching, not research. Unlike many countries (e.g., Korea, China), the goal is not to have a certain number of institutions placing high in global rankings (Trilokekar and Embleton 2011). To some extent, this sets up a mismatch for potential Canada-India linkages, as the Indian partners tend to be more focused on teaching and graduating well-trained students and the Canadian partners more focused on international research partnerships.

A final consideration is that, assuming India does manage to grow its higher education system to produce enough graduates for its own needs, it is not clear how much demand there will still be for large numbers of undergraduates to come to study in Canada. Indian families tend to be close, preferring not to have their children studying on the other side of the world. For many in the middle class, it is a huge expense, particularly as the rupee continues to fall in value. If Indian university places of sufficient quality existed, how many students would do their undergraduate studies abroad, except at possibly the most prestigious universities in the world, such as Harvard and Cambridge? And, oddly enough, that would bring us full circle to the situation of almost 100 years ago.

NOTES

1. See http://international.yorku.ca/global/linkages/india.html for an up-to-date list.

2. These were to comprise the "Four Motors"; in addition to Rhône-Alpes and Baden-Württemberg, there were Lombardy (Italy) and Catalonia (Spain), and there was later talk of a fifth, Wales. In the end, only the first two ever happened, and the funding for those was cut off during the Harris government funding cuts in the mid-1990s. The cultural exchanges ceased immediately, but the universities found the programs sufficiently valuable that they decided collectively to continue, with the program administered by OCAV (an affiliate of the Council of Ontario Universities). Each participating university paid a levy, proportional to its size, to fund the infrastructure of placement and advising.

3. With ORA and OBW, European students can afford it, and they receive some help from their home jurisdictions; with OJS, the Chinese government pays the costs for their students.

4. Details about the various collaborations are at http://oia.uvic.ca/?q=node/406, accessed 14 July 2013.

5. See http://www.uwinnipeg.ca/index/uw-news-action/story.496/title. uwinnipeg-forges-stronger-ties-to-india-.

6. The most recent example is the cancellation of DFAIT's Understanding Canada program in the 2012 federal budget. Together with severely reduced funding for the Shastri Indo-Canadian Institute, this has caused serious concern in both the Indian government and individual institutions, who again question Canada's commitment to India.

7. Disclaimer: I do not personally have a problem with this as Canada needs many skilled and semi-skilled workers and these people may well be satisfying that crucial need, to mutual benefit. As long as we are clear on what is happening and make it more transparent, not pretending that this is about academic linkages when it is in fact about immigration, there is nothing wrong with this.

8. See http://www.istpcanada.ca/international_programs/India/.

9. At http://www.iccrindia.net/chairs.html.

10. When MITACS (Mathematics of Information Technology and Complex Systems) was formed, it was part of the Networks of Centres of Excellence (NCE) program. It has now ceased to be an NCE and has changed its name to Mitacs (and is no longer an acronym).

REFERENCES

Advisory Panel on Canada's International Education Strategy. 2012. "International Education: A Key Driver of Canada's Future Prosperity." At http://www.international.gc.ca/education/report-rapport/strategy-strategie/index.aspx (accessed 10 July 2013).

Agarwal, P. 2009. *Indian Higher Education: Envisioning the Future.* New Delhi: Sage Publications.

Altbach, P. 2010. "India's Open Door to Foreign Universities: Less Than Meets the Eye." *International Higher Education* 60:16–18.

Embleton, S., and H. Neemuchwala. 2011. "India in Focus (CIEC)." Presentation at "Being Global 2011: Strategies and Models for Internationalizing Canadian Higher Education," Higher Education Strategy Associates Conference, Toronto, 14 January.

Onley, D.C. 2010. "Open Ontario Plan." Speech from the Throne, 8 March. Toronto.

Seethapathy, R., and D. Johnston. 2004. "Institutional Linkages: Academic/Government/Private Partnerships in the Canadian & Indian Science & Technology Sector." Ottawa: Government of Canada.

Shubert, A., G. Jones, and R.D. Trilokekar. 2009. Introduction to *Canada's Universities Go Global*, ed. R.D. Trilokekar, G.A. Jones, and A. Shubert, 7–15. CAUT Series. Toronto: James Lorimer.

Thorat, S. 2006. "Higher Education in India: Emerging Issues Related to Access, Inclusiveness and Quality." Nehru Memorial Lecture, University of Mumbai, Mumbai, 24 November.

Touhey, R.M. 2009. *A New Direction for the Canada-India Relationship*. Toronto: Canadian International Council. At http://www.opencanada.org/wp-content/uploads/2011/05/A-New-Direction-for-the-Canada-India-Relationship-Ryan-M.-Touhey1.pdf (accessed 10 July 2013).

Trilokekar, R.D. 2010. "International Education as Soft Power? The Contributions and Challenges of Canadian Foreign Policy to the Internationalization of Higher Education." *Higher Education* 59 (2):131–147.

Trilokekar, R.D., and S. Embleton. 2011. "Access, Social Equity and the Challenges of Internationalizing Higher Education: Implications for Canada & India." Paper presented at the CSSHE Autumn Conference "Higher Education, Globalization, & Social Justice," Vancouver, 3–4 November.

AFTERWORD

CHAPTER 18

CONDUCTING POLICY ANALYSIS IN HIGHER EDUCATION: ISSUES AND PROSPECTS

JANE GASKELL

The range of theories, observations, and styles displayed in the chapters of this book is daunting. The chapters demonstrate the many approaches that can be taken to policy in higher education as well as the diversity of social science and humanities scholarship that is relevant to informing it. Despite claims that higher education is reluctant to examine itself, this volume shows how interesting and engaging scholarship in higher education can be. "Policy" in post-secondary education surrounds and frames an incredible range of issues, from faculty workloads to student aid, from the use of technology to the priority of teaching and research, from levels of funding to forms of leadership. They have all been discussed in this book.

Policy can be looked at through many different lenses: historical, political, economic, narrative, structural, Marxist, feminist, poststructural, and much more. As more analysis appears, it becomes less unified in its approach, defying the conventional wisdom that suggests research converges on a single version of the truth. And policy is formed in many places, from international organizations to national, provincial, and municipal governments; from the president's office at universities and colleges to departments, business units, and unions; from social movements to media as diverse as the *New York Times* and YouTube.

So there is plenty of scope for creativity and difference. Diverse approaches and frameworks do not coexist easily in a single field of

Making Policy in Turbulent Times: Challenges and Prospects for Higher Education, ed. P. Axelrod, R.D. Trilokekar, T. Shanahan, and R. Wellen. Kingston: School of Policy Studies, Queen's University.

research or a department of higher education, or perhaps in this book. But displaying the differences encourages a debate about which issues are most important, which frameworks are most revealing, and which actors are most important in these "turbulent times." Each of the chapters has somewhat different, and somewhat conflicting, answers, but brought together, they allow us to consider the range of possible approaches.

In these concluding thoughts, I will focus first on what the chapters suggest are the important policy questions in higher education today and then reflect on two issues that emerge in virtually all of the chapters in different ways: the role of research in higher education policy and the impact of internationalization on the directions that higher education will take in the future. By considering some of the differences and similarities among the chapters, these concluding thoughts will not resolve, but try to clarify, some differences among the priorities for scholarship in higher education in the next decade.

POLICY IN HIGHER EDUCATION: WHAT ARE THE ISSUES THAT NEED ATTENTION?

Which policy issues are most important in today's environment of fiscal constraint and neo-liberal politics? Is the changing landscape of higher education altering the policy issues we should be talking about?

Much of the literature on educational policy on the K–12 system observes that policy comes in waves and rarely seems to move forward (Tyack and Cuban 1997). We centralize educational systems to ensure cost-effectiveness and systematic approaches to learning; then we decentralize them to encourage innovation and local ownership; then we centralize them again. We criticize teacher-directed learning, dismissively calling it "chalk and talk," "sage on the stage," or "full-frontal teaching"; then we revert to teacher-centred patterns, perhaps with the help of technology; then we encourage student-centred learning again. We want more relevance and applied learning, and then we rediscover the importance of the traditional academic canon. Most "new" ideas in education have been articulated over the last century, but they regain traction at different times in different places.

It is clear that the post-secondary system has become larger, more internationally connected, more research-driven, more diverse, more rhetorically linked to the economy, and more expensive over the last 50 years. But has that changed the issues that are debated? We have had economic downturns before, and arguments about autonomy and student debt and equity, but do they sound different today?

Many of the chapters in this book trace recurrent tensions within a policy framework. Glen Jones tracks the continuing and not terribly successful lobbying in Ontario to increase funding, and he shows that attempts to differentiate institutions by academic function have gained

little traction. Stromquist sees the central issues as being resource generation, governance, faculty workloads, and internationalization. These are
not new issues, although she argues that deregulation and privatization
are changing the "policyscapes" in post-secondary education around
the world.

Perhaps the issues are changing more in some places than others. But
in Europe, the chapters again emphasize continuity. Shattock describes a
policy process in England that has continued to make institutional autonomy a policy issue in the face of a centralized state trying to bring about
change. Although there have been large increases in participation rates,
alongside dramatically lower levels of state funding and an increased
concern with research since 1945, the key issues remain similar. Callender
argues that what is billed as a radical reform in student funding in Britain
in the 2011 white paper reflects the continuing pressures of an expanding
system with less state funding, continuing concerns about equity and
institutional autonomy, and a continuing trend to making students and
their families bear more of the cost, all the while allowing more market
choice and competition. Any radical change, she argues, seems unlikely.

Certainly in China, the landscape and the discourse are remarkably
different today than they were in the 1970s, when Maoist thought framed
educational thinking, many universities were closed, and much of the
academic and economic elite was sent to the countryside. However, Zha
and Yan remind us that the old, underlying tensions around politics
and control of universities are still shaping the evolution of Chinese
universities.

As Vidovich puts it, quality and equity are the key drivers of policy
rhetoric, for good reasons, even though their interpretation is different
in different jurisdictions by different policy actors. In these papers and
in higher education policy circles, cost-sharing (among government,
students, families), expansion (how fast and for whom), and university
autonomy (or public engagement and regulation) are major preoccupations that have been around for a long time in different guises.

The social changes we are experiencing today seem, however, to be
putting a new priority on equity issues. In the *New York Times*, journal-
ist Thomas Edsall (2012) announced that higher education had stopped
being a springboard to social mobility, as it was after the Second World
War, and had become an increasingly powerful mechanism for the
intergenerational reproduction of privilege. Growing inequality in the
United States is reflected in increasing differentiation within the higher
education system, as the privileged become remarkably successful at
ensuring that their children attend the most competitive universities
(Carnevale 2012). The achievement gap between students from higher-
and lower-income families has widened over the last 50 years, as test
scores are increasingly linked to family income and the dollar value of
a university degree in the labour market has risen (Reardon 2011). The

increase in global inequality and mobility means that this process is occurring in and across many jurisdictions. Chinese students are applying to Harvard in accelerating numbers.

That higher education is a means of reinforcing class stratification is no surprise to anyone who has read Bourdieu or other sociologists of education. But the statistics on the increasing disparities between college-educated youth and those without higher education, and between those with a good post-secondary education and those with a marginal one, are striking. And in the context of widening income inequality (Stiglitz 2012), the cultural divide chronicled in Charles Murray's (2012) book on the increasing cultural stratification of American society, and the recent Canadian Ekos poll (2012) showing deep and disturbing fractures between how university-educated and college-educated people view the world, this creeping inequality deserves more policy focus. Much of the research suggests that this is not an issue that can be addressed simply through tuition and student aid policy as it reflects deep cultural beliefs and expectations about the value and cost of education (Swail and Heller 2004).

For at the same time that the wealthy are making sure their children get higher education, others are increasingly sceptical about its value. *Academically Adrift* (Arum and Roksa 2011) provides evidence that many students do not get any better at reading critically after they spend time in most colleges in the US. And law schools are facing litigation from indebted and unemployed students because they claim inflated employment rates for their graduates. If higher education cannot increase students' literacy, or find them a job, its legitimacy should come under serious scrutiny. But differences among institutions are increasing in most countries, and scepticism about the value of post-secondary education could serve to ensure that the system remains dominated by the relatively well-off.

Policy rhetoric is fascinating, as it changes or stays the same, reflects critical issues, or skirts them. But its actual effects can be contradictory. The politics of policy implementation are as interesting, difficult, and complex as the politics of policy formation. While policy talk comes and goes, much of the post-secondary system continues to operate from day to day in the same old ways, for this is a very loosely coupled system, where the autonomy of institutions and faculty members is prized and protected, and union rules often dictate how things are carried out, whatever the strategic plan or the fiscal framework.

Policy can be seen as the verbal performances that are necessary to maintain the viability and legitimacy of higher education for a variety of audiences, sometimes the government, sometimes the students, and sometimes the voters. It can also be seen as the hot air, with accompanying documentation and meetings, that comes from presidents or deans or government officials and makes few inroads into how the work is actually done, much to the frustration of those politicians and presidents. Weingarten points out that "governments appear increasingly frustrated at the lack of responsiveness of post-secondary institutions, their slow pace of change, and, in the view of some, their resistance to accountability." Policy wonks should pay more attention to how policy discussions work at an institutional level as, so often, new initiatives fail to have the impact they claim. The chapters in this book illustrate the failures of ambitious plans for the Lisbon Strategy in Europe, for differentiation in Ontario, and for student aid in Britain.

So many policy issues stay the same over time, at least at a very general level, but in the current climate, issues around equity and implementation have particular relevance. Will new policies in post-secondary education exacerbate inequality or provide opportunities for marginalized groups? Will they change the internal dynamics of higher education institutions or simply circulate in the policy air?

RESEARCH AND THE POLICY PROCESS

As they are researchers, and research is critical to the mandate of universities, the authors in this book frequently touch on the nature of research in post-secondary education and its role in influencing the development of policy.

Research is an important part of the rationale for public support of higher education. De Boer and van Vught stress that since 2000, the innovation agenda with its promise of economic prosperity has rallied support for higher education in Europe and that researchers must "actively, strategically, and commercially engage in interactions with external stakeholders" if the system and Europe itself is going to thrive. This call for engagement and policy relevance is echoed by many, but questioned by critics who see the independence of university research as a platform for speaking truth to power and the research mandate as drawing resources from the student experience, as Stromquist and Dill discuss.

But in the field of higher education, do researchers engage with current policy issues, and is their research heeded? Has it improved policy, or been ignored, or made things worse? What should we do to make it more relevant and useful, or should we just accept its marginality? Are we really in a new age of evidence-based policy, or is that a convenient myth?

The answer to the first question seems clear. The chapters conclude that the role of research in influencing policy in higher education is minimal. And there is no consensus that higher education research should be directed to engage with policy as articulated by governments or university leaders.

Several chapters describing the policy process show how personal connections, serendipity, and politics, not evidence, are the key determinants of policy. The process is complex and often chaotic, as Trilokekar et al. point out. Personal wisdom and good communication skills are key for those in positions of leadership, as Woodsworth and Weingarten describe, and they are enhanced by alliances, connections, and networks of people who are grappling with the same issues, as Embleton, Slowey, and Stensaker demonstrate in different ways.

Given the marginal place of research, the advice Weingarten provides to university lobbyists is something like, Talk nicely, use anecdotes, and you may get what you want because there really is an alignment between the public good and what presidents want for universities. Governments make policy based on "stories, anecdotes, stereotypes, intuitions, ideologies, and personal experiences," all of which are available when research evidence is not. The "leadership industry," as Woodsworth puts it, has expanded as quickly as research, and it has an equally important role to play. This leaves research evidence, particularly research evidence critical of power, on the sidelines. While research evidence can be useful if available, policy direction relies instead on the good judgment and public-spiritedness of the powerful.

This still allows for an argument that research can be influential and helpful. Clark and Norrie argue that research has had a marginal impact because, despite the commitment of the sector to research, there is little relevant and useful scholarly inquiry in higher education in Canada, and the sector is reluctant to act on the evidence that does exist. They contend that post-secondary scholars in Canada publish specialized and theoretical critiques in learned journals, rather than interdisciplinary empirical studies aimed at improving learning outcomes and influencing politicians.

Stromquist sees the uses of research somewhat differently, although she agrees it has not had much effect. Her concern is that universities ally too closely with corporate interests and that researchers must challenge the global policy changes that are undermining academic quality and critically engage with policy-makers at all levels in order to bring about social transformation. This position identifies research quite positively with critique and scholarship with providing legitimacy to the production of counter-narratives that challenge the common sense of the powerful. But like Clark and Norrie, it urges researchers to write about issues that undermine the quality of the academic experience.

Research and policy influence each other. The research that frames and discusses policy change affects how it is understood. The public becomes interested in financial aid, the employment of university graduates, and an increasing class divide because of the number of new reports and evidence about them. Research provides a lens that shapes the debate for and against policy change. And research is influenced by policy change because policy defines new problems and produces new funding (or withdraws it), and it can change the conditions under which we do research.

One of the signs of a mature academic field is its theoretical diversity and innovation. The variety of theories and concepts designed to let us understand the world of post-secondary policy – policyscapes, structural theories, "more dynamic" theories, historically situated action, critical theory, neo-institutional theory, and poststructuralism – all provide the assumptions on which factual claims about evidence are made. They complicate any discussion of what counts as evidence. As the Hsieh and Huisman chapter points out, "behind the general theoretical debate on trends and factors, there is an equally important conceptual-methodological debate on how to measure policy change."

For example, the claim by Hattie and Marsh (1996) that there is no correlation between research productivity and teaching effectiveness relies on correlations among measures of poorly defined concepts. It does not allow for the structural and historical arguments that others would mount. When Janet Hallowell looks at the evidence, she concludes that "it is not evident that much will be gained by HEQCO [the Higher Education Quality Council of Ontario] simply pursuing the question of what is the 'evidence' on the existence, or lack thereof, of the connection between teaching and research in Canada other than to enter into a rather non-productive debate on the nature of the methodology employed or the assumptions underlying any specific study" (Hallowell 2008, 12).

As with policy issues, research evidence is undoubtedly more important in some places and at some times. In Canada, the lack of a federal department of education and the tradition of university autonomy militate against the funding of policy-relevant research. The discussion by Trilokekar et al. of the complex and chaotic policy process in Canada, where individuals get things done, and the economic and social environment frames possibilities, is illuminating. The other Canadian chapters (Jones, Weingarten, Embleton, Clark and Norrie) all stress the importance of personal experience, political skill, and interest group politics over the importance of research findings. Similarly, the evidence from Britain, the US, Europe, China, and India portrays a world in which the findings of research studies on higher education have little direct impact on policy. Research, to the extent that it is relevant, is interpreted, filtered, and used strategically by the people involved in the policy process.

This all suggests taking a more careful look at the processes whereby research evidence can be incorporated into policy development. Sá, Tamtik, and Kretz offer an empirical study of how organizations that fund research, institutions presumably even more committed to research than universities, use evidence. They point to the varied ways that research evidence can be used in agenda-setting, program design, monitoring, and evaluating. And they find that they use evidence, but often in the form of professional expertise rather than in the form of quantitative studies.

This emphasis on the expertise of people who know a research field is echoed by Dill's chapter on how information can be best used to inform higher education policy. Face-to-face communication, collective action, and self-organization are more likely to promote the public good than externally funded and monitored assessments. Evidence must be interpreted by knowledgeable and public-spirited actors to make sense. As he explores the uses and misuses of evidence in government schemes to make universities serve the common good, Dill concludes that the collection of data has many limitations and that collegial approaches serve us best.

The increasing amount of research on higher education around the world signals an increased economic importance for the sector, new communication networks, and a more complex policy process. But it is the way that people with power in a political world make sense of increasingly disparate research studies that will affect policy directions and thus the research program in higher education over a longer term.

INTERNATIONALIZATION

A book with contributors from around the globe raises a lot of questions about the impact of internationalization on post-secondary education. Do the increasing connections among post-secondary institutions and policy-makers in different jurisdictions mean that the sector is converging on fewer models of excellence, or does it allow for increasing differentiation? Does the pressure to internationalize provide more possibilities for learning, or does it restrict local options as a single view of what counts as a world-class university comes to dominate what were discrete local discussions?

Many are concerned that we are observing the production of a single international hierarchy of institutions, where elites around the world agree on the most prestigious institutions, work effectively to ensure that their children gain access, and compete madly to create these institutions in their own countries. Global rankings proliferate, and while there are differences among them, there is a great deal of underlying agreement. Stromquist asserts that "universities throughout the world are becoming alike" due to rankings and shared economic and political ideologies, despite some diversity and resistance. She points to the homogenization of programs, increased external monitoring, rising tuition, expansion without resources, internationalization, managerialism, more part-time faculty, and the erosion of tenure.

Stensaker also sees trends toward convergence and stratification, although he calls for more investigation of an ongoing and dynamic process. He points out that university networks perform symbolic, political, and cultural functions that are likely to maintain and emphasize the inequality among universities on a global scale, even while they take disparate forms and provide possibilities for more effective local political action and better student experiences.

China provides a clear example of how global connectedness leads to differentiation and hierarchy. The amazing increase in university attendance in China, from 1976, when universities were closed, to the current population of over 31 million students (and growing rapidly) marks the significance the Chinese government attaches to the economic role of post-secondary education in a globally competitive economy. This global awareness has led to the expansion of local, low-status places, along with the protection and increased funding of a few elite universities. None of this is without tension. Policy oscillation on centralization and decentralization, equity and expansion, ideological control and freedom of inquiry, reflects the historical traditions and conflicts of the Chinese state despite international models and globalization pressures.

Technology may exacerbate the trends. Marginson, among others, sees MOOCs (massive open online courses) and other online learning opportunities as game-changers. "It's free, dirt cheap to run, rigorous in standard and brings you the world experts. Physics from Higgs or Hawking beats the local science teacher – especially if you don't have one.... A tiny handful of producers and products dominate the global market, overwhelmingly. There is only one Elvis, and only one Harvard" (Marginson 2012, n.p.).

Hsieh and Huisman are more guarded about the emergence of a single, uniform global system. Despite attempts by elites to create Europe as a new unified policy space, depoliticized by the use of standards and data, a policy space developed by experts on "a rising tide of indicators and benchmarks," as Lawn and Grek (2012) put it, they find no evidence of convergence in the quality assurance processes used in England, the Netherlands, and Denmark. Despite more communication about what quality assurance means, each nation state persists in its own system instead of adopting one from another jurisdiction.

If this book had been organized in Jakarta or New Delhi, the arguments might sound different, and the evidence would come from different places. The Indian government is not driven by international rankings in the way that China is. The support of local elites continues to be necessary for viable and effective post-secondary institutions, and pressure to please local elites means substantially different things in Jogjakarta, Cairo, and Winnipeg. Local politics and cultural and religious differences have not disappeared, even as a global elite becomes more wealthy, more mobile, and more unified. Difference is likely to persist in higher education.

CONCLUSIONS

Like any good academic discussion, this book ends with questions rather than firm conclusions, debates and differences rather than any clear consensus. While some trends are clear, even the best-informed analysts can make only provisional statements about their meaning and their future implications. Policy questions arise from social and economic changes that affect families, governments, and students as well as from the preoccupations of those primarily involved in the post-secondary system. Higher education policy is closely tied to the political economy of the nation state, even while international models and networks have an impact. Research reflects as well as influences policy, being embedded in the same politics of meaning and evidence. But more of it should help us all work our way through the tangle of claims about how the post-secondary system can best serve the public good.

REFERENCES

Arum, R., and J. Roksa. 2011. *Academically Adrift: Limited Learning on College Campuses.* Chicago: University of Chicago Press.

Carnevale, A. 2012. *How Increasing College Access Is Increasing Inequality and What to Do about It.* Washington: Georgetown University Centre on Education and the Workforce.

Edsall, T.B. 2012. "The Reproduction of Privilege." *New York Times,* 12 March.

Ekos. 2012. "The Return of Ideology? A Starkly Divided Canada." At www.ekos.com/admin/article.asp?id=498 (accessed 10 July 2013).

Hallowell, J. 2008. *The Nexus of Teaching and Research: Evidence and Insights from the Literature.* Toronto: Higher Education Quality Council of Ontario.

Hattie, J., and H. Marsh. 1996. "The Relationship between Research and Teaching: A Meta-analysis." *Review of Educational Research* 66 (4):507–542.

Lawn, M., and S. Grek. 2012. *Europeanizing Education: Governing a New Policy Space.* Oxford: Symposium Books.

Marginson, S. 2012. "Yes, MOOC Is the Global Higher Education Game Changer." *University World News* 234, 12 August. At http://www.universityworldnews.com/article.php?story=2012080915084470 (accessed 10 July 2013).

Murray, C. 2012. *Coming Apart: The State of White America 1960–2010.* Crown Publishing Group.

Reardon, S.F. 2011. "The Widening Academic Achievement Gap between the Rich and the Poor: New Evidence and Possible Explanations." In *Whither Opportunity? Rising Inequality, Schools, and Children's Life Chances,* ed. G.J. Duncan and R.J. Murnane. New York: Russell Sage Foundation.

Stiglitz, J.E. 2012. *The Price of Inequality: How Today's Divided Society Endangers Our Future.* New York: W.W. Norton.

Swail, W.S., and D. Heller. 2004. *Changes in Tuition Policy: Natural Policy Experiments in Five Countries.* Montreal: Canada Millennium Scholarship Foundation.

Tyack, D., and L. Cuban. 1997. *Tinkering toward Utopia: A Century of Public School Reform.* Cambridge, MA: Harvard University Press.

LIST OF ACRONYMS

AAC&U	Association of American Colleges and Universities
AAU	Academic Audit Unit
AAUP	American Association of University Professors
ABRC	Advisory Board for the Research Councils
ACAATO	Association of Colleges of Applied Arts and Technology of Ontario
ACE	American Council on Education
ACER	Australian Council for Educational Research
AGB	Association of Governing Boards
AHELO	Assessment of Higher Education Learning Outcomes
AIU	Association of Indian Universities
ALTC	Australian Learning and Teaching Council
ATOP	Access to Opportunities Program
AUCC	Association of Universities and Colleges of Canada
AUQA	Australian Universities Quality Agency
BBA	bachelor of business administration
BC	British Columbia
BIS	Department for Business, Innovation and Skills
BITS Pilani	Birla Institute of Technology and Science
BRIC	Brazil, Russia, India, and China
CAAT	Colleges of Applied Arts and Technology
CAT	Colleges of Advanced Technology
CBIE	Canadian Bureau for International Education
CCL	Canadian Council on Learning
CCP	Chinese Communist Party
CDP	Committee of Polytechnic Directors
CEO	chief executive officer

CEPA	Comprehensive Economic Partnership Agreement
CFI	Canada Foundation for Innovation
CFS	Canadian Federation of Students
CHE	Center for Higher Education
CHEPA	Center for Higher Education Policy Analysis
CHERD	Centre for Higher Education Research and Development
CHERI	Centre for Higher Education Research and Information
CIC	Citizenship and Immigration Canada
CIDA	Canadian International Development Agency
CIEC	Canada India Education Council
CIES	Canada India Education Society
CIHE	Center for International Higher Education
CIHR	Canadian Institutes of Health Research
CII	Confederation of Indian Industry
CIRCE	Canada-India Research Centre of Excellence
CLA	Collegiate Learning Assessment
CLASSE	Classroom Survey of Student Engagement
CMEC	Council of Ministers of Education, Canada
CMSF	Canada Millennium Scholarship Foundation
COU	Council of Ontario Universities
CPR	Center for Postsecondary Research
CRC	Canada Research Chairs program
CREPUQ	Conférence des recteurs et des principaux des universités du Québec
CSHE	Center for Studies in Higher Education
CSHE	Centre for the Study of Higher Education
CSHPE	Center for the Study of Higher and Postsecondary Education
CSR	Common Sense Revolution
CVCP	Committee of Vice-Chancellors and Principals
DAAD	German Academic Exchange Service
DCU	Dublin City University
DES	Danish Evaluation System
DES	Department of Education and Science
DES	Department of Education and Skills
DFAIT	Department of Foreign Affairs and International Trade
DfEE	Department for Education and Employment
DfES	Department for Education and Skills

DIT	Dublin Institute of Technology
DRHEA	Dublin Region Higher Education Alliance
DTI	Department of Trade and Industry
EC	European Commission
ECB	European Central Bank
ECSC	European Coal and Steel Community
EdD	doctor of education
EDP	excessive deficit procedure
EEC	European Economic Community
EHEA	European Higher Education Area
EMU	Economic and Monetary Union
ENQA	European Network for Quality Assurance
EQAR	European Quality Assurance Register
ERA	European Research Area
ERA	*Excellence in Research for Australia*
ERC	European Research Council
ESG	European Standards and Guidelines
ESU	European Students' Union
ETS	École de technologie supérieure
EU	European Union
EUA	European University Association
EURASHE	European Association of Institutions in Higher Education
EVA	Danish Evaluation Institute
EVC	Centre for Evaluation and Quality Assurance of Higher Education
FE	further education
FICCI	Federation of Indian Chambers of Commerce and Industry
FP	Framework Programme
GATS	General Agreement on Trade in Services
GDP	gross domestic product
GER	gross enrolment ratio
GITA	Global Innovation & Technology Alliance
GPRA	*Government Performance and Results Act*
GRE	Graduate Record Examinations
HE	higher education
HEA	Higher Education Authority
HEER	Higher Education Empirical Research

HEFCE	Higher Education Funding Council for England
HEI	higher education institution
HEQC	Higher Education Quality Council
HEQCO	Higher Education Quality Council of Ontario
HOAK	Higher Education: Autonomy and Quality
HRSDC	Human Resources and Skills Development Canada
IADT	Institute of Art, Design and Technology
IARU	International Alliance of Research Universities
IAU	International Association of Universities
IC-IMPACTS	India-Canada Centre for Innovative Multidisciplinary Partnerships to Accelerate Community Transformation and Sustainability
ICCR	Indian Council for Cultural Relations
ICTs	information and communications technologies
IIE	Institute of International Education
IIFA	India International Film Awards
IIM-A	Indian Institute of Management, Ahmedabad
IIM-B	Indian Institute of Management, Bangalore
IIT	Indian Institutes of Technology
IITB	Indian Institute of Technology Bombay
IITM	Indian Institute of Technology Madras
IMBA	international master of business administration
IMF	International Monetary Fund
INQAAHE	International Network for Quality Assurance Agencies in Higher Education
IRCHSS	Irish Research Council for the Humanities and Social Sciences
IRCSET	Irish Research Councils for Science, Engineering and Technology
IRHEFSF	Independent Review of Higher Education Funding and Student Finance
ISTPCanada	International Science and Technology Partnerships Canada
ITAL	Institute of Technology and Applied Learning
ITB	Institute of Technology Blanchardstown
ITT	Institute of Technology Tallaght
JNU	Jawaharlal Nehru University
JPG	Joint Planning Group for Quality Assurance in Higher Education

LEAP	Liberal Education and America's Promise
LERU	League of European Research Universities
MBA	master of business administration
MDI	Management Development Institute
MITACS	Mathematics of Information Technology and Complex Systems
MOA	memorandum of agreement
MOOC	massive open online courses
MOU	memorandum of understanding
MRI	Ministry of Research and Innovation
MTCU	Ministry of Training, Colleges and Universities
NAB	National Advisory Body for Public Sector Higher Education
NAUBCS	National Association of University Board Chairs and Secretaries
NCE	Networks of Centres of Excellence
NCIHE	National Committee of Inquiry into Higher Education
NDP	New Democratic Party
NGO	non-governmental organization
NGS	National Graduates Survey
NIH	National Institutes of Health
NPM	new public management
NSERC	Natural Sciences and Engineering Research Council of Canada
NSF	National Science Foundation
NSSE	National Survey of Student Engagement
NUIM	National University of Ireland, Maynooth
NUS	National Union of Students
NVAO	Dutch-Flemish Accrediting Organisation
OBR	Office for Budget Responsibility
OBW	Ontario-Baden-Württemberg
OCAD	Ontario College of Art and Design
OCAV	Ontario Council of Academic Vice-Presidents
OCUA	Ontario Council on University Affairs
OCUFA	Ontario Confederation of University Faculty Associations
OECD	Organisation for Economic Co-operation and Development
OFFA	Office for Fair Access

OISE	Ontario Institute for Studies in Education
OJS	Ontario-Jiangsu
OLT	Office for Learning and Teaching
OLT	Office of Learning Technologies
OMG	Ontario-Maharashtra-Goa
ORA	Ontario-Rhône-Alpes
OSAP	Ontario Student Assistance Program
OUPID	Ontario Universities Program for Instructional Development
PCC	private career college
PEQAB	Postsecondary Education Quality Assessment Board
PES	Public Expenditure Survey
PESC	Public Expenditure Survey Committee
PISA	Programme for International Student Assessment
PMO	Prime Minister's Office
PRIA	Participatory Research in Asia
PRTLI	Programme for Research in Third-Level Institutions
PSE	post-secondary education
QA	quality assurance
QAA	Quality Assurance Agency
QAC	Quality Assessment Committee
R&D	research and development
RAE	Research Assessment Exercise
S&T	science and technology
SBE	Social, Behavioral & Economic Sciences
SCOP	Standing Conference of Principals
SED	Scottish Education Department
SEP	Standard Evaluation Protocol
SFI	Science Foundation Ireland
SFU	Simon Fraser University
SHEEO	State Higher Education Executive Officers
SIF	Strategic Innovation Fund
SLA	service level agreement
SME	small and medium-sized enterprise
SoTL	Scholarship of Teaching and Learning
SPP	Student Partnership Program
SSHRC	Social Sciences and Humanities Research Council of Canada

STEM	science, technology, engineering, and mathematics
TCD	Trinity College Dublin
TEAC	Teacher Accreditation Education Council
TEQSA	Tertiary Education Quality and Standards Agency
TESM	Treaty Establishing the European Stability Mechanism
TQA	Teaching Quality Assessment
TSCG	Treaty on Stability, Coordination and Governance in the Economic and Monetary Union
UBC	University of British Columbia
UCAS	Universities and Colleges Admissions Service
UC Berkeley	University of California, Berkeley
UCD	University College Dublin
UFC	Universities Funding Council
UFV	University of the Fraser Valley
UGC	University Grants Committee
UK	United Kingdom
UNESCO	United Nations Educational, Scientific and Cultural Organization
UOIT	University of Ontario Institute of Technology
UOM	University of Michigan
US	United States
UUK	Universities UK
VSNU	Association of Cooperating Universities in the Netherlands
YITS	Youth in Transition Survey

ABOUT THE CONTRIBUTORS

Paul Axelrod is a professor and former dean of the Faculty of Education at York University.

Claire Callender is professor of higher education studies at the Institute of Education and professor of higher education policy at Birkbeck, University of London.

Ian D. Clark is a professor in the School of Public Policy and Governance at the University of Toronto and former president of the Council of Ontario Universities.

Harry de Boer is senior research associate at the Center for Higher Education Policy Studies, University of Twente.

David D. Dill is professor emeritus of public policy, Department of Public Policy, University of North Carolina at Chapel Hill.

Sheila Embleton is a professor and former vice-president academic and provost, York University.

Jane Gaskell is a professor and former dean of the Ontario Institute for Studies in Education (OISE), University of Toronto.

Chuo-Chun Hsieh is an assistant professor in the Department of Educational Administration and Management at the National Dong Hwa University, Taiwan.

Jeroen Huisman is professor of higher education at the University of Ghent, Belgium.

Glen A. Jones is a professor and holds the Ontario Research Chair in Postsecondary Education Policy and Measurement at OISE, University of Toronto.

Andrew Kretz is a PhD student in the Higher Education program at OISE, University of Toronto.

Ken Norrie is professor emeritus at McMaster University and former vice-president (research) at the Higher Education Quality Council of Ontario.

Creso M. Sá is academic director, graduate education, and associate professor of higher education at OISE, University of Toronto.

Theresa Shanahan is an associate professor and former associate dean in the Faculty of Education at York University.

Michael Shattock is visiting professor, Centre for Higher Education Studies, Institute of Education, University of London, and founding joint director of the MBA in Higher Education Management.

Maria Slowey is professor and director of the Higher Education Research Centre at Dublin City University.

Bjørn Stensaker is a professor in the Department of Education, University of Oslo.

Nelly P. Stromquist is a professor in the International Education Policy Program at the College of Education, University of Maryland.

Merli Tamtik is a PhD student in the Higher Education program at OISE, University of Toronto.

Roopa Desai Trilokekar is an associate professor in the Faculty of Education at York University.

Frans van Vught is honorary professor at the Center for Higher Education Policy Studies of the University of Twente and president of the board of the European Center for Strategic Management of Universities.

Lesley Vidovich is Winthrop Professor in the Graduate School of Education at the University of Western Australia.

Harvey P. Weingarten is president and chief executive officer of the Higher Education Quality Council of Ontario and former president of the University of Calgary.

Richard Wellen is an associate professor in the Department of Social Science at York University.

Judith Woodsworth is a professor in the Département d'études françaises at Concordia University, former president of Concordia University, and former president of Laurentian University.

Fengqiao Yan is a professor and associate dean in the Graduate School of Education at Peking University.

Qiang Zha is an associate professor in the Faculty of Education at York University.

INDEX

cost decreases, 155, 233, 363
cost effectiveness, 43, 61, 134, 191–92, 204, 209–14, 319, 360, 372
cost increases, 13, 25, 129, 143, 156–57, 191, 224
costs,
  for expansion, 21
  for research, 87, 128, 191–92
  for student support, 13, 25, 147, 153, 155–56, 161
  linked to performance measures, 191
  of borrowing, 148
  of capital, 13
  of education, 142–44, 154, 191
  of living, 20, 141–46
  operating/unit, 17, 21, 27, 139, 145, 201–02, 207
cost savings, 235, 362
cost sharing, 143–46
cost-sharing policy, 144–46, 243n3, 409
Council of Ministers of Education, Canada (CMEC), 34
Council of Ontario Universities (COU), 34, 53, 100, 102–04, 106–09, 112, 114nn3&5, 124, 401n2
Council of Regents, 105
Creating Opportunity: The Liberal Plan for Canada, 45
Creative Dublin Alliance, 365
Crosland, Tony, 10, 15, 20
curriculum, 205–06, 208, 211, 330, 335n4, 365, 379, 385
Cutler report, 172, 181

D

DAAD. *See* German Academic Exchange Service
Danish Evaluation Institute (EVA), 282–84
Davis, William C., 102
Day, Stockwell, 126
Dearing Committee. *See* National Committee of Inquiry into Higher Education
Decision on Deepening Educational Reform and Pressing Ahead with Quality Education in an All-Round Way, 321
Decision on the Reform of the Education System, 319
degree-granting. *See under* colleges; universities
Degree Granting Act, 57n3, 104
Denmark, 233–34, 238, 270, 272, 281, 285, 286t2, 287, 288–89, 306, 415. *See also* Scandinavia

Department for Business, Innovation and Skills (BIS), 27, 29, 147, 153–54
Department for Education and Skills (DfES), 23
Department of Biotechnology, 396
Department of Education and Science (DES), 142
Department of Education and Skills (DES), 11, 15–17, 20–21, 25–26, 28–29
Department of Foreign Affairs and International Trade (DFAIT), 47–48, 383, 387, 396
Department of Science and Technology, 396
Department of University Affairs, 102
deregulation, 224
differentiation, 253, 328t1, 409, 414
  among institutions, 4, 100, 104, 107–14, 125, 128, 190–91, 198–99, 203, 209–10, 310n6, 329, 363, 411, 415
  of research capability, 22,
distance education, 301, 399, 401
doctoral degree/program/students, 44, 114n1, 125, 128, 228–29, 232, 255, 299, 304, 308, 329, 379, 398
Dodge, David, 39, 90
double cohort, 44, 88, 123, 134n1
dropout, 197, 348
Drummond report, 111–13
Dublin City University (DCU), 368, 379
Dublin Institute of Technology (DIT), 368, 378
Dublin Region Higher Education Alliance (DRHEA), 367–72, 378–79
duplication, 344–45, 360, 371–72
Dutch-Flemish Accrediting Organisation (NVAO), 281

E

École de technologie supérieure (ETS), 393
economy,
  benefits for, 74, 130, 140, 143
  drivers of, 2, 9, 42, 155, 169
  growth of, 3–4, 19, 34, 45, 76, 143, 147, 192, 299, 332, 341, 343, 349, 351, 363
  knowledge. *See* knowledge economy
Economic and Monetary Union (EMU), 340–41
economic challenges 134, 147, 262
economic development, 74, 143, 172, 306
economic efficiency, 3, 149, 169, 183, 192, 209, 240, 353, 374. *See also* efficiency
economic ideology, 180, 183

National Development Plan 2007–2013, 378

National Institute for Learning Outcomes Assessment, 194, 211

National Institutes of Health (NIH), 65–66, 70, 82

National Outline for Medium- and Long-Term Educational Reform and Development, 317

National Research Council, 299

National Science Foundation (NSF), 65–66, 68–73, 82, 304

National Spatial Strategy, 378

National Strategy for Higher Education to 2030, 371–72

National Survey of Student Engagement (NSSE), 194–95, 200, 205

National Union of Students (NUS), 10, 27

National University of Ireland, Maynooth (NUIM), 368, 378

natural sciences, 64, 74, 237–38, 307

Natural Sciences and Engineering Research Council of Canada (NSERC), 65–67, 71–72, 74, 76, 82, 397

neo-liberalism, 2, 129, 182–83, 222, 224, 238, 243n3, 295, 299, 322, 362, 365, 408

Netherlands Accreditation Organisation, 281

Netherlands, the, 270, 272, 278–81, 285, 287–89, 304, 308, 310n6, 340, 361, 415

network governance, 365

networks, 35–36, 51, 56, 59, 105, 171, 175, 226, 354, 386, 412

institutional, 249–263, 364–65, 372, 414, 416

lobbying, 2,

policy, 99–02, 168, 183, 342

quality assurance, 270

regional, 308

strategic, 5, 359–61, 373–74

See also university networks; lobbying

Networks of Centres of Excellence (NCE), 396, 402n10

New Democratic Party (NDP), 37–38, 50, 53, 107–08

new public management (NPM), 17, 25, 28, 276, 365

New York University, 239

non-governmental organization (NGO), 225, 395–96

Nortel Networks, 43

Northern Ontario School of Medicine, 127

Note of Reservation, 14–15

nursing education, 392

NVAO. *See* Dutch-Flemish Accrediting Organisation

O

Observatory PASCAL, 365

Office for Fair Access (OFFA), 163n7

Office for Learning and Teaching (OLT), 176

Ontario, 391

compared with, 28, 34, 41, 88, 96n1, 193–95, 201–02, 214n4, 307, 386, 388–91, 411

exchange programs with, 389

policy development for, 28, 33–56, 86, 93, 96, 99–101, 107–13, 191

Ontario: A Leader in Learning, 41

Ontario-Baden-Württemberg (OBW), 389–90, 402n3

Ontario College of Art and Design (OCAD), 105, 110–11

Ontario Colleges of Applied Arts and Technology Act, 2002, 109

Ontario Confederation (formerly Council) of University Faculty Associations (OCUFA), 103, 207

Ontario Council of Academic Vice-Presidents (OCAV), 389, 401n2

Ontario Council on University Affairs (OCUA), 104–08, 109–10

Ontario Federation of Students, 103

Ontario Institute for Studies in Education (OISE), 110, 201

Ontario-Jiangsu (OJS), 390, 402n3

Ontario-Maharashtra-Goa (OMG), 381, 388–90

Ontario Research Chairs in Public Policy, 202

Ontario-Rhône-Alpes (ORA), 389–90, 402n3

Ontario Student Assistance Program (OSAP), 38

Ontario Trillium Scholarships program, 44

Ontario Universities International, 390

Ontario Universities Program for Instructional Development (OUPID), 201

Open University, 200

O'Reilly Runte, Roseann, 387

Organisation for Economic Co-operation and Development (OECD), 76–77, 163n3, 168–72, 176–77, 179–84, 192–93, 224–26, 297, 299, 303, 305, 363, 365, 367, 372

Queen's Policy Studies
Recent Publications

The Queen's Policy Studies Series is dedicated to the exploration of major public policy issues that confront governments and society in Canada and other nations.

Manuscript submission. We are pleased to consider new book proposals and manuscripts. Preliminary inquiries are welcome. A subvention is normally required for the publication of an academic book. Please direct questions or proposals to the Publications Unit by email at spspress@queensu.ca, or visit our website at: www.queensu.ca/sps/books, or contact us by phone at (613) 533-2192.

Our books are available from good bookstores everywhere, including the Queen's University bookstore (http://www.campusbookstore.com/). McGill-Queen's University Press is the exclusive world representative and distributor of books in the series. A full catalogue and ordering information may be found on their web site (**http://mqup.mcgill.ca/**).

For more information about new and backlist titles from Queen's Policy Studies, visit http://www.queensu.ca/sps/books.

School of Policy Studies

Intellectual Disabilities and *Dual Diagnosis: An Interprofessional Clinical Guide for Healthcare Providers*, Bruce D. McCreary and Jessica Jones (eds.) 2013. ISBN 978-1-55339-331-3

Building More Effective Labour-Management Relationships, Richard P. Chaykowski and Robert S. Hickey (eds.) 2013. ISBN 978-1-55339-306-1

Navigationg on the Titanic: Economic Growth, Energy, and the Failure of Governance, Bryne Purchase 2013. ISBN 978-1-55339-330-6

Measuring the Value of a Postsecondary Education, Ken Norrie and Mary Catharine Lennon (eds.) 2013. ISBN 978-1-55339-325-2

Immigration, Integration, and Inclusion in Ontario Cities, Caroline Andrew, John Biles, Meyer Burstein, Victoria M. Esses, and Erin Tolley (eds.) 2012. ISBN 978-1-55339-292-7

Diverse Nations, Diverse Responses: Approaches to Social Cohesion in Immigrant Societies, Paul Spoonley and Erin Tolley (eds.) 2012. ISBN 978-1-55339-309-2

Making EI Work: Research from the Mowat Centre Employment Insurance Task Force, Keith Banting and Jon Medow (eds.) 2012. ISBN 978-1-55339-323-8

Managing Immigration and Diversity in Canada: A Transatlantic Dialogue in the New Age of Migration, Dan Rodríguez-García (ed.) 2012. ISBN 978-1-55339-289-7

International Perspectives: Integration and Inclusion, James Frideres and John Biles (eds.) 2012. ISBN 978-1-55339-317-7

Dynamic Negotiations: Teacher Labour Relations in Canadian Elementary and Secondary Education, Sara Slinn and Arthur Sweetman (eds.) 2012. ISBN 978-1-55339-304-7

Where to from Here? Keeping Medicare Sustainable, Stephen Duckett 2012. ISBN 978-1-55339-318-4

International Migration in Uncertain Times, John Nieuwenhuysen, Howard Duncan, and Stine Neerup (eds.) 2012. ISBN 978-1-55339-308-5

Life After Forty: Official Languages Policy in Canada/Après quarante ans, les politiques de langue officielle au Canada, Jack Jedwab and Rodrigue Landry (eds.) 2011. ISBN 978-1-55339-279-8

From Innovation to Transformation: Moving up the Curve in Ontario Healthcare,
Hon. Elinor Caplan, Dr. Tom Bigda-Peyton, Maia MacNiven, and Sandy Sheahan 2011.
ISBN 978-1-55339-315-3

Academic Reform: Policy Options for Improving the Quality and Cost-Effectiveness of Under-graduate Education in Ontario, Ian D. Clark, David Trick, and Richard Van Loon 2011.
ISBN 978-1-55339-310-8

Integration and Inclusion of Newcomers and Minorities across Canada, John Biles,
Meyer Burstein, James Frideres, Erin Tolley, and Robert Vineberg (eds.) 2011.
ISBN 978-1-55339-290-3

A New Synthesis of Public Administration: Serving in the 21ˢᵗ Century, Jocelyne Bourgon,
2011. ISBN 978-1-55339-312-2 (paper) 978-1-55339-313-9 (cloth)

Recreating Canada: Essays in Honour of Paul Weiler, Randall Morck (ed.), 2011.
ISBN 978-1-55339-273-6

Data Data Everywhere: Access and Accountability? Colleen M. Flood (ed.), 2011.
ISBN 978-1-55339-236-1

Making the Case: Using Case Studies for Teaching and Knowledge Management in Public Administration, Andrew Graham, 2011. ISBN 978-1-55339-302-3

Centre for International and Defence Policy

Afghanistan in the Balance: Counterinsurgency, Comprehensive Approach, and Political Order,
Hans-Georg Ehrhart, Sven Bernhard Gareis, and Charles Pentland (eds.), 2012.
ISBN 978-1-55339-353-5

Security Operations in the 21st Century: Canadian Perspectives on the Comprehensive Approach, Michael Rostek and Peter Gizewski (eds.), 2011. ISBN 978-1-55339-351-1

Institute of Intergovernmental Relations

Canada and the Crown: Essays on Constitutional Monarchy, D. Michael Jackson and
Philippe Lagassé (eds.), 2013. ISBN 978-1-55339-204-0

Paradigm Freeze: Why It Is So Hard to Reform Health-Care Policy in Canada, Harvey Lazar,
John N. Lavis, Pierre-Gerlier Forest, and John Church (eds.), 2013.
ISBN 978-1-55339-324-5

Canada: The State of the Federation 2010, Matthew Mendelsohn, Joshua Hjartarson, and
James Pearce (eds.), 2013. ISBN 978-1-55339-200-2

The Democratic Dilemma: Reforming Canada's Supreme Court, Nadia Verrelli (ed.), 2013.
ISBN 978-1-55339-203-3

The Evolving Canadian Crown, Jennifer Smith and D. Michael Jackson (eds.), 2011.
ISBN 978-1-55339-202-6

The Federal Idea: Essays in Honour of Ronald L. Watts, Thomas J. Courchene, John R. Allan,
Christian Leuprecht, and Nadia Verrelli (eds.), 2011. ISBN 978-1-55339-198-2 (paper)
978-1-55339-199-9 (cloth)

The Democratic Dilemma: Reforming the Canadian Senate, Jennifer Smith (ed.), 2009.
ISBN 978-1-55339-190-6